BINATIONAL COMMONS

BINATIONAL COMMONS

Institutional Development and Governance on the U.S.-Mexico Border

■ ■ ■

EDITED BY

TONY PAYAN & PAMELA L. CRUZ

THE UNIVERSITY OF
ARIZONA PRESS

TUCSON

The University of Arizona Press
www.uapress.arizona.edu

ISBN-13: 978-0-8165-4142-3 (hardcover)
ISBN-13: 978-0-8165-4105-8 (paper)

Cover design by Derek Thornton / Notch Design
Interior design and typesetting by Sara Thaxton
Typeset in 10/13.5 Garamond Premier Pro (text) and Bebas Neue Pro (display)

Library of Congress Cataloging-in-Publication Data
Names: Payan, Tony, 1967– editor. | Cruz, Pamela Lizette, editor.
Title: Binational commons : institutional development and governance on the U.S.-Mexico border / edited by
    Tony Payan and Pamela L. Cruz.
Description: Tucson : University of Arizona Press, 2020. | Includes bibliographical references and index.
Identifiers: LCCN 2020011732 | ISBN 9780816541423 (hardcover) | ISBN 9780816541058 (paperback)
Subjects: LCSH: International cooperation. | Mexican-American Border Region. | United States—Relations—
    Mexico. | Mexico—Relations—United States.
Classification: LCC HF1456.5.M6 B56 2020 | DDC 320.90972/1—dc23
LC record available at https://lccn.loc.gov/2020011732

Printed in the United States of America
♾ This paper meets the requirements of ANSI/NISO Z39.48-1992 (Permanence of Paper).

CONTENTS

ABBREVIATIONS

ACA	Affordable Care Act
ACJS	accusatorial criminal justice system
ACLU	American Civil Liberties Union
ACS	American Community Survey
AGEB	*área geoestadística básica*
AHEC	Area Health Education Center
AMA	American Medical Association
AMC	Arizona-Mexico Commission
AMLO	Andrés Manuel López Obrador
AMO	Air and Marine Operations
AOBH	Arizona Office of Border Health
APF	Ley Orgánica de la Administración Pública Federal (Organic Law for Federal Public Administration)
ASEA	Agencia de Seguridad, Energía y Ambiente (Agency for Safety, Energy and Environment, also known as National Agency for Industrial Safety and Environmental Protection)
ATF	Bureau of Alcohol, Tobacco, Firearms and Explosives
AZMC	Arizona-Mexico Commission
BBHM	Border Binational Health Month
BEA	Bureau of Economic Analysis
BECC	Border Environment Cooperation Commission
BEF	Border Energy Forum
BEIF	Border Environmental Infrastructure Fund

BEST	Border Enforcement Security Task Force
BGC	Border Governors Conference
BHC	Border Health Commission
BIDS	Border Infectious Disease Surveillance
BIE	Banco de Información Económica (Economic Information Bank)
BLC	Border Legislative Conference
BLM	Border Liaison Mechanism
BLS	Bureau of Labor Statistics
BORSTAR	Border Patrol Search, Trauma, and Rescue Unit
BTA	Border Trade Alliance
BTS	Bureau of Transportation Statistics
CALTRANS	California Department of Transportation
CAMLA	California Anti-Money Laundering Alliance
CAP	Community Assistance Program
CBP	U.S. Customs and Border Protection
CBX	Cross Border Xpress
CC	Colibrí Center
CCIS	Center for Comparative Immigration Studies
CDM	Centro de los Derechos del Migrante
CDT	Consejo de Desarrollo Económico de Tijuana (Economic Development Council of Tijuana)
CEC	Commission for Environmental Cooperation
CENAGAS	Centro Nacional de Control del Gas Natural (National Center for Natural Gas Control)
CFPP	Código Federal de Procedimientos Penales (Federal Code of Penal Procedures)
CHIP	Children's Health Insurance Program
CHW	community health worker
CIABSUTEP	Center for Inter-American and Border Studies, University of Texas at El Paso
CILA	Comisión Internacional de Límites y Aguas (International Boundary and Water Commission)
CILASUCSD	Center for Iberian and Latin American Studies, University of California, San Diego
CISEN	Centro de Investigación y Seguridad Nacional (Center for Research and National Security)
CITES	Convention on Trade in Endangered Species of Wild Flora and Fauna

CMSA	core metropolitan statistical area
CNBV	Comisión Nacional Bancaria y de Valores (National Banking and Securities Commission)
CNH	Comisión Nacional de Hidrocarburos (National Hydrocarbons Commission)
COBINAS	Consejos Binacionales de Salud (Binational Health Councils)
COG	Council of Governments
COLEF	El Colegio de la Frontera Norte (College of the Northern Border)
COMEXI	Consejo Mexicano de Asuntos Internacionales (Mexican Council on Foreign Relations)
CONAPO	Consejo Nacional de Población (National Population Council)
CPS	Current Population Survey
CRE	Comisión Reguladora de Energía (Energy Regulatory Commission)
CRS	Congressional Research Service
CSG	Council of State Governments
CTA	Center for Transportation Analysis
CTPAT	Customs Trade Partnership Against Terrorism
DCL	designated commuter lane
DEA	U.S. Drug Enforcement Administration
DHS	U.S. Department of Homeland Security
DOC	U.S. Department of Commerce
DOE	U.S. Department of Energy
DOI	U.S. Department of the Interior
DOJ	U.S. Department of Justice
DOL	U.S. Department of Labor
DOS	U.S. Department of State
DOT	U.S. Department of Transportation
DTO	drug trafficking organization
EIA	U.S. Energy Information Administration
EMIF Norte	Encuesta sobre Migración en la Frontera Norte de México (Survey of Migration at Mexico's Northern Border)
ENEU	Encuesta Nacional de Empleo Urbano (National Survey of Urban Employment)
ENOE	Encuesta Nacional de Ocupaciones y Empleo (National Survey of Occupations and Employment)
EPA	U.S. Environmental Protection Agency

EPIC	El Paso Intelligence Center
EPN	Enrique Peña Nieto
EWIDS	Early Warning Infectious Disease Surveillance
FAF4	"Freight Analysis Framework Data Tabulation Tool"
FAST	Free and Secure Trade
FBI	Federal Bureau of Investigation
FCC	Foundation for the Children of the Californias
FDI	foreign direct investment
FERC	Federal Energy Regulatory Commission
FHWA	Federal Highway Administration
FMM	Forma Migratoria Múltiple (Multiple Migratory Form)
FPLEU	Foreign Prosecution and Law Enforcement Unit
FPU	Foreign Prosecution Unit
FQHC	Federally Qualified Health Center
FSS	U.S. Federal Statistical System
FTC	Federal Trade Commission
GAO	U.S. Government Accountability Office
GDP	gross domestic product
GHG	greenhouse gas
GIS	geographic information system
GNEB	Good Neighbor Environmental Board
GRP	gross regional product
GSA	General Services Administration
HAC	Hague Abduction Convention of 1980
HG	Hilarious Givers
HHS	U.S. Department of Health and Human Services
HLCG	High Level Contact Group
HLED	High Level Economic Dialogue
HPSA	Health Professional Shortage Area
IBEP	Integrated Border Environmental Plan
IBOEP	International Bridge Offices of El Paso
IBWC	U.S. International Boundary and Water Commission
ICE	U.S. Immigration and Customs Enforcement
ICF	International Community Foundation
IDP	Institutional Development and Cooperation Program
IIRIRA	Illegal Immigration Reform and Immigration Responsibility Act
IMIP	Instituto Municipal de Investigaciones y Planeación (Municipal Institute for Research and Planning)

IMPLAN	Instituto Metropolitano de Planeación (Metropolitan Institute of Planning)
IMSS	Instituto Mexicano del Seguro Social (Mexican Institute for Social Security)
INA	Immigration and Nationality Act
INAFED	Institución Nacional para el Federalismo y Desarrollo Municipal (National Institute for Federalism and Municipal Development)
INDAABIN	Instituto de Administración y Avalúos de Bienes Nacionales (Institute for Administration and Appraisal of National Property)
INEGI	Instituto Nacional de Estadística y Geografía (National Institute of Statistics and Geography)
INM	Instituto Nacional de Migración (National Migration Institute)
INS	Immigration and Naturalization Service
INSABI	Instituto de Salud para el Bienestar (Health Institute for Well-Being)
IRCA	Immigration Reform and Control Act
IRS	Internal Revenue Service
ISSSTE	Instituto de Seguridad y Servicios Sociales de Los Trabajadores del Estado (Institute for Social Security and Services for Government Employees)
ITA	International Trade Administration
JWC	U.S.-Mexico Joint Working Committee on Transportation Planning
LNG	liquified natural gas
LPOE	land port of entry
MCN	Migrant Clinicians Network
MCO	Managed Care Organization
MLAT	Mutual Legal Assistance in Criminal Matters Treaty
MMB	Mainly Mozart Binational
MMP	Mexican Migration Project
MOU	Memoranda (also Memorandum) of Understanding
MPO	Metropolitan Planning Organization
MPP	Migrant Protection Protocols
MUA	Medically Underserved Area
NAAEC	North American Agreement on Environmental Cooperation
NACEI	North American Cooperation on Energy Information

NADB/NADBANK — North American Development Bank
NAFTA — North American Free Trade Agreement
NAICS — North American Industry Classification System
NASC — North American Strategy for Competitiveness
NASS — National Agricultural Statistics Service
NEEC — Nuevo Esquema de Empresas Certificadas (New Scheme of Certified Companies)
NEPA — National Environmental Policy Act
NGO — nongovernmental organization
NIPA — national income and product accounts
NMOBH — New Mexico Office of Border Health
NSC — National Security Council
OCG — organized crime group
OEA — Operadores Económicos Autorizados (Authorized Economic Operators)
OFO — Office of Field Operations
OGA — Office of Global Affairs
OIG — Office of the Inspector General
ONDCP — Office of National Drug Control Policy
PAG — Pima Association of Governments
PAHO — Pan American Health Organization
PAN — Partido Acción Nacional (National Action Party)
PASE — Programa de Asistencia Estudiantil (Student Assistance Program)
PCIP — Pacific Council for International Policy
PDAP — Project Development Assistance Program
Pemex — Petróleos Mexicanos (Mexican Petroleum)
PGR — Procuraduría General de la República (Attorney General's Office)
PND — Plan Nacional de Desarrollo (National Development Plan)
PNHF — Paso del Norte Health Foundation
POE — port of entry
PPACA — Patient Protection and Affordable Care Act of 2010
PPP — public-private partnerships
PRI — Partido Revolucionario Institucional (Institutional Revolutionary Party)
PRONAP — Programa Nacional Fronterizo (National Border Program)
RFID — radio frequency identification
RMA — Regional Mobility Authority

RRC	Railroad Commission of Texas
SANDAG	San Diego Association of Governments
SAT	Servicio de Administración Tributaria (Tax Administration Service)
SBI	Southwest Border Initiative
SCAG	Southern California Association of Governments
SCIAN	Sistema de Clasificación Industrial de América del Norte (North American Industrial Classification System)
SCT	Secretaría de Comunicaciones y Transportes (Secretariat of Communications and Transportation)
SCTG	Standard Classification of Transported Goods
SDAGBC	San Diego Association of Governments, Borders Committee
SDNHM	San Diego Natural History Museum
SEAGO	Southeastern Arizona Governments Organization
SEDENA	Secretaría de la Defensa Nacional (Secretariat of National Defense)
SEDUE	Secretaría de Desarrollo Urbano y Ecología (Secretariat of Urban Development and Ecology)
SEGOB	Secretaría de Gobernación (Secretariat of the Interior)
SEMAR	Secretaría de Marina (Secretariat of the Navy)
SEMARNAT	Secretaría de Medio Ambiente y Recursos Naturales (Secretariat of Environment and Natural Resources)
SENER	Secretaría de Energía (Secretariat of Energy)
SENTRI	Secure Electronic Network for Travelers Rapid Inspection
SESA	Secretarías Estatales de Salud (State Health Services)
SHCP	Secretaría de Hacienda y Crédito (Secretariat of Finance and Public Credit)
SIE	Sistema de Información Energética (Energy Information System)
SNA	System of National Accounts
SNSP	Sistema Nacional de Seguridad Pública (National Public Security System)
SPP	Security and Prosperity Partnership of North America
SRE	Secretaría de Relaciones Exteriores (Secretariat of Foreign Affairs)
SSA	Secretaría de Salubridad y Asistencia (Secretariat of Health and Welfare)
SSA	U.S. Social Security Administration

STPS	Secretaría del Trabajo y Previsión Social (Secretariat of Labor and Social Welfare)
SVMPO	Sierra Vista Metropolitan Planning Organization
SWBA	Southwest Border Anti-Money Laundering Alliance
TAAP	Transboundary Aquifer Assessment Program
TBIUSD	Trans-Border Institute at the University of San Diego
TCEQ	Texas Commission on Environmental Quality
TCO	transnational criminal organization
TCWECM	Trilateral Committee for Wildlife and Ecosystem Conservation and Management
TGLO	Texas General Land Office
TSA	Transportation Security Administration
UN	United Nations
UNSD	United Nations Statistics Division
USBP	U.S. Border Patrol
USCIS	U.S. Citizenship and Immigration Services
USIBWC	U.S. Section, International Boundary and Water Commission
USMBHA	U.S.-Mexico Border Health Association
USMBHC	U.S.-Mexico Border Health Commission
USMBPP	U.S.-Mexico Border Philanthropy Partnership
USMCA	United States-Mexico-Canada Agreement
VAT	Value Added Tax
WACOG	Western Arizona Council of Governments
WHO	World Health Organization

BINATIONAL COMMONS

Introduction

Governing the Binational Commons

Tony Payan and Pamela L. Cruz

In February 2016, with the U.S.-Mexico border back in the headlines as the U.S. presidential election was heating up, the Center for the United States and Mexico at Rice University's Baker Institute for Public Policy launched a major research project on the U.S.-Mexico border.[1] The organizers convened expert practitioners and scholars from academia, government, civil society, and business sectors to a workshop in Houston, Texas, for an extensive discussion on the central issues facing the binational border. The workshop began with a dynamic discussion on specific issues affecting governance in the binational borderlands. It ended, however, with a consensus among the participants around the need to find ways to prevent the border from becoming hostage to political rhetoric—something that would eventually occur during the campaign and would only intensify in the following years with the election of Donald Trump to the presidency in November of that same year. Thus the conversation, which continued through 2016, had gone from a discussion on how to deal with specific border issues—including economics and trade, security and public safety, human mobility and migration, the environment and water and boundary issues, public health, physical infrastructure, civil society and democracy, political and public policy interfaces, at different governmental levels (binational, federal, state, and local)—to exploring ways to show the border in a positive light under a new administration that seemed hostile to the region and clearly intended to use it as a political pawn. To do this, it was evident that the workshop participants needed to answer the following question: How can a region and its population, as complex as the U.S.-Mexico border, resist attempts to define it negatively for political purposes, create and project its own image under challenging conditions, and show resilience in the face of rhetorical assaults? The answer to this question was to be found perhaps in political mobilization—something difficult on the borderlands as cross-border coordination is already a difficult thing to achieve—or maybe in campaigns to display the many contributions of the border to both countries, such as trade and cultural diversity, and so forth. None of these, however, would be enough. President Trump's assault on the image of the border has been perhaps the biggest constant of his administration and no mobilization or proborder campaign would counter his ability to reach all Americans throughout the country and define the border from his stand. The long-term answer to defend the border and its contributions to American and Mexican life was to be found on the state of the institutions that the border itself had generated to govern itself and their ability to withstand political hostility and survive a particularly hostile presidency. Thus, the first question to answer was: What is the state of cross-border institutions? Other questions followed: Can they help counter the image of the border as defined in Washington, D.C.? And, additionally, how do they contribute to good governance of the binational commons?

To examine the state of the U.S.-Mexico border institutional scaffolding was to require theoretical frameworks and models to understand the history of the border's institutional development and a survey of all the institutions that aid in governing it. An assessment of the current state of the border's institutional development—identifying its strengths and weaknesses—would presumably suffice to protect the borderlands from political profit by opportunistic politicians. At a first glance, participants of the workshop were not optimistic about the condition of cross-border institutions. Some areas appeared more institutionally developed than others. Others were relatively new and much less developed. Many of the participants agreed that governance on the border is uneven and lacking and the overall state of U.S.-Mexico border institutional development falls well short of providing the quantity and quality of venues not only to tackle the problems facing borderlanders—problems that require good solutions if border residents are to live and thrive in a complex environment such as the U.S.-Mexico border—but also to enable the border to resist political assaults and showcase its own accomplishments as a region. At the end of the workshop, the project's focus had shifted to the state of institutional development and governance at the U.S.-Mexico border.

To follow up on this agenda, toward the end of 2016, the Center for the United States and Mexico held a second workshop to refocus the discussion on the state of cross-border institutional development. Many of the mechanisms created by both countries to *govern* the border were examined—including treaties, organizations, commissions, committees, working groups, forums, and so forth—as well as their character and historical evolution. The goal of this second workshop was to carry out a clear-eyed assessment of the state of the mechanisms linking the two countries along and across the borderline and whether they are adequate to provide good governance for the twenty-first century—and provide the material to shield the border's image before national constituencies. However, over the course of these discussions, it became even clearer that the U.S.-Mexico border is a place of uneven institutional development. The border is a field of action where issues move at different speeds in the development of their governance instruments and draw only sporadic and even erratic attention, primarily when the governance mechanisms can no longer provide even moderately adequate solutions to problems and crises ensue. To understand the state of governance at the border it is necessary to describe and examine the degree of institutional development in each of the many different areas and understand how this development evolved through history. Only then would we detect the way cross-border institutions have developed and then be able to craft proposals for more effective governance in the twenty-first century—governance that is not only effective but also resistant to political opportunism. Under this focus, some of the key questions placed on the discussion table were: What is governance at the border? What are the institutions that "provide" governance at the border within and across issues? How have they evolved over time? What is the nature of these institutions? What is their current state? Are there specific issue areas that are more effective at good governance than others? Can some issue stakeholder communities learn from more successful experiences of others when it comes to border governance? Are the institutions overall adequate to deal with the multiplicity and complexity of the issues facing the region? Are the central and regional governments politically prepared to give the border a degree of autonomy to create the institutions that they require to effectively govern the border?

By the end of the year, participants in the two 2016 workshops agreed that, although there is much literature on the U.S.-Mexico border addressing different issues, and even a solid bibliography dealing with governance on many different issues, there was no single volume comprehensively looking at institutional development as a central problem of governance at the U.S.-Mexico border, and certainly not one volume that brings together an assessment of institutional development over many different areas, old and new. This volume attempts to do just that—to bring some of the foremost experts' minds to think through institutional development in their area of expertise, and to make a comprehensive assessment of the many experiences in developing institutions to provide cross-border governance.

Why Study Institutional Development?

Studying institutional development is not only about empowering communities to withstand political buccaneering. It is also about generating effective and democratic governance so that all the members of a community can enjoy the benefits of social life. In this sense, there is a consensus in the social sciences that quality governance is a factor of the degree of institutional development. In effect, governance in a substantive field—markets, security, infrastructure, human mobility, energy, and so on—or a geographic region reflects the quantity and quality of the institutions generated to facilitate and order social intercourse and enable individuals to grow and thrive. Where formal institutions are lacking, informal mechanisms often evolve to provide governance, but in such cases the issue area or geographical location is much more susceptible to capture by more sinister actors and interests who fill the voids created by the dearth of institutions. This means that to be successful, communities must develop meaningful, robust, and democratic institutions, which consist of laws, organizations, regulations, norms, and processes that provide all actors, individual and collective, in the field with clear signaling on behaviors that the members of the community believe enhance the welfare of its members and minimize dysfunctions or the pull of perverse incentives.[2] In general, institutions embody and give meaning to the practices, beliefs, and channels of interaction that control behavior to produce outcomes to the benefit of community members. Thus, institutions provide context to action, structure behavior by providing choice within constraints (Udehn 2002), and help organize collective action for problem solving. In the end, what a community is able to accomplish depends very much on effective governance, which in turn depends on the design and resilience of its institutions. Studying the origin, evolution, and state of institutions in a given context becomes then a prerequisite to understand the condition of governance in it. The resilience of a well-governed community vis-à-vis aggressive political rhetoric and opportunism is a byproduct of good institutional development.

Deep down, this book is concerned with border governance, but judgments on its effectiveness and inclusiveness cannot be understood without an in-depth analysis of the institutions that have been developed by those who claim a certain degree of jurisdiction over the border region and the many and complex issues that run through it. Without a thorough assessment of the institutions that govern specific issue areas along the border and how they come together as a system of governance, it is impossible to judge whether the border region is poised to prosper in the remainder of the century. Without a good analysis of the existing border institutional scaffolding, it is also difficult to craft recommendations to procure the kinds of institutions that will produce outcomes of governance that serve the security of all borderlanders and ultimately both countries.

Additional Challenges to Governing a Binational Commons

Studying institutions and governance in a substantive or geographic area contained within a national context is difficult enough—and generates important theoretical debates among social scientists on means and outcomes. There are many books and academic articles looking at institutions in governance in finance, trade, security, labor unions, technology, environmental issues, resources, human rights, and so forth—most of them evidently focused on specific issue areas, although some do focus on certain geographic regions. Looking at institutions and the categories of governance they produce in *border contexts* is more complicated, however. Borders are not just part of what Manuel Castells calls spaces of place, but they are also spaces of flows (1996, 29). Borders are dual spaces. Borders are where some institutions break off and others begin. They are places where institutions must interface, even when they originate in very different political, social, cultural, and economic traditions. Borders are places that blend but also separate sharply one institutional tradition and history from another. In other words, borders, in many ways, supersede national spaces because, by their sheer existence, borderlines create additional dimensions in social relations (Haselsberger 2014), including multiple levels of interaction (horizontal, vertical, and diagonal) (Torfing et al. 2012); new modalities of contact (hierarchical, cooperative, and competitive relationships, often occurring simultaneously); new bundled and unbundled functions (Cooper and Perkins 2011); new resources and limits on access to them (Sohn 2013); hybrid identities (Cunninghame 2008); and so on, all this in addition to the political-administrative institutions of the state-centric model of governance. Borders produce their own dynamics, unlike those of a more uniform reality in the middle of one country. Border infrastructure, for example, is not simply thinking about unification of standards, budgets, and other such issues, which, though important, can be solved by the institutions of a national policy context. It also requires thinking about the institutions that constitute each other's interlocutors to achieve agreement on basic issues whose nature may be quite different from one national context to another. On the U.S.-Mexico border, when it comes to border ports of entry, construction and expansion of new bridges or gateways often involve direct contact between a local authority in the United States (say, a city or county government) and a federal authority in Mexico (the Secretaría de Comunicaciones y Transportes [SCT, Secretariat of Communications and Transportation]), in what could be called a diagonal relationship. In some ways, the organizations that interact for that purpose must deal with an additional layer of reality—ensuring that a bridge coming from one side over the river meets the other half in exactly the same place and the same way.

Clearly, a key issue in governing the borderlands also has to do with how we view the border space and the dimensions it creates by virtue of its existence. It is true that borders are spaces that divide, but they are also spaces that unite, where water and air sheds, animal and plant species, mineral resources, and even languages and cultures straddle the borderline. Those issues are not easily divisible—they are wholes that need management as totals. In some sense, the borders are what Elinor Ostrom (1990) would call a *commons*. In effect, governing the borderlands requires that the spectator contemplate not a space that ends at a line on the sand or a river but a space that is deeply interconnected and where people, goods, services, and capital want to flow. The border, however, suffers from a state-centric approach to its definitional character. Central governments conceive borders as containers of national sovereignty (Ikeotu-onye 2007), and under this paradigm sovereignty is generally considered extinguished at the borderline. Thus, if two adjoining states fail to build solid institutions to govern the border commons, at a minimum it is possible to expect deficient governance and at a maximum outright conflict and in extreme cases even war. Thus, it becomes possible to ask whether the state (and its overarching institution — the government) is there to function as primarily a gatekeeper or whether it is there to coordinate the building of institutions that can both preserve and reinforce the sovereignty implied in its actions vis-à-vis the abutting state *and* to reach a degree of comfort in its neighborhood so as to pool its sovereignty with its neighbor to build institutions that can enhance governance mechanisms, maximize the border as a resource, and expand the welfare of its people, especially those living along the borderline. This is a question particularly relevant at a border that has institutionally evolved at a slower pace than the flows that cross it — the U.S.-Mexico border. In other words, institutional capacity for good governance at the border has not kept up with the outburst of activity across and along the borderline. And the answer to this question is even more pressing if we consider that there is an increasing political environment within the United States to see the border as a source of serious problems for the country rather than as an invaluable resource.

The question of institutional development is hardly a trivial question. Developing good governance in contexts of defensive sovereignty requires enormous political will — the kind of political will that Europe mustered in creating the union and then its Euroregion programs (Durà et al. 2018). It is possible to understand why states are protective of their sovereignty and why borders are places where states feel particularly insecure — as "creating and guarding borders is one of the most pervasive features of modern states" (Erb 2014, 122). In effect, border regions are more often seen as "front lines" rather than contact zones (Blatter 2004, 532). This partly explains the hesitancy of states to pool their sovereignty to create the right kind of institutions to govern borders seamlessly. Nonetheless, issues do emerge at borderlines and borderlands and states must come together to deal with them. To be sure, there has been some political will and institutional innovation on the U.S.-Mexico border. This volume is full of examples of this. But a key question is whether this amounts to solid and comprehensive institutional scaffolding that can provide good governance and, something more pressing today, withstand the political storms that from time to time clobber the border. The answer would likely be no, as the border has struggled to create wide-ranging institutions to ensure that the border regions are governed as what they are, a commons. Thus, as the reader progresses through this volume, it will become evident that Mexico and the United States have responded to different issues less with a wide-ranging plan to govern their commons and more by reacting to specific crises or issues that arise and cannot be avoided. Empirically, both countries understand the complexity of the border—with all the issues at stake, the many jurisdictions that need to be called to the table, the intensity of the flows both legal and illegal across the border, and so forth—but notionally it has been hard to transcend historical inertias and the low institutional innovation levels of leadership toward better border governance.

Institutional Development by Accretion

Over the course of the project that gave rise to this volume, several important observations emerged on the way the institutions that provide governance to the U.S.-Mexico border emerged. The first is that both countries never really had an intention to manage the border jointly, even when they identified issues that required cooperation. Of course, after the Mexican-American War of 1848 and the Gadsden Purchase of 1853, the priority was to establish the commission that would draw the line that today divides the two countries. This was a painstaking task accomplished by land surveyors, who took years to complete this duty (Werne 2007). By the late 1890s, it had become evident that drawing the line and leaving markers along it was not going to be enough, and the two countries founded the International Boundary Commission, tasked with maintaining the borderline. By the middle of the twentieth century, however, population growth put enormous pressure on the water resources and the two countries simply expanded the commission to add water management to its mandate. It became the International Boundary and Water Commission (IBWC). By the late twentieth century, it was again evident that pollution and other issues required attention, and they again expanded the mission to include sanitation, water quality, flood control, and other environmental issues (IBWC n.d. ["Mission"; "Synopsis"]). The growth of the commission and the expansion of its mandate to include new issues as they appeared along the way is a good example of how border institutions evolved—always reactively, always by accretion, and always ensuring the reinforced *national* rather than *binational* management of the border. The commissions, in effect, reinforced sovereignty; they did not pool it.

This growth by accretion resulted in the evolution of different issues at different speeds (see Sergio Peña's chapter in this volume). Some key issues, like the boundary and water management, are located within well-established organizations like the IBWC; other issues, like transportation infrastructure, are managed through coordinating mechanisms like the U.S.-Mexico Joint Working Committee on Transportation Planning (JWC), which includes representatives from federal, state, and local agencies charged with transportation infrastructure (JWC n.d.). This joint working committee does not have the binding nature of the decisions made by the IBWC, signaling that the issue has evolved at a different speed or is given less importance than boundary maintenance and watershed management. Other areas have seen their coordinating bodies disappear, such as the Pan American Health Organization (PAHO) office in the border region, charged with public health management. Perhaps it disappeared because public health management at the border and the national systems of health care have evolved so as to make it fairly easy to manage the issue without it, or perhaps cooperation on cross-border public health issues is not viewed as important by the two countries—certainly not as much as, say, binational trade, which does get a lot of attention. When it comes to law enforcement, the United States prefers to deal with issues through each nation's capital, trickling the mandates to border agencies and leaving local officers to develop their own informal channels—something that clearly shows that collaboration on this issue moves practically on a case-by-case basis and is managed strictly nationally. On other important and emerging issues, institutions are scarce but the markets function to introduce order to cross-border exchanges and to govern them. Energy is one such issue. In the last few decades, the two countries have seen increasing integration in electricity markets—as in the Cali-Baja Region—and a flurry of cross-border pipelines that bring natural gas from the United States to fuel Mexico's manufacturing competitiveness. These markets, although regulated by national legislation, are clearly integrated and rely on market forces for their governance, and there are close to no binational agencies regulating these exchanges. It may also be because many of them travel either underground (natural gas) or above ground (electricity), or because they cross the border as part of the large cross-border trade in goods. Markets, nonetheless, are institutions and do provide governance (Brunet-Jailly 2012).

What all these examples of how different issues have evolved in their own governance scaffolding show is that institutions, even when they are informal, have evolved gradually, sometimes over and integrating old structures and norms instead of replacing them; at different speeds, with some relatively well-organized issue areas and others relying on much less formal mechanisms for collaboration; and depending largely on the interest of agents who sometimes live quite afar from the border itself, sometimes involving negative attention or reactions to events on the ground at or away from the borderline. The consequence is that institutional development at the U.S.-Mexico border has remained essentially uneven, depending on the issue at hand and many different factors and governance frameworks pertaining to that issue, and depending on the attention the issue area gets from actors in the centers of power or the sense of urgency that envelops that one issue at any given point in time. To be sure, however, it may be that a single institutional design may not serve all issues equally well or that linking all issues into a single coordinating agency is simply too difficult and perhaps not possible or desirable, although clearly there are structures of incentives that could facilitate issue linkage and the construction of cross-border cooperation mechanisms that are more effective and efficacious than what we have today. In other words, this volume does not want to argue that centralized governance schemes are possible or desirable. It simply seeks to illustrate that border institution building has evolved by accretion and at different speeds and often reactively so that current mechanisms are not enough to provide the kind of governance that the borderlands require in the complex, more globalized system of the twenty-first century. That is, the system of institutions must be evaluated comprehensively and vis-à-vis the needs of the growing border population and contemplate even decentralized systems of governance, which can help make life better for all involved. All approaches to institution building should be considered. Single purses of resources for which agencies working together across the border could only apply together might, for example, incentivize them to develop stronger links, even across issues, and formalize their interaction channels. The European Union border regions program has done it relatively successfully, even if it has had its own critics (AEBR 2019).

The factors that impede institution building have to do not only with structural issues—including the overarching constraints that national sovereignty imposes, a mutual historical distrust that persists to this day, incompatibility of governing systems, and so on—but also with uninterested, neglectful, and even adverse agency and a dearth of political will. Moreover, the U.S.-Mexico border has always been a political football, especially in the United States. Indeed, the border can often be a good focal point to profit politically, distract the attention of constituencies, create imagined menaces, or focus blame for other failures. Border institution building, as a result, has suffered from political opportunism—with the field advantage generally going in favor of the border's detractors. This implies that effective institution building depends excessively on the "developers" of a political system and the leadership that they can bring to bear on the construction of organizations, laws, rules, norms, and procedures. It also means that the great degree of political will and creativity required to build institutions in a border context is often missing. Consequently, there is never enough momentum to build more or quickly enough, and because most institutions operate as silos, confined to an issue area or a specific territory, there is little potential for linkages in institution building. In effect, few institution developers have paid the kind of sustained attention that the border requires or brought forth the talents that it calls for. In fact, while few politicians view institution building on the border as a good opportunity to advance their careers, many see political opportunity in creating public hazards (Brown 2011), real or imagined, at the borderlands precisely because they can profit from doing so. The result has been that many of them have held the border region hostage to their political goals—not the least of which in the last few years has been Donald Trump (Heyer 2018). Federal agencies too have viewed the border as an opportunity to assert their organizational interests, well above the idea of effective binational governance (Payan 2018). In effect, the absence of institutions sometimes favors certain actors precisely because it allows them enormous discretion in rule making and rule enforcing. Law enforcement at the border, for example, has hijacked the border policy agenda, gradually increasing its power and influence (Heyman and Campbell 2012) and absorbing jurisdictional authority over many other issue areas. One instance is the U.S. federal government's ability to waive environmental laws to expedite the construction of border barriers (Bear 2009). In effect, sometimes the border is the object of policy by bureaucracy.

The Border and Political Will

Building institutions for border governance requires and will continue to require a high degree of political will. This important ingredient for institution building has been relatively sparse along the U.S.-Mexico border. The European experience, on the contrary, is a clear example of the kind of political will that is required to convince national publics, government agencies, elected leaders, and even local actors to pool sovereignty (Peterson 1997), to break national molds, and to legislate and direct resources that can create incentives to increase binational management policies and systems and deepen cooperation on a multitude of issues unique to border regions. Political will, however, is only one component. Sometimes it exists but other ingredients are missing, and it leads nowhere. Another ingredient is political creativity. Indeed, creating institutions in the twenty-first century for a complex environment such as the border also requires high doses of political creativity (Beamer 1999, 1–10). The relationship between political will and creativity at the border, both of which combine into effective leadership, is not yet well explored. The border has seldom had the kind of leadership that combines both. More often, issues have emerged, derived in a crisis, and leadership has had to respond to them by creating mechanisms to deal with them—some of which disappear over time and some of which have fortunately remained in place and even evolved and become more complex. At other times, it is the demands of the local populations that have made leadership respond. But this too is rare at the U.S.-Mexico border. In a normal context—say, in the middle of the country—local politics bubbles up to the national level. Not so at the border. Along the borderline, this logic is largely reversed. National politics bubbles down to the local level, and decisions about the border get made by people who barely understand the complex dynamics generated by bordered spaces. Trump's rhetoric surrounding the border shows just that. And this is what points to the idea that borders are often the object of negative attention, as opposed to positive and proactive attention in the direction of creating the right management institutions for effective and democratic governance (Soroka and McAdams 2015). Moreover, the dynamics of the Trump administration toward the border are a sign that there might be vested interests in maintaining the border as a problem because it is politically more profitable than exercising political will and seeking creative policy responses to bring about better governance. It is, after, all a curious fact that we often pay attention to problem solving but we seldom pay attention to problem maintenance. At the border, there are actors who prefer to maintain the problem that gives them purpose than to solve it.

But building institutions is complicated; it should be thought of as a long-term investment instead. In other words, political will and creativity among the leaders at the top is not enough to generate institutions. There are other ingredients that contribute to institution building. Leaders and communities must also invest financial resources, cultivate specific skills, and invest energy and time in addition to a sustained degree of enthusiasm around the cause of institutions. Financial resources adequately structured to incentivize certain cooperative behaviors are needed. Institutions require individuals who look after them, maintain them, and ensure compliance—and maybe even punish violations. These same institutions necessitate a degree of what is often referred to as task maturity—that is, the necessary skills to exercise administrative leadership on a day-to-day basis and to respond to demands and implement changes in the institutions when the environment dictates it. In other words, institutions are also made up of human capital that is uniquely prepared to deal with the issues at hand. Complex border contexts such as the U.S.-Mexico border region often require bilingual and bicultural people who can move seamlessly from one side to the other and from one Weltanschauung to another and can themselves be individual bridges when dealing with difficult disagreements. Institution building also requires psychological maturity—the zeal and enthusiasm to commit to crafting the right institutions. At the U.S.-Mexico border, clearly there are people and leaders who are convinced and passionate about their mission. And this kind of conviction and passion is irreplaceable when dealing with the border. It is not difficult to understand that institution building at the U.S.-Mexico border is complex, but even more so if any of these ingredients are missing. Not surprisingly, many different variables must be aligned correctly for institutions to emerge and be effective over a long time. Very often, local politicians will possess one or more ingredients but lack something or may have them all but run into key obstacles, not the least of which is hardened sovereignty, lack of mutual trust, and even vested interests in the status quo, in addition to a democratic deficit, as local actors are seldom consulted on the kind of border they would like to see (Payan 2010).

In general, building institutions that can effectively manage the border commons requires that many ingredients be right and that many forces relent to allow new definitions of the region, the issues, and the actors. Achieving this in a convoluted historical timeline and among intricate issues is itself a nearly insurmountable challenge. And this in turn may explain why institutional development on the U.S.-Mexico border is uneven, primarily reactive, and lacking in both effectiveness and democracy. It may also explain why those interests that are most powerful rhetorically, better funded, more politically adept, and simplistic in their understanding of social life—for example, security in the twenty-first century—end up prevailing at the expense of good governance.

The Twenty-First-Century Governance Challenges

It is already worrisome to get to the third decade of the twenty-first century with a high degree of institutional underdevelopment on the border. Social, political, cultural, and economic change continues apace and does not wait for leaders to meet all the requirements for institution building or for all the ingredients to be just right to do so. The borderlands are expected to continue to grow demographically, doubling their population by 2050—from fifteen million to nearly thirty million residents. This will require a new human mobility system—one that is more open and empowering of borderlands to use the border as a resource. Trade and economic integration, whether under the North American Free Trade Agreement (NAFTA) or its successor, the United States-Mexico-Canada Agreement (USMCA), which is scheduled to enter into force on July 1, 2020, will continue. On the heels of that, the infrastructure that will carry increased traffic is already overwhelmed and the framework that coordinates its expansion and modernization has already proven largely ineffective. Other areas are emerging and will become important, including energy integration (see Adrián Duhalt's chapter in this book). Environmental and natural resources challenges will also become more acute, as global warming accelerates—something that could endanger the sustainability of the entire region. And security cooperation will probably become more important as the global strategic game changes and U.S. hegemony is challenged around the world.

All these changes, many of which are already underway, require a binational vision and a binational strategy. Dealing with them requires sharp theoretical and historical understanding of the issues (see Peña's chapter in this book). It also requires that we have a good idea of what comprises the border, with solid and practicable yet flexible definitions of the borderlands (see Tony Payan and Pamela L. Cruz's chapter in this volume). It requires that the leadership in both countries view the border as a resource for both nations and that they have the vision to build the right institutions. Unfortunately, now, both countries seem to have abandoned the idea of a North America (Pastor 2011) and have resorted to inward-looking nationalistic approaches to problem solving. The elections of Donald Trump in the United States in 2016 and Andrés Manuel López Obrador in Mexico in 2018 are clear signs that the consensus of the last three decades is breaking down—if it ever was true. The two countries seem to be drifting apart in a way not seen since the 1970s. The border remains a poorly understood area and the state of its institutions are such that they do not appear to be able to withstand political capture—exemplified by Trump's insistence on the border wall. Cross-border civil society, as argued later in this book (see Víctor Daniel Jurado Flores and Cecilia Sarabia Ríos's chapter), is also too weak to resist the ever-present temptation to turn the border into a source of problems instead of a source of opportunities. And local leadership appears to be bound by larger, more powerful concepts—for example, sovereignty—to be able to exert power in building institutions that work for the border region (see Manuel A. Gutiérrez and Kathleen Staudt's chapter). Overall, the tide is not in the borderlands' favor. But borderlanders are not powerless. They have found ways to carve niches of cooperation in the past and they can do so in the future. However, their efforts will not render lasting fruit. For that, they will have to push for the construction of institutions that can guarantee good governance that can transcend individuals and reduce the turbulence of national political shifts. Unfortunately, the dearth of institutions—or their uneven development—will only doom the border to a condition of economic and political disadvantage and will continue to erode the quality of life and the cross-border intimacy that many borderlanders long for (Payan and Vasquez 2007).

Goals of This Volume

Borders are unique laboratories to study policy, and they are certainly invaluable places to study institutions and institutional development. If one wants to study health-care systems, for example, artificial lines on the ground, dividing similar populations, such as Ciudad Juárez and El Paso, can help measure effectiveness in delivery or outcomes based on institutional design. Sister cities divided by a borderline can nearly become natural social experiments for students of borders. In other words, borders may serve as places of encounter, but they also provide a clear line between institutional environments that permit the examination of how institutions affect development, social life, political dynamics, markets, and so forth. Borders, in other words, provide the opportunity to study specific phenomena as if they were natural experiments. The U.S.-Mexico border is no exception. The binational border examined in this book, however, does not focus on national institutions to examine the different outcomes they provide. Instead, the border provides a unique opportunity to examine institutional development to govern the binational *commons*, especially institutional development that promotes good governance in transborder spaces as *transborder* spaces, not as spaces contained in a *national* envelope. As already mentioned, borderlines produce their own reality, and it is often different from the two distinct national realities, which a line on the sand separates. In that sense, border spaces also provide unique opportunities for studying the requirements for building institutions that provide governance in spaces of exclusive sovereignty. That too provides a unique opportunity to compare institutions and governance as it is built to function on both sides on a given issue. Thus, this book does not focus on the differences between institutions that abut each other but on institutions—or the lack thereof—that are meant to straddle the borderline.

Without getting ahead of the reader, we can anticipate that, after reviewing some of the evidence, it can be argued that the U.S.-Mexico borderlands exhibit a medium to low level of institutional development or, alternatively, an uneven institutional development, depending on the field of activity—security, trade and economics, water and the environment, human mobility, infrastructure development, and so on. In other words, the U.S.-Mexico border has not reached the level of institutional development that, for example, many of the Euroregions exhibit, but it is also not an alienated border with little or no institutional activity. This leads us to understand that what this volume offers is a diagnosis that can aid politicians and policy makers as well as students of borders in understanding the state of the institutions that govern our border, with the ideal that it can also offer a rough guide to what is still missing to achieve higher levels of institution development and thereby better governance—governance for the twenty-first century.

More specifically, while there are organizations, laws, and regulations that govern certain border spaces—again, in specific areas—others are treated as unilateral despite the strong evidence that they are border spaces that require a greater level of governance. At the same time, a degree of governance complexity exists between the United States and Mexico that stems from the nature and structure of their respective political systems. In each country, different border spaces are governed by different organizations that exist at different levels of government. Thus, governance can often originate differently from separate points of action and power in distinct public policy areas, constituting a multicentric space with overlapping and crisscrossing jurisdictions, but it may not add up to the kind of governance that the U.S.-Mexico border requires in the twenty-first century. In that regard, the U.S.-Mexico borderlands are made up of distinctive and overlapping policy spaces with a long but uneven history of institutional development that present an ideal case for the study of border space governance.

At a chapter-by-chapter level, the goal of this book is to examine where there are strong levels of institutional governance, where it is failing, and what can be done to improve the governance needs of the U.S.-Mexico borderlands. The book examines the entire border region and highlights specific examples from different cases (e.g., Tijuana–San Diego, Nogales-Nogales, El Paso–Ciudad Juárez, Laredo–Nuevo Laredo, and Matamoros-Brownsville, among others). In the process, the book seeks to make a significant contribution to the study of institutional cross-border governance, specifically on the U.S.-Mexico border, including sectors that are fully institutionalized and evident but also the informal networks and hidden actors that may lie underneath and help carry out regional governance. In sum, this edited volume will make a contribution toward filling the institutional development knowledge gap that exists at the U.S.-Mexico border, and each chapter will discuss key policy issues and end with clear policy recommendations to improve cross-border governance.

Organization of the Book

The twelve chapters that follow are organized into two parts. Part I provides a panorama on the theoretical and conceptual perspective of issues that institutions might face. Each chapter examines complex issues such as historical and theoretical concepts of space and place governance; overlapping and inconsistent territorial definitions of the border; data collection, interpretation, and distribution; and the structure of social networks within the binational context of the U.S.-Mexico border.

In chapter 1, "Place and Space Governance at the U.S.-Mexico Border (1944–2017)," Sergio Peña explores the theoretical and historical concepts of space and place to understand governance structures and how these concepts shape institutions and processes. Peña addresses the evolution of governance frameworks at the U.S.-Mexico border in the last fifty years from a spatial perspective. He uses three main schools of thought—positivist, structuralist, and poststructuralist perspectives—to examine U.S.-Mexico border governance and policy. In the end, understanding the history of the border and its governance is quintessential to figure out the routes for institution building in the future.

In chapter 2, "Defining the Border and the Borderlands: A Precondition for Institutional Development?," Tony Payan and Pamela L. Cruz explore the theoretical and empirical problems of defining the U.S.-Mexico border and the difficulty in providing a concise territorial definition of the border. They outline different territorial definitions of the U.S.-Mexico border across political-administrative units, federal entities, and formal binational agreements, and point out the disadvantages of these overlapping and conflicting definitions. Moreover, Payan and Cruz argue that what constitutes the border should be an important element for current and future binational institutions because current territorial definitions complicate the management of population growth, climate change and other environmental challenges, and crossborder activities, both legal and illegal. The myriad definitions are insufficient to effectively manage the border region's policy issues, which affect local, state, national, and international interests.

In chapter 3, "Data for U.S.-Mexico Border Studies: A Comparison of U.S. and Mexican Data Collection and Distribution," James Gerber and Jorge Eduardo Mendoza Cota delve into an issue that is not widely researched—data comparability and data collection institutions of the United States and Mexico. They discuss the differences in data collection and interpretation and the institutional frameworks under which data is compiled and distributed. Furthermore, as Gerber and Mendoza Cota explore, the two greatest limitations to border studies in terms of data collection are that both countries, but especially Mexico, need to provide more municipal-level data, and that both countries need to provide data sources that directly measure crossborder interactions. Better data and comparable data lead to data-driven public policy that works for better governance.

Part II delves into the institutional universe and its governance at the U.S.-Mexico border issue by issue. Each sector has its own institutions, mechanisms of cooperation, lessons to be learned, shared practices, and areas for improved governance. Each chapter deals with a different sector, providing an in-depth view of the institutions that govern and concrete public policy recommendations. The sectors explored in part II are local governments, environment, health, security, human mobility, transportation, trade, and energy.

Chapter 4, "Collaborative Social Networks: An Exploratory Study of the U.S.-Mexico Border," by Víctor Daniel Jurado Flores and Cecilia Sarabia Ríos, focuses on binational institutions and organizations along the U.S.-Mexico border and the social networks of collaboration that exist between institutions in similar fields. The U.S.-Mexico border space is made up of a universe of institutions with a common objective to achieve better governance. Jurado Flores and Sarabia Ríos argue it is important to analyze binational institutions' social networks in order to better understand levels of participation and institutional mediation/management of binational institutional projects, programs, and institutional tendencies to identify interinstitutional social capital.

In chapter 5, "Governing the Borderlands Commons: Local Actors at Work," Manuel A. Gutiérrez and Kathleen Staudt discuss local and state governments, legislative conferences, agency-to-agency work, city-to-city goals, metropolitan region–to–metropolitan region aims, and other "official efforts" to provide quality border governance. Gutiérrez and Staudt argue that both the United States and Mexico enact legislation at the federal level that affects the border region, but it is not common to see one aimed at local-level institutions. They discuss current models for best practices, as seen in San Diego–Tijuana and Laredo–Nuevo Laredo, as well as a model of constraints and lack of cooperation exhibited in El Paso–Ciudad Juárez. They end their chapter with recommendations for governing bodies in the borderlands.

In chapter 6, "Environmental Governance at the U.S.-Mexico Border: Institutions at Risk," Irasema Coronado and Stephen Mumme explore the institutional dimension of environmental governance along the U.S.-Mexico border, with an emphasis on environmental capacity accrual and resilience of the bilateral and cooperative environmental agencies and policies currently in place. Coronado and Mumme lay out the evolution of environmental governance, looking at institutional arrangements, trends, and key agreements. They also examine the binational agencies and programs engaged in border environmental protection. Coronado and Mumme address the challenge of governance along the border and conclude with public policy recommendations for environmental agencies and programs.

In chapter 7, "Health Institutions at the U.S.-Mexico Border," Eva M. Moya, Silvia M. Chavez-Baray, and Miriam S. Monroy examine health institutions and health-care delivery in the United States and at the U.S.-Mexico border. They briefly review the health-care systems in the United States, Mexico's health system, and where the two systems meet and address border and binational health cooperation, including a discussion on binational programs and initiatives. They also address issues specific to the U.S.-Mexico border, such as barriers to health-care access, binational health insurance, and medical tourism. Moya, Chavez-Baray, and Monroy find that a pattern of development exists where cross-border health care has gained presence and momentum and offer public policy recommendations to address the complex realities of health care on the U.S.-Mexico border.

In chapter 8, "From the Institutional to the Informal: Security Cooperation Between the United States and Mexico," Octavio Rodríguez Ferreira provides a background of institutional security cooperation and relationship between the United States and Mexico. He examines historical and political struggles of shared problems between the two countries and explores the cooperation mechanisms, national-level collaboration agreements, field-level interagency collaboration, and "on-the-ground informal networks" that exist in law enforcement and intelligence sharing.

In chapter 9, "U.S.-Mexico Law Enforcement and Border Security Cooperation: An Institutional-Historical Perspective," Guadalupe Correa-Cabrera and Evan D. McCormick consider to what degree the binational relationship has evolved so that cross-border collaboration has proven durable enough to survive the negative rhetoric of the Trump administration. They historically analyze U.S.-Mexico border security cooperation and transnational law enforcement from an institutional perspective.

In chapter 10, "Transportation Institutions Along the U.S.-Mexico Border," Kimberly Collins examines current transportation networks and institutions in the U.S.-Mexico border region. She addresses binational coordination on regional planning and management and local institutions and interactions. Collins also discusses cross-border transportation and infrastructure challenges and ends with a discussion on transportation and the future of cross-border travel.

Chapter 11, "Human Mobility at the U.S.-Mexico Border," by Tony Payan, Pamela L. Cruz, and Carla Pederzini Villarreal, discusses the system of cross-border human mobility and its regulations—including immigration—and impacts on the U.S.-Mexico border. They contend that understanding the institutional scaffolding of human mobility and its governance at the U.S.-Mexico border is crucial to facilitating the flow of legitimate trade and travel. And with human mobility and migration, as with many other issues, it is clear that efficient institutions are now required, as new restrictions in human mobility flows and law enforcement may end up creating burdensome transaction costs for only very marginal returns on security and other such concerns.

Finally, in chapter 12, "Governance and Energy Trade on the U.S.-Mexico Border," Adrián Duhalt explores the extent of U.S.-Mexico cross-border interdependence and integration on energy issues. He focuses on several factors that shape energy border governance, including the recent developments in the energy sector in Mexico, drivers of energy trade, gaps in energy data, and gaps in both formal and informal institutional arrangements that facilitate their interaction and cooperation. Duhalt concludes that while there are vast opportunities in energy institutional innovation at the border, issues such as infrastructure, social opposition, and local community input need to be taken into account to strengthen governance structures and cross-border cooperation.

This volume concludes with a discussion of the public policy recommendations and implications for border governance. It is vital that we look at these institutions, and it is essential for borderlanders to organize to demand of their political leadership stronger institutions for better governance of their binational commons in the twenty-first century. Without stronger political demands, institutional building, and mechanisms for collaboration, good governance will remain elusive and the border will doubtless turn into a nearly unlivable space, prey to interests that diminish democracy, extract enormous costs from its residents, and allow politicians to play games with few consequences.

Notes

1. In August 2019, the Baker Institute's Mexico Center changed its name to the Center for the United States and Mexico.

2.   This does not mean that institutions are quintessentially good. Laws, organizations, regulations, norms, and processes can also be used to exclude, repress, and so forth. In general, governance will reflect the intention of the institutions built, and the outcomes may not necessarily be all good.

References

AEBR (Association of European Border Regions). n.d. Gronau, Germany. Accessed April 30, 2020. https://www.aebr.eu/en/index.php.

Beamer, Glenn. 1999. *Creative Politics: Taxes and Public Goods in a Federal System.* Ann Arbor: University of Michigan Press.

Bear, Dinah. 2009. "Border Wall: Broadest Waiver of Law in American History." Center for International Environmental Law, Washington, D.C., February. http://www.ciel.org/Publications/BorderWall_8Feb09.pdf.

Blatter, Joachim. 2004. "'From Spaces of Place' to 'Spaces of Flows'? Territorial and Functional Governance in Cross-Border Regions in Europe and North America." *International Journal of Urban and Regional Research* 28 (3): 530–48.

Brown, Lara M. 2011. *Jockeying for the American Presidency: The Political Opportunism of Aspirants.* Amherst, N.Y.: Cambria Press.

Brunet-Jailly, Emmanuel. 2012. "Theorizing Borders: An Interdisciplinary Perspective." *Geopolitics* 10 (4): 633–49.

Castells, Manuel. 1996. *The Rise of the Network Society.* Oxford: Blackwell.

Cooper, Anthony, and Chris Perkins. 2011. "Borders and Status-Functions: An Institutional Approach to the Study of Borders." *European Journal of Social Theory* 15 (1): 55–71.

Cunninghame, Patrick Gun. 2008. "Hybridity, Transnationalism, and Identity in the U.S.-Mexican Borderlands." In *Hybrid Identities: Theoretical and Empirical Examinations*, edited by Keri Iyall Smith and Patricia Levy, 13–40. Boston: Brill.

Durà, Antoni, Andrea Noferini, Matteo Berzi, and Franceso Camonita. 2018. "Euroregions, Excellence and Innovation Across EU Borders: A Catalogue of Good Practices." Universitat Autònoma de Barcelona, Spain. https://ec.europa.eu/futurium/en/system/files/ged/recot_crii_catalogue_0.pdf.

Erb, Maribeth. 2014. "Borders and Insecurities in Western Flores." *Asian Journal of Social Science* 42 (1–2): 122–63.

Haselsberger, Beatrix. 2014. "Decoding Borders: Appreciating Border Impacts on Space and People." *Planning Theory and Practice* 15 (4): 505–26.

Heyer, Kristin E. 2018. "Internalized Borders: Immigration Ethics in the Age of Trump." *Theological Studies* 79 (1): 146–64.

Heyman, Josiah, and Howard Campbell. 2012. "The Militarization of the United States-Mexico Border Region." *Revista de Estudos Universitários* 38 (1): 75–94.

IBWC (International Boundary and Water Commission). n.d. "Mission." Accessed April 30, 2020. https://www.ibwc.gov/mission.html.

IBWC (International Boundary and Water Commission). n.d. "Synopsis." Accessed April 30, 2020. https://www.ibwc.gov/About_Us/synopsis.html.

Ikeotuonye, Festus. 2007. "The 'Container Model' Paradox: Borders, Frontiers, and the State's Own Image of Itself." Paper presented at the Sixth Pan-European Conference on International Relations, University of Turin, September 12–15.

JWC (U.S.-Mexico Joint Working Committee on Transportation Planning). n.d. "Who We Are." Accessed April 30, 2020. https://www.fhwa.dot.gov/planning/border_planning/us_mexico/.

Ostrom, Elinor. 1990. *Governing the Commons: The Evolution of Institutions for Collective Action.* Cambridge: Cambridge University Press.

Pastor, Robert. 2011. *The North American Idea: A Vision of a Continental Future.* Oxford: Oxford University Press.

Payan, Tony. 2010. "Crossborder Governance in a Tristate, Binational Region." In *Cities and Citizenship at the U.S.-Mexico Border: The Paso del Norte Metropolitan Region,* edited by Kathleen Staudt, Julia Fragoso, and César Fuentes, 217–44. New York: Palgrave Macmillan.

Payan, Tony. 2018. "Paper Tigers and Imagined Risks: Organizational Culture and Bureaucratic Politics at the U.S.-Mexico Border." Paper presented at the conference Frontière et Murs Frontaliers: Un Nouvelle Ere? Sécurité, Symbolisme et Vulnérabilité, September 25–29.

Payan, Tony, and Amanda Vásquez. 2007. "The Costs of Homeland Security." In *Borderlands: Comparing Security in North America and Europe,* edited by Emmanuel Brunet-Jailly, 231–58. Ottawa, Ontario: University of Ottawa Press.

Peterson, John. 1997. "The European Union: Pooled Sovereignty, Divided Accountability." *Political Studies* 45 (3): 559–78.

Sohn, Christophe. 2013. "The Border as a Resource in the Global Urban Space: A Contribution to the Cross-Border Metropolis Hypothesis." *International Journal of Urban and Regional Research* 38 (5): 1697–1711.

Soroka, Stuart, and Stephen McAdams. 2015. "News, Politics, and Negativity." *Political Communication* 32 (1): 1–22.

Torfing, Jacob B., Guy Peters, Jon Pierre, and Eva Sørensen. 2012. "Interactive Governance: Advancing the Paradigm." Oxford Scholarship Online, May. http://www.oxfordscholarship.com/view/10.1093/acprof:oso/9780199596751.001.0001/acprof-9780199596751.

Udehn, Lars. 2002. *The Limits of Public Choice: A Sociological Critique of the Economic Theory of Politics.* New York: Routledge.

Werne, Joseph Richard. 2007. *The Imaginary Line: A History of the United States and Mexican Boundary Survey, 1848–1857.* College Station: Texas Christian University Press.

PART I

...

FRAMING INSTITUTIONAL DEVELOPMENT AT THE U.S.-MEXICO BORDER

1

Place and Space Governance at the U.S.-Mexico Border (1944–2017)

Sergio Peña

This chapter studies the evolution of governance frameworks at the U.S.-Mexico border over the last fifty years from a spatial perspective. The time frame is bounded by two key events and what happens in between—namely, the 1944 signing of the Treaty Between the United States of America and Mexico for the Utilization of Waters of the Colorado Rio and Tijuana Rivers and of the Rio Grande (hereafter 1944 Treaty) and the election of Donald Trump in 2016 with a strong anti-Mexican rhetoric. These historical events represent inflection points in the way border space is conceived and managed. The 1944 Treaty is an example of cross-border collaboration and cooperation, whereas the latter signals the opposite—unilateralism and confrontation. These cases represent debordering and rebordering processes (Blatter 2004; Brenner 1999; Brenner et al. 2003; Jessop 2002; Newman 2003; Newman and Passi 1998). This chapter places special attention on place and space as key conceptual categories to understand governance structures and their relationship to rebordering and debordering processes at the U.S.-Mexico border. It is important to have a good conceptual grasp of the meaning of place and space for a better understanding of border governance and institutions. Different authors (Agnew 2015; Blatter 2004; Blatter and Ingram 2000; Brenner et al. 2003; Peña 2011) hypothesized that the institutional architecture, broadly defined as the rules and norms that govern the border, had embedded a conception of space and place that shapes the processes, practices, and policy actions (governmental and nongovernmental). Even today, despite integration and intense cooperation, the U.S.-Mexico border is still being governed by conceptions of space as a container (Taylor 2003) rather than in relational spatial terms (Healey 2000; Lefebvre 1991).

I explore further the concepts of space/place and how these conceptual categories can be used as analytical tools to frame the study of border governance. Moreover, I rely on historical analysis to bring together time and space as analytical categories of social systems (Giddens 1984). The analysis will show that time and space are not lineal processes of border governance, as some authors have inferred (Martínez 1994), going from alienated borders that lack cooperation toward integrated transnational spaces. Rather, the process can move one step forward and two steps backward. That is, a process could undo cooperation and integration and lead toward conflict and alienation. Also, as John Agnew (2015, 42) points out, "a priori evolutionism," which divides history into evolutionary stages, is unable to explain when "features of one stage persist into another, or when stages are bypassed or fail to appear."

This chapter is divided into three sections. The first section is a theoretical discussion of the meaning of space and place to draw some inferences regarding the structures, processes, and practices of border governance associated with a particular spatial conception. Different authors provide different classifications and typologies of border approaches and theories (Agnew 2015; Brenner et al. 2003; Kolossov 2005; Newman 2003, 2006; Newman and Passi 1998; Passi 2009), and it is hard to find a common thread among them that would provide guidelines about border governance. However, other works (Davoudi and Strange 2008; Mandanipour, Hull, and Healey 2016) provide synthetic analyses that I consider useful to explore the issue of border governance from a spatial perspective. There are three main schools of thought regarding space and place governance (Davoudi and Strange 2008; Mandanipour, Hull, and Healey 2016): (1) positivist, (2) structuralist, and (3) poststructuralist. The main characteristics of each approach as well as the notions of space and place will be discussed in more detail, as well as how each approach can be extrapolated to the study of border governance. The next section identifies, characterizes, and discusses different programs, policies, and plans that have emerged at the U.S.-Mexico border since 1944, applying the theoretical framework outlined in the previous section. Examples of those programs and actions are the 1944 Treaty; U.S. president Richard Nixon's Operation Intercept in 1969; different operations in the mid-1990s, such as Operation Hold the Line in Texas, Gatekeeper in California, and Safeguard in Arizona; the La Paz Agreement in the 1980s; the Border Industrialization Program; the North American Free Trade Agreement (NAFTA) in 1994; the creation of the Border Environment Cooperation Commission (BECC); the different border programs such as Border 2012 and Border 2020; and state-driven anti-immigrant legislation such as Arizona SB1070 and Bill SB4 in Texas, among others. Finally, U.S. president Donald Trump's proposal to build a wall along the U.S.-Mexico border is addressed. The methodology employed to analyze the programs is based on content analysis. The third section explores the main approaches to border governance and their shortcomings based on the dominant notions of space and place. Also, it includes a reflection on how border governance could be strengthened by using alternative spatial/place frameworks and some policy suggestions.

Space and Place

This section focuses on relevant theoretical works to clarify the concepts of space and place. Borders are the scenario where notions of space and place not only play an important and concrete role but also shape structures, processes, and practice of governance. The academic debate around the meaning of space and place is not new. It dates to Aristotle and Plato in ancient Greece and was then revived in the nineteenth century (Agnew 2011). A point of convergence between structuralist and poststructuralist approaches is the need to move beyond the positivist notion of geographical Euclidean space. The positivist notion treats space as fixed and as a container of social processes that sorts who is in and out (Davoudi and Strange 2008; Mandanipour, Hull, and Healey 2016; Taylor 2003). In the view of Agnew (2015), political space is associated with the territory and sovereignty of the nation-state. Neil Brenner et al. (2003) associate this notion with Max Weber's idea of rational organization and the legitimate use of violence of the state within a given territory. Space is clearly bounded and scales (political and social) perfectly juxtapose with the processes. It is defined as state-centric, and methodologies focus on the nation-state's raison d'être as the main unit of analysis of the international system (Brenner 1999, 2004; Giddens 1984; Harvey 1985; Jessop 2002; Swyngedouw 1997).

Henri Lefebvre's (1991) reflection on the production of space constitutes a point of departure from the positivist or Euclidean analysis, and it has had an important influence among scholars studying space and place from critical postpositivist perspectives (Agnew 2015; Brenner 1999, 2004; Castells 2000; Harvey 1985; Soja 1989). Lefebvre's (1991) main contribution is to open a new line of inquiry by looking at space not as a "thing" with a life of its own but as a product that is the outcome of social relations; space is produced and reproduced by social groups. The social space is the outcome of contradictory dialectic processes that at the same time "unify and fragment," creating a tension between exchange and use value, among other contradictions.

According to Simin Davoudi and Ian Strange (2008, 12–14), the traditional Euclidean geography notion of space was challenged by Gottfried Wilhelm Leibniz and Albert Einstein, who favored a more relational view of space; that is, an object in space (e.g., housing) acquires meaning not by itself or because of its intrinsic characteristics but in relation or relative to another object(s). However, "an important feature of the distinction between an absolute (i.e. Newtonian or Liebnizian) and a relational approach to space is the way in which they conceptualize place. From a Newtonian perspective, space and place are seen as either synonymous or binaries, whereas a relational view of space considers them as internally related to one another" (Davoudi and Strange 2008, 14). As mentioned previously, Lefebvre's (1991) work marks an important point of departure on the conceptualization of space. Lefebvre opts for a dialectical approach to make visible the multiple contradictions, tensions, and conflicts of social relationships that take place around space. Lefebvre was not an exception on reflecting about the role of the state in managing space by arguing that "only the State is capable of taking charge of management of space 'on grand scale' — highways, air traffic routes — because only the State has at its disposal the appropriate resources, techniques, and 'conceptual' capacity" (2009, 238). Furthermore, borders, in Lefebvre's view, are associated with "phallic spaces," which "symbolizes force, male fertility, masculine violence. . . . Phallic brutality does not remain abstract, for it is the brutality of political power, of the means of constraint: police, army, bureaucracy" (1991, 287). The political power and its use are of special interest from the perspective of border governance.

Anthony Giddens (1984, 110–61) offers a different path to understand space and place — structuration theory. Giddens's point of departure is the relationship that exists between agency and structure to shape processes and practice in a social system. Whereas some emphasize that agency, based on individual purposeful, rational action, is enough to explain social systems (e.g., utilitarianism), others emphasize mostly structure, which is defined as constraining agents' social actions. Giddens argues that structuration, unlike structuralism, is focused not only on analyzing social constraints but also on understanding structure's enabling functions. Agency and structure mutually reconfigure each other. Thus, Giddens argues that explanation should focus on "how social theory should confront — in a concrete rather than abstractly philosophical way — the 'situatedness' of interactions in time and space" (1984, 110). The focus of inquiry should therefore be the routines and daily life of an agent vis-à-vis another agent, which Giddens refers to as "co-presence," occurring in time and space. Giddens defines place as the "locale," and "regional" refers to "the use of space to provide the settings of interactions in turn being essential to specifying its contextuality" (1984, 118). Giddens's structuration analysis offers an avenue of inquiry to think of border space as a constraint (physical or symbolic) that not only sanctions but also enables social action in space; agency and structure produce and reproduce places but not at random, instead following a historical path dependency trajectory. Furthermore, Giddens's work moves the unit of analysis from the macro aspects of state power (high politics) toward the local (low politics) or place governance (Mumme and Grundy-Warr 1998; Peña 2011). Inquiry moves from grand theory to midrange theory (Faludi 2002).

The influence of previous works is reflected in recent efforts to clarify the distinction between space and place (Davoudi and Strange 2008; Healey 2000; Mandanipour, Hull, and Healey 2016). Several authors agree (Davoudi and Strange 2008; Hillier 2016) that space and place can be conceptualized and distinguished by the notion that places are socially constructed. This social construction can be based on images and identities. Place is shaped by the "power struggle between the images, aspirations and values of various actant-networks" (Mandanipour 2016, 20, citing Hillier's conclusions). Davoudi and Strange (2008) argue that there are two traditions to understand space and place—the naturalist and the interpretative. The first is based on a natural order of things where cause and effect can be established; the second focuses on the meaning of actions. Thus, social actions attempt to embed places with meaning. Manuel Castells's (2000) widely cited phrase that "space is society," rather than just reflecting it, acquires importance when space is seen as a product of social action, human intentions, and competing meanings. Lefebvre concludes, "Spatial practice thus simultaneously defines: places—the relationships of local to global; the representation of that relationship; actions and signs; the trivialized spaces of everyday life; and, in opposition to these last, spaces made special by symbolic means as desirable, undesirable, benevolent or malevolent, sanctioned or forbidden to particular groups" (1991, 288). Similarly, Agnew (2011, 2015) argues that the notion of place is derived from two perspectives—a geometrical conception as simply part of space (location on the surface) and a phenomenological one, which investigates the essence or being. In Agnew's (2015, 5–6) view, place, as an empirical object, can be defined based on three dimensions: locale, location, and sense of place. *Locale* refers to the structured "microsociological" content of place—the settings of everyday, routine social interactions provided in a place. *Location* refers to the representation in local social interaction of ideas and practices derived from relationships between places. In other words, location represents the impact of the "macro-order" in a place (uneven economic development, uneven effects of government policy, segregation of social groups, etc.). *Sense of place* refers to the subjective orientation that can be engendered by living in a place. This is the geosociological definition of self or identity produced by a place.

It is important to have a clear distinction between space and place because definitions shape institutions, processes, and practices of governance (Davoudi and Strange 2008; Healey 2000; Mandanipour, Hull, and Healey 2016; Peña 2011). Patsy Healey (2000) argues that the practice, as far as space governance is concerned, is transformed from a Euclidean notion, where the aim is to locate objects where they belong for their efficient functionality, and where the planner is in charge of assembling the "jigsaw puzzle" into a relational practice, where the search is for creating and producing common meanings and images through communicative means in the arenas of debate. However, there is another poststructuralist approach, which, instead of seeing social relationships as capable of producing shared meanings and images through inter-subjective ways, argues that power—often linked to the state—is capable of shaping meanings and images and devising ways to control, punish, and discipline subjects, deviant actions, and countercultures by regulating and controlling space (Flybvjerg and Richardson 2002; Foucault 2009).

It is important to consider these analytical approaches to space and place and what each means for border governance. Each is linked to specific forms of governance; each approach represents a form of a governing regime operating simultaneously (Peña 2002, 2011). The traditional Euclidean positivist notion of space overlaps with inter-pretivist or phenomenological notions of place and time, also known as poststructur-alist. Next, I consider three paradigms (positivist, structuralist, and poststructuralist) and ground them in the way border scholars have made use of them and the arguments and ideas put forward.

The Governance of Space/Place and Borders

The previous discussion makes clear the importance of moving away from the notion of space as mere physical location toward space as a place or locale; this is particu-larly true for understanding the governance of borders and the role that structure, agency, and place play (Agnew 2011, 25–43). The cross-border metropolises along the U.S.-Mexico border are a case in point—cities on both sides of the border share a common location in a geographical grid of coordinates of latitude and longitude. However, urban areas are completely different places because of being the product of two different social organizational systems with a specific history. Thus, time and space context matters in the process of place making (Agnew 2015; Giddens 1984; Lefebvre 1991). Agnew argues that one of the advantages of structuration theory is precisely that "this approach allows for the historical specificities and uniqueness of place while proposing that these 'multiple outcomes,' if you will, are the product of a 'one to many correspondence'" (2015, 42).

Davoudi and Strange (2008, 40–41) not only offer a summary of the entire debate between space and place but also provide a framework useful to guide the discussion in relation to the governance of border space and place. I will adapt the criteria employed by these authors as a framework to analyze the literature of cross-border governance of space and place from three main paradigms in the social sciences: (a) positivist, (b) structuralist, and (c) postmodern. Five categories or dimensions are employed to compare and contrast the paradigms: (1) the role of public officials, (2) knowledge and skills, (3) methods of engagement, (4) institutional governance structures and power relations, and (5) modes of implementation.

The Governance of Space and Borders from a Positivist Perspective

Some authors (Agnew 2011; Brenner et al. 2003) argue that under the geographical or Euclidean notion of space, public officials or professionals represent the nation-state interests (sovereignty). Other scholars (Blatter and Ingram 2000, 445) argue that the main role of the official is that of administration, adjudication, liaison investigation, and the use of technical commissions whose institutional design is to rely on scientific, technical information or a judicial approach to depoliticize border issues (Blatter 2004). An example of such a rational organization is the U.S. International Boundary and Water Commission (IBWC) on the U.S.-Mexico border. The IBWC dates to the Guadalupe-Hidalgo Treaty between Mexico and the United States, when the border was negotiated between the two countries. Originally, the name did not include "water" until the 1944 Treaty. The way the commission operates is through the coordination of two sections, each representing a sovereign nation. Telling the history of the IBWC is beyond the scope of this chapter, but the IBWC fits some of the characteristics described above. It is a technical commission that relies on expert scientific knowledge to determine the rules and norms that guide water allocation between two countries. The IBWC is in tune with Joachim Blatter's (2004, 535) idea that this type of commission values two types of professions: engineering and law. The 1944 Treaty, Article 2, establishes that the commissioners in both countries must be engineers. Each section (U.S. and Mexico) of the commission's organizational chart has a foreign affairs secretary, a diplomat, and legal advisers as needed. Border governance is approached as diplomatic engineering (Mumme 1986), focusing on issues that are prone to technical solutions, including land disputes resulting from the shift of the Rio Grande. For instance, the 1963 Chamizal Treaty resolved a land dispute by means of a diplomatic solution (Mumme and Grundy-Warr 1998) based to a great extent on technical knowledge.

Institutions are designed to perform certain functions and roles to achieve their missions. The way institutions behave is based on certain types of knowledge and skills that officials, professionals, or public administrators acquire. The knowledge and skills of certain professions are not exempt from the debate in social sciences linked to the type of epistemologies or knowledge employed. The production of knowledge about border governance includes the typical Weberian state based on a rational bureaucracy (Brenner et al. 2003). The Weberian state is a typical case of positivist epistemology applied to border governance (Brenner et al. 2003). Knowledge must be scientifically and factually based, and decisions must follow a logical sequential order. Knowledge employed is universal and lacks place-based contexts. Neil Brenner (2004, 29) describes this notion as "state-centric epistemological frameworks." The methods of engagement go from very limited forms of communication, normally top-down, to open deliberation. There are few studies (Lemos and Luna 1999; Peña and Cordova 2001; Sánchez 1993) about public participation at the U.S.-Mexico border, all of them focused on analyzing the public participation processes undertaken by the IBWC (Sánchez 1993) or BECC, now the North American Development Bank (NADB) (Lemos and Luna 1999; Peña and Cordova 2001), which are the main bilateral/ binational institutions at the border. To characterize existing public participation processes and practices applying the three main paradigms, I use Archon Fung's (2006) framework to analyze public participation and governance based on a three-dimensional model that looks at (1) types of authority and power, (2) forms of communication and decision mode, and (3) typology of participants.

Based on Fung's (2006) tridimensional model, it can be argued that the traditional mode of public participation associated with the type of institution related to the Weberian state (Brenner et al. 2003) relies on power and authority that is directly and legally assigned to some institution that exercises the authority. The form of communication and decision-making is based on technical expertise; the participants in the decision-making process are expert administrator(s). The IBWC, in its original institutional design, is an example of this model of public participation. The 1944 Treaty delegates the authority to the IBWC to deal with water and boundary issues and establishes the operational mechanisms of the commission. The 1944 Treaty has not a single mention of the word *participation*. The word *public* is found four times and refers to public waters or that each section of the IBWC "may make use of any competent public or private agencies in accordance with the laws of their respective countries" (1944 Treaty, Art. 20). The main stakeholders of the IBWC are the U.S. and Mexican federal governments and their respective foreign affair departments (U.S. Department of State [DOS] and Secretaría de Relaciones Exteriores [SRE, Secretariat of Foreign Affairs]). The border is conceived by the IBWC more as a container (Taylor 2003), with political scale well established, and the border is the limit of the container. Border affairs are managed by two professional commissions, one in each country, which represent a sovereign nation-state. These types of public participation protocols have received severe criticism (Mumme and More 1999; Sánchez 1993), precisely for being top-down and shutting off lay opinions or nonprofessional stakeholders. It is fair to say that the IBWC in the last decade has made important strides to incorporate public participation through its respective Citizen Forums, which incorporate both professional and lay stakeholders. These forums are the instrument that the IBWC employs to receive public input and make its actions more transparent. The aspect of governance and power relations is very important and perhaps one of the topics that has caught the most attention of scholars (Agnew 2011; Blatter 2004; Brenner 2004; Brenner et al. 2003; Jessop 2002; Paasi 2009; Newman 2006; Newman and Paasi 1998; Swyngedouw 1997).

The debate revolves around the influence and link between the nation-state and the locale and, thus, the borders.

From a positivist notion, which evolves from a state-centric approach (Brenner 2004; Brenner et al. 2003) that has the nation-state as the main actor, the following concepts characterize the power relations between the national and the locale. First, authors describe the power relations of politics and place as hierarchical and top-down where local places are "devalued" vis-à-vis the national elites; national territorial space is naturalized, and regions and place are forgotten or have no place in modern history (Agnew 2011). This power relationship assumes that "all social relations are organized within self-enclosed, discretely bounded territorial containers" (Brenner 2004, 38). Socioeconomic and political processes perfectly overlap with state boundaries. Ansi Paasi argues that territory and borders are linked in a "marriage" relationship where the state has the "administrative monopoly over territory" (2009, 217). According to David Newman, "demarcation and management of borders are closely linked to each other" (2006, 6). An important issue relevant to study from a governance perspective is who oversees the border and how it is governed. From the U.S.-Mexico perspective, a legal framework exists that forbids local governments from signing treaties with other governments. Thus, only the national government formally oversees border relations. In Mexico, local governments are limited to manage territory within their jurisdictional boundaries except the international borderline and international waters (Peña 2002), whereas in the United States, state and local governments have complete control except in areas where the U.S. Constitution's Tenth Amendment explicitly assigns it directly to the federal government. The IBWC in the United States and the treaties determined the federal jurisdiction. Multiple federal agencies are assigned different roles—for instance, the IBWC is responsible for boundary demarcation and water, U.S. Border Patrol (USBP) for undocumented migration, U.S. Immigration and Customs Enforcement (ICE) for immigration and customs, and so forth. The organizational political structure of power relationships is like the "Russian dolls" where the local is contained within the state and the state at the same time within the national (Jessop 2002; Swyngedouw 1997). Spatial and administrative functions of federal agencies are mutually exclusive and at the same time complementary.

From the spatial perspective of positivism, the mode of implementation of policy is command and control, and different institutions are assigned specific functions to perform. The mode of implementation is a state-centric federalist approach where directions and commands trickle down from the high to the lower level of governance. Joachim Blatter and Helen Ingram (2000) define this approach as "territory-centered governance," whose main function is to be a border "gatekeeper." The type of cross-border cooperation and governance that takes place is based on an "instrumental logic" of matching means to ends. We can argue that the "territory-centered governance" at the U.S.-Mexico border is evolving and transforming the top-down control and command modes of implementation as lower levels of government (i.e., states) are assuming "gatekeeper" functions for themselves. For example, the USBP, a federal agency, has the mission to prevent unlawful border crossings of people or goods. But Arizona SB1070 and Texas SB4, state initiatives, undertake immigration functions to complement federal law enforcement by allowing local police to detain undocumented immigrants and turn them over to immigration authorities or require them to cooperate with federal immigration authorities.

The Governance of Space and Borders from a Structuralist Perspective

Borders are not sealed to flows. Trade is more intense between neighbors, particularly if there is adjacency of structural differences (Alegría 1992). From a structuralist or, more specifically, a structuration perspective, border officials are there not only to constrain or prevent flows considered unlawful but also to facilitate those that the state certifies as lawful. Brenner (2004, 5–6) argues that borders are open to flows of investment, money, trade, and labor, producing localized agglomeration economies or "super clusters" as new engines of growth. State and local officials, along with local business interests, will push for changes to facilitate the flows across borders. According to Saskia Sassen (2007), the state transfers some of its sovereignty to transnational bureaucracies to promote localities' competitiveness. Environmental issues are not exempt from this perspective of flows (Morehouse 1995), particularly how environmental externalities associated with the flows are managed and minimized (Blatter and Clement 2000). The institutional architecture of the Border Environment Cooperation Commission (BECC, now NADB), based on a binational bureaucracy, seems to fit this description and purpose. The main mission of BECC/NADB is to deal with environmental externalities produced by economic integration from a more collaborative perspective where a unified bureaucracy from the two countries works side by side, instead of using separate commissions, such as the IBWC, allowing for potential mutual learning and empathy.

Structuralism, and particularly structuration theory, argues that place-based knowledge that is context specific is key in explaining structure (rules and resources) and agency (local actor action). Giddens (1984) and Agnew (2011) define the type of knowledge that is contextually grounded and place based as "practical consciousness." The main idea is that truth is not something that we discover but rather it is context specific and produced through communicative means (dialogue, debate, narratives) that allow social actors to act. The truth is temporary (fallible) and changes as new evidence and values emerge.[1] Knowledge then is not objective and value free. Rather, it is linked to power, real or symbolic (Bourdieu 2014). Border scholars (Paasi 2009,

227) argue that knowledge based on "practical consciousness" helps reproduce identities and narratives of a spatial image of the border. Border people either contest or accept narratives of homogenization produced by the nation-state reproduced by the social body in an invisible or unconscious way (Bourdieu 2014). But most important, narratives not only constrain but also should "enable" (Giddens 1984) actors to act to improve their places and the way they live them daily. Border governance thus becomes how local narratives develop a tacit knowledge and become a resource to adapt or transgress rules to local needs and goals. Chambers of commerce and local nongovernmental organizations (NGOs) are important sources of context and place-based knowledge that cooperate around specific interests.

The top-down and expert-based public participation processes and practices discussed previously proved to be limited as new challenges emerged with the economic integration of the two countries and the resulting exponential population and urban growth, particularly on the Mexican side of the border. Thus, new institutions and organizations emerged, such as the Border Governors Conference (1980), the La Paz Agreement (1983), NAFTA (1994), the BECC/NADB (1994), Border 2012, and Border 2020 (2003), among others. Applying Fung's (2006) model, some institutions, such as BECC, would rely on power and authority to co-govern certain processes (e.g., environment), incorporating professional representatives or stakeholders as participants to deliberate and negotiate. The Border 2012 and then Border 2020 programs, which focus on environmental cooperation, were similar to BECC, with the exception that the communication and decision mode will be more focused on developing preferences. The Border Governors Conference (BGC) was a form of participation of state officials with direct authority to make decisions and communication as aggregation and bargain, and the main participants were professional state representatives and agencies. According to Blatter, this type of organizational structure emerges to overcome obstacles that hinder the "exploitation of positive externalities and synergies" (2004, 535), thus forming coalitions to lobby for strategies to promote flows that induce economic growth or programs to manage the border environment in a more holistic way. Susan E. Clark calls this type of public participation "paradiplomacy" or "constituent diplomacy" (2002, 5), which describes perfectly the fact that despite local interest and efforts, the federal government still has authority to support or veto some actions. Peter Haas characterizes this as an epistemic community, which is defined as "a network of professionals with recognized expertise and competence in a particular domain and an authoritative claim to policy-relevant knowledge within that domain or issue area" (1992, 3). In summary, as Giddens (1984) and Agnew (2011) suggest, daily life influences how actors perceive place. Actors' and agencies' strategies and structure combine in time and space to promote place-based strategies (e.g., Border 2020) that will make their quality of life better (e.g., cleaner air, safer water).

From a structuralist perspective, border institutions are understood as structures (i.e., rules and resources) that constrain human agency. According to Newman (2003), institutions create order needed to exercise control. However, human agency often challenges the order of things. For example, the scales of origin and destination of economic processes linked to globalization (trade, finance, labor) make the "container leak" (Taylor 2003). Zygmunt Bauman, using Ulrich Beck, describes the institutions as "zombie like" (2012, 6) to illustrate the fact that social reality makes them look dead but still alive, especially after 9/11. In other words, place and locality and borders are revalued against the national. Thus, there is a need for a restructuring of power relations between the national and local spaces (Agnew 2011) or, according to Brenner, there is a "relativization of the primacy of the national scale and emergence of subnational and supranational scales in such processes" (2004, 44). To overcome the fact that socioeconomic processes and natural ecosystems do not exactly overlap the political structures of power and boundaries, the state will allow some spatial and organizational reconfiguration. Brenner states that the power relations are reconfigured as "polycentric, multi-scalar and non-isomorphic" rather than the typical "Russian dolls" power scales (2004, 4–6). NAFTA, BECC, the U.S.-Mexico Border Health Commission (USMBHC, which monitors health and epidemic threats across borders), and other similar organizations are designed as functional institutions (Blatter 2004) with specific purposes. The process of power reconfiguration becomes a "muddling through" (Lindbloom 1959) process of learning by doing or reorganizing as new problems emerge and become visible and impossible to ignore. In summary, this perspective describes how power structures (rules and resources) are modified and changed to incorporate new functions as place-locality and reality of the border become more complex and diverse. For example, private sector funding contributes to ICE to make the flows more agile, such as the Secure Electronic Network for Travelers Rapid Inspection (SENTRI) line program or the Cross Border Xpress (CBX) skywalk bridge that connects the Tijuana, Mexico, airport with the U.S. side in San Diego.

Structuralism focuses on how to redistribute functions and resources. Thus, the mode of implementation of policy and governance moves from control-command to shared responsibilities and functions among different levels of governmental and nongovernmental institutions. The purpose is to overcome the "constraints" (rules, laws, etc.) imposed by the geographical physical line and make it more fluid (Bauman 2012). According to Blatter (2004), this mode of implementation means shifting the focus from territorial or space-based policies to place-based actions by creating special-purpose governments. Brenner describes this mode as "entrepreneurial urban governance," where all levels of government focus on "growth-oriented approaches" and the mode of implementation is through "horizontal networking, trans-local linkages, and crossborder cooperation initiatives" (Brenner 2004, 2, 6). The type of governance that can emerge goes from "supranational" to "limited functional" integration (Clark 2002; McCormick 1996, 15–23). From the perspective of the border, this "entrepreneurial urban governance" policy approach has been implemented since the mid-1960s. Examples of this "entrepreneurial" governance policy are the Border Industrialization Program (1965), the establishment of the Free Zone (1972), NAFTA (1994), and the Maquiladora promotion (1998). In the 1990s, the SENTRI lane was put in place to more easily facilitate commuters' travel across the borderlands. The CBX in the Tijuana–San Diego area that started operations in 2017 facilitated border crossings for air travelers. In conclusion, the border is simultaneously a physical spatial constraint and a locational resource (Sohn 2014), which enables businesses and entrepreneurs to exploit synergies resulting from "adjacency" (Alegría 1992) of comparative advantages of border localities.

Postmodernism and the Governance of Border Space

From a poststructuralist perspective, there are two perspectives—those of Habermas (communicative rationality) and Foucault (power as a disciplinary and control tool)—to understand the role of public officials and professionals. One emphasizes identity formation and development of a common narrative of place and the future. Public officials thus facilitate the dialogue among actors to produce an "agreement of the situation" based on honest and open dialogue (Habermas 1985) and an action framework. The other, from a critical perspective, argues that professionals' role should be to make visible the invisible, particularly power relations taking place at the border on a daily basis (oppression, exploitation, control, violation of human rights, etc.). The "discomfort with borders" from critical theorists arises because they become "instruments of control" (O'Dowd 2010, 1039). Official and non-official actors should advocate for those that lack power vis-à-vis capitalism (Heyman 2012). For example, border human rights networks and activists are the main advocates, and NGOs emerge as political actors of place-based initiatives. These NGOs have been crucial in the fight against anti-immigrant state legislation such as Arizona SB1070 and recently Texas SB4. Both laws were passed as an attempt by state governments to deal with undocumented migration, arguing that the federal government was not doing enough and giving local police authority to detain and hold undocumented people for future deportation by federal immigration authorities.

Knowledge related to space and place associated with postmodern theories comes from different streams, such as dialectical inquiry, history or historic materialism, hermeneutics, and semiotics, among others. Marxist scholars linked to historical materialism, such as Immanuel Wallerstein (1978), analyze how capitalism restructures labor division and world space in a hierarchical functional way to ensure capital accumulation. Thus, the center periphery is just a spatial organization of capitalism. Thus, borders often are associated with peripheral places in the world's spatial hierarchy (Soja 1989). History is the base of reliable knowledge (O'Dowd 2010, 1033, citing Charles Tilly); that is, space and time should be analyzed in tandem. Social knowledge is "intrinsically time-space dependent"; knowledge is "situated knowledge" and is bound up with positionality (Paasi 2009, 222). Lefebvre (1991, 2009) opts for a dialectical approach to demonstrate contradictions linked to spatial practice and the capitalist mode of production. The concept of phallic space is useful to understand how borders are scenarios where the state must demonstrate its force and virility. Brenner (1999) emphasizes dialectical analysis as well to illustrate how borders are places where the process of bordering and debordering takes place (see also Newman 2003). Finally, hermeneutics and semiotics focus on the meaning of signs and symbols; borders are interesting not for their physical or geographical location but because of the psychosocial (Agnew 2011; Giddens 1984) meaning and what they represent— borders are mental or subjective constructs. Border governance becomes an exercise to construct and deconstruct border institutions and practices to promote alternatives, often focusing on social justice issues (Heyman 2012; Staudt and Coronado 2002), counterpower strategies (Flyvbjerg and Richardson 2002; Foucault 2009), biopolitics, and border surveillance (Salter 2006).

Postmodernism focuses on a broader definition of social actor participation, incorporating not professional stakeholders but lay stakeholders or everyone who is affected by decision-making. Based on Fung's (2006) framework, postmodernism would argue for public participation, where participants would be both professional stakeholders and everyone interested. Participants would not only be heard but also be listened to and understood and have communicative influence (their concerns genuinely considered), and the communication mode would be to express preferences and deliberate and bargain. Blatter defines this form of engagement as "consociations," which influence individuals by "symbolizing ideas and the image of crossborder political community" (2004, 534–35). A good example of this political activism was the opposition by people from all walks of life to the opening of a low-level radiation nuclear waste site in Sierra Blanca, Texas, about eighty-seven miles east of El Paso and near the Mexican border. Using Robert Axelrod's (1984) words, the "shadow of the future" fostered cooperation. Uncertainty about the future overcame class, ethnicity, and nationality. The emphasis of postmodern border studies is to imagine transnational communities that operate in a relational space that overcomes the artificial geographical boundaries of the spatial container and, as Peter Taylor (2003) has said, makes the container leak and eventually disappear, as Europe has done.

Postmodern perspectives, unlike structuralism, consider not only institutional structures in the public domain but also those in the private sphere. The new mantra becomes public-private partnerships (PPP) co-governing. But what exactly does it mean? In terms of organizational scales, PPPs become "fuzzy" and relational (Brenner 2004). Rather than being bounded to a container (Taylor 2003) and mediated through state practices and norms (Agnew 2011), social relations across borders acquire a life of their own. Boundaries "are now understood as multifaceted semiotic, symbolic, and political-economic practices through which state power is articulated and contested" (Brenner 2004, 71, using Newman and Paasi's 1998 ideas). According to Blatter (2004), institutions, instead of exercising power to "constrain" human agency, now function as identity providers. Bauman (2012) refers to this as a process of liquefying institutions created in a mode of modernity (e.g., Weber's rational organization), which were "solid" and unable to deal with challenges posed by globalization. In terms of U.S.-Mexico border governance, this power structure of developing a common identity and making the border seamless is more of a desire than a reality. Institutions such as environmental coalitions and human rights networks are very few and operate on the margins of the gravity center of border policy. The semiotics of the border for many people across the United States is still associated with violence, drugs, cartels, corruption, and lawlessness. As the study of Blatter (2004) shows, the U.S. border approach still revolves pretty much around functional power structures. While environmental uncertainty may unite and provide common semiotics, the negative side of globalization (socioeconomic uncertainty) and the fear of open society produces a "mixophobia" and reinforcement of borders—physically and semiotically (Bauman 2012). The power structures in Washington (e.g., U.S. Drug Enforcement Administration [DEA], U.S. Department of Homeland Security [DHS], among others) and at the state level (Arizona SB 1070 and Texas SB4) are not in a "zombie" stage yet. They are succeeding in making the "social corpus" accept the narrative of securitization since the mid-twentieth century when U.S. president Richard Nixon put in place Operation Intercept in 1969, when inspections at the border were so detailed that the border was practically sealed to force Mexico to cooperate with the War on Drugs policy.

U.S.-Mexico Border Governance: Final Thoughts and Conclusions

Understanding the meaning of time and space is important to analyze border governance and policy. There are important contributions to study the relationship between territory and the nation-state (Agnew 2011; Brenner 1999, 2004; Brenner et al. 2003; Jessop 2002; Swyngedouw 1997; Taylor 2003). There are also analyses that have studied cross-border governance from a spatial perspective (Alegría 1992; Blatter 2004;

Blatter and Ingram 2000; Clark 2002; Newman 2006; Paasi 2009; Peña 2011; Sohn 2014). Several U.S.-Mexico border studies were written in the context of globalization in general and particularly the economic integration between the United States and Mexico. Thus, it is important to reflect about the border in the context of rising Mexiphobia during the Trump administration and what it means in terms of border governance. So, the main question is: Is Trump's governance and policy different, from a spatial perspective, compared to previous administrations? The short answer is that it is different only in the form but not in its content. At the beginning of this chapter, I hypothesized that despite integration and intense cooperation, the U.S.-Mexico border is still being governed by a conception of space as a container (Taylor 2003) rather than in relational postpositivist policy frameworks (Healey 2000; Lefebvre 1991). So, the conclusion is that, from a spatial perspective, Trump's border policy is not different in the substance but only in the form by trying to sensationalize the topic. The last column in Table 1.1, for example, shows a total of twenty-two border policy actions (treaties, programs, operations, laws, etc.). Nine (41 percent) of them are classified as containing a Euclidean spatial notion of the border as a container, eight (36 percent) are characterized as spaces of flows, and only five (23 percent) are classified as containing some form of relational notions of space. Those classified as Euclidean spatial actions deal with border demarcation, undocumented migration, and natural resources allocation. The programs classified as spaces of flows deal with trade, expedited border crossings, environmental externalities, and drugs. Those classified as relational spaces or places are related in order of importance to the environment, public health, and urban development.

The analysis here shows U.S.-Mexico border policy still embedded in a Euclidean notion of space that emphasizes differentiation rather than local "place-based" identity policy narratives. Trump has not only emphasized the phallic notion of space by his bravado and by sensationalizing the border but has also exploited the fear and anxiety of people in the United States who, as Bauman (2012) suggests, are afraid of an open society and economy, thus supporting "mixophobic" policies that shield them from outsiders. Thus, the border's function is still to divide (Newman 2006) and exclude those whom the nation-state and its citizens fear. Border governance policy and power structure remain state-centric and top-down. The nation-state has never gone away; it is still very much present in the life of border residents and more so for border crossers, who must endure the procedures and practice of a bureaucracy trained to sort out those who belong and those who need to be excluded. Trump's immigration policy reform proposal sketched out in his 2018 State of the Union speech reflects exactly the exclusion of immigrants who do not look like people from Norway. Furthermore, it is interesting to study what has happened to the Border Governors Conference. Originally, this organization was supposed to gather state officials to exchange ideas and learn from each other and then to lobby their respective governments for local place-based policies. However, since the passage of anti-immigration initiatives by Arizona (SB1070) and then Texas (SB4), the BGC is in disarray and is more a photo opportunity for politicians than a forum and arena to debate and propose "action frameworks" to facilitate flows or construct an identity narrative.

In the renegotiation of NAFTA, the spaces of flows were threatened by Trump, who argued it is the worst deal in history and Mexico has taken advantage of the United States. The facts, goals, and objectives are often contradictory regarding the notion of space that Mexico and the United States have in mind. The Trump administration wants to impose mechanisms to prevent manipulation of currency, reduce deficits, and improve wages and labor conditions in Mexico. Mexico argues that those issues would limit its sovereignty to manage its economic affairs. To have a sense of what NAFTA represents, in 2015 bilateral trade between the United States and Mexico accounted for US$584 billion (Wilson 2017, 7), but, most important, the main issue is that intra-industry trade accounts for 53 percent of total trade (Wilson 2017, 9). In other words, half of what is being traded between the two countries are inputs and not final goods. Trump's skepticism about NAFTA threatened the entire chain of industrial production of North America. Mexican border cities are important centers of production and spaces of flows. That is their lifeblood. There is no question that NAFTA needed to be upgraded or modernized. New industries have appeared since 1994 (e.g., e-commerce). But the objectives (reduction of trade deficit, fair and reciprocal trade) put forward by the Trump administration showed that he had a misunderstanding of what international trade and NAFTA are all about (exploiting comparative advantages). Deficits with Mexico are because the value of inputs used to assemble goods is less than the value of the finished good (inputs plus labor costs) being exported through the border. Spaces of flows are what make the border important, and they account for a good number of U.S. jobs and lower prices that consumers pay. The goals of the Trump administration, improving labor standards and wages paid to Mexican workers, deserve discussion and could represent an opportunity. This could make border cities move away from a race to the bottom-of-the-line production based on cheap labor into a higher value-added industry.

Instead of spending billions of dollars in building a wall that separates the two countries, the nations should instead support BECC/NADB's mission, which has been critical in building environmental infrastructure such as water treatment plants, drinking water facilities, and paved roads, among others. These actions have made a big difference in the quality of life of border residents. However, this approach may not be politically acceptable, since the industrial surveillance complex in the United States (DHS, DEA, etc.) is powerful and benefits from the traditional Euclidean notions of space. Trump's budget proposals signal a strengthening of the idea of the border

TABLE 1.1 Border programs, policies, and actions

Border action	Year	Objective	Category	Spatial notion
Water treaty	1944	Set up the framework to distribute the waters of the Colorado and Rio Grande Rivers	Natural resources	Euclidean
Chamizal Treaty	1963	Resolve the land dispute produced by shifts in the channel due to floods in the Rio Grande	Border demarcation	Euclidean
Mexico's Programa Nacional Fronterizo (PRONAF)	1962	Make the border more attractive and change its image	Urban development	Relational
Mexico's Border Industrialization Program	1965	Establish the basis that allows the location of maquiladoras at the border in Mexico	Trade	Flows
Operation Intercept by U.S. Border Patrol	1969	Enforcement of federal narcotic laws	Drug trafficking	Euclidean
Free Zone establishment by Mexico	1972	Allow goods and services across the border to be imported free of duties and taxes	Trade	Flows
Border Governors Conference (BGC)	1980	Foster cooperation among border states	Multi-issue but trade is the driving force	Relational
La Paz Agreement	1983	Cooperation to protect border environment	Environment	Flows
Immigration Reform and Control Act (IRCA) in the United States	1986	Provide legal status to undocumented immigrants in the United States	Migration	Euclidean
Operation Blockade/Hold the Line/Gatekeeper in the United States	1993	Deter and prevent undocumented crossings from Mexico into the United States	Migration	Euclidean
Border Environment Cooperation Commission (BECC)	1994	Cooperation to protect border environment from possible harms done by free trade agreement	Environment	Relational

Name	Year	Description	Category	Type
North American Free Trade Agreement (NAFTA)	1994	Reduce barriers to trade and investment	Trade	Flows
Maquiladora promotion	1998	Maquiladoras can locate in Mexico outside border zones	Trade	Flows
Secure Electronic Network for Travelers Rapid Inspection (SENTRI)	2000s	Expedite clearance of border crossings	Border crossings	Flows
US-Mexico Border Health Commission (USMBHC)	2000	Monitor public health and prevent epidemic outbreaks by disseminating information	Public health	Relational
Border 2012 / Border 2020	2003	Cooperation to protect border environment	Environment	Relational
Real ID Act / Patriot Act, Public Law 109-13	2005	Exempts U.S. federal government from environmental requirements to clear the legal hurdle to build the border fence	Border demarcation	Euclidean
Mérida Initiative	2008	Cooperation to deal with drug trafficking	Drug trafficking	Flows
Arizona SB1070	2010	Authorized local law enforcement to undertake immigration duties	Migration	Euclidean
Cross Border Xpress (CBX) Bridge	2017	Facilitate cross-border crossings of air travel passengers in the Tijuana–San Diego area	Border crossings	Flows
Texas SB4	2017	Requires local authorities to cooperate with federal immigration officials, with penalties for failure to cooperate	Migration	Euclidean
Trump border wall	2017	Attempt to build a border wall in the United States	Border demarcation	Euclidean

Source: Adapted from Fung 2006, 70–72.

as a container and getting away from limited structuralist and postmodern notions of space.

Finally, this chapter has provided a discussion regarding different paradigms about border governance—positivism, structuralist, and poststructuralist. It demonstrated that border governance is a general concept that deals with multiple issues or policy problems. Border policy problems (e.g. drugs, undocumented migration) that are difficult to define and build consensus around are more prone to power relations and state-centric solutions, but there are also policy issues that could be more prone to dialogical and social learning solutions (e.g., air, water, health). Border problems are diverse, and thus it is almost impossible to characterize border governance based on a single model and institutional architecture. There are multiple models and institutional designs that coexist and overlap, as this chapter has shown.

Note

1. Charles Peirce, James Williams, and John Dewey are considered to provide the classical ideas of the philosophy known as pragmatism. Contemporary scholars include Richard Bernstein, Richard Rorty, Hilary Putnam, and Jürgen Habermas, among others. Pragmatism is considered to provide the basis for the communicative turn in social science (see Blanco 1994).

References

Agnew, John A. 2011. "Space and Place." In *The SAGE Handbook of Geographical Knowledge*, edited by John A. Agnew and David N. Livingston, 316–30. London: SAGE.

Agnew, John A. 2015. *Place and Politics: The Geographical Mediation of State and Society*. Political Geography 1. New York: Routledge.

Alegría, Tito. 1992. *Desarrollo urbano en la frontera México-Estados Unidos: Una interpretación y algunos resultados*. Mexico City: Consejo Nacional para la Cultura y las Artes.

Axelrod, Robert. 1984. *The Evolution of Cooperation*. New York: Basic Books.

Bauman, Zygmunt. 2012. *Liquid Modernity*. Cambridge, UK: Polity.

Blanco, Hilda. 1994. *How to Think About Social Problems: American Pragmatism and the Idea of Planning*. Westport, Conn.: Greenwood.

Blatter, Joachim. 2004. "'From Spaces of Place' to 'Spaces of Flows'? Territorial and Functional Governance in Cross-Border Regions in Europe and North America." *International Journal of Urban and Regional Research* 28 (3): 530–48.

Blatter, Joachim, and Norris Clement. 2000. "Cross-Border Cooperation in Europe: Historical Development, Institutionalization, and Contrasts with North America." *Journal of Borderland Studies* 15 (1): 13–54.

Blatter, Joachim, and Helen Ingram. 2000. "States, Markets and Beyond: Governance of Transboundary Water Resources." *Natural Resources Journal* 40 (2): 439–73.

Bourdieu, Pierre. 2014. *On the State: Lectures at the College of France 1989–1992*. Malden, Mass.: Polity.

Brenner, Neil. 1999. "Beyond State-Centrism? Space, Territoriality, and Geographical Scale in Globalization Studies." *Theory and Society* 28 (1): 39–78.

Brenner, Neil. 2004. *New State Spaces: Urban Governance and the Rescaling of Statehood*. Oxford: Oxford University Press.

Brenner, Neil, Bob Jessop, Martin Jones, and Gordon MacLeod, eds. 2003. *State/Space: A Reader*. Malden, Mass.: Blackwell.

Castells, Manuel. 2000. *The Rise of the Network Society*. The Information Age: Economy, Society, and Culture 1. Malden, Mass.: Blackwell.

Clark, Susan E. 2002. "Spatial Concepts and Cross-Border Governance Strategies: Comparing North American and Northern Europe Experiences." Paper presented at the EURA Conference on Urban and Spatial European Policies, Turin, April 18–20.

Davoudi, Simin, and Ian Strange, eds. 2008. *Conceptions of Space and Place in Strategic Spatial Planning*. New York: Routledge.

Faludi, Andreas, ed. 2002. *European Spatial Planning*. Cambridge, Mass.: Lincoln Institute of Land Policy.

Flyvbjerg, Bent, and Tim Richardson. 2002. "Planning and Foucault: In Search of the Dark Side of Planning Theory." In *Planning Futures: New Directions for Planning Theory*, edited by Philip Allmendinger and Mark Tewdwr-Jones, 44–62. New York: Routledge.

Foucault, Michel. 2009. *Security, Territory, Population: Lectures at the College de France, 1977–1978*. Translated by Graham Burchell. New York: Picador.

Fung, Archon. 2006. "Varieties of Participation in Complex Governance." *Public Administration Review* 66 (1): 66–75.

Giddens, Anthony. 1984. *The Constitution of Society: Outline of the Theory of Structuration*. Berkeley: University of California Press.

Haas, Peter. M. 1992. "Introduction: Epistemic Communities and International Policy Coordination." *International Organization* 46 (1): 1–35.

Habermas, Jürgen. 1985. *The Theory of Communicative Action*. Vol. 2, *Lifeworld and System: A Critique of Functionalist Reason*. Boston: Beacon.

Harvey, David. 1985. *The Urbanization of Capital*. Oxford: Blackwell.

Healey, Patsy. 2000. "Planning in Relational Space and Time: Responding to New Urban Realities." In *A Companion to the City*, edited by Gary Bridge and Sophie Watson, 517–30. Malden, Mass.: Blackwell.

Heyman, Josiah McConnell. 2012. "Political Economy and Social Justice in the U.S.-Mexico Border Region." In *Social Justice in the U.S.-Mexico Border Region*, edited by Mark Lusk, Kathleen Staudt, and Eva Moya, 41–59. New York: Springer.

Hillier, Jean. 2016. "Imagined Value: The Poetics and Politics of Place." In *The Governance of Place: Space and Planning Processes*, edited by Ali Mandanipour, Angela Hull, and Patsy Healey, 69–101. New York: Routledge.

Jessop, Bob. 2002. "The Political Economy of Scale." In *Globalization, Regionalization and Cross-Border Regions*, edited by Markus Perkmann and Ngai-Ling Sum, 25–49. London: Palgrave Macmillan.

Kolossov, Vladimir. 2005. "Border Studies: Changing Perspectives and Theoretical Approaches." *Geopolitics* 10 (4): 606–32.

Lefebvre, Henri. 1991. *The Production of Space*. Translated by Donald Nicholson-Smith. Oxford: Blackwell.

Lefebvre, Henri. 2009. *State, Space, World: Selected Essays*. Edited by Neil Brenner and Stuart Elden. Translated by Gerald Moore, Neil Brenner, and Stuart Elden. Minneapolis: University of Minnesota Press.

Lemos, Maria Carmen de Mello, and Antonio Luna. 1999. "Public Participation in the BECC: Lessons from the Acuaférico Project, Nogales, Sonora." *Journal of Borderlands Studies* 14 (1): 43–64.

Lindblom, Charles E. 1959. "The Science of 'Muddling Through.'" *Public Administration Review* 19 (2): 79–88.

Mandanipour, Ali. 2016. "Concepts of Space." In *The Governance of Place: Space and Planning Processes*, edited by Ali Mandanipour, Angela Hull, and Patsy Healey, 69–101. New York: Routledge.

Mandanipour, Ali, Angela Hull, and Patsy Healey, eds. 2016. *The Governance of Place: Space and Planning Processes*. New York: Routledge.

Martínez, Oscar J. 1994. *Border People: Life and Society in the US-Mexico Borderlands*. Tucson: University of Arizona Press.

McCormick, John. 1996. *The European Union: Politics and Policies*. Boulder, Colo.: Westview.

Morehouse, Barbara, 1995. "A Functional Approach to Boundaries in the Context of Environmental Issues." *Journal of Borderlands Studies* 10 (2): 53–73.

Mumme, Stephen P. 1986. "Engineering Diplomacy: The Evolving Role of the International Boundary and Water Commission in US-Mexico Water Management." *Journal of Borderlands Studies* 1 (1): 73–108.

Mumme, Stephen P., and C. Grundy-Warr. 1998. "Structuration Theory and the Analysis of International Territorial Disputes: Lessons from an Application to the El Chamizal Controversy." *Political Research Quarterly* 51 (4): 969–85.

Mumme, Stephen P., and S. T. Moore. 1999. "Innovation Prospects in US-Mexico Border Water Management: The IBWC and the BECC in Theoretical Perspective." *Environment and Planning: Government and Policy* 17 (6): 753–72.

Newman, David. 2003. "On Borders and Power: A Theoretical Framework." *Journal of Borderlands Studies* 18 (1): 13–25.

Newman, David. 2006. "The Lines that Continue to Separate Us: Borders in Our 'Borderless' World." *Progress in Human Geography* 30 (2): 1–19.

Newman, David, and Ansi Paasi. 1998. "Fences and Neighbours in the Postmodern World: Boundary Narratives in Political Geography." *Progress in Human Geography* 22 (2): 186–207.

O'Dowd, Liam. 2010. "From a 'Borderless World' to a 'World of Borders': 'Bringing History Back In.'" *Environment and Planning D: Society and Space* 28 (6): 1031–50.

Paasi, Ansi. 2009. "Bounded Spaces in a 'Borderless World'? Border Studies, Power and the Anatomy of Territory." *Journal of Power* 2 (2): 213–34.

Peña, Sergio. 2002. "Land Use Planning on the US-Mexico Border: A Comparison of the Legal Framework." *Journal of Borderlands Studies* 17 (1): 1–19.

Peña, Sergio. 2011. "Regímenes de planificación transfronteriza: México–Estados Unidos." *Región y sociedad* 23 (50): 115–51.

Peña, Sergio, and Gustavo Córdova. 2001. "Public Participation and Water Supply: The Case of Two Communities on the USA-Mexico Border." *Water International* 26 (3): 390–99.

Salter, Mark B. 2006. "The Global Visa Regime and the Political Technologies of the International Self: Borders, Bodies, Biopolitics." *Alternatives: Global, Local, Political* 31 (2): 167–89.

Sánchez, Roberto, 1993. "Public Participation and the IBWC: Challenges and Options." *Natural Resources Journal* 33 (2): 283–98.

Sassen, Saskia. 2007. *A Sociology of Globalization.* New York: W. W. Norton.

Sohn, Christophe. 2014. "The Border as a Resource in the Global Urban Space: A Contribution to the Cross-Border Metropolis Hypothesis." *International Journal of Urban and Regional Research* 38 (5): 1697–1711.

Soja, Edward W. 1989. *Post Modern Geographies: The Reassertion of Space in Critical Social Theory.* New York: Verso.

Staudt, Kathleen, and Irasema Coronado. 2002. *Fronteras No Más: Toward Social Justice at the U.S.-Mexico Border.* New York: Palgrave Macmillan.

Swyngedouw, Erik. 1997. "Neither Global nor Local: 'Glocalization' and the Politics of Scale." In *Spaces of Globalization: Reasserting the Power of the Local,* edited by Kevin Cox, 137–66. New York: Guilford.

Taylor, Peter J. 2003. "The State as a Container: Territoriality in the Modern World System." In *State/Space: A Reader,* edited by Neil Brenner, Bob Jessop, Martin Jones, and Gordon MacLeod, 101–14. Malden, Mass.: Blackwell.

Wallerstein, Immanuel. 1978. "World-System Analysis: Theoretical and Interpretative Issues." In *Social Change in the Capitalist World Economy,* edited by Barbara Hockey Kaplan, 219–36. Beverly Hills: SAGE.

Wilson, Christopher. 2017. *Growing Together: Economic Ties Between the United States and Mexico.* Washington, D.C.: Mexico Institute, Woodrow Wilson International Center for Scholars.

2

Defining the Border and the Borderlands

A Precondition for Institutional Development?

Tony Payan and Pamela L. Cruz

At the heart of this book lies the issue of *governance* on the U.S.-Mexico border. Within that core is the conviction that governance, especially *good* governance, is closely related to institutional development. In fact, without institutions, it is impossible to speak of governance—unless imposed by brute force. In effect, institutions—defined as an established organization, law, practice, or custom (Olsen 2010)—help focus attention, energy, and resources on solving problems in the broader environment and disciplining policy action, directing it to solve those problems in a way that is generally accepted and legitimate. The nature and state of the relationship between governance and institutional development are particularly important in complex environments, where there is a multiplicity of actors, issues, interests, and interactions. In such complex environments, institutions address themselves to specific issues—the market, security, the environment, elections, finance, infrastructure, and so on—helping focus attention, energy, and resources on particular concerns. Similarly, institutions organize collective action because they are charged with addressing questions within well-delineated territories—such as a city, a state, a region, or a country. Likewise, institutions address themselves to regulating relations and interactions among the members of a community and the methods and manners by which they must solve the challenges they face; that is, they provide for channels of communication and cooperation on how actors are to relate to each other in addressing an issue. Despite justifiable criticism of institutions and institution building as a panacea to many problems (Cox 2000; World Bank 2012), they remain the sine qua non for providing good and stable governance and ways for people to participate in governance processes legitimately and in an orderly fashion. In fact, over time, people come to expect institutions and those who occupy them to provide leadership and to achieve effective resolution of broader and specific policy problems.

The picture of the relationship between institutional development and governance outlined above, however, applies quite well when dealing with domestic issues—those that are fully contained within a political or territorial jurisdiction. There are, however, other more complicated scenarios, such as border regions, where territory and sovereignty function in ways that tend to structurally sever consolidated, even if sometimes politically conflictual, approaches to policy problems. For John A. Agnew (2015), for example, political space is associated with the territory and sovereignty of the nation and ontologically implies all-inclusive policy approaches to common problems. But such is not the case in spaces divided by an international borderline—unless there are institutions built precisely to bridge the gaps created by international territorial demarcations by pooling sovereignty for problem solving. In border contexts, a single issue straddling a borderline may in fact be addressed by institutions in mutually exclusive terms. In such politically complex arenas, where two sovereign nations meet and have established *national* institutions of governance but face *common* problems, the issue of institutions is particularly difficult to sort out. The border is, after all, where one nation-state and one set of national institutions ends and where the other begins, and they each claim absolute and exclusive jurisdiction, even when policy problems require well-coordinated institutions of governance precisely because they occur or evolve independently of national desires and sometimes because of the borderline. In these cases, policy makers are called to build institutions jointly and collaboratively to solve problems that transcend the lines—for example, governing cross-border flows in a way that increases national security, regulates migration in a legal and orderly way, establishes mechanisms to share and maintain water and air sheds, enforces the rule of law, and so forth. But building effective cross-border institutions is hardly easy. Doing so is accompanied by the presumption that shared problems will be addressed through institutional constructs that at once adhere to mutually exclusive national sovereignty—itself a foundational institution—and build institutions that dictate solutions that cross the borderline, that give the "other" a say and preferably a legitimate mandate in how a problem is resolved on the opposite side of the border. Cross-border institutions must, therefore, preserve and even reinforce national sovereignty as an underlying institution and at the same time pool that sovereignty to resolve common problems. This tension is not easily resolved and often requires considerable political will (Leibenath et al. 2008). Sovereignty pooling also frequently entices a great deal of political resistance from more nationalistic groups and constituents.

Indeed, as the European Union case shows, convincing national publics to pool sovereignty to govern border areas jointly via *supranational* institutions is not easy (Durà et al. 2018). Yet a degree of institutional thickness—that is, a sufficient number and a certain quality of binational institutions—is fundamental to ensure successful joint problem definitions, effective common programmatic responses, and compatible evaluations that allow for recalibrating policy to ensure resolution of specific policy issues and ultimately overall development. Moreover, the presence of strong institutions, when they include processes that generate public involvement and stimulate dialogue on public policy issues, gives legitimacy to government action and increases the degree of democracy in the communities they are meant to serve (on both sides of a border). Hence, institutions, especially well-developed, responsive, transparent, and well-funded institutions, are the sine qua non of good governance—and they do not come easy to border contexts as they often elicit virulent nationalistic reactions from domestic publics. Without institutions that do both—preserve sovereignty and pool it at the same time—however, there is a higher degree of uncertainty, more arbitrary decision-making processes, lower levels of democracy, lesser degrees of legitimacy, and more opportunities for certain actors to hijack the governance system for their purposes, much as we have seen a perverse degree of militarization at the U.S.-Mexico border, with a much greater emphasis on law enforcement and national security and less concern with human and due process rights (Dunn 2010). In border regions, in fact, governance often depends on individuals and their political will rather than on the work of permanent, solidly built institutions (Payan 2010). Thus, poor governance in border zones is largely driven by the dearth of binational institutions to address thorny binational issues jointly. Under such circumstances, not only is good governance difficult, but problems often persist and even worsen over time. And the border itself becomes a burden and a transaction cost and can even operate in detriment to the welfare of residents on both sides of the line. Thus, at the center of the discussion on institution building for good governance in border contexts are two concepts that complicate our reflection on institution building and governance—sovereignty and territory. In this chapter, we set aside the complex issue of sovereignty and seek to tackle the issue of territory in institution building and governance at the U.S.-Mexico border. Elsewhere we address the more abstract concept of sovereignty and its own complications.

When thinking about institution building, governance, and territory, a question arises: Are two adjacent nations required to enjoin a territorial or spatial definition of the *border* to be able to build institutions that are effective in solving common problems? The research team for this project set out to create a database of existing binational or bilateral institutions on the U.S.-Mexico border—including organizations, formal agreements, and practices that *govern* the border—and a key finding was that there is no single territorial definition of the border. In fact, the research team found institutions that addressed themselves to different issues, depending in part on their own territorial definition of the border; or to specific places, regardless of the proximity of other spaces and demarcations on the ground. Moreover, the team found that some institutions remain stubbornly national, such as law enforcement, while others have had a degree of success in governing broader cross-border issues, such as water sharing. Some were more or less well organized, such as the International Boundary and Water Commission (IBWC), covering the Rio Grande watershed, while others operated more like networks, such as many groups dedicated to defending the rights of migrants, refugees, and asylum seekers. Thus, as the project progressed, it became quite evident that the border was, territorially speaking, many different things to many different actors—some very aware of their territorial reach and others barely even thinking about space. An important conclusion of these findings was that institutional development of the U.S.-Mexico border is likely to be a reflection of that irregular relationship that many different actors keep with territory—perhaps with the sole exception that every one of them is cognizant that they are dealing with a borderline. This led the members of the research team to ask: Can a definitive demarcation of the borderlands help build institutions to provide more effective or *good* governance for the fifteen million people who live in cities and towns in proximity to the borderline? Should the border be defined territorially so that, once constrained from many, overlapping, and even conflicting territorial definitions, borderlanders can be free to build well-grounded institutions to provide governance on the manifold issues that affect the borderlands? The experience of the European Union was, to some extent, a guide for the team, as Europeans had more carefully thought through the relationship between territory and governance than North America had (Noferini et al. 2019).

The next step in this process of understanding the relationship between territory and institution building (for good governance) in border contexts was to take a series of territorial definitions of "the U.S.-Mexico border" and overlap the different maps used by different actors exercising authority to see what the common border core was, what lay at the periphery, and what was extraordinarily outside any potentially useful consolidated territorial definition of the border. In reviewing the many *territorial* understandings of the U.S.-Mexico border, the team ran into yet another important discovery: there were quite a few territorial definitions of the border, with no obvious core territorial definition. The conceptions of border from the perspective of its territory varied considerably—some were very narrowly defined as only those jurisdictions or narrow strips of land adjacent to the borderline, and some reached well into U.S. or Mexican land. Yet the team continued searching for a core territorial definition of "the border," partly motivated by the conviction that having a clear understanding of what the border encompasses territorially is a prerequisite to build institutions that can address border issues and the provision of good governance for the benefit of the populations they are meant to serve. Yet to the researchers, over time it became clear that there was no single territorial definition of the border but many, depending on who speaks of the border, and this appeared to be a problem to building solid institutions for good governance across issues and along the entire borderlands. Faced with this, the team had to ask whether a fixed territorial definition of the border was absolutely necessary in addressing institution building in cross-border contexts—specifically, whether having a territorial definition of the border was absolutely necessary to build effective cross-border institutions for good governance. The answer to this quandary is important, given that the wide variety of definitions around the U.S.-Mexico border, or the lack of a consensus around the spatial demarcation of the border, raise the question over whether it is possible to resolve *border* issues if the institutions are not built with a specific territorial scope that can allow for clear jurisdictions and less overlaps or conflicting claims in addressing different problems and population. The confusion is further exacerbated by the fact that various agencies define the border for their own purposes, without consideration to other agencies' needs and without coordination. In other words, when faced with multiple actors, each working on its own definition of the border, there is much room for them to find definitions that serve their interests and not those of the citizens of the borderlands. In sum, the practice is that the border is a different thing for different actors, depending on their view of it—and some prefer a territorially defined jurisdiction over it while others prefer an issue-based definition of the border. Some definitions of the borderlands are highly technical, such as border watersheds, while others are highly political and even imperialistic, such as the U.S. Border Patrol's one hundred air miles definition (discussed later in this chapter). We hypothesized, therefore, that these overlaps and contradictory definitions are at least partly responsible for the uneven institutional development of the border, which in turn makes governance more difficult and encapsulates a deeper degree of uncertainty for all border users. Worse, the open manipulation of territorial definitions of the border could hide more perverse behavior by agents who benefit from having no common understanding of the borderlands.

Given this set of interesting questions, the rest of this chapter explores and explains the various definitions of the border, the borderlands, and the border region, showing the difficulty of achieving good governance in a territorially fragmented space, when institutions have evolved by accretion, quite unevenly, and largely as a reaction to issues that have waxed and waned over time. Understanding this lack of consensus around the spatial/territorial understanding of the border may also help explain why the region remains politically mired by the perception of chaos, lawlessness, disorder, and unruliness. It can also help understand why the border remains an easy prey of political rhetoric and manipulation, and is interchangeably interpreted as a land of great opportunity as well as a source of problems. Finally, this may also explain why the ultimate response to the border has become a military-like enforcement of rules at the expense of due process rights, human rights, and democratic accountability by the agencies that claim jurisdiction over the border and its users. In the end, this chapter exposes the tension that is created by institutional underdevelopment at the U.S.-Mexico border, the desires of borderlanders for more open and democratic governance, and the opportunities that territorial lack of definition has created for agencies to assert themselves over and above the very vision that many borderlanders may have of their own homeland. Clearly, the U.S.-Mexico border residents share more than a borderline. They share a common history and culture, social and economic ties, and environmental, security, energy, and public health concerns. Even so, defining the border *territorially* has been elusive in detriment to their image of themselves. There are variable characterizations of the spatial dimensions of the border, depending on the issue at hand, and policy makers and scholars often avoid this prickly question altogether by simply talking about "the border" without defining the area it includes. In the next sections, this chapter outlines the different territorial descriptions of the U.S.-Mexico border across federal entities, formal binational agreements, and political-administrative units; explores the complexity of defining the border region; and points out the disadvantages of its overlapping and conflicting definitions—and the necessity of defining its territorial lines to develop and implement effective public policies that address the region's issues. This is done not with the idea that there should be a single definition of the border—different issues may call for different spatial boundaries—but with the idea that haphazard institutional evolution results in degrees of governance that may create more problems than they solve.

The Boundary, the Border Region, and Public Policy

To understand the importance of defining the border territorially, a distinction must be made between the boundary and the border region and their relationship to public policy. The boundary line between Mexico and the United States stretches 1,951 miles. It was largely set in the mid-nineteenth century by the 1848 Treaty of Guadalupe Hidalgo and the 1853 Gadsden Purchase. The Treaty of Guadalupe Hidalgo, signed on February 2, 1848, ended the two-year Mexican-American War, with the United States acquiring territory from Mexico that makes up present-day Texas, California, Nevada, Utah, parts of Colorado and Wyoming, and most of Arizona and New Mexico. The treaty also established the Rio Grande as the border between Texas and Mexico. However, it led to another boundary dispute—the location of the border west of El Paso, Texas (Griswold del Castillo 1990, 55–61). Tensions lingered over a disputed territory, the Mesilla Valley, what is now the border between southern New Mexico and Arizona and Mexico. Negotiations by James Gadsden and Antonio López de Santa Anna, and finalized in 1854, the Gadsden Purchase, settled the issues regarding the boundary, with the United States acquiring nearly thirty thousand square miles of Mexican territory in exchange for US$10 million. Other land disputes have occurred since then, mainly the Chamizal Border dispute, but they were minor and fully resolved by the 1960s (Payan 2016).

The boundary, however, is *not* the border or the border region. As already mentioned before, the *border* has in fact many different definitions depending on the issue, the agency, or even the perspective of the different political actors or functionaries who speak about the border or handle specific issues along or across the borderline. Conceptually, it can be said that the border is in constant motion (Konrad 2015)—with its extension depending on the actor or the policy issue at hand. The following sections explain the different definitions, organizing them by level of government and agency and showing the difficulty of addressing the complicated matrix of territory, policy issues, and actors' preferences. At the end of that discussion, what will be made clear is that resolving the location of the borderline on the sand (the boundary) would only be the beginning, not the end, of the search for effective institution building for good cross-border governance. The 1848 and 1854 establishment of the boundary was indeed the beginning of the possibility of building institutions to govern the region. Reviewing the history of the U.S.-Mexico borderlands, however, shows that there never emerged and there is in fact no clear consensus on what truly encompasses the border region (Ganster 2000). Unlike the U.S.-Mexico boundary line, "the border region" has had a more convoluted meaning, one that follows intricate but not coterminous political, administrative, economic, cultural, and social interests and views. Moreover, the advance of globalization—including economic and trade integration, regional and global security concerns, migration flows, climate change threats, and so forth—continues to engulf greater swaths of territory into what can be labeled the *border region*, primarily because more and more communities are impacted by cross-border activity. Thus, not having a standard territorial definition of the U.S.-Mexico border region has consequences for public policy and makes the border more vulnerable to political exploitation and ulterior motives than almost any other region of the country. Particularly problematic is the fact that treaties usually define the border region by miles/kilometers on either side of the international boundaries, covering only small portions of some counties and severing the defined political-administrative units (i.e., counties and *municipios*) of both countries.[1] This makes it difficult to advocate for programs and resources or analyze the populations who are truly in need of services; impedes local political organization; incentivizes local governments and federal agencies to manipulate the definition based on organizational rather than regional interests; and makes cooperation and joint territorial management difficult. Setting an agreed territorial definition of the border would solve most of these issues. This difficult political task upstream would likely help ease political issues downstream—as the institutional scaffolding with specific powers to negotiate and resolve issues would lower opportunistic advances by other actors and agencies downstream who would take advantage of the lack of territorial definition to advance their organizational interests and mute local participation in governance. In other words, a broader debate on how to organize border governance and how to delegate problem solving in a way that encompasses the border region would improve research, data analysis, and public policy implementation to help depoliticize border management down the line and ultimately serve the long-term planning and implementation of regional development.

Interestingly, it may be worth adding here that the word *border* itself is coming into question as something that can be tied down to a territory or, at a minimum, must be somewhat objectively related to a borderline. Indeed, there are people who have argued that the border is now something that can be found in spaces well away from the borderline. For example, the United States has been quite effective at establishing an effective borderline at Canadian and other airports, where passengers are screened before they board the plane, or at manufacturing plants, where goods are inspected even before they are sent off on their way to the *true* borderline. This spatial projection of the borderline further complicates the relationship between territory, institution building, and governance and must be taken into account in the future, as we deterritorialize the very concept of border but border many other spaces that do not lie immediately adjacent to any borderline (Bersin 2012).

Varying Definitions of the Border: The Local Perspective

When defining the border, one of the most influential demarcations comes from local communities and governments. They are, after all, the actors most closely affected by what the border means. Map 2.1 illustrates the primary approach most local political and bureaucratic actors but also most academics, policy makers, and the media employ to talk about the U.S.-Mexico border region. The area is roughly composed of local political administrative units that directly touch the official boundary line, and it includes twenty-three U.S. counties and thirty-six Mexican municipios (shown in medium gray). This definition is arbitrary, however, given that border issues are not limited to those that concern local political-administrative units adjacent to the borderline. No one would say that environmental issues, public safety, or natural resources issues follow the political lines of counties and municipios. For this reason, border counties and municipios that do not directly touch the boundary are often included by others as part of the border region, depending on the issue at hand, such

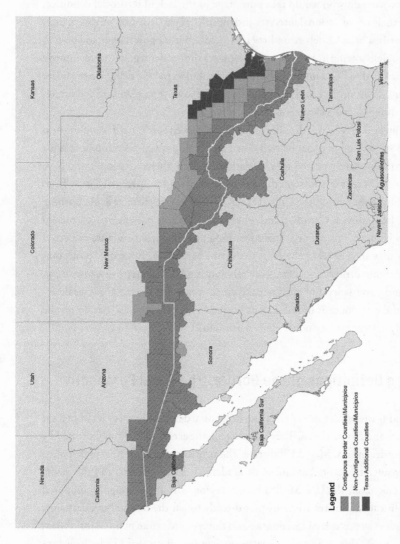

MAP 2.1 Counties and municipios on the U.S.-Mexico border, showing three different definitions of the border. Map produced by Pamela Cruz, with assistance from Rice University's Baker Institute of Public Policy and GIS/Data Center, using data from Natural Earth, the U.S. Census Bureau, and the Instituto Nacional de Estadística y Geografía (INEGI) (http://www.naturalearthdata.com/downloads).

as shared natural resources, sociocultural ties, economic interactions, legal and illegal cross-border flows, and demographic similarities (such counties and municipios are shown in light gray).

Defining the U.S.-Mexico border region by local political-administrative units is analytically useful, as most statistical data are collected at that level and local governments can articulate the border's interests to aid in the analysis, creation, and implementation of public policy. But it would further help if there were a consensus on the definition—which does not exist even among academics.[2] The United States–Mexico Political Analysis Tool (USMexPAT) project of Arizona State University, for example, defines the border as thirty-seven U.S. counties and seventy-eight Mexican municipios (Rex 2014), which clearly differs from alternative definitions among academics (Ganster 2000). As Joan Anderson and James Gerber put it:

> This focus does not resolve a number of additional problems, however, as it still remains to determine how "deep" the border is. That is, how far into the United States and Mexico do border influences extend? This is an area of investigation for future research. Given the state of border studies, any definition we might offer now would be somewhat arbitrary. (2008, 11)

What is clear from this map is that there is a need to understand not just where the borderline or boundary is but also the territorial demarcation of the *border* around the issues above ground shared by local communities, many of which arise along the borderline and gradually fade out as one moves away from the boundary. A definition of the border must include, therefore, not just a pure territorial dimension but also an aboveground dimension that goes more directly to the issues affecting local communities by virtue of their being adjacent to or near the borderline.

Varying Definitions of the Border: The State Perspective

Statewide political motivations also interfere with a broad consensus on a territorial definition of the border region. Through Senate Bill 501 in 1999, for example, the legislature of the State of Texas, which covers the longest stretch of the U.S.-Mexico border, added several counties (dark gray in Map 2.1) to the border region—including Bexar County, which contains the San Antonio metropolitan area. This definition had also previously been used by John Sharp, then Texas comptroller of public accounts (Sharp 1998). The legislature cited the growing population of the Texas-Mexico border and the number of residents of the region who lack access to state agency resources and services as reasons for the expanded definition.[3] S.B. 501 brought the number of

Texas counties considered part of the border region to forty-three and linked them directly to state public policies for the border region.

Another definition includes all the states adjacent to the borderline. This definition encompasses ten states—four in the United States and six in Mexico—with a combined population of one hundred million people (DOS 2016). This definition allows a broader understanding of the concerns, issues, and opportunities regarding the border shared by state authorities (e.g., trade, environmental resources, labor markets, infrastructure), but it—absurdly—includes places like Northern California and the Texas Panhandle as part of the border, which is difficult to justify. This state-based definition of the border region is used by the Border Governors Conference (BGC) established in 1980 (New Mexico Border Authority n.d.). A border governors' meeting is held periodically, although political considerations and partisan disagreements often get in the way—the 2010 BGC was derailed by Arizona's controversial S.B. 1070 and the conference has not met since 2012 (Lee and Wilson 2014, 16, 47).[4] The BGC produces joint declarations but has little power to force issues onto the national policy agenda (Lee and Wilson 2014, 36). A similar group, the Border Legislative Conference (BLC), is composed of federal and state legislators who represent regional districts, but legislators participate on a voluntary basis (Border Legislative Conference n.d.). Moreover, it appears to have no influence on agenda setting for the border. Both groups are constrained by the supremacy of the federal agenda over that of state and local officials. Clearly, the BGC and the BLC discuss economic development, tourism and travel, agriculture and livestock, science and technology, energy, environment, water, wildlife, customs and logistics, border crossings, migration, security, education, public health, and emergency management, but with minimal impact on the border policy agenda as set in the national capitals. Furthermore, their border definition often considers state interests in areas such as taxation, public services, public/ private partnerships, trade, and law enforcement, areas in which the states sometimes compete with one another.

Varying Definitions of the Border: The National Perspective

The third and most fragmented territorial definition of the U.S.-Mexico border region comes from the federal government. The most common definition of the border by the U.S. and Mexican governments is found in the 1983 "Agreement Between the United States of America and the United Mexican States on Cooperation for the Protection and Improvement of the Environment on the Border Area," also known as the La Paz Agreement. U.S. president Ronald Reagan and Mexican president Miguel de la Madrid Hurtado signed the agreement in response to environmental problems in the U.S.-Mexico border region. Article 4 defines the "border area" as one hundred kilometers (sixty-two miles) on either side of the inland and maritime boundaries between the United States and Mexico. This definition includes the border cities and towns along the boundary where pollution and other environmental problems could spill to the other side. Even so, the definition does not cover the full geographical extent of cross-border watersheds and sub-watersheds (Ganster 2014). Complicating this definition further, the La Paz Agreement area includes in whole or in part forty-four counties and eighty municipios, because the definition refers to a linear measure (kilometers/miles), which does not conform to the boundaries of political-administrative bodies (counties and municipios) (HHS n.d.).

Two institutions—the Border Environment Cooperation Commission (BECC) and the North American Development Bank (NADB), created in 1993 through the North American Free Trade Agreement (NAFTA)—first operated with the same one-hundred-kilometer border definition. Their charter agreement also allows projects eligible for assistance outside their border definition if it remedies a transboundary environmental or health problem. In July 2000, however, the NADB published a draft document titled "Utilizing the Lending Capacity of the NADB," in which one of its recommendations was expanding its geographic jurisdiction from one hundred kilometers on each side to three hundred kilometers on both the U.S. and Mexican sides (Doughman 2002, 202). Concerns were raised on such an expansion because it could potentially pit economically disadvantaged border communities in competition with wealthier communities like Los Angeles, Phoenix, and Monterrey (Reed and Kelly 2000). In 2004 the U.S. Congress passed legislation redefining the border region, and the charter was amended to define the border region as one hundred kilometers north of the boundary in the United States and three hundred kilometers south into Mexico.[5] The Pan American Health Organization (PAHO), a binational international agency focused on health, also has its own definition of the border, which it says consists of forty-eight U.S. counties and ninety-four municipios (PAHO 2012, 698–99).

In law enforcement and policing, the definition of the border encompasses an even broader geographical area. According to the Immigration and Nationality Act (INA) § 287 (codified in 8 U.S.C. § 1357), which outlines immigration enforcement, U.S. agencies can refer to a "reasonable distance from any external boundary of the United States," and any officer or employee of the service designated by the attorney general may—without a warrant—board and search any vessel, railway car, aircraft, conveyance, or vehicle for the "purpose of patrolling the border to prevent the illegal entry of aliens into the United States."[6] "Reasonable distance" was later defined as one hundred air miles from any external boundary of the United States.[7] U.S. Customs and Border Protection (CBP) agents can thus set up immigration checkpoints in a much larger geographical area than almost any other U.S. agency. It is not clear why one hundred air miles was chosen and why the populations that live within that zone were not consulted, but nearly two-thirds of the U.S. population falls within that definition of the border (ACLU n.d.) (see Map 2.2).

Mexico has an even more complex definition of the border region for customs and law enforcement purposes. It designates an area of twenty kilometers (12.42 miles) from Mexico's side of the boundary as the border. When traveling south from Ciudad Juárez, Chihuahua, for example, it is possible to run into the old Customs House located exactly on what the locals knew as "Kilómetro 20," the place where every vehicle and individual was subjected to customs inspection. At other times, the Mexican government lists entire municipios as part of the border region, with no explicit or specific justification for including one and not the other (Secretaría de Economía n.d.). Interestingly, in Mexico, border towns and cities are border "free zones"; U.S. citizens and residents may travel there without obtaining a visitor's permit (Forma Migratoria Múltiple [FMM, Multiple Migratory Form]), and Mexican citizens may bring in via land crossing US$300–500 worth of merchandise with only a system of random checks for tax collection purposes (Programa Paisano 2019; DOS n.d.). It used to be that U.S. citizens could even return to the United States without a passport, something that changed as CBP now requires every single person entering the United States to have a passport. Entry is of course not denied to citizens, but not having proper documents can subject the border crosser to considerable harassment. The requirement, however, remains a U.S., not a Mexican, requirement.

Overlapping and Conflicting Definitions of the Border

It is evident, as already stated a few times and in different ways, that the border is many things to many actors—depending on the level of government where a particular problem is to be addressed, the issue and the actor or government agency addressing it, the territorial or jurisdictional understanding of the problem to be addressed, and even the different political, civil, social, and economic actors that interact on one side or across the borderline. There are also different overlapping and conflicting territorial definitions of the U.S.-Mexico border region. Map 2.3 shows how the southwest border region overlaps under different definitions.

Similarly, and under conditions of the kind of conceptual stretching that the lack of a territorial definition of the border leads to, on this map, cities as far away from the borderline as Monterrey, Nuevo León, and San Antonio, Texas, can be considered the border, even though anyone walking on its streets may clearly sense that the border effect has largely faded out.

MAP 2.2 Territorial definition of the border for U.S. federal law enforcement agencies. Map produced by Pamela Cruz, with assistance from Rice University's Baker Institute for Public Policy and GIS/Data Center, using data from "The Government's 100 Mile Border Zone" map by the American Civil Liberties Union (ACLU) (https://www.aclu.org/know-your-rights-governments-100-mile -border-zone-map).

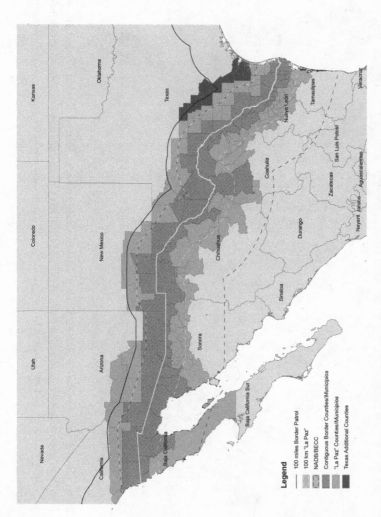

MAP 2.3 Overlapping territorial definitions of the U.S.–Mexico border. Map produced by Pamela Cruz, with assistance from Rice University's Baker Institute for Public Policy and GIS/Data Center, using data from Natural Earth, the U.S. Census Bureau, the Instituto Nacional de Estadística y Geografía (INEGI), the U.S. Environmental Protection Agency (EPA), the Texas Commission on Environmental Quality (TCEQ), the North American Development Bank (NADB), the Border Environment Cooperation Commission (BECC), and the American Civil Liberties Union (ACLU).

Now there are, of course, arguments for having different definitions of the border. For academics, for example, a consistent operationalization may be difficult, as it depends on what they are researching and how (Gerber 2009, 32). Another argument is that public policy issues do not necessarily coincide with a single territorial definition and forcing a single definition based on territorial demarcations might complicate the work of different agencies, diluting their focus on the borderlands that might be closer to the borderline and require greater attention. What is more, border watersheds may stretch well beyond a territorial definition useful to law enforcement, trade, or environmental issues. However, border issues have become increasingly complex. A standard understanding of the border's parameters is necessary to create the binational institutions that eventually evolve into effective joint territorial managers of these issues. Part of the inability of the border region to advocate for its own interest is precisely the fact that no one knows what the border region really encompasses.

Why Is It Important to Agree?

The political environment in the United States today has become poisonous. The common border with Mexico has turned into a focal point to articulate much of that vitriolic rhetoric and a place to blame for many socioeconomic ills in the country. Starting with the U.S. elections of 2016, the environment turned even more toxic. There is continued advocacy for the construction of a border wall, under the assumption that a massive barrier between the United States and Mexico can help simplify and solve border issues. There is also a call for restricting migration and even legal human mobility at the border, something that is bound to deprive borderlanders of a precious resource (Sohn 2013). Attention to the effective administration of joint natural resources and environmental management has taken a back seat to national priorities. U.S. president Donald Trump has in fact been clear—the nation-state, as defined by its boundary line, is the sole legitimate container of all policy solutions, implying that cross-border institution building and cooperation rank very low in his political priorities (Ponsot 2017). This border management model, however, is not sustainable in the long run. The border region is, by definition, a place of interactions—economic, social, and cultural—with people, goods, capital, and services continually flowing back and forth across the border. Moreover, the region is growing and developing at a fast pace and requires solid institutions to govern these exchanges in a way that is participative, transparent, and effective. A dearth of institutions complicates the management of population growth, orderly urbanization and infrastructure development, good natural resource management, climate change and other environmental challenges, and dealing with cross-border activities, legal and illegal (Staudt and Coronado

2002, 10–15). The lack of territorial definition around the borderlands complicates institution building and, thereby, good governance on this and many other issues. The myriad definitions of the border constitute an obstacle to effectively manage the border region's policy issues, which affect local, state, national, and international interests. There are powerful reasons to seek a joint definition of the border, although there are also reasons to remain flexible when talking about the border.

Some of the key advantages but also disadvantages to defining the border were already identified in the La Paz Agreement of 1983 when the border was defined as one hundred kilometers on either side of the borderline. The importance of defining the borderlands was further recognized in 2004, when the borderlands south of the boundary line extended to three hundred kilometers. This was the most important attempt at defining the border territorially, as it was recognized that without a spatial definition, it was nearly impossible to define problems, create policy, and respond effectively to border issues. Recognition of the border as a territory, unique unto its own and carrying its own distinct policy needs, came with the idea that unilateral approaches to managing the U.S.-Mexico border region are questionable because segregating markets by separating cross-border communities, rather than taking advantage of their joint potential, impoverishes populations and sets back economic development. The region was recognized as a dynamic territory, with borderlanders using resources to maximize individual and household wealth—working, shopping, investing, and carrying out activities in areas they believe their resources will be more efficiently allocated. Impeding these calculations will force people to spend more resources than required on a particular good and consequently lead to a loss of individual and collective wealth—and also damage the cultural and social ties that support healthy communities and facilitate the larger political and diplomatic work needed to build effective governance institutions on both sides of the border. A territorial definition of the border also helps plan policy for the long term, answering questions on population growth and investment in cities and helping define who qualifies for specific benefits. The B1-B2 visa for border residents, for example, grants a benefit on the basis of territory—full mobility within the band of twenty-five miles north of the boundary line. All visitors must obtain an additional permit (I-94) if they are to travel further beyond the border territory as recognized by the nature and character of that visa.

Territorial definition also helps coordination. Effective regional management evidently requires close political coordination among all three levels of government—local, state, and national—within each country and across the boundary line. This is a multilayered, complex political landscape that calls for an overarching set of institutions. If the appropriate governments are identified through their territorial jurisdiction, calling the right authorities from the right places becomes easier. For instance, a border commission would certainly call to the table all the right mayors, governors, and agency heads who need to be at the table to discuss the various issues affecting their communities and create standardized responses to specific issues. These groups, backed by federal and political will, can then designate specific functionaries to work on certain issues and create working groups that could coordinate the multiple agencies that govern the border space and articulate the needs of communities clearly encompassed within a specific territory. Moreover, these venues, forums, or channels can identify the populations that need to be consulted and queried about their own interests and vision, something that could not only help democratize responses to the pressing issues of specific areas and populations but also help provide legitimacy to solutions crafted by joint administrative systems. A broad territorial approach to border issues would also create a greater degree of balance and access to all the different interests that need representation in governance—from human rights to environmental issues to law enforcement. Not defining the border would not only impede coordination but create vacuums that give opportunities to specific interests and agencies to capture governance for their own purposes. This has already been the case on the U.S.-Mexico border, where law enforcement has pushed its way into vacuums created by the lack of institutions and coordination in many areas and crafted a governance system that privileges security over many other visions of the border and shoved aside many other economic, social, and cultural concerns to advance its own organizational interests. What we have seen at the U.S.-Mexico border, in effect, is policy by bureaucracy, where specific agencies, namely law enforcement, define the border, set the agenda, choose the response, control all other actors, and become the primary interlocutor for the border in a way that sacrifices the true diversity of the border and nullifies the desires of border residents. Around 90 percent of law enforcement agents, for example, support the border wall, whereas the population of the United States at large is divided, and around 80 percent of border residents oppose it (Corchado and Pedroza 2016; Friedersdorf 2019). In effect, this is the equivalent of policy by bureaucracy. Moreover, the absence of a territorial definition of the border can incentivize some nonborder actors to seek a definition of the border to capture funding and programs that would and should be designated to aid border populations. This is partly what happened when the Texas state legislature decided to include a number of counties far away from the borderline so as to funnel resources to their development, something that allowed Bexar County, where the city of San Antonio sits, to compete aggressively and successfully with much needier border counties for precious state resources (see Map 2.1, dark gray shading). Without a clear, agreed-upon definition of the border, the word becomes nimble and easily captured by political interests that may not necessarily serve the interests of border communities. Thus, a binational, agreed-upon territorial definition of the border region would facilitate governance, enhance democracy, and support the well-being of border residents. Although this model appears counter to the concept of sovereignty, a border commission to coordinate the work of all agencies involved in border management could reinforce sovereignty while bringing order and coordination to a region whose many agencies appear to be operating independently and without regard to the activities of others—and often not solving their own agendas and worsening those of other actors.

The issue of defining the border territorially, however, is not as easy as its potential advantages may suggest. Straitjacketing the region into a hard spatial domain might also impede the kind of flexibility that is required to manage different issues according to their own characteristics and needs and to create institutions that move at different speeds, depending on the issue at hand. The examination of the different territorial definitions of the border clearly shows that it is very difficult to encase specific issues within a well-demarcated limit. Watersheds, for example, are complicated, and although their greatest visibility may be the Rio Grande between Texas and Mexico, the tributaries of the river may be as far away from the borderline as Colorado or south-central Chihuahua State. Managing the water resources of the Rio Grande, therefore, does not lend itself to easy territorial definition of the border. Similarly, cross-border trade is vital not only to the border region but also to the entire economic health of both nations. Thus, confining trade facilitation to a border region, without considering the state of the overall road and rail system well beyond a simple territorial definition of the border, would likely be a mistake. Roads and railways are the arteries of a much greater system that can extend well beyond the borderline. The problem here is much more than having a territorial definition of the borderlands, but not thinking about the way the two national systems interconnect at the border ports of entry can nonetheless be a problem, as ports of entry become clogged and end up constituting an important transaction cost, precisely because there are low levels of coordination in understanding, building, and managing border infrastructure jointly. This all indicates that a single territorial definition of the border may not serve all issues well, as issues and territory are not always coterminous and may require different definitions of what the border is.

Clearly, a fixed or standardized territorial definition of the border is a complicated issue. There are both advantages and disadvantages to having one. To advocate for territorial demarcations of the border requires, therefore, taking stock of the advantages and disadvantages of doing so. Overall, however, we believe that a territorial definition of the border, even if such definition maintains a degree of flexibility, would allow for policy solutions that might be more comprehensive, serve border communities more directly with a focus on their needs and interests, prevent policy hijacking by specific actors, and provide greater opportunities for local communities to participate in decision-making. This would in turn allow for better governance with clear jurisdictions and responsibilities that allow for greater democracy, accountability, responsiveness, and efficiency in policy. The current territorial structure of the border has evolved by accretion, creating in its path structural inefficiencies to good policy making and implementation. The importance of the relationship between policy and territory comes into focus more sharply when such a process is viewed through the lens of a borderline, where institutions both reinforce sovereignty and pool it as required for effective problem solving.

Conclusion

At the end of this reflection, we can safely conclude that current territorial demarcations of the U.S.-Mexico border region do not facilitate the creation of institutions that provide good governance for all borderlanders; they do not leverage the border as a resource (Sohn 2013) for binational prosperity and security and create instead enormous transaction costs on all border users; and they do not represent the interests of borderlanders. Instead, they are often sets of arbitrary, and at times unilateral, definitions of what is fundamentally a shared space with problems that know no boundaries. Moreover, multiple territorial conceptions of the border provide plenty of opportunities for various actors to push their very narrow interests (e.g., law enforcement) and exclude many other important agents from the decision-making processes or from expressing their own views on issues that affect everyone (e.g., workers, families, human rights advocates). In the end, this results in a serious democratic deficit at the border (Payan 2010). In effect, the current territorial definitions of the border—although we acknowledge that there can be several and there does not have to be one definition alone—do not facilitate joint problem solving for the good of all and often make problems worse. Management of the region should be shared at a basic level, and that begins by reconsidering more useful territorial definitions of the border region. Fragmented territorial definitions impose excessive costs on borderlanders, who have to spend increasing amounts of money, time, and energy if they want to interact with each other across borderlines. The general suspicion is that territorial fragmentation does benefit certain interests at the expense of general welfare. This approach, in the long run, is unsustainable. The twenty-first-century U.S.-Mexico border requires a territorial reorganization and a common definition(s) to create effective governance mechanisms for a competitive and sustainable region.

Notes

1. A municipio is the Mexican political administrative unit equivalent to a U.S. county.
2. James Gerber, Francisco Lara-Valencia, and Carlos de la Parra (2010) include forty municipios and twenty-four counties adjacent to the boundary. Marie Mora and Alberto Dávila (2009) confine the border to twenty-three counties and thirty-five municipios, which

they also say are "adjacent" to the boundary line. Joan Anderson and James Gerber (2008) include twenty-five counties and thirty-eight municipios, which they argue touch the borderline. Federico Gerardo De Cosío and Andrés Boadella argue that "perhaps there is one legal border definition, which is the 'imaginary line' that divides Mexico and the United States [but] there are many operational definitions of the border. Each definition responds to the specific needs of the defining organization. Any consensus is unlikely as to what is meant by the border region. . . . In addition, for some observers, the border should also include other metropolitan areas that are far beyond the boundary because either they are influenced by the border, or they influence the border. San Antonio, Texas, and Monterrey, Nuevo León, are classic examples since these two cities consider themselves the gateway to the United States or to Mexico" (1999, 2–3).

3.   Texas legislature, S.B. 501, 76th Regular Session, 1999, http://www.lrl.state.tx.us.

4.   Senate Bill 1070, formally titled the Support Our Law Enforcement and Safe Neighborhoods Act, was an anti-immigration bill signed by former Arizona governor Jan Brewer on April 23, 2010. The law "compelled police to ask for papers and allowed officers to arrest a person without a warrant if the officer believed the person has committed an offense that makes them deportable. The law also made it a crime to fail to carry registration papers and for people in the country illegally to solicit work." See Duara 2016.

5.   Public Law 108-215, 108th Congress, 118 Stat. 579, April 5, 2004, https://www.congress .gov/108/plaws/publ215/PLAW-108publ215.htm. See also NADB 2017, chapter VI, Article II, p. 24.

6.   8 U.S. Code §1357, Powers of Immigration Officers and Employees, 2011 edition, https:// www.govinfo.gov/content/pkg/USCODE-2011-title8/html/USCODE-2011-title8 -chap12-subchapII-partIX-sec1357.htm.

7.   Code of Federal Regulations, Title 8, Aliens and Nationality, https://www.gpo.gov/fdsys /pkg/CFR-2001-title8-vol1/xml/CFR-2001-title8-vol1-sec287-1.xml.

References

Agnew, John A. 2015. *Place and Politics: The Geographical Mediation of State and Society*. Political Geography 1. New York: Routledge.

American Civil Liberties Union (ACLU). n.d. "Fact Sheet on Customs and Border Protection's 100-Mile Zone." Accessed May 5, 2020. https://www.aclu.org/other/aclu-factsheet -customs-and-border-protections-100-mile-zone?redirect=immigrants-rights/aclu-fact -sheet-customs-and-border-protections-100-mile-zone.

Anderson, Joan B., and James Gerber. 2008. *Fifty Years of Change on the U.S Mexico Border: Growth, Development, and Quality of Life*. Austin: University of Texas Press.

Bersin, Alan. 2012. "Lines and Flows: The Beginning and End of Borders." *Brooklyn Journal of International Law* 37 (2): 388–406.

Border Legislative Conference. n.d. "What Is the Border Legislative Conference?" Accessed May 5, 2020. http://www.borderlegislators.org/description_eng.htm.

Corchado, Alfredo, and Courtney Pedroza. 2016. "Common Ground: Poll Finds U.S.-Mexico Border Residents Overwhelmingly Value Mobility, Oppose Wall." *Dallas Morning News*, July 18.

Cox, Robert W. 2000. "Gramsci, Hegemony and International Relations." In *International Relations: Critical Concepts in Political Science*, edited by Andrew Linklater, 1207–22. New York: Routledge.

De Cosío, Federico Gerardo, and Andrés Boadella. 1999. "Demographic Factors Affecting the U.S.-Mexico Border Health Status." In *Life, Death, and In-Between on the U.S.-Mexico Border: Así Es la Vida*, edited by Martha Oehmke Loustaunau and Mary Sánchez-Bane, 1–22. Westport, Conn.: Bergin & Garvey.

Doughman, Pamela M. 2002. "Water Cooperation in the U.S.-Mexico Border Region." In *Environmental Peacemaking*, edited by Ken Conca and Geoffrey D. Dabelko, 190–219. Washington, D.C.: Woodrow Wilson Center Press; Baltimore: John Hopkins University Press.

Duara, Nigel. 2016. "Arizona's Once-Feared Immigration Law, SB 1070, Loses Most of Its Power in Settlement." *Los Ángeles Times*, September 15.

Dunn, Timothy J. 2010. *Blockading the Border and Human Rights: The El Paso Operation That Remade Immigration Enforcement*. Austin: University of Texas Press.

Durà, Antoni, Andrea Nosferini, Matteo Berzi, and Francesco Camonita. 2018. "Euroregions, Excellence and Innovation Across EU Borders: A Catalogue of Good Practices." Università Autónoma de Barcelona, Spain. https://ec.europa.eu/futurium/en/system/files/ged/recot_crii_catalogue_0.pdf.

Friedersdorf, Conor. 2019. "Why Did the Border Patrol Union Switch Its Position on the Wall?" *The Atlantic*, January 15.

Ganster, Paul, ed. 2000. *The U.S.-Mexican Border Environment: A Road Map to a Sustainable 2020*. San Diego: San Diego State University Press.

Ganster, Paul. 2014. "Evolving Environmental Management and Community Engagement at the U.S.-Mexican Border." *Eurasia Border Review* 5 (1): 19–39.

Gerber, James. 2009. "Developing the U.S.-Mexico Border Region for a Prosperous and Secure Relationship: Human and Physical Infrastructure Along the U.S. Border with Mexico." Baker Institute, March 26. https://www.bakerinstitute.org/media/files/Research/0214b170/LAI-pub-BorderSecGerber-032709.pdf.

Gerber, James, Francisco Lara-Valencia, and Carlos de la Parra. 2010. "Re-Imagining the U.S.-Mexico Border: Policies Toward a More Competitive and Sustainable Transborder Region." *Global Economy Journal* 10 (2).

Griswold del Castillo, Richard. 1990. *The Treaty of Guadalupe Hidalgo: A Legacy of Conflict*. Norman: University of Oklahoma Press.

Konrad, Victor. 2015. "Toward a Theory of Borders in Motion." *Journal of Borderlands Studies* 30 (1): 1–17.

Lee, Erik, and Christopher Wilson, eds. 2014. "The U.S.-Mexico Border Economy in Transition." Wilson Center, February. http://naresearchpartnership.org/wp-content/uploads/2013/07/US-MEX-Border-Economy-in-Transition.pdf.

Leibenath, Markus, Ewa Korcelli-Olejniczak, and Robert Knippschild, eds. 2008. *Crossborder Governance and Sustainable Spatial Development: Mind the Gaps!* Berlin: Springer.

Mora, Marie T., and Alberto Dávila. 2009. *Labor Market Issues Along the U.S.-Mexico Border.* Tucson: University of Arizona Press.

New Mexico Border Authority. n.d. "Border Conferences." Accessed May 5, 2020. http://www.nmborder.com/Border_Conferences.aspx.

Noferini, Andrea, et al. 2019. "Cross-Border Cooperation in the EU: Euroregions amid Multilevel Governance and Reterritorialization." *European Planning Studies Journal* 28 (1): 1–22.

North American Development Bank (NADB). 2017. "Agreement Between the Government of the United States of America and the Government of the United Mexican States Concerning the Establishment of a Border Environment Cooperation Commission and a North American Development Bank," November 10. https://www.nadb.org/uploads/content/files/Policies/Charter_Eng.pdf.

Olsen, Johan P. 2010. *Governing Through Institution Building: Institutional Theory and Recent European Experiments in Democratic Organization.* Oxford: Oxford University Press.

Pan American Health Organization (PAHO). 2012. "United States–Mexico Border Area." In *Health in the Americas*, 698–721. Washington, D.C.: Pan American Health Organization. https://www.paho.org/salud-en-las-americas-2012/index.php?option=com_docman&view=download&category_slug=hia-2012-country-chapters-22&alias=153-us-mexico-border-153&Itemid=231&lang=en.

Payan, Tony. 2010. "Crossborder Governance in a Tristate, Binational Region." In *Cities and Citizenship at the U.S.-Mexico Border: The Paso del Norte Metropolitan Region*, edited by Kathleen Staudt, César M. Fuentes, and Julia E. Monárrez Fragoso, 217–44. New York: Palgrave Macmillan.

Payan, Tony. 2016. "How a Forgotten Border Dispute Tormented U.S.-Mexico Relations for 100 Years." *Americas Quarterly*, Winter. https://www.americasquarterly.org/content/how-forgotten-border-dispute-tormented-us-mexico-relations-100-years.

Ponsot, Elisabeth. 2017. "Watch the Recording of Donald Trump's Full Speech Before the United Nations." *Quartz*, September 19. https://qz.com/1081446/unga-2017-donald-trump-full-video-and-transcript-at-united-nations-general-assembly/.

Programa Paisano. 2019. "¿Qué mercancías puedo ingresar al país?" Blog, November 1. https://www.gob.mx/paisano/es/articulos/que-mercancias-puedo-ingresar-al-pais.

Reed, Cyrus, and Mary Kelly. 2000. "Expanding the Mandate: Should the Border Environment Cooperation Commission and North American Development Bank Go Beyond Water, Wastewater and Solid Waste Management Projects and How Do They Get There?" Texas Center for Policy Studies, San Antonio, July.

Rex, Tom R. 2014. "The Geography and History of the United States and México, with a Focus on the Border Area." Arizona State University, Tempe, April. http://usmexpat.com/wp-content/uploads/2014/04/Volume-I.pdf.

Secretaría de Economía. n.d. "Franja Fronteriza Norte y Región Fronteriza." Accessed May 5, 2020. https://www.gob.mx/se/acciones-y-programas/franja-fronteriza-norte-y-region-fronteriza-cupos-de-importacion-de-productos-basicos-para-empresas-de-la-frontera.

Sharp, John. 1998. "Bordering the Future." Office of the Comptroller of Public Accounts, Austin, Texas.

Sohn, Christophe. 2013. "The Border as a Resource in the Global Urban Space: A Contribution to the Crossborder Metropolis Hypothesis." *International Journal of Urban and Regional Research* 38 (5): 1697–1711.

Staudt, Kathleen, and Irasema Coronado. 2002. *Fronteras No Más: Toward Social Justice at the U.S.-Mexico Border*. New York: Palgrave Macmillan.

U.S. Department of Health and Human Services (HHS). n.d. "The U.S.-Mexico Border Region." Accessed May 5, 2020. https://www.hhs.gov/about/agencies/oga/about-oga/what-we-do/international-relations-division/americas/border-health-commission/us-mexico-border-region/index.html.

U.S. Department of State (DOS). 2016. "U.S. Relations with Mexico." Bureau of Western Hemisphere Affairs, Bilateral Relations Fact Sheet, July 12. https://2009-2017.state.gov/r/pa/ei/bgn/35749.htm.

U.S. Department of State (DOS). n.d. "Mexico International Travel Information." Bureau of Consular Affairs. Accessed May 5, 2020. https://travel.state.gov/content/passports/en/country/mexico.html.

World Bank. 2012. *The World Bank's Approach to Public Sector Management 2011–2020: Better Results from Public Sector Institutions*. Washington, D.C.: World Bank.

3

...

Data for U.S.-Mexico Border Studies

A Comparison of U.S. and Mexican Data
Collection and Distribution

James Gerber and Jorge Eduardo Mendoza Cota

The asymmetries of the U.S.-Mexico border region are a serious obstacle to comparative research and analysis. Differences exist in data collection systems, the primary concerns of data programs, and the geopolitical units below the state level. Some researchers get around these obstacles by looking at only one side of the border, conducting qualitative studies, or presenting their results at such a highly aggregated level that it is difficult to compare border communities or to know the extent and limits of their integration. To be sure, there will always be a need for qualitative and one-country research, but quantitative analysis is essential for deepening our knowledge of the border region and, ultimately, U.S.-Mexico integration. Comparable quantitative measures of border communities and border issues may seem impossible given the difficulties of meeting the data requirements. For example, if concepts and measurement methods are substantially different, then cross-border comparisons are not possible; or if the unit of measurement in Mexico is different from in the United States, then comparisons are not relevant. In effect, there are three requirements for cross-border quantitative analysis: (1) there must be a close similarity or identity in data concepts (what is measured); (2) methods must be the same (how it is measured) or, given the socioeconomic differences, must lead to measurements of a similar population; and (3) the unit of observation must be the same (level of aggregation) so that both sides are using the same or similar geopolitical units for their measurements.

National data collection programs, including those of the United States and Mexico, are designed to use standard frameworks, norms, and recommended best practices. These are mostly a result of international collaboration within the United

Nations (UN) and the United Nations Statistics Division (UNSD).[1] The existence of a widely followed set of guidelines for national data programs ensures at least some comparability in the concepts, data collection, and methods. The degree of comparability should not be overestimated, however. Differences in economic conditions, political organization, and social values also mean that there are significant differences not just in data collection but also in the relative importance that countries assign to the different uses of the data.

The home page of the UNSD's website lists the topics and subtopics for national data programs, shown in Table 3.1. These are not identical to the categories used by the United States or Mexico, but they give a general idea of the main topics covered in their data collection and distribution programs. Many of the topics in Table 3.1 are national in scope and are not disaggregated to state or local levels in the United States or Mexico, although some are. All the topics in Table 3.1 are covered by the United States and Mexico, along with many additional subtopics that are not specified in Table 3.1 or that are rolled into a broad subtopic such as "basic economic statistics." Examples include transportation statistics; statistics related to specific economic sectors such as agriculture, mining, manufacturing, services, and construction; and other sectors that are grouped together in Table 3.1 under the "basic economic statistics" category.

The fact that data collection programs in the United States and Mexico have many similarities and are more or less aligned with the UN guidelines does not mean that their censuses, household surveys, and other data collection programs are equivalent or always comparable. Conditions in each country vary in ways that create different needs for statistical information while the institutional history of data collection programs causes variations in both subject areas and the specific questions asked in surveys. For example, the United States has no Census of Ejidos, for very obvious reasons, but Mexico needs to have one. Thus, even when the same purpose motivates data collection, there are variations in the specific information sought. For example, the United States and Mexico conduct censuses of population that provide information about housing and social characteristics of the population (as well as head counts), but Mexico's larger share of the population living below an acceptable minimum standard results in more questions about housing construction materials, sewage and water connections, and other details not found in the U.S. census. Mexico uses this data in various ways, including the construction of an index of marginalization, something the United States has not thought to worry about. (The United States does, however, have data on poverty, although it is a bimodal category rather than an index derived from many variables.)

Occasionally, the United States and Mexico compile the same statistic using more-or-less identical methods, but the meaning of the statistic cannot be interpreted in the

TABLE 3.1 Topics of UN-recommended data collection

Topic	Subtopics
Development indicators	Millennium Development Goals
	Sustainable Development Goals
Economy	Basic economic statistics
	Energy statistics
	Industrial statistics
	National accounts
	Tourism statistics
	Trade statistics
Environment	Environmental-economic accounting
	Environment statistics
Population and society	Civil registration and vital statistics
	Disability statistics
	Gender statistics
	Household surveys
	Migration statistics
	Population and housing census
	Time-use statistics

Source: UNSD, https://unstats.un.org/home/, accessed April 28, 2020.

same way. A prime example of this obstacle to comparability is the unemployment rate. At the national level, countries measure unemployment using nearly identical definitions and methods. In Mexico, however, it is relatively easy for laid-off workers to find work in the country's large informal labor market. These jobs are frequently poorly paid, do not offer benefits, and may have limited hours, but they meet the formal definition of employment. Hence, Mexico's unemployment rate is usually lower than that of the United States, but it is misleading if it is not contextualized and examined more closely with additional measures of conditions in the labor force.

In addition to the differences in data collection and interpretation that stem from differences in economic conditions, the institutional framework under which data is compiled and distributed is very different in the two countries. Specifically, Mexico's efforts are much more centralized than are efforts in the United States. Mexico's primary data collection agency is the Instituto Nacional de Estadística y Geografía (INEGI, National Institute of Statistics and Geography), an autonomous organization that is governed by a board appointed by the president of Mexico (INEGI n.d. ["Quiénes somos"]). INEGI is the primary data provider in Mexico but not the only one. Other data compilers and distributors of interest to border scholars include

TABLE 3.2 Political-statistical units at the subnational level

	United States	Mexico
Primary subnational unit	States	States
Substate	Counties	Municipalities (*municipios*)
Submunicipal and subcounty	Metropolitan statistical areas, census tracts, block groups, and census blocks	*Localidades, áreas geoestadísticas básicas* (AGEBs)

Sources: U.S. Census Bureau n.d. ["Concepts and Definitions"]; INEGI 2016.

the Secretaría de Economía and the Consejo Nacional de Población (CONAPO, National Population Council). Increasingly, Mexico is using the INEGI web portal to centralize access to data from different federal agencies. In contrast, the U.S. Census Bureau is INEGI's closest equivalent in the United States. It is the principle agency of a decentralized U.S. Federal Statistical System (FSS). The FSS is a conglomeration of thirteen separate agencies, including the Census Bureau.[2] Many of these thirteen agencies provide disaggregated data for state and local jurisdictions, but some do not, and no one site provides access to the data compiled by different agencies.

A final consideration is the comparability of the subnational political or administrative units for which data are available. As shown in Table 3.2, the degree of similarity between the United States and Mexico is perhaps surprising. Both countries have states that serve broadly similar roles and for which most national data are disaggregated and apportioned. The fact that state-level data are nearly as good as national data is one reason why some border scholars choose to define the border as the ten states that share the border.[3] Below the state level, the United States is divided into counties and Mexico into *municipios* (municipalities). These are similar divisions in that they include all the territory of every state, they include both rural and urban areas, and they are a primary geographical unit for many statistical purposes—for example, the population censuses. Municipalities and counties have different political functions in the state and national systems of the two countries and also have their own administrative subunits. Nevertheless, the relative geographical similarity of U.S. counties and Mexican municipalities together with the fact that data collection efforts in both countries prominently display county and municipal data make these administrative units useful for border scholars and especially for cross-border comparisons.

Below the level of counties (United States) and municipalities (Mexico), the geographical units of analysis become somewhat more complicated and less similar. Mexico's population and housing censuses provide submunicipal data for *localidades*. These are composed of "*áreas geoestadísticas básicas*" (AGEBs). AGEBs are the primary geospatial reference area and are combined to make up a localidad. Localidades are either urban or rural. Urban ones are places of 2,500 or more inhabitants or the principal offices of a municipality (*cabecera*), while rural ones have fewer than 2,500 inhabitants and are not centers of municipal government. The United States has a variety of substate units in addition to counties, including census tracts, block groups, and census blocks. Each of these are subcategories that are defined primarily for census purposes. In addition, the United States compiles a wide variety of data for urban areas, often referred to as a "core metropolitan statistical areas" (CMSAs). These have one or more core urban places and significant socioeconomic integration, even if it crosses state boundaries.

Primary Data Sources for Border Scholars: The Censo de Población y Vivienda and the Census of Population and Housing

A census is an attempt to count all units of whatever is counted, be it people, houses, businesses, governments, or any other subject. Most likely, the word *census* evokes the idea of a census of population and housing. There is good reason for this since the census of population has a long history in both the United States and Mexico. In the former, it is a constitutional mandate that is required for the purpose of apportioning congressional representation.[4] The Mexican census began in its modern form in 1895 when Porfirio Díaz initiated a census to help diagnose the country's needs for economic growth (INEGI 1996). Furthermore, census counts are major undertakings that require years of planning and a nationwide effort to engage the cooperation of the entire population. Everyone or nearly everyone is aware of the census population count when it occurs. Censuses of population also usually include questions about housing, a wide range of social and demographic questions, and some questions about household incomes. The censuses of the United States and Mexico have substantial areas of overlap, in part because they both conform to the general principles suggested by the United Nations.[5] In addition, they are conducted in the same year (every ten years during years that end in zero). In general, censuses are useful because they count individuals, they are universal in coverage over a defined territory, they are carried out quickly so there is an element of simultaneity, and they are conducted with a defined periodicity.

A key issue for any census is the definition of who is a resident in a state, county, or smaller unit and who is a visitor. This is particularly important when there is a large population of migrants, or what is referred to in Mexico as the *población flotante* (floating population). The presence of squatter communities that sometimes appear overnight or groups of people that seem to lack permanency in the place they occupy when the census is conducted poses conceptual and definitional challenges for the statistical agency. In the United States, a somewhat similar problem occurs when the Census Bureau tries to count the relatively large homeless population. Homeless individuals often do not want to be counted, and given their lack of a specific place of residence (unlike at least some of the floating population in Mexico), they are perhaps harder to enumerate.

This issue requires Mexico and other countries to define residency in terms of the amount of time a person is in a particular locale or intends to be there. The cutoff employed by INEGI is six months. For example, a migrant from Guadalajara to Tijuana who spends less than six months in Tijuana, either in terms of actual time spent or time spent plus future plans, is not considered a resident of Baja California or Tijuana and will be counted as a resident of Jalisco and Guadalajara. Mayors of border communities in Mexico often view this as unfair, since they have the costs associated with the migrant population and do not receive a proportionate share of the federal funding that is population based. Nevertheless, some definition of residency is required and a six-month definition is within guidelines suggested by the United Nations. Obviously, a person on vacation in Los Cabos should not be counted as a resident, nor should business travelers who work outside their home community for a period of time. The six-month standard is one way to deal with this issue.

INEGI conducts a Censo de Población y Vivienda (Census of Population and Housing) every ten years in years ending in zero. Since 1995 it has supplemented the census with an intercensal population count (Conteo de Población) that is less detailed and is conducted in years ending in five (1995, 2005, 2015). The population censuses and counts provide a wealth of data at the state, municipal, and submunicipal levels and are readily available on the INEGI website.[6] The U.S. census is in the same years as the Mexican, and similar to INEGI's Conteo, the Census Bureau has the American Community Survey (ACS). In the twentieth century, census data were collected on a short form that asked a handful of basic demographic and housing questions and a long form that only a subset of the population answered and that covered more extensive and detailed questions. After 2000 the long form became the ACS and was changed to a format that continually samples the U.S. population every month to produce annual estimates for states, counties, and other subunits. Places with more than 65,000 people have annual estimates, places with more than 20,000 and up to 65,000 have three-year estimates, and all places, regardless of population, have five-year estimates. This makes the ACS similar to the Conteo, although for places with 20,000 or more, there are more frequent estimates (every one or three years, depending on size). During the year, there are about 3.54 million individuals included in the sample. The fact that the monthly samples are aggregated to obtain one-year, three-year, and five-year averages means that it is not a snapshot at a specific point in time, as are censuses.

The censuses of population and housing in the United States and Mexico are relatively similar and have many areas of overlap. Both censuses cover basic demographic, social, and economic characteristics such as age, gender, education, work, income, marital status, and family size. Housing questions cover the size of the dwelling, number of bedrooms and access to plumbing, kitchens, and technologies for information and communications. Given that both countries follow UN guidelines, it is not surprising that there is substantial similarity in the questions asked. Not all the questions are asked in the same format, however, and there are also some substantial differences.

The primary differences in the censuses of population and housing reflect the most characteristic differences between the two countries. Mexico's per capita income is about one-fourth that of the United States, it has a much larger share of its population that is indigenous, and it has experienced a high level of emigration in the last several decades. Consequently, it has questions not found in the U.S. census relating to housing construction, food security, and infant mortality, which give a more complete picture of socioeconomic marginalization. In addition, there are several questions that seek to measure the size and language characteristics of the indigenous population, and the population that has migrated. The United States, on the other hand, is more concerned about the race, ethnicity, and ancestry of its population. In addition, it has more questions about housing costs and whether the inhabitants are owners or renters.

The differences in the censuses of population and housing are significant by themselves, but they also enable each country to generate supplementary descriptive statistics that cannot be duplicated across the border. For example, Mexico's more extensive collection of data related to poverty—including substandard housing and the lack of electricity, food insecurity, illiteracy, and infant mortality—provides the basis for an index of socioeconomic marginalization or social exclusion. CONAPO creates an index of marginalization for all AGEBs, municipalities, and states. Data are available for 1990–2015, in five-year increments (CONAPO n.d.). This program combines data from the census of population and housing to classify the administrative units into one of seven strata reflecting the degree of deprivation or marginalization in the population of the territorial unit. The index of marginalization is based on a statistical methodology that combines nine measures of housing, education, income, and geographical isolation. The fact that it is a multidimensional measure gives it added robustness. The United States has nothing comparable to this attempt to measure marginalization at the local level, although it does provide indicators of poverty, according to the national definition (U.S. Census Bureau n.d. ["About"]). The United States also measures poverty, household income, and income per capita at the substate level, albeit not within the census.[7] Given that U.S. border regions are some of the poorest and presumably most marginalized in the United States, a similar program to measure social exclusion or marginalization on the north side of the border would increase our understanding of the challenges faced by border communities. And an effort by INEGI to estimate income per capita at the municipal level would also be worthwhile.

Other Censuses: Agriculture and Economics

The United States and Mexico carry out several other censuses in addition to the census of population and housing (see Table 3.3). INEGI conducts three additional censuses of the economy, agriculture, and governments, while the Census Bureau performs an economic census and a census of governments but leaves the agricultural census to the National Agricultural Statistics Service (NASS), which is part of the Department of Agriculture. The economic and agricultural censuses have data on units smaller than states, and Mexico's census of governments also has some limited data for municipalities. The U.S. Census of Governments only reports a state total for substate political units such as counties, cities, and special purpose governments such as school districts. Unfortunately, with the exception of some censuses of government, they are not conducted in the same years.

Agriculture Censuses and Surveys

All agricultural censuses focus on crop and livestock production, as well as providing supplemental data on inputs, demographics, and other relevant information about

TABLE 3.3 Agriculture, economy, and government

Census	United States	Mexico
Agriculture	National Agricultural Statistics Service. Every 5 years in years ending in 2 and 7.	INEGI. Irregular, at least once every decade.
Economy	Bureau of the Census. Every 5 years in years ending in 2 and 7.	INEGI. Every 5 years in years ending in 4 and 9.
Government	Bureau of the Census. Every 5 years in years ending in 2 and 7. Does not include data for individual substate political units.	INEGI. Federal and state, every year. Municipalities, every odd year.

Source: U.S Census Bureau n.d. ["NAICS Codes"]; INEGI n.d. ["Censos y conteos"].

farms and agricultural production units. The Mexican agricultural census, or Censo Agropecuario, also includes detailed information about Mexican ejidos.[8] As with the population and housing census, Mexico's agricultural census contains questions that are relevant to the country but not to the United States. For example, there are questions about indigenous identity, whether the farm owners or operators receive remittances from abroad, materials used to construct the farm dwelling, water availability, sanitation and electrical services, and more. Information for most items is available at the municipal level, and historical data back to 1991 are easily downloadable from the INEGI website (INEGI n.d. ["Censos y conteos"]). The agency responsible for the U.S. Census of Agriculture, the NASS, also implements a variety of surveys on a much more frequent basis than the census. Current and historical data, some of which reach as far back as 1850, are available on the NASS website (NASS n.d. ["Census of Agriculture Historical Archive"; "Home"]).

Economic Censuses

Economic censuses provide a clearer and more detailed picture of businesses and economic activity in general, including not only manufacturing but also transportation, utilities, services, construction, mining, and other sectors. Together with the censuses of agriculture and government, the intent is to cover most, if not all, economic activities inside the territorial boundaries of a county.

With the negotiation, signing, and implementation of the North American Free Trade Agreement (NAFTA) in the early 1990s, the three countries began to harmonize the classification of economic activities. The result was the North American Industry Classification System (NAICS), or Sistema de Clasificación Industrial de América del Norte (SCIAN) in Spanish. The three countries first used the NAICS in the economic censuses of 1997. Since then, it has been revised for each census, but in relatively minor ways. For example, in 2012 the category of electricity generation was disaggregated to include biomass, wind, solar, and geothermal categories. The NAICS method adopted by the NAFTA countries uses a six-digit hierarchical classification system. An example is given in Table 3.4. The first two digits indicate the sector, in this case manufacturing. Each additional digit narrows the definition to a more specific type of manufacturing within the same sector as the original two digits (Castillo Navarrete 2007; INEGI 2013; U.S. Census Bureau n.d. ["Introduction to NAICS"; "NAICS Codes"]). In Table 3.4, 33 (manufacturing) is the sector, 336 is the subsector (manufacturing of transportation equipment), 3361 is the industrial group or *rama* (motor vehicle manufacturing), 33611 is the industry or *subrama* (auto and light duty motor vehicle manufacturing), and 336111 is the class or *clase* (auto manufacturing).

TABLE 3.4 An example of the NAICS (SCIAN) classification system

NAICS code	Economic activity	Hierarchical name
33	Manufacturing	Sector/*Sector*
336	Transportation equipment manufacturing	Subsector/*Subsector*
3361	Motor vehicle manufacturing	Industry group/*Rama*
33611	Auto and light vehicle manufacturing	Industry/*Subrama*
336111	Auto manufacturing	Class/*Clase*

Source: U.S. Census Bureau n.d. ["NAICS Codes"].

Canada, Mexico, and the United States have harmonized their classification systems for the first four hierarchical levels, but the fifth and final level, which is the most specific and detailed, remains under the discretion of each country. The purpose is to allow flexibility in meeting the data needs and specific characteristics of each country. There are a few additional national differences or idiosyncrasies. The United States has not yet incorporated forestry, agricultural support, rail transportation, and employment by private households. Certain government-sponsored or government-operated enterprises may be in the census of governments in one country and in the economic census of another. These include mail services, public utilities, and a number of others (U.S. Census Bureau ["NAICS Codes"]). And a few U.S. industry groups and industries have data that are found in a separate source, called "County Business Patterns" (U.S. Census Bureau n.d.). Most of these limitations are relatively minor, so that the economic censuses cover nearly all the economic sectors of a country, particularly when combined with information in the censuses of agriculture and government. Furthermore, the data are nearly all available at the county level or Mexican municipality level and frequently at levels representing even smaller geographical units. Table 3.5 lists the sectors and the two-digit sector code for each of the twenty sectors covered by the economic censuses.

The questions asked in the two economic censuses have a significant amount of similarity. These include questions about the number of firms in each sector; the number of employees and some of their characteristics; investments in fixed capital, labor costs, and output; and a number of additional areas. The actual comparability of the two censuses is quite limited, however, due to two basic problems, one relatively minor and the other very serious. First, the censuses are not administered in the same years. This is a minor problem, however, because there are survey programs that provide some of the same data during the intervening years, particularly for employment, although not as much for firm characteristics.[9] A more serious problem is that the economic censuses do not capture information about economic activity that originates

TABLE 3.5 Sectors covered in the economic censuses of the United States and Mexico

Sector name	Code	Sector name	Code
Agriculture, forestry, and fishing	11	Real estate, rentals, and leasing	53
Mining	21	Professional, technical, scientific services	54
Utilities	22	Management of corporations and enterprises[a]	55
Construction	23	Administrative, support, waste management, and remediation	56
Manufacturing	31–33	Education	61
Wholesale trade	43	Health and social assistance	62
Retail trade	46	Arts, entertainment, and recreation	71
Transportation and warehousing	48–49	Accommodations and food and beverage services	72
Information	51	Other services	81
Finance and insurance	52	Government[b]	91

Sources: INEGI 2015; U.S. Census Bureau n.d. ["Comparing Historical Data"; "NAICS Codes"].

[a]Management services are difficult to measure and not included in Mexico's census; in the U.S. census they are only reported at the state level.

[b]The government sector is not included in the U.S. Economic Census but can be found in the U.S. Census of Governments.

in the informal sector. This is very significant for Mexico and causes the census to be a snapshot of only part of the Mexican economy.[10] For example, the latest economic census (2014) lists total employment as 21,576,358. This is the sum of employment in all the economic units it measures, although it does not include government. Mexico also conducts a monthly labor market survey, however, called the Encuesta Nacional de Ocupación y Empleo (National Survey of Occupations and Employment). According to the survey, 49,415,412 people were employed during the same period (INEGI n.d. ["Indicadores económicas de coyuntura"]). The census number is just under 44 percent of the survey number, meaning that approximately 56 percent of the labor force is not included in the economic census. (Outside estimates of the informal labor force in Mexico put it at just under 60 percent.) The differences between the survey and the census are mainly a result of differences in methodology and purpose. The employment survey is a household survey, while the economic census is a count of businesses and their employees. Employment surveys are designed to measure conditions in the labor force, while economic censuses measure businesses in the formal sector primarily. Informal businesses are not explicitly excluded, but the fact that their employees are not registered with national pension and benefit programs puts them mostly outside the purview of the economic census. Employment or labor market surveys are an important part of most countries' national data collection systems and are discussed in more detail in the next section.

Other Censuses and Surveys

In addition to censuses and their near-cousins, the United States and Mexico conduct a large number of regular and special surveys.[11] The largest of these in the United States is the American Community Survey (ACS). The ACS fills the gap between census years and provides a continuous snapshot of the U.S. population and its characteristics. The closest Mexican equivalents to the ACS are the Conteo de Población and the Encuesta Intercensal (Inter-censal Survey). The latter is a survey that provides detailed information on population and housing at the state, municipality, and localidades levels. Again, like the ACS, the purpose is to fill the gap between census years.

Summing up so far, there are five main sources of information about Mexico and its population that have state-level and municipal-level data. These are: (1) Censo de Población y Vivienda, (2) Conteo de Población, (3) Encuesta Intercensal, (4) Censo Económico, and (5) Censo Agropecuario. The U.S. counterparts are as follows: (1) Census of Population and Housing, (2) American Community Survey, (3) Economic Census, and (4) Agricultural Census. Most municipal-level data comes from one of these sources, or one of a handful of surveys that are regularly administered on a special topic, or from an administrative data set—for example, on municipal finances. The longest run of historical data is available in the censuses of population and housing and the census of agriculture. All the sources have municipal or county data as well as state and national data, and some variables have information at the submunicipal or subcounty levels.

The ACS and the Encuesta Intercensal are household surveys and not censuses, but there is an effort to provide population information at national, state, and local levels that is nearly as reliable as a census. Additional household surveys are conducted in both the United States and Mexico. Typically, however, these are valid only at the national level since it is usually the case that the sample sizes for local areas are not large enough to allow valid inferences. In many cases, even state-level data samples are not large enough to measure conditions at that level. Household surveys are frequently the primary source of information on work and wages for households and labor markets that is not captured by a census. Household surveys are also the main source for measuring inequality, poverty, and marginalization, but again usually only at the national level. When the survey is directed toward working conditions, it is a labor market survey. These sometimes overlap with household surveys, and both tend to be available in large data sets that require some technical expertise. Labor market surveys (economic sector, occupation, hours of work, wages, etc.) come in a variety of forms in both the United States and Mexico. The main drawback for border scholars is the aforementioned problem of sample size at the local level.[12]

Labor market data in the United States are not solely or even primarily the responsibility of the Census Bureau. Under the decentralized organizational format of the FSS, the Bureau of Labor Statistics (BLS) is responsible for most labor market data and analysis. Some of its work is performed in collaboration with the Census Bureau—for example, the measurement of the national unemployment rate—but the BLS has numerous additional programs such as estimates of consumer prices, employment by sector and occupation, working hours and wages, and productivity. Many of these variables are measured at subnational levels of states, counties, and cities. The availability of this data at regional levels, often including the possibility of obtaining continuous time series estimates, is perhaps one of the primary differences between U.S. and Mexican data. Many of the variables available on the BLS website are also available for Mexico from INEGI but much less commonly at the municipal level, and never in a continuous, annual time series. Border scholars who want to obtain similar data for Mexico must rely on the census, the population count, and the intercensal estimates. Since these data programs are not intended primarily to measure labor market conditions, they have much less detailed information about occupations, wages, and economic sectors. While there is nothing on INEGI's website that is comparable to the BLS data on labor markets and working conditions, Mexico's data collection efforts provide a single point of access for many of the data series available at the state and municipal levels.

Economic Data: GDP and the National Income and Product Accounts

One of the most elusive answers to a question about the border is the extent of economic integration in border communities. If we define the border as the counties and municipalities (municipios) touching the border, then nearly 80 percent of border residents live in one of nine twin-city conurbations that are spaced along its two-thousand-mile length. Consequently, cities play a central role in the border economy. Large numbers of people cross every day through border crossings that are reported to be among the busiest in the world. Most of the trade between the United States and Mexico passes through a land port of entry (LPOE). Mexico's border region is the location of a disproportionately large share of the foreign direct investment it receives and is also home to a large part of its manufacturing industry and manufactured goods exports. Border communities have a great deal of interaction, but how much?

Missing Information

Ideally, border scholars would be able to look at the global value chains of firms and industries that have production facilities on both sides of the border. In that way, we could trace the movement of a good as it moved across the border for additional processing or as it moved back and forth several times, as some goods do. The global value chain can be thought of as having three main activities. In the initial stages of production, there are high-value-added research and design; in the middle stages there are low-, medium-, and high-value-added processing; and in the final stage there are high-value-added marketing, logistics, and after-product servicing. It is easy to imagine a product in a sector such as electronics, where the research and design are primarily in the United States; some or all of the manufacturing is in Mexico; and the marketing, logistics, and after-market servicing are back in the United States. This may sound like a highly stylized description of the economic relationship between border communities, but it closely resembles the actual relationships of some firms in San Diego and Tijuana in the fields of medical devices and some electronics.

The human counterpart to the movement of goods across borders is the movement of people. Ideally, border scholars would like to know not just the number of border crossers but their relationship to the labor force and the impacts they have once they cross. While there is a fair amount of estimation of cross-border shopping effects, we still only have educated guesses about the number of people who cross daily or weekly to work while maintaining a residence on the other side of the border, or their occupations or the sectors in which they work. Importantly, it would also be good to know the impact they have on the communities where they reside but do not work. For example, if forty thousand Tijuanenses work in San Diego (or Los Angeles) and cross once a week, how much of their U.S. wage is spent in Tijuana and, collectively, how much does this add to Tijuana's income? Similarly, how many people live in the United States and work in Mexico? Neither the United States nor Mexico has data programs that would help to understand the phenomenon of cross-border workers.

Available Economic Information

The economic censuses count the number of formal businesses, their employees, investments, and other activities related to the business. They are an important piece of the statistical portrait of economic activity, but they are not the main sources of regular information about the economy. That category of information is called the national income and product accounts. As with the censuses of population and housing, there is an internationally used system for measuring the overall level of economic activity, also sponsored by the United Nations, called the System of National Accounts (SNA).

The primary measurement of economic activity is gross domestic product (GDP), defined as the market value of all final goods and services produced in a given time period (usually a year or a quarter) in a country or a region. It measures services as well as goods, and only final goods and services, since counting intermediate inputs would lead to double counting: once as an intermediate input and again in the final value of the good or service produced. GDP is the most comprehensive measurement of economic activity, and every country in the world measures it regularly, with the exception of countries at war or suffering some other disaster that prevents them from gathering data. In the United States, GDP estimates are the responsibility of the Bureau of Economic Analysis (BEA), also (like the Census Bureau) housed in the Department of Commerce. In Mexico, INEGI estimates GDP and produces Mexico's national income and product accounts (NIPA). At the subnational level, GDP is sometimes called gross regional product (GRP). The concept is the same as national GDP but measured for a defined subnational geographic region. In the United States, the BEA produces estimates of GDP for states and metropolitan areas (many of which are equivalent to counties) and has historical data back to 2001 and older in some cases.[13] The BEA also estimates personal income for counties and states, where personal income is a subcomponent of GDP and is a measure of all the income received by individuals.[14] Consequently, if border scholars want to know per capita personal income in the Brownsville-Harlingen metropolitan area, annual data are available back to 1969.[15] INEGI's estimates for Mexico are much more limited, in terms of both regional measures and time series. First, INEGI does not produce estimates below the state level. Hence if researchers want to compare GDP or personal income per person in the two Nogales, it cannot be done with official data since there are no estimates for Nogales, Sonora.[16] Second, the estimates of state GDP are a continuous annual series back to 2003, but for prior years, the series is not continuous and methodological changes make the prior data not strictly comparable to 2003 and later years. The lack of official estimates of income or total output below the level of Mexican states is perhaps one of the most serious deficiencies and greatest obstacles to comparable U.S. and Mexican data in the border region.

Economic Data: Trade and Foreign Investment

Statistics on international trade and investment suffer from most of the same problems as regional GDP data, and then some. Probably most everyone would agree that we would know much more about border communities if we had some idea of what they produced and exported and especially if we could know what part of the United States or Mexico receives the exports from an exporting border city. That is, it would tell us a great deal about the economy of a county or municipality—say, Ciudad Juárez—if we knew what it exports and imports. Further, it would be even more helpful to our understanding of border economies if we knew where its exports go and where its imports come from: that is, if we knew the regional economies that are its trading partners. Unfortunately, it is impossible to obtain this data given the current state of data gathering.

Gathering local export and import data is difficult and full of pitfalls. Consider local export data, for example. Customs officials measure the flow of goods across borders, and the Bureau of Transportation Statistics (BTS) provides data on commodity flows, both internationally and domestically. Commodity flows measure the movement of goods in trucks, planes, aircraft, pipelines, and ships from one point to another. Between customs and the BTS, we have data on the flow of goods entering and exiting the United States. This is not enough to measure regional exports, however, since we do not know where the good was produced. Is the good leaving the United States and entering Mexico through Nuevo Laredo a product of Laredo, Texas, or of somewhere else in Texas, somewhere else in the United States, or even a product imported into the United States from another country and re-exported to Mexico? It is often possible to trace the origin of the export good back to the place of its production but not always. Goods may be shipped from one place—say, Cleveland, Ohio—to a warehouse in another place, then eventually moved again. At some point, the shipper will declare that they are exporting the good, but if that is not done by the producer, the good may not be correctly identified as an export of the region where it is produced.

Imports are even more problematic to measure at the subnational level. Imports enter a country and then move in any direction, including toward an eventual re-exportation after some degree of processing or warehousing. The ultimate destination is often ambiguous or even unknown at the time the goods enter a country. Consider a large retail chain such as Costco or Walmart or Soriana. Their distribution centers are constantly supplying them with the products they need for stocking the shelves of individual stores, but the state or city that receives a particular good is unknown until the order is placed. Keeping track of the movement of all goods entering the country, from their origin to their ultimate destination, would place an enormous burden on firms and, for the most part, is not done. Therefore, the data reported to national data programs is limited.

Both Mexico and the United States attempt to measure exports by state of origin. In the Mexican case, the data reaches back to 2007 and can be found in the Banco de Información Económica (BIE, Economic Information Bank). For the United States, the International Trade Administration (ITA) tracks exports by state of origin and imports by state of destination. It also estimates exports by metropolitan area. These data are useful but less reliable than national-level data, given the aforementioned problems of determining the origin of exports and the destination of imports.

Services are a further obstacle to gathering and reporting trade data at the subnational level. Recall that international trade includes both goods and services.[17] Furthermore, the cross-border ties of border cities imply that international services trade is most likely an important component of the border economy. Accounting and legal services, business consulting and health services, among others, are visibly important in the cross-border business networks of border cities. Yet neither the United States nor Mexico measures services trade at any level below the national level. It might be theoretically possible to measure the supply of accounting services, for example, that are provided by Tijuana firms to U.S. customers, but determination of the origin of the purchaser of the service and establishing whether it is in San Diego or another firm located somewhere else in the United States that has an affiliate in San Diego is conceptually difficult, expensive, and outside the reach of national data programs.

Another component of cross-border economic networks is the flow of international investment. In particular, inward foreign direct investment (FDI) is especially important to Mexican border communities where the Border Industrialization Program sought to build an export processing sector after its beginning in 1965. The program became the maquiladora program, and now, after legal and tax changes, has become part of general Mexican manufacturing. The Secretaría de Economía tracks and reports the inward flow by state (see Secretaría de Economía n.d.). The United States does not provide equivalent data, nor does either country provide data at the county or municipal level. Further, it is impossible to know the origin of the FDI, other than the country. For example, it is impossible to know how much San Diego invests in Tijuana, given that financial resources are fungible and relations between corporate headquarters and affiliate enterprises are often complex and opaque. Furthermore, the FDI is but one type of financial flow. All the other forms, such as bank loans, stock and bond transactions, and other more complicated forms, are not measurable below the national level for many of the same reasons that limit reporting on the FDI. The primary online sources other than the economic censuses for locating available economic data are the Bureau of Economic Analysis for the United States and the Banco de Información Económica for Mexico.

Migration Data Sources

Both the United States and Mexico have developed databases to capture migration patterns at the national and regional level. The Censo de Población y Vivienda, the Encuesta Nacional de Ocupaciones y Empleo (ENOE, National Survey of Occupations and Employment), and CONAPO's Migración Interna are the main sources of information in Mexico. In addition, El Colegio de la Frontera Norte (COLEF, College of the Northern Border) publishes the Encuesta sobre Migración en la Frontera

Norte de México (EMIF Norte, Survey of Migration at Mexico's Northern Border) from data it gathers with the support of Mexican government agencies.

Mexico's Censos de Población y Vivienda include information on the population that has moved from one state to another, from one municipality to another, and from subunits of municipalities to different ones. It also has data on immigration from outside Mexico. The census data include information from the previous five years, with the objective of measuring the volume and direction of internal and external migratory movements. The EMIF survey is conducted by COLEF and sponsored by the Secretaría del Trabajo y Previsión Social (STPS, Secretariat of Labor and Social Welfare) and CONAPO. It was developed in the early 1990s in order to discover the volume and determinants of migratory flows, particularly the temporary migration flows from Mexico to the United States and vice versa. The survey is administered on the Mexican side of the border to migrants returning to Mexico from the United States and also asks where they intend to settle in Mexico. It measures both temporary and permanent migration, and migrants sent back by the U.S. Border Patrol (USBP).

On the U.S. side, the Census Bureau's Current Population Survey (CPS) provides information about the population born outside the United States and distributes the data in both the CPS and the ACS. The definition of foreign-born population is defined as individuals who do not have U.S. citizenship at birth and includes naturalized citizens, lawful permanent residents, refugees, legal nonimmigrants, and persons residing in the country without authorization. An important nongovernmental source of information is the Mexican Migration Project (MMP). It is survey data gathered through random interviews with households across Mexico and over many decades. The MMP has a wealth of precise and comprehensive data on migrations topics. The MMP, like most other sources on migration, does not focus on border communities, although there are sufficient samples for some states. Data comparability is another main problem with measuring migration flows. Sample populations, time periods, and methodology are different for each data source. For instance, the ACS has annual data for urban areas but Mexico does not. The EMIF is a survey of flows and the MMP is a survey of households. The MMP survey is precise at the municipal level for the municipalities it samples, but it is not statistically representative of the whole country.

Other Data Sources for Border-Related Data

There are a number of additional agencies within the U.S. decentralized system that collect national, state, and local data. It is not possible to list every source of data, but a few of the main ones are the National Center for Health Statistics, the National Center for Education Statistics, the Bureau of Justice Statistics, and the Bureau of Transportation Statistics.[18] The websites of these organizations have both local and more geographically aggregated data on some of the main topics of concern to citizens and communities in the border region. For example, the BTS is a useful source for border-crossing data, disaggregated by type (pedestrian, passenger cars, trucks loaded, trucks empty, etc.) and port of entry, with monthly estimates back to 1996. Data are available for inbound traffic from Mexico, Canada, and other places of origin.

There are beginning to be some changes to the domination of INEGI in Mexico's more centralized system of data gathering and distribution. The relatively new federal government website claims to have data from 280 (2019) institutions in its new "Datos Abiertos" system. More recently, it has affiliated with the open data system called datamx, which describes itself as "La plataforma cívica de datos abiertos de México" (The civic platform for open data in Mexico) and has open databases from 82 (2019) civil society and governmental organizations.[19] Unlike all the other sources mentioned in this chapter, it has publicly available private sector data as well as governmental data.

In addition to these newer federal governmental and private data sources, there are many state-level sources with county- or city-level data. For example, state departments of health or health services in the United States have a wide range of public health data, some of which can be matched with Mexican data from "Registros Administrativos," on the INEGI website. Similarly, state offices of public instruction have substate-level data on schooling and education, and state tax offices have local data on retail sales and sales taxes. Again, the match to INEGI-provided data is not perfect, but some comparisons are possible with the censuses (education). Local revenue data is more complicated since the functional differences between Mexican municipalities and U.S. cities and counties cause their finances to be structured differently with completely different revenue and expenditure streams.

Finally, both countries provide access to microlevel data consisting of the individual households or enterprises that are the subject of censuses and surveys. Not surprisingly, there is an international standard for distributing what are called "public use micro-samples." Not only do both countries adhere to the standard but they also both provide large samples of their household data to the organization IPUMS-International (see IPUMS-International n.d.). Mexican census data are available from 1960 to the present, as well as population counts for 1995, 2005, and 2015, and U.S. census data have similar coverage.

Five Proposals for Improving Data Collection

No description of U.S. and Mexican data sources for border research can provide a complete guide. This chapter has focused on publicly available governmental data since those are official, are usually part of long-term historical data collection and distribution efforts, and are embedded in an officially mandated program of data gathering. These characteristics create some comparability over time within each country and also make it unlikely that there will be radical changes in the data gathering in the near future. Indeed, the main changes in both countries over the last few decades have been to make the data more available and easier to access electronically. Many of the limitations of existing data have been mentioned throughout the chapter. In sum, there are at least five categories where the lack of data hinders our understanding of the interactions between border communities and their residents. Each of these categories have specific subsets of data that could be collected and reported and that would considerably further our understanding of the border. The five areas are briefly presented here.

Proposal 1: Expanding Information on Local Income and Economic Status

Income and economic status could be expanded at the substate level. There are two pieces to this proposal, one for the United States and one for Mexico. In the United States, the use of an income threshold to define poverty produces a binary, yes/no measurement. In Mexico, INEGI should estimate municipal-level income. CONAPO has done this previously when it estimated human development indices for all municipalities for the year 2000, and Joan Anderson and James Gerber (2008) developed an estimation methodology to measure municipal income in several census years. These two examples show that statistical estimation procedures could be used with existing data and could then be examined for reliability with a set of more specific, follow-up investigations. Mexico's creation of an index of marginalization results in a more complex and comprehensive indicator of inclusion and exclusion than the binary categories of poverty/not poverty. The index is continuous and takes into account a number of variables beyond income. The United States could easily adopt a similar measure with existing data sources.

Proposal 2: Measuring the Informal Economy

Measurements of economic informality are complicated and do not enjoy a consensus methodology or definition. Nevertheless, it is clear that large sectors of economic activity are omitted from Mexico's economic census, which then gives a distorted picture of overall economic activity. Some of the omissions are provided in the labor market surveys, but those contain little information about business enterprises. A more intensive effort to measure the activities of informal business enterprises would supplement the Mexican economic census and make it more comparable to the U.S. version of the census. The importance of this effort is highlighted by the fact that overall economic growth appears to be held back by the increases in the number of very small, undercapitalized, and low productivity business enterprises (Bolio et al. 2014; Levy 2018). This initiative could occur within the framework of the existing economic census program or via a new program in Mexico that is similar to the U.S. "County Business Patterns."

Proposal 3: Capturing Data on Cross-Border Commuters

Increasingly large numbers of U.S. citizens choose to live in Mexico and commute to work in the United States. Mexican border cities have always had a share of their labor force that commuted across the border, while the maquiladora industry and other economic activities in Mexico have received workers who reside in the United States. We know very little about the population of cross-border commuters even though they probably constitute one of the primary forms of economic and social integration in the border region.[20] Mexico's Encuesta Nacional de Empleo Urbano (ENEU, National Survey of Urban Employment) formerly contained estimates of the percentage of the labor force resident in Mexico that worked in the United States.[21] Presumably these were cross-border commuters since they maintained a Mexican residence, but the frequency of crossing (daily, weekly, or less regular) was not queried, nor the type of activity they performed in the United States. The question was only available for large cities surveyed by ENEU, and it dropped this question some years ago. The U.S. American Community Survey estimates average commute times for every county in the United States, but like the earlier ENEU survey, the data is residence based, not work based. Therefore, there are few questions about work, no questions about leaving the United States to work, and the work focus means that even if there were such questions about international border crossings, it would shed light on the north-to-south commute only and not on the commute from south to north. Given that the ACS already measures commute times, it should not be overwhelmingly difficult to expand the analysis to include destinations, occupations, wages, and expenditures. Mexico's census, Conteo de Población, and the Conteo Intercensal could also be modified in similar ways. This would not provide annual estimates, but it would create a basis for a more complete understanding of economic and social integration in border communities. Among the more important questions worth investigating are absolute numbers of cross-border commuters, frequencies of their commutes, work locations, industry and occupation, wages, and expenditures.

Proposal 4: Regional Disaggregation of Foreign Direct Investment

Inward foreign direct investment (FDI) is an important indicator of economic activity in the Mexican border communities where the maquiladora program has become part of general Mexican manufacturing. Both the Secretaría de Economía and the Federal Trade Commission (FTC) should coordinate to create data at the county or municipal level for both countries, and the United States should develop a database at the state level. The objective is complicated because of difficulties in estimating the origin of the FDI. Corporate headquarters and affiliate financial movements and stock and bond transactions tend to limit the reports on FDI. Nevertheless, this would be an important variable to evaluate the degree of economic integration between both countries.

Proposal 5: Migration Data Compatibility

Databases for migration movements between Mexico and the United States lack comparability, which is an obstacle for estimating and tracking migration flows. The U.S. and Mexican databases, both governmental and nongovernmental, have been designed with different sample populations, time periods, and methodology. It would be helpful for the analysis of migration flows if efforts to make those sources of information more compatible could be coordinated by the different sources of migration statistics.

A Final Word

There are many other potential areas of inquiry, including a combined public use micro-sample of census data that covers all counties and municipalities on the border, or measures of education for students who cross the border to go to school, or spending (and taxes paid) by people who cross the border to shop. We know little about people who cross the border to worship or people who belong to civic or professional organizations on the other side, or the use of health care by border crossers. Border scholars know these are important activities for many individuals and border communities, but we have no idea of the general magnitude or trends. Mexico and the United States are geographically destined to interact in profound and continuous ways. The degrees of collaboration and conflict may vary over time, but the trend for many decades has been toward deeper integration. Geography is a fundamental driver of this trend, but it is aided by technological changes that make cross-border communications easier and more extensive. Deeper integration is also driven by the advantages it conveys to both countries as our economic and social lives become increasingly intertwined. It would be a further advantage to border scholars, policy makers, businesses, educators, and others if our data collection and distribution systems could keep up with the changes happening on the ground. One does not have to be much of a visionary to be able to recognize that the many forms of integration in the border region are integral to the success of the U.S.-Mexico partnership.

Notes

1. See the website of the United Nations Statistics Division, accessed April 28, 2020, https://unstats.un.org/home/.

2. In addition to the U.S. Census Bureau, the FSS includes the Bureau of Labor Statistics, the National Center for Education Statistics, the National Agricultural Statistics Service, the National Center for Health Statistics, the Energy Information Administration, the Bureau of Economic Analysis, the Economic Research Service, the Bureau of Justice Statistics, the National Center for Science and Engineering Statistics, the Statistics and Income Division of the Internal Revenue Service, the Bureau of Transportation Statistics, and the Office of Research, Evaluation and Statistics of the Social Security Administration.

3. See, for example, Ganster and Lorey 2016. A major exception to the claim that national data are also available at the state level is international trade statistics. It is difficult to trace the location of the production of exports (often it is not clear they are exports until some time has passed and they have moved across state boundaries), and the ultimate destination of imports is even more difficult to determine consistently and accurately.

4. Constitution of the United States, Article 1, section 2.

5. See United Nations 2015 for a guide to the recommended methods and topics for population and housing censuses.

6. The INEGI website, http://www.inegi.org.mx, provides easy and free access to all its census data. For the population censuses, data are available online back to 1895 and the first modern census count. For the population censuses and counts, see INEGI n.d. ["Censos y conteos"].

7. Both U.S. and Mexican censuses ask questions about income, but these are limited and problematic given that both rely on self-reporting by the respondent. Furthermore, the U.S. and Mexican questions do not ask the same thing. Mexico asks about income from work, whereas the U.S. question is simply about income.

8. Ejidos are collectively owned farming units that give individuals the use rights to a piece of property but maintain collective ownership. Individuals are not free to sell or rent the land they control. Ejidos were greatly expanded after the Mexican Revolution.

9. See, for example, U.S. Census Bureau n.d. ["NAICS Codes"]. INEGI and U.S. agencies also conduct labor market surveys that provide some of the same employment information in the economic census. However, detailed information about firms and firm characteristics is not available in those surveys.

10. According to the International Labour Office (2014), nearly 60 percent of Mexican workers have informal jobs.

11. INEGI's "Programas" page has links to all the censuses, household and establishment surveys, and much more. See INEGI n.d. ["Censos y conteos"].

12. On the U.S. side, an important monthly survey is the Current Population Survey (CPS). The CPS is sponsored by the Department of Labor and conducted by the Census Bureau. The CPS is administered monthly to approximately sixty thousand households and is the source for estimates of national employment and unemployment as well as a variety of data on migration, education, income, and other topics that help define the U.S. population. Unfortunately, it is a national survey with limited samples from any specific region. Individual observations or groups of observations can be extracted from the CPS, but border communities do not provide enough observations to reach a reasonable level of statistical reliability. In Mexico, an important labor market survey is the Encuesta Nacional de Ocupación y Empleo (ENOE). Unlike the CPS, it is designed to provide reliable state-level data, but there are no data for municipalities.

13. Metropolitan areas are urban agglomerations that often correspond to counties.

14. GDP, unlike personal income, includes a variety of taxes and subsidies paid or received by businesses and does not subtract depreciation of capital equipment used in production.

15. For a complete list of regional income and GDP estimates, see Bureau of Economic Analysis n.d. Note also that the Brownsville-Harlingen metropolitan area is identical to Cameron County, Texas.

16. Note that Joan Anderson and James Gerber (2008, 2017) developed a method for dividing state GDP into its municipal shares.

17. Services are an increasingly important part of trade. For the United States, they are equal to 40 percent of its merchandise goods trade (2019) and are an area with a large trade surplus. Mexico's services exports and imports are less important in relative terms (7 percent of merchandise goods trade) but still important absolutely and are equal to US$66.6 billion. See IMF 2020.

18. The respective websites are National Center for Health Statistics, https://www.cdc.gov/nchs/; National Center for Education Statistics, https://nces.ed.gov; Bureau of Justice Statistics, https://www.bjs.gov; and Bureau of Transportation Statistics, https://www.bts.gov.

19. The federal website is https://www.gob.mx; the website of datamx, a project of CodeandoMéxico, is http://datamx.io. See CodeandoMéxico, http://www.codeandomexico.org.

20. Note that there are various studies of border crossers and their reasons for crossing. There are also estimates of the effects of cross-border shopping and some estimates of tourism in the border region. None of these studies tackle the more difficult problems of cross-

border workers and the effects they have on the sending and receiving border communities, nor do they dig into the cross-border business ties of local firms.

21. ENEU data provide the percent of the *población económicamente activo* (PEA, economically active population) resident in a Mexican city and working in the United States. There was no additional data such as absolute numbers, occupation, wages, whether the commute was daily or some other frequency, or expenditure patterns.

References

Anderson, Joan B., and James Gerber. 2008. *Fifty Years of Change on the U.S.-Mexico Border: Growth, Development, and the Quality of Life.* Austin: University of Texas Press.

Anderson, Joan B., and James Gerber. 2017. "The US-Mexico Border Human Development Index, 1990–2010." *Journal of Borderlands Studies* 32 (3): 275–88.

Bolio, Eduardo, Jaana Remes, Tomás Lajous, James Manyika, Eugenia Ramirez, and Morten Rossé. 2014. "A Tale of Two Mexicos: Growth and Prosperity in a Two Speed Economy." McKinsey Global Institute, March. https://www.mckinsey.com/global-themes/americas /a-tale-of-two-mexicos.

Bureau of Economic Analysis. n.d. "Regional Data Table Availability." Accessed April 28, 2020. https://www.bea.gov/regional/docs/DataAvailability.cfm.

Castillo Navarrete, Eva. 2007. "An Analysis of SCIAN at Ten Years of Its Creation: A Retrospective." INEGI, Dirección General de Estadísticas Económicas, Aguascalientes.

Consejo Nacional de Población (CONAPO). n.d. "Índice de marginación." Accessed April 28, 2020. https://datos.gob.mx/busca/dataset/indice-de-marginacion-carencias-poblacionales -por-localidad-municipio-y-entidad.

Ganster, Paul, and David Lorey. 2016. *The U.S.-Mexican Border Today: Conflict and Cooperation in Historical Perspective.* 3rd ed. Lanham, Md.: Rowman & Littlefield.

Instituto Nacional de Estadística, Geografía y Infomática (INEGI). 1996. *Estados Unidos Mexicanos: Cien años de censos de población.* Aguascalientes: Instituto Nacional de Estadística, Geografía y Infomática.

Instituto Nacional de Estadística, Geografía y Infomática (INEGI). 2013. *Sistema de clasificación industrial de América del Norte.* Aguascalientes: Instituto Nacional de Estadística y Geografía.

Instituto Nacional de Estadística, Geografía y Infomática (INEGI). 2015. *Censos económicos 2014: Resultados definitivos.* Aguascalientes: Instituto Nacional de Estadística y Geografía.

Instituto Nacional de Estadística, Geografía y Infomática (INEGI). 2016. *Manual de cartografía geoestadística.* Aguascalientes: Instituto Nacional de Estadística y Geografía.

Instituto Nacional de Estadística, Geografía y Infomática (INEGI). n.d. "Censos y conteos." Accessed April 28, 2020. https://www.inegi.org.mx/datos/default.html#Programas.

Instituto Nacional de Estadística, Geografía y Infomática (INEGI). n.d. "Indicadores económicas de coyuntura: Población ocupada por sector de actividad económica: Total." Encuesta Nacional de Ocupación y Empleo, Banco de Información Económica. Accessed April 28, 2020. http://www.inegi.org.mx/sistemas/bie/.

Instituto Nacional de Estadística, Geografía y Infomática (INEGI). n.d. "Quiénes somos." Accessed April 28, 2020. https://www.inegi.org.mx/inegi/quienes_somos.html.

International Labour Office. 2014. "Informal Employment in Mexico: Current Situation, Policies and Challenges." *Notes on Formalization.* Programme for the Promotion of Formalization in Latin America and the Caribbean. https://www.ilo.org/wcmsp5/groups/public /---americas/---ro-lima/documents/publication/wcms_245889.pdf.

International Monetary Fund (IMF). 2020. "IMF Committee on Balance of Payments Statistics: Annual Report 2019." Washington, D.C., February 18. https://www.imf.org/en/Publications /Balance-of-Payments-Statistics/Issues/2020/02/18/IMF-Committee-on-Balance-of -Payments-Statistics-Annual-Report-2019-49062.

IPUMS-International. n.d. "Harmonized International Census Date for Social Science and Health Research." Accessed April 28, 2020. https://international.ipums.org/international /index.shtml.

Levy, Santiago. 2018. *Unrewarded Efforts: The Elusive Quest for Prosperity in Mexico.* New York: Inter-American Development Bank.

National Agricultural Statistics Service (NASS). n.d. "Census of Agriculture Historical Archive." Accessed April 28, 2020. http://agcensus.mannlib.cornell.edu/AgCensus/home page.do.

National Agricultural Statistics Service (NASS). n.d. "Home." Accessed April 27, 2020. https:// www.nass.usda.gov.

Secretaría de Economía. n.d. "Competitividad y normatividad / Inversión Extranjera Directa." Accessed April 28, 2020. https://www.gob.mx/se/acciones-y-programas/competitividad-y -normatividad-inversion-extranjera-directa?state=published.

United Nations (UN). 2015. *Principles and Recommendations for Population and Housing Censuses.* Revision 3. New York: United Nations. https://unstats.un.org/unsd/publication /seriesM/Series_M67rev3en.pdf.

U.S. Census Bureau. n.d. "About: How the Census Bureau Measures Poverty." Accessed April 28, 2020. https://www.census.gov/topics/income-poverty/poverty/about.html.

U.S. Census Bureau. n.d. "Comparing Historical Data: Changes in Census Scope." Accessed April 28, 2020. https://www.census.gov/programs-surveys/economic-census/guidance /historical-data.html.

U.S. Census Bureau. n.d. "Concepts and Definitions: Geographic Hierarchy." American Community Survey, Geography and the American Community Survey. Accessed April 28, 2020. https://www.census.gov/programs-surveys/acs/geography-acs/concepts-definitions.html.

U.S. Census Bureau. n.d. "County Business Patterns." Accessed April 28, 2020. https://www
.census.gov/programs-surveys/cbp/about.html.

U.S. Census Bureau. n.d. "Introduction to NAICS." Accessed April 28, 2020. https://www
.census.gov/eos/www/naics/.

U.S. Census Bureau. n.d. "NAICS Codes and Understanding Industry Classification Systems."
Accessed April 28, 2020. https://www.census.gov/programs-surveys/economic-census
/guidance/understanding-naics.html.

PART II

. . .

ISSUES, ACTORS, AND STRUCTURES AT THE U.S.-MEXICO BORDER

4

Collaborative Social Networks

An Exploratory Study of the U.S.-Mexico Border

Víctor Daniel Jurado Flores and Cecilia Sarabia Ríos

T he U.S.-Mexico border region is considered to be a space of contrasts. On the one hand, it has been stereotyped as a space of asymmetries, insecurity, and drug trafficking; on the other hand, it can be considered a space of exchange, cooperation, interconnection, integration, and cooperation with a particular dynamic that responds to cross-border or binational action. In this cross-border or binational region, the dynamic shows specific problems and its solutions acquire different nuances due to the intervention of the traditional actors of civil society, private initiative, and government; and the presence of international actors contributes to provide effective responses for both contexts.

Along the border, there are many examples of cooperation and innovative solutions to joint problems.[1] No matter how difficult it may be to generate good cross-border governance—with such complicated sets of issues, focuses, actors, organizations, interests, and sovereign claims and a constant struggle to define and redefine the border itself—there are increasing expectations of cooperation in all areas among diverse actors from civil society at large, economic entrepreneurs, and government agents and policy makers. They increasingly expect all networks, formal and informal, to conform to certain standards of governance and to build this governance based on the needs established by the actors' closeness and their interests and dynamics, as well as the need for mutual accessibility for problem solving. Interestingly, even as the nation-state asserts itself at the borderline, there is also a growing understanding that border areas require a level of governance that goes beyond national limits. Governance must be agreed to by parties on both sides, something that, by definition, is difficult to achieve. Accordingly, Luis Aguilar Villanueva defines governance as "the process by which actors of a certain society make decisions around their objectives in coexistence—both fundamental and relevant to the current situation—and over how to coordinate to achieve these objectives: their sense of direction and leadership skills" (2006, 90). This is a suitable conceptual approach to the issue of cross-border governance because it includes all the key components—processes, actors, objectives, coordination, and capacities—that should be reflected in understanding cross-border governance: the human factors, the institutional structures, the process design, management experience, as well as other external factors, which may influence them, including sovereignty and autonomy and various issue triggers (Ramos and Villalobos 2013). All analysis of cross-border governance must be this comprehensive if it is to succeed in explaining cross-border governance and sorting out the most successful practices that lead to it.

The resolution of complex problems requires the integration of capacities of various scales, sectors, and levels of social organization and governance systems. Governance networks not only accept resources; they are structured to take advantage of each actor or participant of a sector that provides different resources. These networks combine the political will and legitimacy of the civil society sector with the financial resources, interest in business, enforcement and regulations, and the coordination and capacity building of states and international organizations. They create bridges that allow participants to exploit the synergies between the resources that they provide, the grouping of knowledge, the exchange of experience, and the generation of a feasible institutional framework for successful collaboration. Because they link socioeconomic, political, and cultural differences, governance networks can transform in collaborative and constructive relationships between public, private, and civil society sectors.

Adriaan Schout and Andrew Jordan (2003) recognize two network governance models: one model proposes the active management by governments like a centralized governance authority; the other model focuses the governance networks as self-organized, governing systems. Currently, the dominant model is the active management of governance networks that allows centralized governance authorities to maintain a higher level of modular intermediation. This allows a greater capacity to open and close the process of political will, the decentralization of governance processes in which a variety of actors interact with a certain level of autonomy and self-organization to achieve functions for problem solving and thus governance goals. In this way, the strategies to achieve network governance can be placed in a cycle based on the level of autonomy and self-organization that is delegated to a governance network in terms of achieving organizational functions and governance goals.

Previous studies that have analyzed cross-border networks have had one of two focuses. The first focus is based on the examination of a closed group—for example, the people who work in an organization. This line of research takes a close look at the relationships among the people who interact within that organization or with an organization dealing with the same issue across the border. This is a narrow focus, more akin to a case study of the individuals and organizations that deal with a single issue. The second approach focuses on considering specific actors and attempting to understand their social relationships in their environment—that is, examining their behavior outside their immediate organizations and the way they move their agendas in the larger socio-ecological setting. The first approach is most appropriate in contexts of institutional betweenness, or interaction among peers, especially considering the advantages of remote communication and physical interactions used to craft, implement, and evaluate cross-border programs or projects in a specific issue area. Interestingly, this focus is an approach that can elucidate how actors and organizations develop into networks that participate in problem solving in specific binational issues and how they get organized to do so. The second approach allows us to see how actors and organizations negotiate and obtain support and legitimation for their actions in the broader field environment and how they interact with other actors in the borderlands space to garner resources of all kinds to aid in solving the issue at hand. The advantage of this approach is that it shows how issue-focused actors and organizations negotiate their broader context, often through cultivating relationships across different but relevant issues. Overall, observing these intra-issue and extra-issue connections and placing them in a single diagram shows how networks structure themselves and also allows us to analyze the existing relationships between individuals and organizations until they become part of a larger governance network across borders, in addition to permitting an examination of the processes of participation and betweenness through the visualization of the flows and exchanges of information and knowledge between institutions on both sides of the border.

To achieve the objective of this chapter, the text has been divided into several sections. The first section outlines the methodology used to conduct this study. The second section outlines the structure of the binational network according to the actors that participated in a survey we distributed. The third section establishes and describes the links between the various actors of the network being studied. The fourth section establishes the degree of centrality, closeness centrality, and betweenness centrality among the actors in the network. The fifth and final section presents considerations for the exploratory study of the collaborative social networks within the binational context of the United States and Mexico.

Methodology: Descriptive Analysis of the Network

To carry out this study of cross-border governance networks—admittedly an exploratory study—a sample of 150 organizations and actors was considered. This sample was chosen because these actors and organizations operate in the binational context between the United States and Mexico and are considered to contribute to the interest at hand: cross-border governance. The database contains the names, the initials, the types of actors or organizations, the field in which they operate, the city and region where they were established, and the year they were founded. The source of this database was elaborated by Víctor Daniel Jurado Flores and Cecilia Sarabia Ríos (2017) using data from the Center for the United States and Mexico at Rice University's Baker Institute for Public Policy with the objective of identifying the various actors and organizations that produce cross-border governance along the border area and geo-referencing them to determine where cross-border governance development is most advanced. This database offers input for the exploratory analysis of cross-border networks. All the actors and organizations in the database were asked to respond to a questionnaire about collaboration in their area, within and with other actors outside their area. The results of this study are based on a sample of the 22 of these actors that responded, out of a total 150 digital surveys. The rest of the actors and organizations did not respond to the surveys or did so well beyond the writing of this chapter. Even so, we consider this number sufficiently representative and certainly revealing of the practices of governance among the actors and organizations under observation. Once the answers were received, these surveys were used to develop graphs of the networks, univariate statistics, and indicators of closeness, centrality, and betweenness to establish reciprocal ties among actors and organizations and to estimate centrality indices so as not to distort the information provided by them. Even so, the sample clearly has limitations, which were fully discussed during the analysis of the data, concluding finally that it is sufficiently representative of the scope and type of networks that exist on the U.S.-Mexico border.

After examining the samples for representativeness, we conducted a network analysis. For this, a series of graphs were created. These graphs contain two types of information. The first type refers to the nodes representing the actors and organizations in the different sectors of the institutional scaffolding in which they are situated. The second graph shows the links—that is, the different relationships between and among actors or the nodes in which they are located. After that, the study identifies the attributes of the nodes where the various actors and organizations are located with the objective of scrutinizing their characteristics, including the governmental level of their positioning within the node, the type of their participation in it, the issue area of their activity, and the geographic location of the institution along the border itself. The following list reflects the specific characteristics analyzed.

1. Name of the institution
2. Governmental level: local, state, federal
3. Participation: unilateral, binational, multinational
4. Issue area: environment, social justice, health care, transportation, economic development, migration, academia, education, governance, infrastructure

5. Geographic location: California, Arizona, New Mexico, Texas, Baja California, Maryland

After this basic information on the various actors and organizations under study was collected and the links among the different types of relationships were measured, the possible collaborations between institutions and organizations that operate in the U.S.-Mexico border area were examined as well. The possible collaborations among actors and organizations were taken from the same sample, based on the responses to a survey sent by email. Although responses were not received from all actors and organizations identified in the database, the number of responses seems sufficient to understand the possible collaborations among them and to map out and illustrate the participation and interinstitutional betweenness throughout the binational region.

The survey text was developed with a series of closed questions. Reducing the range of responses to the survey, without diminishing its nuances, is the easiest way to encode the responses that come in. It also makes the analysis more uniform when creating categories of responses from the answers to the survey. The final survey was sent by email to the actors and organizations identified in the database provided by the Center for the United States and Mexico—all 150 of them. The questions included inquiries regarding the types of collaboration shared with some of the listed actors and organizations—a list that was also provided to the surveyed actors and organizations. Positive responses were encoded with the number 1 and negative responses with a 0, representing institutional collaboration and no institutional collaboration, respectively. Once the surveys were conducted, they were transferred to an Excel database where a matrix of symmetrical data was created. That is, the first column and the first line contain the names of the participating institutions. Additionally, another matrix was created with the attributes of the actors and organizations. This second matrix allowed us to develop the analysis of collaboration and betweenness based on the different attributes considered. In summary, the matrices used for this study have the following structure:

Nodes, in two columns:
1. Actor/Organization Identifier (acronym)
2. Collaboration / No collaboration

Attributes, in five columns:
1. Level of operation
2. Type of participation
3. Sector
4. City
5. State

This information was used to conduct an exploratory analysis of the network, calculating the descriptive indicators related to each actor in the network, including the density of the network and the number of cliques or "set of nodes or actors that have all of the possible links between them" (Quiroga 2003, 45), as well as the links among them along the lines of the centrality measurements outlined above: degrees of centrality, closeness, and betweenness.

The network perspective requires considering multiple levels of analysis. The differences are interpreted according to the limitations and opportunities that exist based on how the actors are immersed in the networks; the structure and behavior of the networks are based on and activated by the local interactions among the actors. Studying the differences in how the individuals are connected can be extremely useful in understanding their attributes and behaviors. Having a lot of connections often means that the individuals are exposed to more, increasingly diverse information (Hanneman 2000).

For the exploratory analysis of the network, calculations were performed for the network's descriptive indicators as listed in the following section.

The Actors or Structure of the Network

Density of the Network

The density of a network is conceptualized as the number of relationships a specific network has compared to the total number of possible relationships it could have. It is calculated by dividing the number of existing relationships by the number of possible relationships and then multiplying by one hundred. The total calculation of relationships is then found by multiplying the total number of nodes by the total number of nodes minus one ($k \times k\text{-}1$) (Hanneman 2000). Calculating the network's density allows us to describe how connected the network is, obtaining results that identify and situate the number of possible relationships according to each attribute of the institutions/organizations analyzed, thereby establishing categories of institutions or actors that create more relationships than others.

Number of Cliques

A clique corresponds to a defined subgroup within a network structure. According to Águeda Quiroga, "a clique is a set of nodes or actors that have established all of the possible links among themselves. A clique must have more than two actors, generally working with three or more members" (2003, 45). Based on the approach to the set of nodes or actors that have established all the possible links among them, or cliques, the network's substructures can be recognized, which emphasizes how the macro can arise from the micro. For this approach, we first focused our attention on the individuals and understanding how they are immersed in the greater structure of the network that is subsequently divided into subgroups, and secondly on the juxtaposed groups. This apparently obvious idea must be highlighted because it is also possible to approach the question of the networks' substructures from a downward perspective. Both aspects are valuable and complementary (Hanneman 2000; Molina and Ávila 2010). Accordingly, the analysis of the cliques or subgroups allows us to understand which actors in a clique also belong to other cliques and which members of the network share cliques. These results are interesting as they allow us to understand which actors in a network interact with other subgroups within the same levels of participation and sectors and, in turn, with institutions and organizations with other levels of participation and different sectors, adding a dynamic aspect to the network's configuration.

Links and Centrality Measures Among Actors

Degree Centrality

Degree centrality or range is understood as the number of direct links an actor (or node) has—that is, how many other nodes it is directly connected to. This measurement allows us to understand, for some specific nodes, the degree or number of connections that are established in the framework of information exchange, interinstitutional collaboration, and financing projects and initiatives. Actors that have more links with other actors may have an advantageous position. By having a lot of links, they may have alternative ways of asserting their presence and institutional influence and, consequently, are less dependent on other institutions. Having more links often allows them to be third parties and to participate in exchanges with others, as they are able to benefit from that position (Hanneman 2000). The calculation of this measurement allows us to understand the level of relationships that are established by certain nodes that are relevant to this study inasmuch as they have greater connections in the interinstitutional collaboration network.

Closeness Centrality

Closeness centrality indicates how close a node is to the rest of the network, which represents the capacity of a node to reach the others throughout the entire structure. According to Robert Hanneman, "Actors that are able to reach the others in shorter path lengths have favorable positions. This structural advantage can be translated to power" (2000, 6). For this study, the calculation of closeness centrality allows us to understand the degree or structural position of an institution or organization in the social structure of the collaboration/participation network based on the position it occupies as a node in the network.

Betweenness Centrality

Betweenness centrality indicates how many times a node appears in the shortest path (or geodesic path) connecting it to two other nodes. In other words, it shows when an institution is an intermediary between two other institutions in the same group that do not interact with each other (which can be called a "bridge institution"). As Hanneman explains, "Betweenness centrality shows an actor with a favorable position inasmuch as the actor is located amid the geodesic paths between other pairs of actors in the network. That is, the more entities or institutions that depend on me to make connections with others, the more influence I have. If, however, two actors are connected by more than one geodesic path and I am not present in all these paths, I lose power" (2000, 13). Accordingly, a node's level of frequency is calculated when it acts as an intermediary between two others in order to achieve access to a project or financing. The following sections present the findings of this exercise.

The Structure of the Network

To understand the relationships among actors and organizations participating in the institutional scaffolding that embodies cross-border governance, the networks that connect them were analyzed with two primary focuses. The first focus includes the actors and organizations and the relationships that exist between/among them in a social context (Clark 2006; Molina 2004). This focus provides a better understanding of the position of each actor or organization within the network and the influence associated with each actor's or organization's position in the network. From there, it is possible to discern how each actor or organization uses his or her position in the network to access resources, including assets, capital, and information—all of which are highly desirable assets for any actor or organization in any network because they facilitate the pursuit of the organization's interests, the implementation of its vision, and the bestowal of legitimacy that is often sought. In the field of organized civil society—economic and academic actors and organizations, for example—this second focus allows us to understand the levels of centrality, closeness, and betweenness.

Interestingly, one specific matter is revealing—information. Since one of the primary resources flowing through the networks is information, applying network analysis to information flows and bottlenecks is extremely useful when trying to understand governance. This analysis not only allows researchers to identify issues with information but also, theoretically, the identification of flows and bottlenecks should lead to better strategies for sharing information among different actors based on existing structures, thereby striving to provide them with incentives rather than replace them (Clark 2006; Molina 2004). Accordingly, studying the networks implies providing strategies that compensate the deficiencies in the networks' structures. Moreover, institutions with a variety of information sources usually belong to various *clusters*, which bestow a certain degree of power in the role of betweenness among institutions that do not have many contacts and, consequently, lack access to better-quality information. Similarly, in order to access resources, the actors in an institution develop ties with actors in other institutions, forming *clusters*, in which the better-positioned institutions are not only better informed but also have greater access to material resources because they have better information.

This kind of analysis in turn allows researchers and students of cross-border governance to know that flows—of information and other assets—within a network are not necessarily equitable. On the contrary, actors and organizations in a network have a specific position in said network, and this position may be one of privilege or disadvantage, thereby establishing hierarchies based on the positions of the actors or organizations within the network (Clark 2006). That also allows the student of cross-border governance to conclude that for the purposes of governance, belonging to certain networks provides access not only to information and material resources but also to other organizations and actors that can help improve the value of these resources, creating a circle of virtue for that actor or organization. Accordingly, actors and organizations arrange and structure their networks to maximize the benefits they can obtain, getting closer to the information and resources available in their environment to turn them into opportunities to consolidate or advance their interests. Consequently, the investment in building networks of relationships to access or mobilize resources with the intention of generating income, obtaining or transmitting information, or establishing oneself as a node of influence in their field is called *building social capital* (Clark 2006; Hanneman 2000; Molina 2004). Social capital is expendable and creates a virtuous circle, attracting greater resources. Prestige, influence, and reputation follow. One has to assume that this circle of influence only strengthens the networks of governance, enhancing certainty and predictability in the environment— although the quality of the values and norms that underlie that power could be studied separately.

An important distinction, however, must be made. While it is essential to study the structure of networks, studying the flows that pass through these networks is equally important, as it allows us to visualize the relationships between the different actors interacting among themselves in any given context—spatial, temporary, or thematic—and to evaluate who is who and what they can achieve within the network. That in turn allows us to make judgments on the quality of governance itself. From this perspective, flows reveal the relative weight of each actor or organization and the degrees of collaboration and betweenness among them, offering a better understanding of the degree of influence they have in the issue area in which they participate. Interestingly, that can also help figure out who really governs in each issue area and whose values and vision prevail. This also enables researchers of governance to visualize the complete picture of the integration of all actors and organizations that share common interests, have a similar vision, and collaborate actively to implement their goals but also figure out what actors and organizations are not well connected to the network and have, therefore, little influence in the way a particular problem is defined, dealt with, and ultimately resolved. Thus, this type of analysis has several functions, including a prescriptive and a corrective function. It may also help actors and organizations to figure out how to plug themselves into the network and participate in governance according to their interests and vision of the issue. This also helps actors and institutions, such as those that participated in our study, to understand how structures work, who has influence, who they must relate to more closely, and their relative positions within the network (Hanneman 2000). Accordingly, the main findings from the survey and the overall analysis of interinstitutional networks reveal that a greater level of collaboration between the actors and organizations located in the United States might be needed and tell us what each of them must do to participate more fully in the governance of their issue area, with a stronger presence in this network. This applies to all areas, economic and business sectors, social justice concerns, academic groups, health-care providers, law enforcement, and so on. Table 4.1 shows the number and attributes of these actors.

Based on the actors and organizations that participated in the study's survey, listed in Table 4.1, we see a network with a certain degree of organization despite the heterogeneity of the surveyed actors and organizations—admittedly self-selected, as only a certain percentage responded to the survey. In other words, there are institutional and intersectoral interactions in this network. Figure 4.1 shows the structure of this network, which covers a significant number of actors all along the border.

Within the network's general structure, the collaboration among various actors and organizations can be considered more specifically at different levels and issue areas. In terms of collaboration at the binational level—that is, the border region—and according to our set of respondents, there is a stronger presence of actors and organizations in the social justice sector (Centro de los Derechos del Migrante, Colibrí Center, Hilarious Givers, International Community Foundation, and U.S.-Mexico Border Philanthropy Partnership), followed by actors in the academic sector (El Colegio de la Frontera Norte), health care (Paso del Norte Health Foundation), and the region's economic development sector (Arizona-Mexico Commission). It is important to point out the centrality of El Colegio de la Frontera Norte in Figure 4.2. That academic organization seems to bring the network together, as it occupies an important position in a central node.

Health-care and social justice organizations have been identified as central in terms of participation, influence, and collaboration at the federal level. Although the organizations are classified as actors with participation at the federal level, it is important to point out that the level of participation is regional, with FEMAP Foundation (FEMAPF) and Paso del Norte Health Foundation (PNHF) as organizations in the health-care sector that are present on both sides of the border (see Figure 4.3). The other actors at this level are the Centro de los Derechos del Migrante (CDM), with headquarters in Baltimore, Maryland, and the U.S.-Mexico Border Philanthropy Partnership (USMBPP), which is a network in and of itself of actors from various philanthropy sectors with many sponsors and social organizations, which are present across ten border states. A similar case is the International Community Foundation, headquartered in California, which finances projects for social development in Baja California and Latin America. At this level, it is important to point out the presence of foundations and financiers, which function as networks of actors dealing with issues such as health care and social development and are present in the United States, although their scope of action extends to the binational region.

An analysis of collaboration at the state level reveals that the actors and organizations with a higher level of collaboration (or networking) among them are mainly academic and health-care organizations. El Colegio de la Frontera Norte (COLEF), the Center for Inter-American and Border Studies at the University of Texas at El Paso (CIABSUTEP), the Trans-Border Institute at the University of San Diego (TBI-USD), and the San Diego Natural History Museum (SDNHM) are the academic actors/organizations in this network that are most active in collaborations among them, although they also reach out to other types of organizations by definition. Academic institutions pride themselves on collaborating and reaching across many different actors in their field environment. Along those lines, the following health-care organizations constitute a central network of close collaboration on the issue of health care and public health: the New Mexico Office of Border Health (NMOBH), the Migrant Clinicians Network (MCN), and the Arizona Office of Border Health (AOBH). An initial approach to Figure 4.4 indicates that issues of migration and border studies connect the organizations and actors in this network, and this figure shows the connections between these actors in their respective areas of activity.

Regarding the type of unilateral collaboration that involves activities at the local level (see Figure 4.5), we can see a broad, heterogeneous network, perhaps broader than at the state level. However, it is important to highlight three organizations, which are essentially the core actors bringing this network together: the Arizona Office of Border Health (AOBH), which deals with health-care issues; the Center for Iberian and Latin American Studies, University of California, San Diego (CILASUCSD);

TABLE 4.1 Actors participating in the survey and their attributes

Name	Initials	Level	Participation	Sector	State	Year Founded
Arizona-Mexico Commission	AMC	State	Binational	Economic development	AZ	1959
Arizona Office of Border Health	AOBH	State	Unilateral	Health care	AZ	
Center for Comparative Immigration Studies	CCIS	State	Unilateral	Migration	CA	1999
Center for Iberian and Latin American Studies, University of California, San Diego	CILASUCSD	Federal	Unilateral	Academia	CA	1976
Center for Inter-American and Border Studies, University of Texas at El Paso	CIABSUTEP	State	Unilateral	Academia	TX	
Centro de los Derechos del Migrante	CDM	Federal	Binational	Social justice	MD	2005
Colibrí Center	CC	State	Unilateral	Social justice	AZ	2006
El Colegio de la Frontera Norte	COLEF	State	Unilateral	Academia	BC	1982
FEMAP Foundation	FEMAPF	Federal	Unilateral	Social justice	TX	2010
Foundation for the Children of the Californias	FCC	Federal	Multinational	Health care	CA	1994
Hilarious Givers	HG	Federal	Binational	Social justice	CA	2014
International Bridge Offices of El Paso	IBOEP	State	Unilateral	Transportation	TX	

Organization	Abbr.	Level	Type	Sector	State	Year
International Community Foundation	ICF	Federal	Binational	Social justice	CA	1989
Mainly Mozart Binational	MMB	Local	Unilateral	Education	CA	1992
Migrant Clinicians Network	MCN	State	Unilateral	Health care	TX	1985
New Mexico Office of Border Health	NMOBH	State	Unilateral	Health care	NM	1993
North American Strategy for Competitiveness	NASC	Federal	Multinational	Transportation	TX	1994
Paso del Norte Health Foundation	PNHF	Federal	Binational	Health care	TX	1995
San Diego Association of Governments, Borders Committee	SDAGBC	State	Unilateral	Transportation	CA	1966
San Diego Natural History Museum	SDNHM	State	Unilateral	Academia	CA	1874
Trans-Border Institute at the University of San Diego	TBIUSD	Local	Unilateral	Environment	CA	
U.S.-Mexico Border Philanthropy Partnership	USMBPP	Federal	Binational	Social Justice	CA	2008

Source: Jurado Flores and Sarabia Ríos 2017.

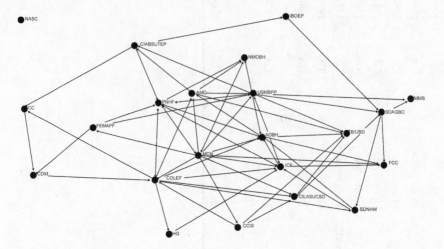

FIGURE 4.1 Network of interactions among actors. *Source*: Jurado Flores and Sarabia Ríos 2017.

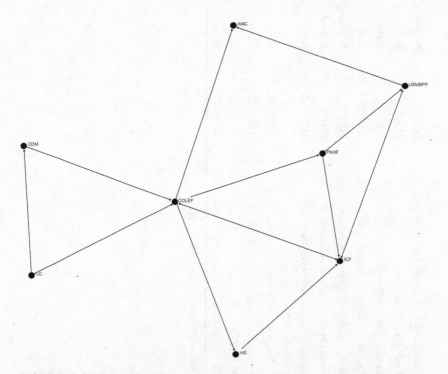

FIGURE 4.2 Network of collaboration at the binational level. *Source*: Jurado Flores and Sarabia Ríos 2017.

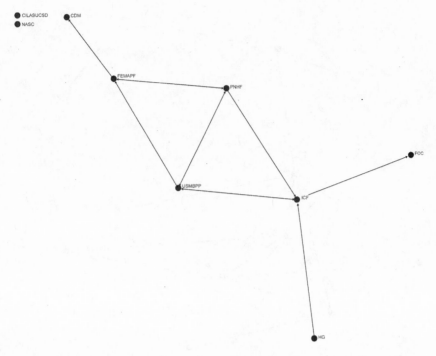

FIGURE 4.3 Network of collaboration at the federal level. *Source*: Jurado Flores and Sarabia Ríos 2017.

and the Transborder Institute at the University of San Diego (TBIUSD). These three central actors/organizations help connect the other institutions in this network.

Figure 4.6 also groups the organizations with more members (health care and academia), showing an organized network with reciprocal ties between central actors/organizations. In this case, the PNHF and the AOBH are the central institutions in this network, which implies that the level of betweenness allows them to extend collaboration and communication networks to the other organizations in the network. That also means that they are higher in the hierarchy of influence among their peers.

Links Between Actors

Essentially, the purpose of examining the links between the different actors and organizations is to establish the centrality, closeness, and betweenness of each actor in the network based on their responses regarding their links to other actors and organizations in the network (see Table 4.2). The estimate of univariate statistics in network

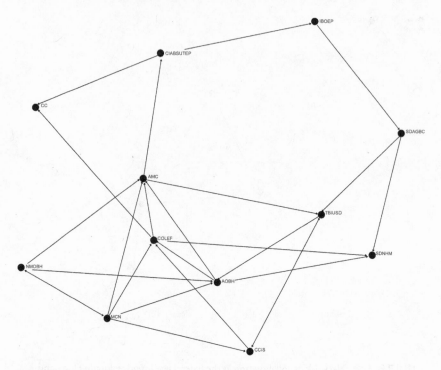

FIGURE 4.4 Network of collaboration at the state level. *Source*: Jurado Flores and Sarabia Ríos 2017.

analysis allows us to explain the role each actor plays as a source of relationships (in an undirected graph, such as in this case). The sum of the connections of an actor or organization with the others (e.g., USMBPP states that it interacts with eleven other actors or organizations) is the out-degree of the node. This degree of nodal points is important because it explains how many connections an actor or organization has. The out-degree of the node is normally a measure of how influential an actor or organization can be. In this case, we can see the first group of actors, USMBPP and MCN, which have the greatest number of connections (eleven and ten, respectively). The second group is composed of ICF, with eight connections; COLEF, also with eight connections; and PNHF, with seven connections. Subsequently, actors AOBH and SDAGBC each have six connections. This number of connections shows that these actors/organizations have a high degree of collaboration with others in the field environment, which may be due to personal networks of civil servants, collaborative work on specific projects, financing projects to local organizations, and so forth.

The actors and organizations in the first group have a high potential for influence. The second group of actors/organizations can be influential or have a strong pres-

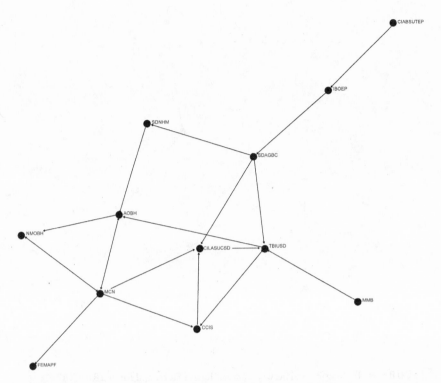

FIGURE 4.5 Network of collaboration in a unilateral context (local). *Source*: Jurado Flores and Sarabia Ríos 2017.

ence, but only if they relate to the indicated actors or organizations—in other words, those that have a significant weight in the structure. Otherwise, they will have little influence within the overall structure. To a certain degree, their influence depends on their capacity to strengthen it through other connections. Furthermore, reviewing the averages shows that USMBPP has a relationship with 52 percent of the actors/organizations in the network and MCN has a relationship with 47 percent of the actors/organizations in the network. Although Table 4.2 shows the out-degree—that is, which actors or organizations they have a relationship with—it is also important to analyze the in-degree of the node: that is, the institutions as recipients of collaboration (see Table 4.3).

The sum (in-degree) of each column in the adjacency matrix is the in-degree node to the vertex: in other words, how many actors/organizations send information (or mention that they have collaborated) with the node being studied. Actors or organizations that receive information from many sources (or that are asked to collaborate in terms of resources, investigations, studies, or consultancies) may be prestigious (in

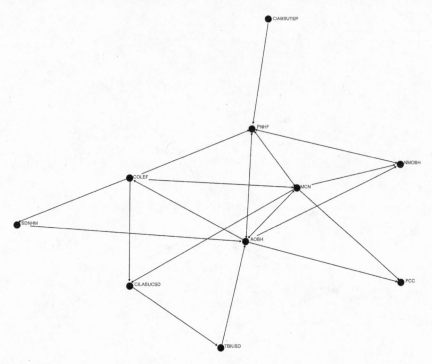

FIGURE 4.6 Intersectoral network. *Source*: Jurado Flores and Sarabia Ríos 2017.

the sense that other institutions want to collaborate with said institution and therefore send it information). Actors and organizations that receive information from many sources may also be more powerful.

Considering the averages, a different pattern can be identified in terms of the out-degree node, as well as a high degree of variation. Actors ICF, PNHF, and TBIUS are very important; likewise, the same actors are also important in sending information (or collaborating)—consequently, they serve as "communicators" and "facilitators" in the system. The second group of actors is composed of USMBP, MCN, AOBH, AMC and COLEF, which receive information (or are asked to collaborate) and have average levels of out-degree. Furthermore, the calculation of the density of relationships in the network of actors/organizations is 17 percent (see Table 4.4). This is an expected result, since it shows a low density in the number of existing relationships, which leads to the conclusion that the interactions between institutions in programs, financing, consultancies, and so on, have a low level of connectivity due to the heterogeneity of the actors analyzed, their different levels of participation, and their belonging to different sectors of activity.

TABLE 4.2 Connections between the actors in the network

Actors	1 Connections (out-degree)	2 Average	3 Standard	4 Variance
AMC	3	0.143	0.350	0.122
AOBH	6	0.286	0.452	0.204
CC	1	0.048	0.213	0.045
CCIS	3	0.143	0.350	0.122
CDM	1	0.048	0.213	0.045
CIABSUTEP	3	0.143	0.350	0.122
CILASUCSD	1	0.048	0.213	0.045
COLEF	7	0.333	0.471	0.222
FCC	1	0.048	0.213	0.045
FEMAPF	2	0.095	0.294	0.086
HG	1	0.048	0.213	0.045
IBOEP	1	0.048	0.213	0.045
ICF	8	0.381	0.486	0.236
MCN	10	0.476	0.499	0.249
MMB	2	0.095	0.294	0.086
NASC	0	0	0	0
NMOBH	3	0.143	0.350	0.122
PNHF	7	0.333	0.471	0.222
SDAGBC	6	0.286	0.452	0.204
SDNHM	2	0.095	0.294	0.086
TBIUSD	2	0.095	0.294	0.086
USMBPP	11	0.524	0.499	0.249

Source: Jurado Flores and Sarabia Ríos 2017.

The calculation of actor/organization cliques is extremely important to understand their impact on cross-border governance. Studying cliques of actors and organizations allows us to visualize how many subgroups exist in the network of organizations in the U.S.-Mexico binational region. Moreover, this analysis allows us to describe the actors in a clique that also belong to other cliques, as well as which members of the network they share cliques with. These results show what actors and organizations in a network have a higher level of social capital, by being mainly connected with other groups. A next step would be to investigate how they use this social capital and for

TABLE 4.3 Degree of the node

Actors	Connections (in-degree)	Average	Variance
AMC	5	0.238	0.181
AOBH	6	0.286	0.204
CC	2	0.095	0.086
CCIS	2	0.095	0.086
CDM	2	0.095	0.086
CIABSUTEP	2	0.095	0.086
CILASUCSD	4	0.09	0.154
COLEF	5	0.238	0.181
FCC	4	0.19	0.154
FEMAPF	3	0.143	0.122
HG	1	0.048	0.045
IBOEP	1	0.048	0.045
ICF	8	0.381	0.236
MCN	5	0.238	0.181
MMB	2	0.095	0.086
NASC	0	0	0
NMOBH	4	0.19	0.154
PNHF	7	0.333	0.222
SDAGBC	3	0.143	0.122
SDNHM	3	0.143	0.122
TBIUSD	7	0.333	0.222
USMBPP	5	0.238	0.181

Source: Jurado Flores and Sarabia Ríos 2017.

what purposes. In our analysis, a subgroup or clique in a network is a group with a minimum number of three members, or a triad (since a relationship is between two actors/organizations, or a dyad, while a group is made up of a minimum of three members).

Interestingly, a total of four subgroups or cliques were found in the network of interorganizational collaboration among the sample under study (see Table 4.5). Most subgroups are composed of three members, allowing us to conclude that, despite the network's heterogeneity, it has substructures of members that interact among themselves but are not strongly connected to each other. Instead, they are connected

TABLE 4.4 Density of the network

	1 Density	2 No. of links
Actors	0.175	81

Source: Jurado Flores and Sarabia Ríos 2017.

TABLE 4.5 Subgroups in the network

Group	Actors in each group
1	MCN, PNHF
2	NMOBH, MCN, PNHF
3	MCN, PNHF, USMBPP
4	ICF, USMBPP, SDAGBC

Source: Jurado Flores and Sarabia Ríos 2017.

through certain key actors/organizations that play a special role and place in the network's structure.

These results show that three actors (MCN, PNHF, and USMBPP) have a high level of importance in the network inasmuch as they share subgroups within the network, while the vast majority have only a few relationships or do not belong to any clique or relationship.

Centrality, Closeness, and Betweenness in the Network

Having outlined the groupings, it is also important to look closely at the nature of their relationships. This section attempts to do just that. It seeks to explain the calculations used to determine degree centrality, closeness, and betweenness in the network. Each of these three important elements of network analysis is examined separately.

Degree Centrality

Degree centrality or range is understood as the number of direct links an actor or organization has; that is, it describes how many other nodes a given actor or organization is directly connected to. At the same time, this allows us to determine which node has the most connections in the network or is connected more than other actors or organizations and, consequently, has a higher level of social capital associated with these

TABLE 4.6 Degree centrality in the network

Actors	Out-degree	In-degree	Normalized out-degree	Normalized in-degree
AMC	3	5	0.143	0.238
AOBH	6	6	0.286	0.286
CC	1	2	0.048	0.095
CCIS	3	2	0.143	0.095
CDM	1	2	0.048	0.095
CIABSUTEP	3	2	0.143	0.095
CILASUCSD	1	4	0.048	0.190
COLEF	7	5	0.333	0.238
FCC	1	4	0.048	0.190
FEMAPF	2	3	0.095	0.143
HG	1	1	0.048	0.048
IBOEP	1	1	0.048	0.048
ICF	8	8	0.381	0.381
MCN	10	5	0.476	0.238
MMB	2	2	0.095	0.095
NASC	0	0	0	0
NMOBH	3	4	0.143	0.190
PNHF	7	7	0.333	0.333
SDAGBC	6	3	0.286	0.143
SDNHM	2	3	0.095	0.143
TBIUSD	2	7	0.095	0.333
USMBPP	11	5	0.524	0.238

Source: Jurado Flores and Sarabia Ríos 2017.

connections. An analysis of Table 4.6 shows that the nodes made up of more actors or organizations with a higher degree centrality are USMBPP, MCN, ICF, PNHF, and COLEF, at 52 percent, 47 percent, 33 percent, and 33 percent, respectively. This in turn allows us to demonstrate that these actors have a greater degree centrality within the network of governance; that is, they constitute, in effect, the most important actors in the network and may have a deeper impact on governance in both depth and breadth. This index also presents the names of the main nodes in the network—namely, the actors that are more important and have significant centrality in terms of interorganizational collaboration within the network, as they allow for connections with other organizations based on information, financing, consultancies, capital, and so forth. In terms of influence (or power), this means that actors or organizations with a higher degree centrality in the structure have more resources, which allows them to pursue and advance their interests better than other actors or organizations.

Degree of Closeness

Degree of closeness indicates the distance of a node to the rest of the network. Closeness centrality represents the capacity of a node to reach the others in the network, which shows the node's capacity to achieve access to information, resources, and consultancies as compared to other actors. Table 4.7 lists the actors that are better positioned in the network: ICF, AOBH, TBIUSD, and PNHF, followed by MCN, USMBPP, COLEF, and AMC. These actors have high social capital, as they have more possibilities of accessing projects, obtaining financing, and getting information, and potentially have greater connections with government organizations (allowing them to influence governance more forcefully), the private sector (allowing them to create stronger lobbying networks), and supranational agencies (helping them achieve legitimacy in the broader environment).

Closeness is important because, in many ways, it indicates the nature of the network in and of itself—of the intersections connecting the network's unifying threads: that is, how the network is interconnected. Simply put, who is close to whom in collaboration agreements, whether formal or informal, is in itself a revealing element for understanding cross-border governance. The following section focuses on the nature of each of the actors and their capacity for betweenness in the network.

Degree of Betweenness

Betweenness indicates the frequency with which a node appears in the shortest path connecting two other nodes—that is, the distance between nodes is central to this analysis. This distance implies and measures the centrality of the betweenness, indicating that an actor serves as an intermediary between two other organizations in the same sector that do not interact with each other or even between sectors that are not closely related to each other. That means that this actor or organization is what could be called a "bridge" organization or actor between other organizations or actors or between sectors. That implies a certain degree of influence in governance as it connects various definitions of problems, solutions, information, and so forth. The betweenness centrality analysis indicates that the organizations or actors with higher betweenness centrality are ICF (92.9 percent) and COLEF (91.8 percent), which clearly serve as intermediaries between other organizations, connecting projects, programs, information exchange, capital and material goods, and so on. Table 4.8 shows the following group of intermediaries resulting from the analysis: USMBPP

TABLE 4.7 Closeness centrality in the network

Actors	Closeness (out-degree)	Closeness (in-degree)
AMC	0.318	0.323
AOBH	0.350	0.350
CC	0.226	0.276
CCIS	0.300	0.292
CDM	0.280	0.259
CIABSUTEP	0.313	0.288
CILASUCSD	0.226	0.318
COLEF	0.368	0.323
FCC	0.273	0.318
FEMAPF	0.288	0.296
HG	0.280	0.256
IBOEP	0.266	0.233
ICF	0.362	0.362
MCN	0.396	0.333
MMB	0.280	0.284
NASC	0.045	0.045
NMOBH	0.318	0.313
PNHF	0.375	0.344
SDAGBC	0.339	0.296
SDNHM	0.300	0.313
TBIUSD	0.280	0.350
USMBPP	0.404	0.328

Source: Jurado Flores and Sarabia Ríos 2017.

(64 percent), PNHF (56 percent) and AOBH (55 percent). It is important to point out that within this group of intermediary actors and organizations or "bridge" actors/ organizations, three belong to the financial sector (which is extremely important due to its centrality in the flow of resources, mainly capital), one is a border health-care office (which is not surprising, given the importance of the public's well-being and its history of cross-border cooperation), and another is a center for academic research (the type of organization that naturally aims to interconnect with other organizations). Interestingly, the academic world and the public health world keep appearing often—although, again, and admittedly, there is some self-selection bias in our sam-

TABLE 4.8 Betweenness centrality in the network

Actors	Betweenness weighted for distance
AMC	26.255
AOBH	54.562
CC	5.033
CCIS	9.021
CDM	21.333
CIABSUTEP	25.867
CILASUCSD	1.850
COLEF	91.876
FCC	1.988
FEMAPF	12.967
HG	0
IBOEP	2.250
ICF	92.936
MCN	40.721
MMB	0
NASC	0
NMOBH	0.567
PNHF	56.026
SDAGBC	24.617
SDNHM	2.000
TBIUSD	35.650
USMBPP	64.481

Source: Jurado Flores and Sarabia Ríos 2017.

ple, there are reasons to suspect that this is probably the case in any event. Table 4.8 shows betweenness weighted according to the distance between nodes.

Final Considerations

All cross-border institutional scaffoldings first begin with networks of individuals and small groups, which interact across borderlines to articulate their interests and vision, something that eventually demands stronger and deeper organizational levels to systematize and order relations to allow these individuals and groups to realize more efficiently the benefits that stem from their interaction. Such has been the case with the U.S.-Mexico border. In fact, the U.S.-Mexico binational region features a unique set of dynamics regarding its institutions of governance. While some of them have become more fully organized over time, such as the International Boundary and Water Commission, others remain much more informal and fluid. All, however, contribute just as much to cross-border governance. At a thirty-thousand-foot view, the entire institutional framework that governs the U.S.-Mexico border comes together in this physical space and deals with all sorts of issues, some quite complex and others less so, with the goal of achieving greater governability of the area *as a binational region*. This network includes multiple actors, individual and collective, and organizations that reside on both sides of the border. Governance at the border also reveals varying degrees of success in dealing with binational issues. Clearly, not all actors and organizations that comprise and populate these cross-border governance institutions maintain the same level of political development, nor do they have the same capacity to contribute to the region's governance. Still, studying this framework along the border reveals examples of successful governance practices. In fact, binational projects and programs, whether unilateral or bilateral, operate within an extremely complex socio-institutional framework where interactions among many different actors can be observed, including local and national governmental and nongovernmental organizations, as well as public and private institutions, all of which operate in local, regional, national, and international spaces. Many of their functions and jurisdictions also overlap. These actors' objectives are focused on security, migration, natural resources and the environment, human rights, infrastructure, economic development, and so forth. Their variety of foci in spatial and thematic scope is further complicated because the borderlands are a territorial stage where binational cooperation tends to focus on short- and medium-term projects, with alliances and competing agendas among various kinds of actors and organizations, not all of whom see eye to eye on what the border should be—something that limits the possibilities of continuity and the consolidation of successful governance experiences. The border is therefore conceived not only as a space of territorial, thematic, or temporary delineations but also as a point of interconnections, an influx of opportunities, a diversity of focuses and interests. It is, in fact, and deceivingly, a much more conflictive space than most would observe. Thus, it is in general a complex space to govern, precisely because it possesses enormous potential for all kinds of exchanges and flows, where the similarities and differences emerge and result in the continuous reconceptualization of the border. This continual struggle to reconceptualize the borderlands, however, provides us with enormous opportunities for institutional innovation (Sohn 2015).

In trying to understand the levels of collaboration, betweenness, and connection between organizations or actors in a network, it is necessary to understand the nature of said network and the attributes of the relationships between the people and organizations in their environment, as well as interconnections that may arise. Based on the knowledge of a network, it is possible to identify who works in said network and how they work, as well as to understand the relationships between the different actors and organizations. In order to understand interorganizational work and make appropriate decisions, it is important to dedicate some time to identifying key actors and organizations and understanding the social relationships between them.

The methodology of analysis for social networks in the social sciences has undergone significant growth in recent years. It has been applied to such diverse topics as public health care, psychology, business organization, and electronic communication. Continuous advances in information and communication technologies are enabling institutions and people to become increasingly more connected, and more intensely connected, both qualitatively and quantitatively. This involves collaborating remotely as well as being aware of the existence of organizations, networks of actors, and the work being carried out by said entities. Consequently, there is a greater awareness of the importance of social relationships on all levels, from virtual networks on a global scale to interorganizational collaboration networks at different levels, based on different issues, to community networks with shared interests, and so on. Furthermore, using the analysis methodology for networks as a diagnostic tool can help us understand levels of participation based on centrality, closeness, and betweenness in binational projects and programs, demonstrating institutional trends that can help identify the alliances and societies that have been created, thereby recognizing the construction of cross-border interinstitutional social capital. Visualizing networks on the local, state, national, and binational levels among organizations and actors, including individuals, allows us to understand the networks that show interactions between organizations that have an influence on a certain topic, in a certain space, and at a specific time.

The results of the exploratory examination of networks of binational actors carried out for this study indicate that, although a model of cross-border governance cannot be identified, the organizations and other actors in the United States have greater disposition for collaborating. The most important actors and organizations standing out from these findings are in issue areas that have the strongest presence in the network, specifically the social justice, academic, and health-care sectors. In other words, despite the heterogeneity of the actors and the organizations that participated in the study's survey, a certain degree of articulation and systematization can be observed; these actors and organizations already form a network with institutionalized and intersectoral interactions. Collaboration at the binational level involves actors and organizations in the area of social justice, followed by the academic, health-care, and economic development sectors.

A cross-sectional analysis of the different levels of government reveals the following results. At the federal level, the actors with a stronger presence in the network include the health-care and social justice sectors, with a strong presence of foundations and financiers. An analysis of collaboration at the state level reveals that the institutions and organizations with a greater degree of collaboration are mainly from the academic and health-care sectors. In regard to collaboration at the local level, there is a broad heterogeneous network, primarily featuring actors in the health-care and academic sectors.

In terms of numbers, the study revealed the following results. The actors with a greater number of connections or with a high degree of interinstitutional collaboration may have access to personal networks of civil servants, perform collaborative work on specific projects, and participate in financing projects to local organizations, among other factors. In regard to actors as recipients of collaboration, those that receive information from many sources are deemed to be more prestigious and, therefore, more powerful or influential within the network. Furthermore, the interactions among institutions in programs, projects, financing, consultancy, and so forth have a low level of connectivity due to the heterogeneity of the actors analyzed, their different levels of participation, and their belonging to different sectors of activity. Therefore, an exploration of the results indicates that there are four subgroups, mainly associated with the health-care and social justice sectors.

The network analysis from many different perspectives reveals that organizations and actors that are the most important in the network are clearly in the social justice, health-care, and academic sectors, largely due to their possibilities of accessing projects, financing, and information, and potentially having closer connections with government organizations, the private sector, and supranational agencies. One could argue that one leads to the other or the other to the one. The reality is that they start in a privileged position and then build cycles of privilege and perpetuate their influence on cross-border governance. Lastly, the actors and organizations identified as intermediaries in the network are from the health-care and academic sectors—not surprisingly in the case of academics, as they dedicate much time to exploring issues of governance and reaching out to many different actors and organizations in many different issue areas. These results are part of an exploratory study, which, despite its limitations, allows us to understand some of the attributes of the actors on the border of Mexico and the United States; nevertheless, the exploration should be continued in order to understand the praxis of the different actors.

Note

This chapter, including quotations from non-English sources, was translated into English by Heather Elizabeth Higle of HH Translations.

1.   The case of the Sierra Blanca nuclear dump in the 1980s is an example where civil society actors from both sides of the border were drastically opposed to the federal waste disposal

policy in that area (Poshman 1999). Another example is the creation of the North American Development Bank (NADB) and the Border Environment Cooperation Commission (BECC) binational institutions, founded in 1983 with the purpose of providing financing for projects aimed at supporting preservation, protection, and improvement of the environment of the border area to increase the well-being of the population of Mexico and the United States (NADB Constitutive Agreement 2017). Another example of cooperation is the binational airport that, through a pedestrian bridge or Cross Border Xpress (CBX), connects the Tijuana International Airport with a terminal of the San Diego airport in the United States without leaving the air terminal and whose purpose is compatible time and crossing costs (CBX n.d.; Grupo Aeroportuario del Pacifico n.d.). In each of these examples, the actors and institutions (which include civil society, government, and entrepreneurs) on both sides of the border maintain a relationship to solve joint problems.

References

Aguilar Villanueva, Luis F. 2006. *Gobernanza y gestión pública*. Mexico City: Fondo de Cultura Económica.

Clark, Louise. 2006. "Manual para el mapeo de redes como una herramienta de diagnóstico." Centro Internacional de Agricultura Tropical, La Paz, Bolivia, March. http://revista-redes .rediris.es/webredes/textos/Mapeo_redes_LC06.pdf.

Cross Border Xpress. n.d. Accessed September 27, 2019. https://www.crossborderxpress .com/en/.

Grupo Aeroportuario del Pacifico. n.d. "Cross Border Xpress." Accessed September 27, 2019. https://www.aeropuertosgap.com.mx/es/tijuana/cross-border-xpress.html.

Hanneman, Robert A. 2000. "Introducción a los métodos de análisis de redes sociales." University of California, Riverside.

Jurado Flores, Víctor Daniel, and Cecilia Sarabia Ríos. 2017. "Collaborative Social Networks." Database.

Molina, José Luis. 2004. "La ciencia de las redes." *Apuntes de Ciencia y Tecnología*, no. 11 (June).

Molina, José Luis, and Javier Ávila, eds. 2010. *Antropología y redes sociales: Una introducción a UCINET6-NETDRAW, EGONET y el análisis comparado con SPSS*. Barcelona: Universidad Autónoma de Barcelona.

NADB Constitutive Agreement. 2017. "Acuerdo entre el Gobierno de los Estados Unidos de América y el Gobierno de los Estados Unidos Mexicanos sobre el Establecimiento del Banco de Desarrollo de América del Norte." November 10. https://www.nadb.org/uploads /content/files/Policies/Charter_2004_span.pdf.

Poshman, Joshua. 1999. "Environmental Justice Case Study: The Struggle for Sierra Blanca, Texas Against a Low-Level Nuclear Waste Site." University of Michigan. http://www.umich .edu/~snre492/blanca.html.

Quiroga, Águeda. 2003. "Introducción al análisis de datos reticulares: Prácticas con UCINET6 y NetDraw1." Versión 1, Departamento de Ciencias Políticas, Universidad Pompeu Fabra, June. http://revista-redes.rediris.es/webredes/talleres/redes.htm.

Ramos, José María, and Alberto Villalobos, eds. 2013. *Gobernanza y prevención transversal en la frontera norte de México*. Mexico City: Colectivo de Análisis de la Seguridad en Democracia; Madrid: Instituto Universitario de Investigación Ortega y Gasset.

Schout, Adriaan, and Andrew Jordan. 2003. "Coordinated European Governance: Self-Organising or Centrally Steered?" CSERGE Working Paper, EDM 03-14. University of East Anglia, Centre for Social and Economic Research on the Global Environment, Norwich. http://hdl.handle.net/10419/80265.

Sohn, Christophe. 2015. "Unpacking the Concept of Cross-Border Integration: The Role of Borders as a Resource." In *Fronteras y procesos de integración regional: Estudios comparados de América y Europa*, edited by María del Rosio Barajas Escamilla, Pablo Wong-González, and Nahuel Oddone, 29–48. Tijuana: El Colegio de la Frontera Norte.

5

• • •

Governing the Borderlands Commons

Local Actors at Work

Manuel A. Gutiérrez and Kathleen Staudt

The late Nobel Laureate political economist Elinor Ostrom made famous the concept of "governing the commons" (1990), focusing especially on ecosystems and on people's ability to manage and overcome the "tragedy of the commons" (Hardin 1968), where self-interest undermines or destroys common resources. We contend, in this chapter, that the fourteen million people and the fourteen twin cities and towns along the nearly two-thousand-mile U.S.-Mexico borderlands should move toward forging a better way to govern their regional and local commons once national self-interest behavior is tamed and made more accountable to local voices.[1] Local voices have been muted in a historic "democratic deficit" that Tony Payan (2010) analyzes about the borderlands. Narratives about the borderlands, continuously manipulated over time to serve national security and trade agendas, have finally begun to be more comprehensive with border studies research and large-scale surveys, such as a 2016 sample of more than 1,400 borderlanders and a 2018 sample of 2,400 central borderlanders.[2]

To show this steady, albeit slow, progress, we bring different perspectives to this analysis, both empirical and normative. We seek to analyze local elective bodies and two federal systems of government. Electoral democracy permits voters—presumably a critical mass of them, as analyzed in percent-voter-turnout terms—to choose representatives who make decisions on residents' behalf. Moreover, we assume that federal governments devolve authority from federal to state and local governments, permitting some discretionary action to foster binational communication to improve the conditions of their regions by working together as opposed to alienating their counterpart. Yet we know that Mexico has a far more centralized federal system of government, with municipal governments heavily dependent on Mexico City for financial support, even after passage of the 1984 decentralization constitutional amendment of Article 115 in which state governments captured sizeable sums from the seemingly decentralized financial resources (Rodríguez 1997). Moreover, in the post-9/11 world, the United States has imposed numerous constraints at borders in the name of national security. And, commonly understood among border scholars, borders are political and social constructions that change over time, the latest of which include both the Chamizal Agreement of the early 1960s, returning a square mile of land to Mexico due to a meandering river boundary; and the U.S. customs clearance process at the Tijuana airport. Shrouding all these, we acknowledge the extreme inequalities that characterize both sides of the U.S.-Mexico border, first established by Oscar Martínez in interdependent power asymmetry terms (1994) and later by Iñigo Moré (2011) and Kathleen Staudt (2017) in numeric terms as situated among the most unequal borderlands in the world.[3] Writing about the Americas, Filippo Celata, Raffaella Coletti, and Venere Stefania Sanna believe that "transnational cooperation has become an important instrument in regard to economic development: the areas of the border are typically peripheral in respect to their national centers, and sometimes they are negatively affected by the policies of their own states" (2013, 170). Therefore, if border cities and towns could operate at the microlevel and cooperate with their neighbor, there could be gains for both sides of the borders to govern their "commons," as Ostrom would call them.

Although local government literature is sparse, we intend to expand on the existing state-centered and business-oriented literature with a theme to emphasize cooperation and best practices. Across our cases of border cities, some pairs display cooperation and a willingness to move in the same direction by establishing workable binational channels.

In some border communities, public space is used to demonstrate and make visible support for neighbors through art and popular culture. Tijuana borderlanders have decorated the border fence with such messages of friendship, hope, harmony, closeness, solidarity, and cooperation as "love trumps hate, *el amor vence al odio*," "humanity cannot be segregated," "make love, not walls," and "*ningún ser humano es ilegal* [no human being is illegal]." A part of the border fence next to the ocean is even painted sky blue to make it seem invisible. In the South Texas region, there is a memorial for all migrants who have died trying to cross the border. People use symbols and signs to show that communities are united and supportive of each other. Border communities can show and expand the idea of unity and mutual respect, though billboards are not present in all twin cities and towns.[4]

While the federal governments have different priorities, at the local level people show that they live and experience a different reality. For example, in 2016 Cronkite News, Univision, and the *Dallas Morning News* conducted a poll that surveyed borderlanders and found that people are "deeply connected. Both share similar concerns for their families on issues such as safety, jobs, and education" (Univision PR Team 2016). In a 2018 survey of 2,400 people on both urban sides of the central borderline, almost half (47 percent) of El Pasoans and more than a third (37 percent) of Juarenses say these are "sister cities," with considerable numbers "crossing" to the other side (Acosta 2019). This is consistent with the idea that borderlanders and their realities are different from what the federal governments and polarizing politicians imply. Cities could try to apply binational models to benefit their region according to aspects of positive cooperation at various levels as analyzed herein.

This chapter is organized into three sections. In the first section, we look at some of the ways federal and state policies incentivize or shape binational cooperation (or its absence). The second section looks at some primary or related issues drawing on political institutions, governmental bodies, civil societies, and voter turnouts at recent elections. The third section discusses current or proposed solutions, where we identify best practices, ideas, and programs in three of the different multiple U.S.-Mexico borderlands. In a concluding section, we offer recommendations for governing our borderlands commons. Among questions we raise with a focus on local institutions, we consider the following: How do federal and state policies shape binational border institutions? Do they incentivize binational cooperation or discourage it, and in which policy areas? What differences exist across municipal governments and is their binational work, if present, visible in local media and with oversight? Do local council border relations committees exist, and if so, what are their missions? As this analysis will show, binational institutions and media coverage are superficial, probably unhelpful to readers and border people.

Federal and State Government-to-Government Efforts

Local and state government-to-government efforts are valuable and pivotal contributors to border governance. There are official efforts at all levels of government to cooperate in different areas, but local governments are the most diverse, despite much nationalist political rhetoric about "border security" that discourages cooperation and generates fear among publics. Thus, an overall assessment of the entire institutional field as it has developed and judgments about the quality of governance they provide are both crucial.

Politically, the field of government-to-government efforts ranges from legislative conferences, to agency-to-agency work, to city-to-city work, to other official efforts. It should also be recognized that nongovernmental organizations facilitate state government-to-government cooperation, such as the Council of State Governments (CSG) West, which aims to bring together governors and state legislators (CSG n.d.).

Energy and environmental issues too provide precedents that shape binational mechanisms of governance. According to the International Water Law Project (1999), cooperation at the federal level is sometimes cemented by a Memoranda of Understanding (MOU). In some other cases, MOUs also occur between neighboring cities, such as an MOU between the City of Juárez Water Utilities and the El Paso Water Utilities Public Service Board, where both companies share the same surface water source (Rio Grande / Río Bravo and the Hueco Bolson). Furthermore, there are also MOUs on cross-border communications and emergency response between El Paso, Ysleta, and Sunland Park in the United States and Ciudad Juárez, Mexico, where some principles and guidelines were drawn to serve as a guide to emergency planning (EPA 2009).[5] And on human mobility, in a federal MOU, the U.S. Department of Homeland Security (DHS) agrees to regulate the flow of persons, particularly on the common border. This MOU was created between the DHS and the Secretaría de Gobernación (SEGOB, Secretariat of the Interior) and the Secretaría de Relaciones Exteriores (SRE, Secretariat of Foreign Affairs) of Mexico, on the Safe, Orderly, Dignified and Humane Repatriation of Mexican Nationals, signed on February 20, 2004 (DHS 2016).

The state level, however, is equally important. Perhaps the best government-to-government example is the U.S.-Mexico governors' conference. At its peak, the CSG facilitated meetings of governors of the four U.S. border states and their six Mexican counterparts hosted biennially in rotating states. According to the Texas Secretary of State, who kept formal documents from the Border Governors' Conference, some interest areas included agriculture, border crossings, economic development, education, environment, health, and tourism. Each of these sections showed a different number of recommendations and accomplishments (Texas Secretary of State n.d.). These meetings served as a forum to discuss topics ranging "from trade and cross-border violence to water rights and infrastructure needs" (Spagat 2011).

These multistate meetings, however, suffered both from diminishing interest by U.S. governors as time progressed and from Mexican governors who boycotted the conference in Arizona to protest governor Jan Brewer's anti-immigration laws. This allowed governors to take a stand on a matter that is typically handled at the federal level, where governors and mayors lack authority. To be sure, local authorities can meet "periodically to discuss issues like immigration and congested border crossings" (Spagat 2011), but they do not have the power to act, as the federal government has the monopoly over these issues.

Lately there have been challenges to federal authority, such as state laws on immigration and border security, many of which are contested in courts. Even so, not all states are friendly to border issues. Texas, for example, allocates approximately $800 million annually for "border security." Still, agencies too can individually facilitate cooperation, depending on the party in power and its ideological orientations.

The Council of State Governments West meetings, for example, called attention to problems and funding needs, sometimes from the federal governments. For instance, the U.S. Environmental Protection Agency (EPA) and its Mexican counterpart, the Secretaría de Medio Ambiente y Recursos Naturales (SEMARNAT, Secretariat of Environment and Natural Resources), collaborated on air quality in the region.

As the environmental chapter in this volume argues, the North American Free Trade Agreement (NAFTA) environmental side agreement created two institutions to address water, sanitation, and other infrastructure in the borderlands: the Border Environment Cooperation Commission (BECC) and the North American Development Bank (NADB/NADBANK), now consolidated under the latter. NADBANK even expanded its jurisdiction further south of the border.

States also establish agency-to-agency cooperation, such as when California provided ambient monitoring certification training for twenty Tijuana technicians (Texas Secretary of State n.d.). Another state-to-state example is the Arizona-Mexico Commission (AZMC). This commission is a regional nonprofit organization that seeks to improve the economic prosperity of the Arizona and Sonora area. The AZMC believes that through trade, Arizona and the U.S. economy will benefit from this binational partnership with Sonora's private and public sectors (AZMC n.d.). Its different areas of focus are advocacy, trade, networking, and information. The AZMC members seek to influence policy and decision-making in areas that impact the bilateral relationship, such as art, education, energy, environment and water, health services, security, tourism, transportation and infrastructure, among others.

Because AZMC tries to influence the decision-making process at the state and federal level, it does not receive funding from those two government levels but is funded through memberships and sponsorships with individual membership dues at $250 and sponsorships at levels from Copper at $1,500 to Diamond at $15,000. The Diamond Sponsorship includes a private dinner with the Arizona governor and the opportunity to travel with the governor and state officials to Mexico on trade missions (AZMC n.d.). Businesses, usually better organized and prepared to engage in binational cooperation albeit in a "pay-to-play" system, have become a powerful driving factor for governments to act and to facilitate cross-border commerce.

States have passed other important and significant agreements to improve their trade capabilities and even cross-national education efforts. At a fanfare ceremonial opening in 2014, the border governors of Chihuahua and New Mexico opened the Union Pacific Railroad's state-of-the-art Intermodal Transport facility, celebrating private-public funding and cooperation at all levels of both governments.[6] Border states often see counterpart states on the other side as more than neighbors, as trade is important for their economies. The states of New Mexico and Chihuahua developed a border master plan (DOT 2015). Realizing that they share an extensive borderline,

New Mexico and Chihuahua put together a plan to enhance the effectiveness of cross-border transportation facilities. The U.S.-Mexico Joint Working Committee on Transportation Planning (JWC) promotes this border master plan. The committee, composed mainly of several federal and state agencies, also operates with a policy advisory committee and technical working group in which local actors participate.

As for education, a successful program implemented at the University of Texas at El Paso by the Texas legislature in 1987 is the Programa de Asistencia Estudiantil (PASE, Student Assistance Program). This program allows "qualified Mexican citizens and permanent residents the opportunity to pay tuition at the Texas resident rate for undergraduate and graduate studies" (KVIA 2016). This program was designed to attract Mexican students who can demonstrate "financial need, meet admission requirements and maintain academic standing" (KVIA 2016). This program allows young Mexican citizens to achieve a degree and become bilingual in the best interests of the binational region, not just one side of the border. Available for more than thirty years, PASE has survived political changes in the state legislature, indicating that the program works and the benefits are visible.

Although nongovernmental, another example of government-to-government cooperation is the U.S.-Mexico Border Mayors Association, an international association of border mayors from Mexico and the United States. Since 2011 this organization has met to discuss issues like trade but also "economic development, industrial recruitment and border security" (USMBMA 2011, 1) in order to remain competitive in a global economy. Ultimately, one clear goal is to establish a recognized authority that can provide policy recommendations to state and federal legislatures as a unified voice with business issues at the helm. Some of the formal documents listed under the Border Mayors Association's website demonstrate its goals and capacities.[7] For instance, in 2011 the U.S. mayors signed a letter to the media where they tried to highlight how the initiative had been working and how investment in manpower, technology, and resources had led to a safer border. This letter also intended to separate the U.S. cities from the drug violence that their "sister cities" suffer. Another document, the 2010 Bilateral Action Plan, mentions that the top priorities will be binational infrastructure coordination; risk management; resumption to ensure coordination after emergency shutdowns, preclearance, prescreening, and pre-inspection of people, goods, and products in order to improve border crossing; cross-border commerce and ties; along with law enforcement and cooperation. If local governments cooperate among themselves more effectively, more power and authority will devolve to the local terrain. According to the Border Mayors Association, "It was obvious, from the panelist and the comments from the mayors, that bi-lateral relationships have largely ignored the needs of the border. On national levels, border communities have been left out of the debate. The national emphasis has only been on security not trade" (USMBMA 2017,

5). Once again, a common theme is trade, discussed at every level and a central issue. Both of the previously mentioned conferences tried to draw some power from the top. However, the agendas seem to be driven by business—the most effectively organized interest group. An important effort by these groups is highlighted under their charters, which is to develop sound policies for the region and to advocate for funding from the state and federal government. Among some of the proposed solutions for trade improvement, the binational group presented an innovative and creative freight shuttle system that could expedite cross-border freight transportation and address the community and commercial needs. However, the lack of funding has deterred mayors from traveling to and attending these meetings.

Federalism in Mexico does not facilitate the idea of cooperation. The Mexican government allocates most of its power at the federal level. This has left local governments with very little power and authority to negotiate and reach agreements with neighboring cities within their region. This issue of centralization is not new. Even Venustiano Carranza, a leader of the Mexican Revolution, governor of Coahuila, and president of Mexico, described Mexico's federal system as a central power that always imposes its will. Carranza's view of Mexico's system has remained accurate. In his view, the states are just instruments used to execute the orders and will that come directly from the center. During the nineteenth century, Mexico experienced an institutions crisis and the federalist system was not an exception. Despite many issues, the federal system has been upheld as one of the fundamental aspects of the constitution. In practice, if the federal and local governments are pitted against each other, the federal government's order will prevail.

In some instances, the evolution of the federalist system has been called federalism in theory but centralism in practice due to the growth of centralized power (Carbonell 1998). In terms of the postrevolutionary period, Article 73, which defines the powers vested to Congress and mentions some explicit powers, including the one that supersedes local governments' authority, has been reformed more than forty times since 1917 (Carbonell 1998). Most of those reforms only transferred more power to the federal government and against local authorities. To this day, in the event that a local proposal or agreement contradicts a federal approach, the federal government has the power to dismiss such agreements. Despite a more decentralized constitution, in practice the federal government has been able to maintain power over the local and state governments. More recently, the relationship of the federal government and the states has been called "coordinated federalism, or of cooperation" (Álvarez del Castillo and Farías 1990, 51, quoted in Valencia Carmona 2016, 376). Yet Mexico's governors, municipal presidents, and state legislators have participated in some of the nongovernmental binational cooperation efforts noted here, without barriers posed by the federal government.

At the federal level, Mexico's current president, Andrés Manuel López Obrador (AMLO), has spoken on different occasions about the relationship between the United States and Mexico. During López Obrador's campaign, he referred to the bilateral relationship as one that needs "mutual respect, friendship with the American people and cooperation for development in order to solve migration, security, and violence issues through well-being, not walls or militarization" (López Obrador 2018).

In addition, López Obrador pushed for a border "free zone." This zone, which covers the entire length of the U.S.-Mexico border and is twenty-five kilometers (15.5 miles) wide, will allow some fiscal incentives in the aforementioned border towns (SRE 2018). These fiscal incentives will allow cities to double the minimum wage, decrease taxes, and sell fuels at the same prices as their U.S. neighbors (Morales 2019). This proposal will reduce income taxes from 30 percent to 20 percent and the Value Added Tax (VAT) for items coming into the country from 16 percent to 8 percent. In terms of the minimum wage, it will increase to 176 pesos (US$8.80) per day. While this increases the wages 100 percent, the wages remain significantly lower than the U.S. counterparts. AMLO believes that "it is a very important project for winning investment, creating jobs and taking advantage of the economic strength of the United States" (Nikolewski 2019).

Furthermore, López Obrador addressed the border in his first government report ("Primer Informe de Gobierno 2018–2019"). He discussed Mexico's disposition to improve the lives of Mexican citizens through cooperation and development. He also expressed his desire to pass and ratify the United States-Mexico-Canada Agreement (USMCA) in order to improve commercial and financial ties with the United States. In terms of border development, López Obrador spoke about binational coordination in order to expand, improve, and foster competitiveness and prosperity. In order to do so, there was an expansion in the Palomas–Columbus international port of entry and modernization at the Reynosa–Pharr point of entry. Investment in these areas will help boost bilateral trade (López Obrador 2019).

From this consideration of ways that the federal and state frameworks shape municipal governments, we now move to compare local governments and, following that, examine models for binational cooperation and governance.

Political Institutions: Democratic Deficit in the Borderlands?

We can observe differences across the entire U.S.-Mexico border, including within institutions, especially types of government and their sizes. In Mexico, a single local government exists, called the cabildo, while in the United States these local units of government are called cities, towns, villages, and county commissioners' courts (legislative bodies, not in the judicial sense). Elections on the Mexican side are partisan. Thus, Mexican municipalities operate under partisanship rules to select members of their cabildo with proportional representation, plurality, or a combination of these two as a selection method. In the United States, they are mostly nonpartisan, based on the so-called progressive reforms of nearly a century ago. For instance, people vote for individuals and not political parties at the local level.

U.S. local governments vary from city council to county commissions and have different management styles. These legislative bodies are open, generate decent attendance (depending on the issue), and, in big cities, can be streamed online and posted as videos on city websites. Minutes are recorded (and approved at subsequent meetings), and agendas must be posted publicly three days in advance.

Across all these borderland municipalities, we observe that seats are filled via proportional representation (PR) (Mexico), single-member district (SMD), or even at-large representation (United States) (see Tables 5.1 and 5.2). Structures like these have consequences for residents' access to representatives, issue-oriented frameworks, and the diversity of council members. Mexican positions are filled on two-, three-, or four-year terms that rarely match the changes in the cast of characters on the neighboring side of the border. Elected officials' salaries in local governments seem overly generous compared to both middle-class salaries in their cities and those in the United States. Few members of the public, if any, attend the public meetings. Thus, when the nongovernmental organization Plan Estratégico de Juárez (Strategic Plan of Juárez) began videotaping meetings—highlighting absenteeism, lack of quorum, and superficial discussion—the oversight seemed to incentivize more reasonable and transparent behavior.[8] The states of Baja California, Sonora, Chihuahua, and Tamaulipas hold these elections every three years, while Coahuila is the exception, holding them every other year. Out of these municipalities, Tijuana has an established border committee that works with its northern neighbors, as does a revived border relations committee in El Paso, while Nuevo Laredo recently instituted one.

Another important aspect to keep in mind is voter turnout (see Tables 5.3 and 5.4). Different electoral rules in these two countries were collected from the last municipal election, though we did not consider the 2016 U.S. presidential election because it would drive up numbers compared to midterm or off-year elections in places with November local government elections. The central interest was in the extent to which people vote for their local representatives, which in turn could potentially intervene to create binational institutions. Participation is uniformly low in most U.S. border cities, except for San Diego, with the highest turnout of 35.52 percent and more similar to Tijuana's turnout. In Texas, since 2018, city and county elections are held in November, along with other state and national elections, likely to increase turnout

TABLE 5.1 Representation in Mexican border cities

City	Number of regidores	Partisan/ nonpartisan	Proportional Representation (PR)	Terms	Border relations committee
Acuña	13	Partisan	9 Plurality / 4 PR	2 years	No
Agua Prieta	6	Partisan	4 Plurality / 2 PR	3 years	No
Camargo	4	Partisan	Plurality	3 years	No
Ciudad Guerrero	6	Partisan	4 Plurality / 2 PR	3 years	No
Ciudad Miguel Alemán	6	Partisan	4 Plurality / 2 PR	3 years	No
Ciudad Juárez	18	Partisan	PR	3 years	No
Matamoros	21	Partisan	14 Plurality and 7 PR	3 years	No
Mexicali	15	Partisan	PR	3 years	No
Mier	6	Partisan	4 Plurality / 2 PR	3 years	No
Naco	5	Partisan	3 Plurality / 2 PR	3 years	No
Nogales	20	Partisan	12 Plurality / 8 PR	3 years	No
Nuevo Laredo	21	Partisan	14 Plurality and 7 PR	3 years	Yes
Ojinaga	14	Partisan	8 Plurality / 6 PR	3 years	No
Palomas	10	Partisan	6 Plurality / 4 PR	3 years	No
Piedras Negras	10	Partisan	Plurality	2 years	No
Reynosa	21	Partisan	14 Plurality and 7 PR	3 years	No
San Luis Río Colorado	21	Partisan	PR	3 years	No
Tecate	10	Partisan	PR	3 years	No
Tijuana	16	Partisan	PR	3 years	Yes

Source: INAFED n.d.

rates. Voters in all northern Mexico municipalities turn out at double-digit rates of 30 percent or more. El Paso's extremely low turnout rate of 8.34 percent in pre-2018 elections calls into question the legitimacy of democratic elections. One might question whether improper practices produce higher voter turnout rates in Mexico, albeit this is an issue we cannot verify here.

An institutional issue of concern involves organizations connecting individuals to government with identity and/or issue-oriented policy frameworks, political parties, and organizations. Democracy theorists have long recognized the importance of intermediary organizations like political parties, raising questions about the supposed professionalism associated with century-old U.S. moves toward nonpartisan local gov-

TABLE 5.2 Representation in U.S. border cities

City	Type of council	Number of members	Partisan/ nonpartisan	Border relations committee
Brownsville	City commission	6 council members	Nonpartisan	No
Calexico	City council	3 council members	Nonpartisan	No
Del Rio	City council	6 council members	Nonpartisan	No
Eagle Pass	City council	4 council members	Nonpartisan	No
El Paso	City council	8 council members	Nonpartisan	Yes
Laredo	City council	8 council members	Nonpartisan	Yes
Los Ebanos	City commission under Hidalgo County	4 council members	Nonpartisan	No
McAllen	City council	6 council members	Nonpartisan	No
Nogales	City council	5 council members and 1 vice mayor	Nonpartisan	No
San Diego	County commission— board of supervisors	5 counties for board of supervisors	Nonpartisan	Yes
Tecate	Under San Diego Council			

Source: Data from each county's website, July 2017.

ernment elections. With the so-called professionalism comes a growth in city bureaucracy and unelected officials, like city managers, their deputies, and city attorneys, who shape the decision-making process. One must also look at who funds local campaigns for candidates. According to an analysis of publicly posted campaign donation information on El Paso's mayor and city council, costly elections tend to be funded primarily by wealthy Anglo developers and contractors, with four of eight city council representatives dependent on big donors of $1,000 or more for one-half to three-quarters of total funds in 2018, thus raising questions about a "pay-to-play" system that masks elite dominance as democracy (Staudt 2020b). Yet in Mexico, despite party "representation," without district-based elections and with party-driven neighborhood groups (the efficacy of which varies based on the party in power), urban spaces often lack effective routine oversight and interaction with their local governments. Mexico is home to a multiparty system, while the U.S. political structure usually produces two major parties along with "third-parties," often considered throwaway votes in presidential elections because the United States lacks direct votes for president (it holds indirect elections, via the Electoral College).

The media play a key role in the oversight of local governments and the ability or failure to pursue binational cooperation. The coverage given to council meetings and,

TABLE 5.3 Voter turnout in Mexican border cities

Election year	City	Registered voters	Participation	Participation percentage
2017	Acuña	104,651	58,861	56.25
2017	Piedras Negras	120,810	65,552	54.26
2016	Camargo	12,788	7,157	55.97
2016	Ciudad Guerrero	2,742	1,586	57.84
2016	Ciudad Juárez	1,031,373	428,639	41.56
2016	Ciudad Miguel Alemán	20,156	12,238	60.72
2016	Matamoros	385,211	190,409	49.43
2016	Mexicali	594,785	195,975	32.95
2016	Mier	4,405	2,769	62.86
2016	Nuevo Laredo	299,617	146,482	48.89
2016	Ojinaga	22,139	11,692	52.81
2016	Palomas	17,764	8,090	45.54
2016	Reynosa	488,143	231,477	47.42
2016	Tecate	72,753	27,163	37.34
2016	Tijuana	1,089,004	348,023	31.96
2015	Agua Prieta	60,686	29,521	48.65
2015	Naco	4,411	3,032	68.74
2015	Nogales	175,374	74,533	42.50
2015	San Luis Río Colorado	139,009	53,996	38.84

Source: Data from INE n.d.

if applicable, border committees across the border also signals accountability and relevance. In an analysis of articles published in Mexican border cities in February 2016, the results are not flattering (see Table 5.5). Few articles exist, and in Mexico, many newspapers do not print letters to the editor, in which ordinary citizens might call into question local government practices. With a focus on northern Mexico media, Ciudad Juárez, Ciudad Guerrero, and Tijuana are the ones that publish more articles on their cabildos. Only in Tijuana, Nuevo Laredo, and Ciudad Juárez did articles mention border relations.

In U.S. border cities, the English-language results show more coverage of local government, largely because of property-tax decision-making, which gives voters and media readers strong stakes in the process (see Table 5.6). The *El Paso Times* once assigned a reporter to cover city council meetings, but subscribership has shrunk and editorial direction and content often come from the news conglomerate Gannett,

TABLE 5.4 Voter turnout in U.S. border cities

Election year	City	Registered voters	Participation	Participation percentage
2017	Calexico	10,616	2,018	19.01
2017	El Paso	418,665	34,897	8.34
2017	McAllen	N/A	7,675	N/A
2014	Brownsville	N/A	8,227	N/A
2014	Del Rio	26,447	8,121	30.71
2014	Eagle Pass	28,852	5,292	18.34
2014	Laredo	N/A	24,102	N/A
2013	Nogales	544	138	25.37
2013	San Diego	683,370	242,747	35.52
2013	Tecate	Under San Diego County		

Source: Data from each county's website, July 2017.

TABLE 5.5 Articles on border relations, Mexican border cities, February 2016

City	Articles about cabildo	Articles about border relations
Acuña	4	0
Agua Prieta	0	0
Camargo	0	0
Ciudad Guerrero	7	0
Ciudad Juárez	8	2
Ciudad Miguel Alemán	0	0
Matamoros	1	0
Mexicali	4	0
Mier	0	0
Naco	0	0
Nogales	0	0
Nuevo Laredo	4	3
Ojinaga	0	0
Palomas	0	0
Piedras Negras	2	0
Reynosa	3	0
San Luis Río Colorado	0	0
Tecate	0	0
Tijuana	5	2

Source: Duran 2016.

TABLE 5.6 Articles on border relations, U.S. border cities, February 2016

City	Articles about city council	Articles about board of supervisors	Articles about border relations
Brownsville	0	5	0
Calexico	0	0	0
Del Rio	6	13	0
Eagle Pass	2	2	0
El Paso	17	0	4
Laredo	8	14	0
Los Ebanos	0	0	0
McAllen	6	4	0
Nogales	7	6	0
San Diego	23	4	0
Tecate	0	0	0

Source: Duran 2016.

which publishes *USA Today*. (Spanish-language media in the United States do a better job of covering Mexico, largely because counterpart or co-owned media cover similar stories on both sides.) English-language media in San Diego have the most coverage out of the entire list, followed by El Paso. El Paso's articles on border relations involve the unique visit of Pope Francis to the border in February 2016.

The lack of reporting and exposure leads us to believe that coverage is superficial, unhelpful to readers, and rarely attentive to border matters. This is problematic because it signals a lack of accountability and interest. In order for formal institutions and nongovernmental organizations (NGOs) to push for and supply greater binational involvement, there must be some demand from residents and readers. If people do not know what is going on or do not indicate that binational cooperation is important, then it becomes more complicated to reach and improve binational ties.

To summarize, clearly local governments offer important examples of the democratic deficit in the borderlands, where border residents are left with little voice except voting in low-turnout elections, and in El Paso, where elections face excessive influence from businesses and their campaign donations. In the first section of this chapter, we analyzed how the United States and Mexico enact legislation at the federal level that affects the border region, with priorities and agendas set in Washington, D.C., and Mexico City. Often, Memoranda of Understanding (MOUs) are distributed across departmental agencies, focused on migration, climate change, health, security, and trade (as other chapters have discussed). Typically, national security trumps other laws. At the local level, cities often depend on what happens to their neighboring cities. In the nations' capitals, the priorities are different. Cooperation is not a zero-sum game; a gain on one side should not be a loss for the other side. Instead, through formal channels and institutions, cooperation can translate into positive dividends for both sides of the border. In "Border Narratives in a Neoliberal Era," Staudt mentions that "institution-building at the border must embrace border people and their local legislative council/*cabildo* representatives in a public format. Business alone cannot speak for employees, consumers, and the unemployed. Local elected officials should interact regularly through border relations committees with appointed members of the public from all walks of life" (2020a, 252). Do models exist for binational cooperation? We discuss these next.

Current or Proposed Solutions: Best Practices, Ideas, and Programs

We will now discuss some of the government-to-government efforts followed by some current solutions, as implemented in three borderlands regions. We have detected regions or areas with adequate practices, ideas, and programs, such as the Cali-Baja model from the San Diego–Tijuana communities. Moreover, it is also worth mentioning that the Paso del Norte region of El Paso, Texas, revived its local border committee, which once attempted to partially perform a similar function as the Cali-Baja one. These committees are composed of members of the city council, the mayor, and/or their appointees from the community. Although federal and state policies affect binational cooperation or alienation, we believe that the best way to promote and achieve true cooperation is at the local level, where some leadership, autonomy, and initiative exist.

We analyzed these pairs of cities across the border with partnerships, resources, and means to interact with their counterpart. Among our cases, we can distinguish how certain city dyads are more effective in providing good governance when they are able to reach across the border and work together for the region. Of course, in dyads with a clear lack of cooperation, cities are stuck with some one-size-fits-all decisions imposed by the federal government. Some municipalities face legal constraints from their state government, such as what Payan (2010) found for establishing and fostering a relationship between El Paso and Ciudad Juárez. During those efforts, the Texas Open Meetings Act was a significant legal obstacle for these tristate meetings because city councils cannot meet outside their jurisdiction. While the 2007 effort was well received by the media and the public, it produced very little because it did not restructure the relationships in the region. Thus, for more impactful change, there is a need of structural and formal changes, not just sporadic or periodic instances of cooperation between local governments and interest groups.

San Diego–Tijuana: A Binational Model of Institutional Cooperation

Even though some issues cannot be addressed solely at the local level, and despite the fact that most cooperation is controlled at the federal level, the "main achievements of cross-border economic cooperation have been accomplished by local private organizations" (Mendoza 2017, 44), and San Diego and Tijuana have shown outstanding willingness to cooperate. According to Lawrence Herzog and Christophe Sohn, "There are important local and regional government agencies that intervene in favour of cross-border cooperation and economic development—these include the San Diego Regional Economic Development Corporation, the Cali-Baja Binational Mega-Region, the Tijuana Economic Development Council, the City and County of San Diego, the municipality of Tijuana, the San Diego Association of Governments (SANDAG), the Metropolitan Transit System (San Diego), and the California Department of Transportation (CALTRANS), among others" (2019, 186). It is worth mentioning that these agencies operate locally, as opposed to some of the larger binational organizations that spring from the federal government. An important example of one of the former groups is the California-Baja California Master Plan, which was drafted in 2008 and is the first of its kind for any U.S. and Mexican states. The plan's purpose is to "coordinate a cooperative approach to the development and planning of all major POEs [ports of entry] along the California-Baja California border. It seeks to permanently institutionalize the planning process" (Herzog and Sohn 2019, 190).

The Cali-Baja region is a case of cooperation and positive relationship across cities, buttressed by state governments. In this region, one can see Tijuana's municipal president attending a city council meeting in San Diego (San Diego Red 2017), a binational meeting for *regidores* and council members (Gómez 2014), and even San Diego's border relations office in Tijuana (Dibble 2013). The San Diego–Tijuana case contains different projects, such as the economic development forum, the planning and coordination committee, marketing/development, tourism promotion, and the recycling market development zone (City of San Diego n.d.). By actively promoting some of these activities, such as tourism, the cities market themselves as a region, not as individuals, and they seek to attract people. This is an example of how cities can win on both sides by cooperating. Moreover, according to council president Mario López, the binational office has been successful and approved by the civil societies and business leaders on both sides of the border (Dibble 2013). Thus, this border relation appears solid. Bob Filner, the San Diego mayor who backed this initiative, had to resign, but the binational office remained open and had full support from the city council and other important figures. This is an example of how a well-established office with a clear purpose can be accepted and survives changes in political office.

The San Diego Regional Chamber of Commerce is an organization that is currently under the leadership of Jerry Sanders, former San Diego mayor. Its goal is to make the San Diego region business friendly, and its committee provides networking, development, and access to business leaders and policy makers. Among its priorities, the Chamber of Commerce has listed NAFTA, immigration reform, the Tijuana River Valley pollution, and border infrastructure and efficiency. Moreover, among its accomplishments, the Chamber of Commerce signed an MOU with Mexico's Senate in which it agreed to the opening of "PedWest Southbound, improving the efficient movement of the 63,000 pedestrians crossing each day" (San Diego Regional Chamber of Commerce n.d.). Overall, the management council is composed of mainly business leaders. Therefore, one can expect that the priority of the group will be related to trade as opposed to other local issues.

In addition, Tijuana and San Diego were included as part of a game theory model study. Linda Fernandez (2013) discusses environmental cooperation between the United States (San Diego) and Mexico (Tijuana). In this study, the author examines water pollution and the actions and reactions by binational institutions in the United States and Mexico. A key discussion is on asymmetries in damages, budgets, and abatement costs between the two countries. The three game theory scenarios include the Nash Equilibrium (NE), a noncooperation game of unilateral decision-making; a cooperation game with water monitoring and information sharing for decisions; and a Stackelberg game with formal financial channels for one country separate from decisions for wastewater pollution reduction of each country. This study demonstrates that "cooperation is optimal for minimizing costs, damages and steady-state pollution stock to lowest levels" (Fernandez 2013, 34). Furthermore, the Stackelberg game "improves considerably the situation for both the US and Mexico compared to the non-cooperative Nash Equilibrium (NE)" (34). This study describes an environmental issue, but cooperation across cities, states, and nations could also alleviate social or economic problems. In fact, Niles Hansen believes that border development requires local and regional cooperation in order to deal with social and economic problems. Frequently, local actors become pivotal players because "local and binational interests do not fit in nation-state logic" (quoted in Tentori and Almaraz Alvarado 2015, 185), and in some cases, "cooperation webs emerge as a response to failed central authorities" (189). In other cases, formal institutions actually silence voices. Therefore, it is pivotal that the private sector contributes and allows for other voices to be heard. In the San Diego–Tijuana area, there are forty organizations with a presence on both sides of the border—most of them from the private sector (205).

San Diego and Tijuana have become a model of good cooperation because, for instance, they have worked together to create a space for people to enjoy themselves.

In order to revitalize Tijuana's downtown area and make walking into Tijuana safer and shorter, there has been a development of cultural venues, restaurants, bars, cafés, and other facilities. The funding source for this project came from government, both Tijuana's municipal government and Baja California's state government, but could not have been possible without the support of the Consejo de Desarrollo Económico de Tijuana (CDT, Economic Development Council of Tijuana), a private sector planning group (Dibble 2017). Some might argue that this is not a successful case or that the relationship between the two cities is not even friendly. Glen Sparrow says that the relationship between San Diego and Tijuana is driven by economics, not trust or friendship, and therefore he doubts that this could be considered a binational city or region. Among his arguments, Sparrow (2001, 73) claims that the clash of cultures, economies, and governments is complex. Moreover, citing Nicole Ehlers and Jan Buurskink, he defines binational cities as "those double cities that are 'divided' by a national border, that share a common hinterland and whose inhabitants have a sense of belonging together" (Ehlers and Buurskink 2000, 187, quoted in Sparrow 2001, 82). According to Sparrow, San Diego and Tijuana have a long way before they can meet this criterion; he instead classifies them as "separate cities within sovereign nations that exhibit numerous asymmetries" (2001, 82).

El Paso–Ciudad Juárez: A Model of Constraints and Limited Cooperation

The Paso Del Norte region is an interesting case, because as much as the region is interdependent, there is no institution similar to the one in the Cali-Baja region. However, a strong binational, tristate business organization exists: the Borderplex Alliance, which drives some of the economic development strategies in the region. The Borderplex Alliance is an NGO with steep annual membership fees ranging from the young entrepreneur rate of $1,000 to $250,000 for capstone investors. (For more detail on its binational influence, see Staudt 2020b.)

In 2018 the city of El Paso reestablished the Committee on Border Relations, which was dormant from 2011 until 2018. This committee, which works "with the Mayor and with interested organization and individuals in El Paso and Ciudad Juarez, shall consider issues and projects affecting the development or relations between the two communities, and affecting the border and the area in proximity to El Paso, and shall make recommendations to the City Council and the Binational Task Force or successor entity of the latter on programs or projects to enhance and benefit the relations between the two communities" (City of El Paso n.d. ["Committee on Border Relations"]).

In the past, the committee's main function—the development of relations between the two communities—was often overlooked or ignored. Aside from these functions, the border relations committee absorbed the duties of another committee related to international cooperation. The International Bridge Commission's main function (in 2009 its duties were transferred to the dormant border relations committee) was to make recommendations to the city council and the mayor on "matters affecting the aesthetic appearance, safety and efficient flow of people and commerce across the international bridges in El Paso" (City of El Paso n.d. ["International Bridge Commission"]). According to the committee's agenda, on March 4, 2008, despite the increase of violence in Ciudad Juárez, the city of El Paso wanted to work on projects such as a binational committee with Ciudad Juárez, a meeting of city councils, a border mayors' conference with an international affairs table, and even projects on binational art, industry, and customs.

Staudt served on El Paso's border relations committee for a year and a half, 2018–19. To provide insight—ethnographic and participant observation style—Staudt encountered a nearly invisible operation hamstrung by many rules, frequent turnover by the economic development staff assigned to oversee the committee, and finally a city manager– and mayor-imposed Code of Conduct in 2019 that forbid city elected officials, volunteers, and political appointees (like herself) to disagree with official policies—that is, in this case, the city's economic development plan. After resigning several months before her term was over, Staudt concluded that more advances could occur through NGOs, informal cross-border networks, and the nonprofit community foundations in both cities.

While the federal governments typically focus on national security issues or trade, it is important that these two cities tried to work on their regional priorities and interests. Furthermore, more recently the cabildo of Ciudad Juárez and El Paso's city council have tried to work on creative and constructive solutions for binational cooperation. For instance, in June 2017, Ciudad Juárez's council prepared a special session to welcome El Paso's city hall as a guest. However, due to issues with their agenda, El Paso had to cancel. This special session got canceled days before the Ciudad Juárez cabildo met to discuss the agenda, which was supposed to include relevant topics for both cities. According to Roberto Rentería Manqueros, the city's secretary, the purpose of this meeting was to strengthen the communication avenues that currently exist with representatives of the neighboring city (Herrera 2017).

It is clear that the Paso del Norte region is not the best example of successful binational cooperation. Evidence shows attempts to create and empower local institutions. This case shows some willingness and efforts by both local governments to establish formal institutions to improve the conditions of El Pasoans and Juarenses. Ciudad Juárez and El Paso have tried to rekindle some formal government-to-government type of cooperation alongside some business-led efforts. In the Paso del Norte region, investors have decided to pursue a similar strategy as in the Tijuana area. In El Paso, local investors have a plan to attract more people and make the area more welcoming. This is an important area because it is located near the international port of entry with

Ciudad Juárez. In a joint city council meeting, representatives from El Paso and Ciudad Juárez pledged to work together in this project. Ciudad Juárez has a multimillion-dollar investment in what it calls a "safety-corridor," where the police monitor the streets. Furthermore, local leaders have decided to join forces and work together to improve the conditions of their historic downtown areas. Instead of creating two separate projects, politicians want to attract people from both sides of the border and boost local businesses. Moreover, both cities are also promoting this joint venture online. One of the objectives is to promote the area for visitors and tourists from El Paso through the website Oh Yes Juárez. According to José Arturo Ramos Andujo, Ciudad Juárez's director of projects, there is reciprocity between the two cities as they promote activities on both sides of the border (*Juárez a Diario* 2015; Montes 2017).

In 2017 Ciudad Juárez and El Paso decided to host a joint session in order to improve relations between the two cities in the Paso del Norte region. This meeting, which all El Paso representatives and twenty city officials from Ciudad Juárez attended to discuss a binational route to improve the region's economic ties, lasted just under two hours (Nylander 2017). Among issues that council members want to tackle are the misconceptions that surround the border region and, in the words of El Paso's mayor, Dee Margo, the desire to accentuate "that we are truly one region" (Pérez 2017). Moreover, this agreement will lead to binational cultural activities, tourism, health, and transportation, among other areas. Another positive example of binational cooperation at the local level was documented on December 5, 2017. The Rio Grande Economics Association monthly luncheon/speaker series hosted the International Bridges for the City of El Paso with Roberto Tinajero, economist, and David Coronado, assistant director. An important topic of discussion was the reduction of wait times—a high-priority, high-cost item. In this meeting, Tinajero discussed a partnership between the city of El Paso and U.S. Customs and Border Protection (CBP) for staff and overtime, which began as a multimillion-dollar pilot program approved by El Paso's city council. This program is paid for by increases in bridge tolls (fifty cents per pedestrian and fifty cents per axle for vehicles, with the average truck having five axles). In the past, these funds would go to the city's discretionary funds, but they are now redirected to the improvements in bridges and traffic and largely paid for by cargo truck traffic. The city and region benefit from business retention and expansion. With this in mind, another initiative is the binational monthly meeting of the Bridges Steering Committee with stakeholders from both sides—agency and business operational (not policy-maker) people. The Bridges Steering Committee conducts north- and south-bound mapping and identifies improvement projects in traffic flow and signage. It envisions the binational committee as a working group on "simple projects to benefit traffic." Coronado mentioned that some Ciudad Juárez municipal and State of Chihuahua funding is paying for overtime and kiosks near the Aduana flow for cargo trucks.

Other studies have focused on similar issues. For instance, Kathleen Staudt and Pamela Cruz (2014) consider links between businesses and local governments in the Paso del Norte region. Their analysis suggests that business leaders also struggle at the local level due to federal constraints, since the national capitals have different priorities. Thus, one can see a trade-off between security and the economy. Moreover, as one of their interviewees said, if "everyone would leave us alone, we'd get a lot done" (Staudt and Cruz 2014) because the national centers do not understand border dynamics as well as the local governments do, or, as another interviewee said, they "work as a region." Furthermore, the issue of federalism is explained by Staudt and Cruz by placing some of the burden of border issues on centralization with policies made so far from the border. They also allude to the incapacity of local authorities, such as the mayor (*presidente municipal*), to make decisions. Other interviewees commented on the availability and the difficulty in obtaining federal resources, the changes in administration (the immediate-no-succession constitution principle, with no civil service), and policy changes that make it difficult for border business to thrive.

Not all past efforts have been welcomed or approved by the other levels of government. In the past, Texas governor Greg Abbott has mentioned that this is not the "United States of Municipalities," in reference to "certain standards that must be met before which local municipalities or counties can establish new regulations" (Svitek 2017). On a similar note, Beto O'Rourke and Susie Byrd, El Paso council members at the time, described an event where the federal and state government squashed an attempt by the local government to take a different measure on an existing issue. In an attempt to have an honest and open discussion about the War on Drugs and the violence in Ciudad Juárez, council members voted for a resolution, which passed unanimously. The mayor vetoed this resolution later that day because he was confronted by Austin and Washington, D.C., and threatened with withholdings of state and federal funds. Following the same direction as the mayor, Silvestre Reyes, El Paso's congressman at the time, asked council members not to move forward with the resolution or they would face some consequences with the funding (O'Rourke and Byrd 2011, 16–17).

Laredo and Nuevo Laredo: A New Beginning

Laredo, Texas, and Nuevo Laredo, Tamaulipas, have officially begun to host four binational committees where the main topics to discuss will be culture, art, education, security, economic development, and sustainability that will benefit both cities. According to a recent article, both the Laredo mayor and the Nuevo Laredo municipal president named the members of each binational committee. One of the goals is to improve infrastructure to offer better transportation across the border and allow residents to enjoy "medical attention, the gastronomy, and recreational areas" (Cárdenas

2017). The main objective of these commissions is to collaborate across cities for a common goal. These committees will meet a minimum of two times per month. As of March 27, 2019, some binational meetings have taken place in order to discuss strategies and projects (*El Mañana de Nuevo Laredo* 2019). Their responsibility is to identify projects that benefit both cities. Only announced on August 19, 2017, it is still early to determine if these new commissions will have a positive outcome for the Laredo region.

Thus far, we have analyzed some cases that show successful and somewhat successful binational institutions at the local level. In the concluding section, we will discuss recommendations for governing bodies of our borderlands.

Conclusions and Recommendations for Better Governance of Our Borderlands

After analyzing some pairs of binational communities with contrasting local government institutions on each side and their limited interactions, it is clear that much is missing in efforts to foster quality governing of the borderlands commons. With federal governments that dominate border policies and that trump most issues in favor of national security, representatives from local governments and municipalities lack seats at the negotiating table, and too few border congressional representatives are able to mount counternarratives of cooperation. However, the efforts of El Pasoans in the Sixteenth Texas District, congresswoman Verónica Escobar and former congressman Beto O'Rourke, offer notable exceptions in their accurate counternarratives, especially with the harsh U.S. asylum-seeker policies in 2018 and thereafter, which prevented scores of thousands of refugees from crossing in the central borderlands under the misnomer "Migrant Protection Policy." Our assessment of U.S.-Mexico local institutions is that they offer few or weak models for constructive binational institution building in the borderlands. Perhaps the only available case that demonstrates an attempt to build local institutions that foster cooperation in our borderlands commons at the local level can be found in the Cali-Baja area. However, even these examples (like the Borderplex Alliance of the central borderlands) are oriented to business and/or infrastructure for trade rather than also for more comprehensive concerns. Clearly, far more research is necessary to analyze and unpack local governments, civil society, media, and participation in the U.S.-Mexico borderlands. We have begun only a superficial but hopefully pioneering start that will lead to more research and action, especially to build and sustain binational relationships among people involving comprehensive policy issues rather than business and trade alone. In conclusion, we make the following recommendations based on findings from this chapter.

- Initiate binational committees in local government legislative bodies and foster regular interaction in them and between local councils, providing them with seed funding to initiate pilot projects.
- Establish and staff offices in city/municipal governments to liaise with the neighboring side.
- Press for better coverage of binational issues in local print and social media, in both English and Spanish, highlighting successes in cooperation. Publish regular op eds and blogs on binational topics that foster interest in our borderlands commons.
- Instigate and fund fact-finding missions to develop ways to increase voter participation when turnout rates (i.e., *abstencionismo* [abstentionism]) fall below 30 percent.
- Build interest and capacity at the state level for fostering local binational relationships. States like California, Arizona, and New Mexico have forged ahead, while Texas remains behind and reliant on funding the border security narrative. (Staudt 2016)
- Use billboards and public space (such as on the border fences/walls) to draw messages that foster cooperation on both sides of the border. The United States should follow Mexico's lead in facilitating beautiful artwork on the fence, especially on the Baja California side of the border. (This may require pressure on the Department of Homeland Security.)
- Foster corporate cultures of social responsibility and civic engagement toward shared prosperity in our borderlands commons. Establish fees for youth and ordinary residents to foster voice and participation that go beyond "pay-to-play" business organizations.[9]
- Renew the spirit of federalism in both self-proclaimed federal systems so that local governments exercise the genuine authority and financial resource base supposedly accorded them.
- With support from regional trade negotiators, establish goals and timetables to foster policy interventions that reduce inequalities in wages and GDP per capita for one of the most unequal borderlands in the world.

Notes

All translations are ours unless otherwise indicated.

1. Population figures are from Staudt and Coronado 2002, drawing on both countries and their 2000 censuses of *municipios* (Mexico) and counties (United States).
2. The results of these surveys, carried out by Arizona Public Radio and the *Dallas Morning News*, most notably illustrate borderlanders' interest in cooperation and interaction without walls. See Univision PR Team 2016. Parts of the "Border Perceptions Index" 2018 study, coordinated by Josiah Heyman, Eva Ross, and Mario Porras, have been summarized

in Acosta 2019. The word *borderlanders* sounds less awkward in Spanish: *fronterizos/ fronterzas/fronterizxs*.

3. Moré used 2004 GDP per capita and purchasing power parity figures to analyze two hundred borders, while Staudt used 2014 GDP per capita, purchasing power parity, and constant dollar figures to analyze pairs of three hundred land borders, with the former Moré analysis locating the U.S.-Mexico border in the bottom twenty-four and the later Staudt analysis in the bottom forty.

4. We traveled along the entire east-to-west border, generating a large digitized picture database of art and billboards in public space focused on border themes.

5. In *Threshold: Emergency Responders on the US-Mexico Border*, Ieva Jusionyte (2018) documents strong informal cooperation between firefighters and emergency responders on both sides of Ambos Nogales in the Arizona-Sonora borderlands as well as the border city of Douglas, Arizona, which paid minimum sums so that firefighters could cross the border in insured vehicles to assist in emergencies and avoid personal liability (often a deterrent in other borderlands).

6. Staudt (2014) attended this grand event and wrote about it for *Newspaper Tree* soon thereafter.

7. Although the association's website is now defunct, some of its historical documents are maintained online by the Center for U.S.-Mexican Studies at UC San Diego.

8. For more on Plan Estratégico de Juárez, see the main website, accessed August 20, 2017, http://www.planjuarez.org, or the website of RegidorMX (a project of the plan), accessed May 17, 2020, https://planjuarez.org/regidormx-juarez/.

9. For example, the Borderplex Alliance in the central borderlands charges annual fees that range from $1,000 to $250,000, clearly beyond the limits of what most people are able to pay.

References

Acosta, Laura. 2019. "UTEP and El Paso Community Foundation Collaborate on Binational Survey." UTEP Communications, June 25. https://www.utep.edu/newsfeed/campus/UTEP -and-El-Paso-Community-Foundation-Collaborate-on-Binational-Survey.html.

Álvarez del Castillo, Enrique, and Urbano Farías. 1990. "El federalismo como decisión política fundamental del pueblo mexicano." In *México: 75 años de Revolución*, vol. 3, *Política*. Mexico City: Fondo de Cultura Económica.

Arizona-Mexico Commission (AZMC). n.d. "Arizona-Mexico Commission." Accessed December 20, 2017. https://www.azmc.org/about-us/.

Carbonell, Miguel. 1998. "El Estado Federal en la Constitución Mexicana: Una introducción a su problemática." *Boletín Mexicano de Derecho Comparado* 1 (91): 81–106.

Cárdenas, Alma. 2017. "Oficializan la conformación de los comités binacionales." *CML Noticias*, August 18. https://www.conmilupanoticias.com/?p=23867, http://primeravuelta.com /2017/08/19/oficializan-la-conformacion-de-los-comites-binacionales/.

Celata, Filippo, Raffaella Coletti, and Venere Stefania Sanna. 2013. "La cooperación trans-fronteriza en la región del Trifinio y la difusión de modelos europeos de gobernanza de las fronteras en América Latina." *Si Somos Americanos, Revista de Estudios Transfronterizos* 13 (2): 165–89.

City of El Paso. n.d. "Committee on Border Relations." Accessed September 29, 2019. http://legacy.elpasotexas.gov/muni_clerk/detail.asp?id=22.

City of El Paso. n.d. "International Bridge Commission." Accessed August 20, 2017. http://legacy.elpasotexas.gov/muni_clerk/detail.asp?id=49.

City of San Diego. n.d. "Economic Development." Accessed August 15, 2017. https://www.sandiego.gov/economic-development/sandiego/trade/mexico/binational.

Council of State Governments (CSG). n.d. "U.S.–Mexico State Alliance Partnership Partner Information." Accessed May 14, 2020. http://www.csgwest.org/programs/usmex-partners.aspx.

Dibble, Sandra. 2013. "Council President: Tijuana-San Diego Relations Still Strong." *San Diego Union-Tribune*, August 7.

Dibble. Sandra. 2017. "Tijuana Launches $13 Million Plan to Improve Pedestrians' First Sight of the City." *Los Angeles Times*, December 25.

Duran, Lucero. 2016. "Final Paper." Unpublished paper written under the supervision of Kathleen Staudt, University of Texas at El Paso, May.

Ehlers, N., and J. Buursink. 2000. "Binational Cities: Peoples, Institutions, and Structures." In *Borders, Regions, and People*, edited by M. van der Velde and H. van Houtum, 182–201. London: Pion.

El Mañana de Nuevo Laredo. 2019. "Se lleva a cabo Reunión Binacional entre NLD y Laredo, Texas." March 27. http://elmananadenuevolaredo.com.mx/se-lleva-a-cabo-reunion-binacional-entre-nld-y-laredo-texas/.

Fernandez, Linda. 2013. "Transboundary Water Institutions in Action." *Water Resources and Economics* 1 (January): 20–35.

Gómez, Ana. 2014. "Realizan foro binacional de regidores." *El Imparcial*, February 27. https://www.elimparcial.com/sonora/mundo/Realizan-foro-binacional-de-regidores-20140227-0261.html.

Hansen, Niles. 1985. *Border Region Development and Cooperation: Western Europe and the U.S.-Mexico Borderlands in Comparative Perspective.* El Paso: Center for Inter-American and Border Studies, University of Texas at El Paso.

Hardin, Garret. "The Tragedy of the Commons." *Science* 162, no. 3859 (December 13, 1968): 1243–48.

Herrera, Isamar. 2017. "Suspenden visita de Cabildo de El Paso a sesión de Juárez." *860 Radio Noticias*, June 5. http://www.860noticias.com.mx/jrz/suspenden-visita-de-cabildo-de-el-paso-a-sesion-de-juarez/.

Herzog, Lawrence, and Christophe Sohn. 2019. "The Co-mingling of Bordering Dynamics in the San Diego–Tijuana Cross-Border Metropolis." *Territory, Politics, Governance* 7 (2): 177–99.

Institución Nacional Para el Federalismo y Desarrollo Municipal (INAFED). n.d. "Enciclopedia de los Municipios y Delegaciones de México." Accessed July 2017. http://www.inafed.gob.mx/work/enciclopedia/.

Instituto Nacional Electoral (INE). n.d. "National Electoral Institute." Accessed July 2017. http://aceproject.org/about-en/regional-centres/ine.

International Water Law Project. 1999. "El Paso-Juarez Memorandum of Understanding." December 6. https://www.internationalwaterlaw.org/documents/regionaldocs/Local-GW-Agreements/El_Paso-Juarez_MoU.pdf.

Juárez a Diario. 2015. "Continúa Municipio Promoviendo el Turismo." July 13. http://www.juarezadiario.com/juarez/continua-municipio-promoviendo-el-turismo/.

Jusionyte, Ieva. 2018. *Threshold: Emergency Responders on the US-Mexico Border*. Berkeley: University of California Press.

KVIA. 2016. "NMSU and UTEP Explain Why Mexican Students Get Tuition Discount." July 1. https://kvia.com/news/2016/07/01/nmsu-and-utep-explain-why-mexican-students-get-tuition-discount/.

López Obrador, Andrés Manuel. 2018. "Boletín campaña-012." April 9. https://lopezobrador.org.mx/entrevistas/page/2/.

López Obrador, Andrés Manuel. 2019. "Primer Informe de Gobierno 2018–2019." September 1. https://lopezobrador.org.mx/wp-content/uploads/2019/09/PRIMER-INFORME-DE-GOBIERNO.pdf.

Martínez, Oscar J. 1994. *Border People*. Tucson: University of Arizona Press.

Mendoza, Jorge. 2017. "Economic Integration and Cross-Border Economic Organizations: The Case of San Diego-Tijuana." *Estudios Fronterizos* 18 (35): 22–46.

Montes, Aaron. 2017. "Investors, City Target Paseo de Las Luces." *El Paso Inc.*, November 27.

Morales, Roberto. 2019. "México da prioridad a zona libre en la frontera: AMLO." *El Economista*, January 3. https://www.eleconomista.com.mx/estados/Mexico-da-prioridad-a-zona-libre-en-la-frontera-AMLO-20190103-0102.html.

Moré, Iñigo. 2011. *The Borders of Inequality*. Tucson: University of Arizona Press.

Nikolewski, Rob. 2018. "New President of Mexico Creates 'Free Zone' Along U.S. Border in Hopes of Boosting Economy, Reducing Migration." *San Diego Union-Tribune*, December 31.

Nylander, Chorus. 2017. "El Paso City Council Hosts Joint Meeting with Juarez Leaders." KTSM, October 30. https://www.ktsm.com/news/el-paso-city-council-hosts-joint-meeting-with-juarez-leaders/847633089/.

O'Rourke, Beto, and Susie Byrd. 2011. *Dealing Death and Drugs: The Big Business of Dope in the U.S. and Mexico; An Argument for Ending the Prohibition of Marijuana*. El Paso: Cinco Puntos Press.

Ostrom, Elinor. 1990. *Governing the Commons: The Evolution of Institutions for Collective Action*. New York: Cambridge University Press.

Payan, Tony. 2010. "Cross-Border Governance in a Tristate, Binational Region." In *Cities and Citizenship at the U.S.-Mexico Border: The Paso del Norte Metropolitan Region*, edited by Kathleen Staudt, César M. Fuentes, and Julia A. Monárrez Fragoso, 217–44. New York: Palgrave Macmillan.

Pérez, Elida S. 2017. "Juárez, El Paso City Councils Hold Joint Meeting to Work on Common Goals." *El Paso Times*, October 30.

Rodríguez, Victoria E. 1997. *Decentralization in Mexico: From Reforma Municipal to Solidaridad to Nuevo Federalismo*. Boulder, Colo.: Westview Press.

San Diego Red. 2017. "Participa alcalde de Tijuana en sesión de cabildo de la asociación de gobiernos de San Diego." May 26. http://www.sandiegored.com/es/noticias/143786/Participa-alcalde-de-Tijuana-en-sesion-de-cabildo-de-la-Asociacion-de-Gobiernos-de-San-Diego.

San Diego Regional Chamber of Commerce. n.d. "Accomplishments." Accessed December 20, 2017. https://sdchamber.org/international/accomplishments/.

Secretaría de Relaciones Exteriores (SRE). 2018. "Discurso completo del C. Presidente Andrés Manuel López Obrador en la toma de protesta." December 13. https://embamex.sre.gob.mx/sudafrica/index.php/discurso-integro-de-andres-manuel-lopez-obrador-al-rendir-protesta-como-presidente.

Spagat, Elliot. 2011. "US-Mexico Governors Conference Languishes." *San Diego Union-Tribune*, September 28.

Sparrow, Glen. 2001. "San Diego-Tijuana: Not Quite a Binational City or Region." *GeoJournal* 54 (1): 73–83.

Staudt, Kathleen. 2014. "New Mexico and Texas Display Contrasting Narratives on Border Trade and Respect for Border Residents." *Newspaper Tree*, May 30.

Staudt, Kathleen. 2016. "Todos Somos Fronterizos (but What About the Workers?)." Chuco-Pedia, August 20. http://www.chucopedia.org. Site discontinued.

Staudt, Kathleen. 2017. *Border Politics in a Global Era: Comparative Perspectives*. Lanham, Md.: Rowman & Littlefield.

Staudt, Kathleen. 2020a. "Border Narratives in a Neoliberal Era: The Central U.S.-Mexico Borderlands." In *North American Borders in Comparative Perspective*, edited by Guadalupe Correa-Cabrera and Victor Konrad, 232–57. Tucson: University of Arizona Press.

Staudt, Kathleen. 2020b. "Political Contributions: The Best Candidates Money Can Buy?" In *Who Rules El Paso? Private Gain, Public Policy, and the Community Interest*, by Carmen E. Rodríguez, Kathleen Staudt, Oscar J. Martínez, and Rosemary Neill, 30–38. El Paso: Community First Coalition.

Staudt, Kathleen, and Irasema Coronado. 2002. *Fronteras no Más: Toward Social Justice at the US-Mexico Border*. New York: Palgrave Macmillan.

Staudt, Kathleen, and Pamela Cruz. 2014. "'Getting It': Business NGOs and Political Actors Talk About the U.S.-Mexico Border Region." Presentation at the Association of Borderlands Studies Conference, Albuquerque, N.Mex.

Svitek, Patrick. 2017. "Gov. Abbott: This Country Isn't the 'United States of Municipalities.'" *Texas Tribune*, March 27.

Tentori, Minerva Celaya, and Araceli Almaraz Alvarado. 2015. "Nuevas fronteras para la innovación tecnológica: Colaboración y cooperación en la región Tijuana-San Diego." *Región y sociedad* 27 (64): 183–219.

Texas Secretary of State. n.d. "Border Governors Conference." Accessed December 20, 2017. https://www.sos.state.tx.us/border/bmaconf.shtml.

U.S. Department of Homeland Security (DHS). 2016. "Local Arrangement for Repatriation of Mexican Nationals." February 23. https://www.dhs.gov/sites/default/files/publications/LRA-Base.pdf.

U.S. Department of Transportation (DOT). 2015. "New Mexico—Chihuahua Border Master Plan." http://dot.state.nm.us/content/dam/nmdot/InternationalPrograms/NM-CHIH_BMP.pdf.

U.S. Environmental Protection Agency (EPA). 2009. "Binational Hazardous Materials Emergency Plan Modification among City of El Paso, Texas Sunland Park, New Mexico, Municipality of Juarez, Chihuahua and Ysleta del Sur Pueblo." August. https://www.epa.gov/sites/production/files/201601/documents/clean_copy_amended_mou_on_emergency_final_with_signatures_secured_2009_0.pdf.

U.S.-Mexico Border Mayors Association (USMBMA). 2011. "Border Mayors Association Resolution." https://usmex.ucsd.edu/_files/documents_resolution_2011.pdf.

U.S.-Mexico Border Mayors Association (USMBMA). 2017. "U.S.-Mexico Border Mayors Association—2017 Binational Summit." https://usmex.ucsd.edu/_files/documents_esc_action_plan.pdf.

Univision PR Team. 2016. "Major U.S.-Mexico Border Poll Finds That Most Border Residents Oppose a Wall and Think the Tone of the 2016 Presidential Election Could Damage Relations Between Both Countries." July 18. https://corporate.univision.com/corporate/press/2016/07/18/major-u-s-mexico-border-poll-finds-that-most-border-residents-oppose-a-wall-and-think-the-tone-of-the-2016-presidential-election-could-damage-relations-between-both-countries/.

Valencia Carmona, Salvador. 2016. "En torno al federalismo mexicano." In *Estudios sobre federalismo, justicia, democracia y derechos humanos: Instituto de Investigaciones Jurídicas*, edited by Antonio María Hernández, 359–80. Mexico City: Universidad Nacional Autónoma de México.

6

...

Environmental Governance at the U.S.-Mexico Border

Institutions at Risk

Irasema Coronado and Stephen Mumme

The international boundary separating the United States and Mexico straddles a remarkably rich array of ecosystems and human settlements. It also separates two distinct societies and political systems whose institutions may bear a familiar resemblance but are not easily coordinated across the international line. It attaches two distinct economies characterized by economic asymmetry but joined by a high degree of interdependence. These facts are fundamental to any evaluation of the state of environmental governance and binational cooperation for environmental improvement and sustainable development in the border region. With these facts in mind, this chapter examines the institutional dimension of environmental governance along the U.S.-Mexico border with an emphasis on environmental capacity accrual and resilience of the bilateral and cooperative environmental agencies and policies currently in place. For our purposes, environmental governance is understood as the set of formally established institutions, policies, and practices that aim at conserving natural resources and protecting human health on a sustainable and transgenerational basis. Such policies and practices address the provision and utilization of water, the preservation of air quality, the protection of soils and land uses, the prevention of contamination and injury from toxic substances, and the maintenance and protection of habitats of species that populate the various border ecosystems.

Our chapter proceeds in three parts, followed by a concluding section with policy recommendations. We first trace the development of environmental cooperation along the border with an emphasis on the key agreements and institutional trends shaping binational cooperation on environmental protection. In this first section, we show how the current institutional arrangements have evolved and how they resemble a multilevel governance assemblage of disparate and loosely connected agencies and practices that fall well short of a highly integrated and strategic commitment to the sustainable management of the border environment. In the second section, we examine the binational agencies and programs engaged in environmental protection along the border and discuss the most pressing stressors weighing on these institutions and programs. In the third section, we summarize and reflect on the institutional trends and challenges confronting binational cooperation for environmental improvement and sustainable development. We conclude with our recommendations for strengthening these institutions and programs.

The Evolution of Environmental Governance Along the Border

Of all the issue areas within the gamut of policies and concerns that define bilateral relations between the United States and Mexico, that of the environment is certainly the youngest and, in the minds of some scholars and pundits, the least compelling. A focus on the transboundary implications of environmental conditions at and along the international boundary emerged in the 1970s, long after other issues were well ensconced in public discourse and on the dockets of presidential summits. Set alongside the attention-grabbing headlines on trade, narcotics, security, immigration, and energy, the environment has often taken a back seat on the bilateral policy agenda.

Among the several implications that flow from this late emergence of environmental concern along the border is the fact that many of the agencies engaged in environmental governance along the boundary are comparatively young. Only the water sector is a clear exception to this rule, and even here most of the institutional rules, structures, and practices date back to the end of World War II. The oldest of these institutions, the venerable International Boundary and Water Commission (IBWC) of the United States and Mexico, endowed with a treaty mandate, was charged with boundary and water management, mostly centered on problems related to water allocation. By the early 1970s, the commission found itself drawn into problems of water quality and pollution, largely through its narrow charge to address transboundary sanitation problems. In the 1970s, a youthful set of domestic environmental agencies in the United States and Mexico was pressed to explore new avenues for binational cooperation on water quality, air quality, solid wastes, hazardous and toxic substances, and other matters. New protocols emerged from these initiatives that only loosely synchronized with the mandate of the IBWC. The signing of the Border Environmental Cooperation Agreement (La Paz Agreement) in 1983 committed both nations to data exchange, consultation, and regular discussion of needs and opportunities for cooperation along the boundary. The La Paz Agreement strengthened the binational foundation for cooperating on environmental problems at the border and broadened the jurisdictional space for bilateral engagement. Even so, that agreement was a diplomatic framework agreement that was additive to preexisting institutions. It did not establish a secretariat or commission with the authority and financing to independently address environmental problems in the border region.

It was largely environmentalists' frustration with the La Paz Agreement and its ad hoc, nonstrategic, low priority, and reactive approach to binational environmental management that galvanized environmental opposition to the proposed North American Free Trade Agreement (NAFTA) in 1990, compelling both governments to address transboundary environmental issues at the border, and at a North American scale, to defuse legislative opposition to the trade accord. Beginning with the Integrated Border Environmental Plan (IBEP) in 1992, the U.S. Environmental Protection Agency (EPA) and Mexico's then Secretaría de Desarrollo Urbano y Ecología (SEDUE, Secretariat of Urban Development and Ecology) sought to elevate border area environmental concerns on the bilateral agenda by organizing and consolidating the various disparate environmental efforts and functions of various federal and state agencies into what could be presented to the public as a unified and coherent effort to prioritize environmental protection in the border area. As many environmentalists observed at the time, this was more in the vein of a public relations initiative than any prioritization of environmental needs or strategic planning for environmental address along the border. At the EPA, a new public environmental advisory body, the Good Neighbor Environmental Board (GNEB), was formed to channel intergovernmental and citizen concerns and advice to the agency.

These efforts proved insufficient to satisfy NAFTA's many critics on both sides of the border. As the agreement neared final approval in 1993, two new side agreements were signed to address environmental criticism. The first, the North American Agreement on Environmental Cooperation (NAAEC), a trilateral agreement, committed the governments to monitor environmental trends across the region, establishing a permanent secretariat for that purpose and inviting citizen groups to denounce instances of national failure to enforce environmental laws. The second, a bilateral agreement to establish a Border Environmental Cooperation Commission (BECC) and a North American Development Bank (NADB), aimed directly at the U.S.-Mexico border, establishing institutional mechanisms for the solicitation, approval, and financing of needed border area environmental infrastructure. Additionally, the governments ramped up their La Paz Agreement cooperative effort with a successor plan to the IBEP, now reconfigured as the Border XXI Program.

Other institutions also gained a boost from the trade negotiations and their side agreements. Notably, and partially in response to the NAAEC accord, binational and regional cooperation among North American wildlife agencies under two international agreements dating to the 1930s and 1940s was strengthened with the creation of a Trilateral Committee for Wildlife and Ecosystem Conservation and Management (TCWECM) in 1996. An initiative to establish a Border Health Commission (BHC) was launched in 1992 and came to fruition in the "Agreement to Establish a United States-Mexico Border Health Commission," signed in 2000.

It is fair to say that the emergence and development of cooperative environmental governance institutions along the border since the early 1970s has proceeded in an ad hoc, semi-integrated fashion in response to particular challenges confronting the governments at the time of their creation. Newer institutions and programs have largely been additive to the mix of those existing at the time, amplifying and strengthening the range of mechanisms available to the governments for environmental protection and addressing public environmental demands in the border area. The newer institutions and programs have brought additional capacity for environmental protection and new synergies among agencies with overlapping mandates in areas like water quality and environmental health. What has emerged, gathering steam in the 1990s, is a multilevel governance framework for binational cooperation on environment and natural resources policy characterized by several well-established binational agencies, other trinational and binational agencies and programs less supported by the governments, and a wide mix of domestic agencies at the federal, state, and municipal level in both countries with jurisdictions, mandates, and interests affecting the border area with limited and conditional ties to one another. Of these, only three—the IBWC, the Commission for Environmental Cooperation (CEC), and the BECC/NADB— are currently established as independent agencies; the other projects and programs are housed in the domestic agencies of the two governments.

Governmental support and funding for these binational agencies and programs has varied considerably over time, with some funded jointly on a sustained basis by the federal governments and others funded separately within each nation and on a case-by-case, project-by-project basis. Over time, environmental protection on the border has seen more interagency partnerships and collaborations in addressing specific problems, but these partnerships, such as those engaged between the IBWC and the national environmental agencies, have been less than systematic, usually undertaken on a problem or project basis with funding assigned accordingly. This checkered history of funding for border environmental protection limits binational environmental capacity and generates considerable uncertainty as to the sustainability of many cooperative environmental programs. The regional division of federal administration for border affairs in both countries arguably adds to policy uncertainty as program priorities and funding streams are affected by regional and state administrative divisions along the border.

In sum, the border region has seen considerable growth in environmental commitment by the governments since the mid-1970s, captured in various international agreements and advanced by the post-1990 expansion of institutions and programs for environmental protection that came along with NAFTA. Unfortunately, what we have witnessed since 2000 is the gradual erosion of government support for some of these agencies and programs. Most agencies and programs endure but confront the challenge of diminished funding and some curtailment of functions. They have also suffered from the U.S. turn to heightened border security and the greater intrusion of border security practices on the authority and funding of environmental and natural resources agencies operating in the border area. To examine this trend, it is useful to look at this multigovernance system through the lens of particular border environmental agencies and programs.

Binational Environmental Agencies and Programs Along the Border: An Overview

In the mix of international institutional mechanisms tasked with environmental protection along the border, four agencies, each endowed with distinct operational missions, exist as established organizations delivering policy outputs for the border community. These agencies—the IBWC, the BECC/NADB, the BHC, and the CEC—vary considerably, not just in mission and functions but in levels of support from the governments. With varying degrees of intersectoral coordination, partnership, and financing, almost all work in tandem with the environmental programs of the two governments as administered by federal agencies in each country, principally the EPA and the Secretaría de Medio Ambiente y Recursos Naturales (SEMARNAT, Secretariat of Environment and Natural Resources) but also engaging other federal and subsidiary agencies in both countries. A brief review of each agency's mandate, functions, and institutional trends is useful for purposes of charting the policy range and reach of these institutions and spotlighting current challenges for binational cooperation on environmental protection in the border area.

International Boundary and Water Commission (IBWC)

Of the various binational institutions with mandates for environmental protection in the border area, the IBWC is certainly the oldest and, arguably, the best established. Established by the U.S.-Mexico Water Treaty in 1944 with antecedents in the International Boundary Commission dating to 1889, the IBWC is charged with administering all U.S. agreements with Mexico on boundary and water matters. The IBWC is composed of two distinct national sections: the USIBWC, based in El Paso, Texas; and the Comisión Internacional de Límites y Aguas (CILA, International Boundary and Water Commission), based in Ciudad Juárez, Chihuahua. Each section is subject to the policy oversight of its respective government's foreign ministries, and the IBWC has the character of an international body when the two sections are joined in formal sessions.

The IBWC's environmental functions were not well specified at the time the 1944 Water Treaty was signed and ratified. Under the treaty's Article 3, the IBWC was given the responsibility for dealing with all border sanitation problems affecting the international boundary. In the 1950s and 1960s, the IBWC was drawn into diplomatic discussions concerning transboundary sewage flows at various locations along the boundary, including Douglas and Agua Prieta; the twin cities of Naco, Arizona, and Naco, Sonora; the twin cities of Nogales, Arizona, and Nogales, Sonora; at Mexicali, Baja California, and Calexico, California; at Tijuana, Baja California, and San Diego, California; as well as sewage spills to the Rio Grande River at Laredo, Tamaulipas. International sewage treatment plants operated under IBWC oversight were built at Douglas–Agua Prieta and Ambos Nogales.

Public pressure to address transboundary water quality and pollution concerns more broadly arose during the historic dispute over the salinity of the Colorado River, settled in 1973, and persisted through the 1970s as sanitation problems worsened at several border locations and were joined by a number of other instances of industrial contamination of transboundary rivers, most notably on the San Pedro River spanning the Arizona-Sonora section of the international boundary. After the EPA struck an executive agreement with Mexico in 1978 to cooperate in resolving environmental problems in the border area to include water pollution threats to public health and wildlife, the IBWC in 1979 reached another agreement, IBWC Minute 261, extending Article 3's application to all transboundary water pollution problems and broadening its original mandate in this issue area (IBWC 1979). Specific applications of Minute 261 authority to instances of transboundary water contamination require additional and more focused agreements.

Under its Minute 261 authority, the IBWC moved to address various transboundary sanitation and pollution problems in the border region. U.S. assistance was extended to Mexico to improve sewage disposal operations in Mexicali, expand sewage treatment at Ambos Nogales, and improve sewage management at Tijuana with the aim of developing an international sewage treatment plant on the Tijuana River in San Diego. In 1983 the IBWC's lead authority for addressing transboundary water quality problems was recognized in the La Paz Agreement on U.S.-Mexico border area environmental cooperation. With La Paz, however, the IBWC was drawn into partnership with the national environmental agencies in addressing transboundary water pollution. This was evident early on as Annex I to the La Paz Agreement (EPA 1985), coupled with IBWC Minute 270 (IBWC 1985), set out cooperative arrangements for mitigating Tijuana's fugitive sewage flows. This partnership deepened with NAFTA and the heightened priority that agreement brought to environmental protection at the border. When the IBWC moved to negotiate construction of an international sewage treatment plant at San Diego, the USIBWC reached a formal understanding with the EPA on sharing U.S. costs, and shortly after, in 1995, a new IBWC agreement, Minute 294, committed the commission to cooperating with the EPA, and the newly established BECC, in developing water and wastewater solutions for qualifying communities along the international boundary (IBWC 1995). In 1998 the commission signed Minute 299, authorizing the signing of a coordination MOU with the BECC and enabling a further partnership in the "planning, development, and execution of wastewater treatment projects" along the border (IBWC 1998). Contributing to the IBWC's environmental turn, the USIBWC incorporated sustainable development into its 2000 strategic plan for operations along the border (USIBWC 2000).

The commission's environmental authority is further enhanced by three recent agreements, Minutes 319 and 323 addressing water sharing and ecosystem restoration in the lower Colorado River region and Minute 320 on environmental cooperation in managing threats to the Tijuana River (IBWC 2012, 2015, 2017). In the former instance, the IBWC broke new ground in authorizing Colorado River water use for restoring riparian vegetation in the limitrophe reach of the river and below the southern international boundary. That agreement, which lapsed in December 2017, was replaced with Minute 323, which extends the earlier minute's shortage sharing and ecosystem restoration provisions for a ten-year term ending on December 31, 2026. Minute 320 works as a framework agreement for addressing sanitation and pollution threats, sedimentation, solid waste contamination, and the development of joint water stewardship benefiting the Tijuana River's riparian environment.

While the IBWC's environmental mandate and functions have grown markedly since the 1970s, it bears remembering that its jurisdiction for environmental protection is very narrow, limited strictly to addressing water quality issues that abut upon or cross the international boundary. The agency has assiduously avoided suggestions that it undertake work that encroaches on the jurisdictions of other domestic agencies in either country. Its operational understanding of its jurisdiction has grown slightly with the agreements struck following the 1983 La Paz Agreement, and particularly in recent years with a broadening of its environmental functionality.

An institutional strength of the IBWC, and a potential weakness, is its treaty marriage of boundary and water management along the border. As a treaty-constituted body of long standing, the IBWC enjoys a high level of binational support, and this is reflected in the organization and status of its national commissions. The IBWC has a reputation as a corps of border engineers charged with a largely technical mission derived from its treaty mandates. Both national sections have enjoyed steady budgetary support over the years. The IBWC's field offices span the international boundary. The U.S. Section is endowed with its own operations and construction capability. Over the years, it has acquired a relatively large professional staff, currently employing more than two hundred engineers, technical specialists, and supporting personnel. The U.S. Section's budget has at times ranged from more than $US200 million during the 1960s at the height of its Rio Grande dam construction phase to its current and more modest support of US$45 million in 2014 (DOS 2014). Measured in budget and staff, it is today the largest and best supported of the binational agencies engaged in environmental protection on the boundary.

The commission is not without its critics, however. Its technical-diplomatic character has drawn accusations of excessive attention to procedure and protocol, bureaucratic monopolism of diplomatic discussions on boundary and boundary water issues, political insularity, and limited capacity to quickly respond to transboundary pollution concerns (Sanchez 1993). Certain problems, notably the management of transboundary groundwater, have largely eluded the commission's capacity to bring stakeholders to the bargaining table.[1] Over time, both sections have tried to address these issues, some of which are simply a function of diplomatic oversight and protocol associated with the commission's oversight by the foreign ministries. Since the 1990s, the U.S. Section, for example, has developed new capacity for public relations and outreach as well as convening citizen advisory groups representing key regions of the international boundary. On the Mexican side, CILA has recently begun to convene advisory groups while working with SEMARNAT's already established Northern Boundary Sustainability Councils (Roberto Salmon, interview with Steve Mumme, 2016). These measures have not stilled all criticism directed at the commission but have certainly helped soften its public image. What must be said is that the IBWC as a binational agency occupies a narrow but important sector of environmental protection with a bearing on the provision and quality of water in much of the border region.

Border Environment Cooperation Commission (BECC) and North American Development Bank (NADB)

The BECC and NADB as a set of paired agencies were established by executive agreement in 1993 and became operational in 1995. The two agencies were established to address the border environmental infrastructure deficit at the time NAFTA was authorized, estimated at the time by the U.S.-Mexico Chamber of Commerce to exceed US$22 billion and expected to worsen as NAFTA trade ramped up after 1993. They are directly a response to environmental criticism of the trade agreement and the governments' efforts to address these criticisms in advance of NAFTA's legislative approval.

Originally chartered as two paired but independent agencies partnered for border environmental infrastructure development, the agencies' initial priority was defined as assisting border communities with water and wastewater treatment. The BECC was designed to encourage, vet, and certify proposed projects in the border zone while the NADB was to assist in financing these projects. Situated in Ciudad Juárez and with an operating budget of US$3.6 million (Kelly and Reed 2000, 11), the BECC was truly binational, headed by a general manager and deputy manager representing the United States and Mexico whose roles and responsibilities reversed every three years, ensuring shared leadership. Proposed projects were to be developed with community participation and support, be financially viable, and meet exacting environmental sustainability standards. A technical assistance program, the Project Development Assistance Program (PDAP), helped border communities with their project proposals. The BECC's administrative oversight was innovative in incorporating representatives of federal government, state government, municipalities, and nonprofit organizations on its board of directors. Decisions on projects and priorities were to be made with a high level of administrative transparency and openness to public input.

The NADB, headquartered in San Antonio, Texas, was structured as a bank functionally dedicated to border environmental infrastructure development. Initially endowed with US$3 billion, configured as US$2.55 billion in callable capital and US$0.45 billion in paid-in capital, contributed equally by each country, 90 percent of its working capital was dedicated to environmental infrastructure and 10 percent to community investment programs in both countries—the latter justified as needed structural adjustment addressing NAFTA's adverse labor force impacts (McKinney 2000, 169, 173). The NADB was authorized to finance up to 50 percent of a BECC-certified project's needs and assist borrowers in locating additional financing to get projects off the ground. The bank's oversight was more insular than the BECC's with a board composed of three members from each country, all representing federal agencies (treasury, foreign affairs, and environment), with little transparency or opportunity for public input.

As authorized, the NADB was initially constrained by an imperative to lend at competitive market rates and avoid any hint of subsidizing border projects. Early on, this proved to be a serious obstacle for poor border communities lacking the means to satisfy the agency's loan repayment requirements. In 1996 an Institutional Development and Cooperation Program (IDP) was created to assist local utilities with their administrative operations. This was helpful but insufficient. In 1997 the NADB established its Border Environmental Infrastructure Fund (BEIF), a funding mechanism that allowed it to accept payments from other government sources, principally the EPA, to finance grants to assist needy border communities in supporting projects. Bolstered with US$170 million from the EPA channeled through the BEIF, the NADB's lending program was invigorated. By 2000 the BECC and NADB's Joint Status Report noted that the BECC had certified forty-four projects, twenty-five of these in the United States and nineteen in Mexico, with NADB financing or assisting with financing in thirty-six of these projects (BECC/NADB 2004). As many as 140 community-based projects were receiving the BECC's technical assistance.

A change of political administrations in 2000 as well as a dramatic reshuffling of U.S. domestic border priorities after 2001 led to binational rethinking of the BECC/NADB arrangement. Though the EPA's contribution to the BEIF had been reduced from US$100 million to US$75 million in 1998, the George W. Bush administration further slashed BEIF grant funding in 2003 (GNEB 2012). In 2004, in response to various Mexican criticisms, including the limited geographic range of their border operations, the BECC and NADB boards were merged and their operational jurisdiction extended from 62 miles (100 kilometers) south of the boundary to 186 miles (300 kilometers) (BECC/NADB 2004). A new NADB Water Infrastructure Investment Fund was created, enabling the agencies to support needed water conservation in Mexico's Rio Conchos basin in support of IBWC efforts to address structural issues in Mexico's treaty compliance on the Rio Grande (IBWC 2002). Critics remained unsatisfied. The NADB was charged with sustaining excessive administrative costs, exceeding its lending portfolio, and inefficiencies in loan processing; defenders noted that the lion's share of its administrative costs was dedicated to administering BEIF grants and technical assistance amounting to nearly US$729 million by 2005 (Martin 2006). U.S. border states, spearheaded by Texas, lobbied successfully to beat back a 2006 effort by the U.S. Treasury to drop the bank altogether (Abel and Sayoc 2006; Hendricks 2006). Even so, the agencies' ability to subsidize environmental infrastructure projects was hampered by the sharp reduction in BEIF funding, which by 2006 had leveled off at US$10 million annually. The loss of grant funding forced both agencies to turn to other funding sources, including public/private partnerships and a greater reliance on state resources in financing needed projects.

By 2012 the BECC and the NADB could boast US$6.307 billion invested in border environmental infrastructure based on 208 certified projects in the border region, 171 of these supported by the NADB (see Table 6.1). Of the 208 certified projects, 94 were U.S. projects and 114 were situated in Mexico. Facilitating project development, though by no means compensating for the loss of BEIF funding for water infrastructure, was a small new Community Assistance Program (CAP), established by the NADB in coordination with the BECC in 2011 and funded from earnings from the NADB's loan portfolio (BECC 2012). Also, in 2011, to achieve greater operating effi-

TABLE 6.1 BECC/NADB-certified projects and funding, 1995–2012

	Mexico	United States	Total
BECC-certified projects	114	94	208
NADB-supported BECC projects	N/A	N/A	171
Financing	US$3.435 billion	US$2.873 billion	US$6.307 billion

Source: BECC 2012.

ciencies, the two agencies initiated a process of adjusting and coordinating procedures, including a joint project pipeline and streamlined certification procedures, with the aim of fully merging the two bodies under a single administrative structure. In 2014 and marking the twentieth anniversary of the two bodies, the joint agencies' board agreed to move forward with the proposed merger. Under the new plan, touted by BECC/NADB officials as doubling overall lending capacity, the BECC is incorporated as a unit of the bank responsible for administering project certification and sustainability compliance criteria (BECC/NADB 2014). The twin parts of the new entity retain their current names and administrative centers (NADB in San Antonio, BECC in Ciudad Juárez). The ten-member board—since 2005 composed of a representative of each federal government's treasury, state, and environment ministries as well as a representative of the states, and another representative from civil society in each country—remains the same, at least at last report. In 2017 both countries authorized the formal merger (BECC/NADB 2017; Chapa 2017).

In sum, when considered over its twenty-five-year trajectory, the BECC/NADB partnership, now better understood as the NADB with the BECC as a subordinate department operating from Ciudad Juárez, has generated vital environmental investments in the border region (Chapa 2017). By 2014 more than US$7 billion was infused in border communities, principally in water-related projects but also including various air, solid waste, and renewable energy investments over the past decade. That the agencies have survived intense criticism by elements of both governments, enduring three administrations in each nation and currently sustained by a fourth, suggests the newly reorganized NADB has gained a strong institutional foothold as a regional development agency, one that enjoys considerable political support among border communities in each country. But when measured against the array of needs identified in the early 1990s, many environmentalists remain disappointed in the overall levels of budgetary support as well as what can be viewed as a retreat from the original goals of a highly responsive, transparent, and participatory BECC representing and advancing the public's environmental interests along the border.

Border Health Commission (BHC)

The U.S.-Mexico Border Health Commission (USMBHC), established by executive agreement in 2000, has antecedents that date back to the 1970s in reports by the El Paso field office of the Pan American Health Organization (PAHO) (Coppege 1978). Rising concern with an array of threats to public health in the sister cities along the boundary, including environmental threats like air and water pollution, heavy metals, and solid wastes, led to informal collaborations between local health authorities on both sides of the border.

In 1988, at the urging of the Texas Medical Association, the American Medical Association (AMA) passed a resolution calling on the U.S. Congress to establish and fund a permanent U.S.-Mexico Border Environmental Health Commission. A year later, in 1989, the Texas Medical Association convened the first annual Border Health Conference in El Paso, Texas, again calling for a Border Health Commission. The AMA's Council on Scientific Affairs followed this call in 1990 with an article in the *Journal of the American Medical Association* calling the border "a virtual cesspool and breeding ground for infectious diseases" and describing broad public support for such a commission among the medical establishment. The AMA argued that the La Paz Agreement and its framework for binational cooperation on environmental problems did not provide a mechanism by which the two countries could address "vector control, rabies, and drinking water quality," nor did it create an institution that could reach binding agreements on dealing with public health problems along the boundary (Council on Scientific Affairs 1990, 3320). The USIBWC, it noted, had been granted further authority by the Ronald Reagan administration in 1988 to reach agreements with Mexico on international pollution problems on the Rio Grande River but did not have the authority to address water and sewage services deficits in the impoverished informal settlements known as *colonias* along the river (Council on Scientific Affairs 1990, 3321). The IBWC, the Council on Scientific Affairs suggested, "was a deliberative authority, not an implementing one" (1990, 3321). Another institution was necessary to fill these and other public health gaps along the border.

The AMA's statement drew considerable notice in the NAFTA debates, which fueled further effort to create a new binational health authority. In January 1993, representatives of the California, Arizona, and Texas medical associations, meeting in Tucson, Arizona, issued a further call for the creation and funding of a U.S. Border Health Authority and a U.S.-Mexico Border Health Commission (USMBHA 1993). Benefiting from the public visibility generated by the NAFTA debate and with the support of all four U.S. border state medical associations and all ten of the border states' governors, the AMA successfully lobbied to get a BHC bill though the U.S. Congress in 1994. On October 22, 1994, President Bill Clinton signed Public Law

103-400 authorizing the U.S. Department of Health and Human Services (HHS) to negotiate with Mexico to establish a U.S.-Mexico Border Health Commission (USMX-BHC).

The USMX-BHC initiative, as originally authorized in the United States, came with modest funding of $800,000 for U.S. activities (Valdez 1998). The new government of Ernesto Zedillo, beset by a drastic devaluation of the Mexican peso, had little incentive to commit to a project widely seen as driven by U.S. medical associations. A debate over wording in the authorizing legislation that seemed to imply that Mexico ought to pay the health costs of its citizens residing in the United States, though apocryphal, did not help matters (Bennet 1997). After protracted negotiations, an agreement was signed in July 2000.

Under the "Agreement to Establish a United States-Mexico Border Health Commission," the BHC is to "identify and evaluate current and future health problems affecting the population in the United States-Mexico Border Area, particularly those in vulnerable, high risk groups" ("Agreement" 2000). Headquartered in El Paso, Texas, the BHC bears a resemblance to the IBWC; it is composed of two national sections, each of which sustains its own national secretariat under the guidance of its national Ministry of Health. Each section has thirteen members, including the delegate from its Ministry of Health. Decisions are reached by double majority—most of the membership of each section and much of the commission as a whole. The BHC is required to meet at least once annually in the border region ("Agreement" 2000).

Since its creation in 2000, the BHC has maintained a comparatively low profile among border environmental agencies, functioning to gather and disseminate needed public health information to the border community, gather research and spotlight worrisome health trends, and partner with other federal programs and state and local health authorities in raising public awareness of border health needs. Among the twenty-seven achievements since its founding, reported in 2016, were (1) sponsoring since 2004 an annual Border Health Week to promote "sustainable partnerships" addressing border health problems; (2) providing training to *promotores* in mental health abuse, substance use, and environmental health issues; (3) partnering with the EPA on environmental initiatives through the Border 2010 Program in coordination with BHC's Healthy Border 2010 Initiative; (4) establishing a U.S.-Mexico Border Reproductive Health Summit in San Diego in 2014; (5) establishing an ongoing Border Obesity Prevention Initiative in 2013; (6) creating the Leaders Across Borders binational training program in 2009, still ongoing; (7) sponsoring the Binational Health Council's strategic planning workshops to build organizational capacity in binational health councils; (8) establishing the Mexico–United States Border Tuberculosis Consortium to strengthen binational efforts to combat TB in the border area; (9) establishing he Binational Border Health Research Expert Panel (2007) to convene border research partners to advise BHC on border health research; and (10) establishing the Border Influenza Surveillance Network (2007) (BHC 2016, 2017).

At its inception, the BHC was funded with a budget of US$5 million or less, roughly 20 percent of which, US$1 million, was contributed by Mexico's Secretaría de Salubridad y Asistencia (SSA, Secretariat of Health and Welfare) and the remainder from the HHS Office of Global Affairs (OGA) (BHC 2003). Funding has since declined. In 2016 the entire budget for the OGA amounted to a little over US$6 million, down from US$16.7 million in 2009. It appears that the BHC has been effective in generating funds from partner agencies and services to sustain its various programs, including the EPA's Border Health Initiative, with which it has collaborated for more than a decade (EPA 2014). Mexico's contribution to these programs cannot be determined from public documents. Even so, recent trends are certainly worrisome for the sustainability of the agency's programs.

Commission for Environmental Cooperation (CEC)

Of the several international agencies engaged in border region environmental management, the Commission for Environmental Cooperation (CEC) is the only one that is trinational in scope, with a mandate and jurisdiction that spans all three North American nations: Canada, the United States, and Mexico. Established by the North American Agreement on Environmental Cooperation (NAAEC), a NAFTA side agreement, the CEC on paper enjoys an expansive mandate (see Table 6.2). In addition to these functions, the CEC is formally charged with administering the NAAEC's provisions for citizen monitoring of compliance with national environmental obligations. Its formal structure consists of a council composed of the heads of the environmental ministries of the member countries, a Secretariat (based in Montreal, Quebec, Canada), and various advisory committees, including a Joint Public Advisory Committee composed of citizens of the three countries. The CEC's Secretariat is financed with equal contributions from member countries and, despite inflation, has remained relatively constant at a total of US$9 million since its founding.

As an agency, the CEC and its Secretariat have little responsibility for implementing environmental policy. It has been previously described as an SOS agency, whose main functions are scaling, organizing, and spotlighting: (1) monitoring and scaling environmental data at a meta scale for the use of the governments and the public; (2) organizing and helping organize epistemic communities of researchers, policy makers, and advocacy groups invested in understanding and managing transboundary environmental problems; and (3) shining a spotlight on transboundary environmental problems that may be neglected by the governments (Mumme et al. 2009).

Though the CEC's focus on the U.S.-Mexican border region has been limited, and arguably it has become more limited over time due to the eroded purchasing power of its budget and retrenchments in its actual functions, the CEC's activities affect the U.S.-Mexico border region in several ways. First, because so much of the CEC's focus is inherently targeted on transboundary phenomena, its data compiling and monitoring activities are valuable for those public and government agencies interested in positioning the border within environmental trends affecting North America. Second, the Secretariat's Article 13 investigative authority has been periodically deployed to draw needed attention to serious environmental problems located in the border region, ranging from conservation problems in the transboundary San Pedro River watershed on the Arizona-Sonora border to a recent study of the problems associated with lead-acid battery recycling and disposal in Mexican border cities. Third, the Secretariat's Article 14 authority to act on citizen-initiated complaints of national noncompliance with environmental law by undertaking rigorous, science-based factual investigations of problems found to have a credible basis has drawn needed high-level attention to a number of serious environmental problems requiring remediation in the border area. In addition to these functions, the CEC has recently renewed its small-grant support for citizen nonprofit environmental groups engaged in environmental mitigation, pollution prevention, and local conservation activities in the border region. These efforts often complement and strengthen those of other environmental agencies and programs along the border.

The La Paz Programs / Border 2020

Apart from the established agencies with mandates for environmental protection and ecological conservation along the border, two border-focused programs established by the governments add to the overall effort for environmental protection in the border zone. These programs operate under the authority of binational executive agreements authorizing the participation of the governments' federal and subsidiary agencies in cooperative activities aimed at improvements in the border environment. The oldest and best established of these programs is the series of coordinated binational efforts undertaken under the umbrella of the La Paz Agreement beginning in 1992. Until 1992 the La Paz Agreement functioned in the form of four binational workgroups organized by the environmental ministries and focused on air, water, hazardous wastes, and emergency responses to environmental threats. At least one La Paz Agreement Annex, or implementing agreement, had been signed in each of these areas (EPA 1991). Inspired by sharp criticism of the governments' ad hoc, crisis-driven priority setting in implementing the La Paz Agreement in the 1980s, the governments initiated what evolved into a sustained series of semi-integrated, or coordinated, interagency environmental protection plans led by their federal environmental ministries but engaging a wide range of national, binational, and subnational agencies in the border area.

TABLE 6.2 The CEC's mandate and responsibilities

NAAEC authority	CEC and parties' responsibilities
Article 1. CEC mandate	Foster the protection and improvement of the environment in the territories of the parties for the well-being of present and future generations
	Promote sustainable development based on cooperation and mutually supportive environmental and economic policies
	Increase cooperation between the parties to better conserve, protect, and enhance the environment, including wild flora and fauna
	Support the environmental goals and objectives of NAFTA
	Avoid creating trade distortions or new trade barriers
	Strengthen cooperation on the development and improvement of environmental laws, regulations, procedures, policies, and practices
	Enhance compliance with, and enforcement of, environmental laws and regulations
	Promote transparency and public participation in the development of environmental laws, regulations, and policies
	Promote economically efficient and effective environmental measures
	Promote pollution prevention policies and practices
Article 2. Parties' obligations within their national jurisdiction	Periodically prepare and make available reports on the state of the environment
	Develop and review environmental emergency preparedness measures
	Promote education in environmental matters, including environmental law
	Further scientific research and technology development in respect of environmental matters
	Assess, as appropriate, environmental impacts
	Promote the use of economic instruments for the efficient achievement of environmental goals
Article 10 (23). CEC Council's authorized functions	Comparability of techniques and methodologies for data gathering and analysis, data management, and electronic data communications on matters covered by this agreement
	Pollution prevention techniques and strategies

Approaches and common indicators for reporting on the state of the environment

The use of economic instruments for the pursuit of domestic and international agreed environmental objectives

Scientific research and technology development in respect of environmental matters

Promotion of public awareness regarding the environment

Transboundary and border environmental issues, such as the long-range transport of air and marine pollutants

Monitoring exotic species that may be harmful

The conservation and protection of wild flora and fauna and their habitat, and specifically protected natural areas

The protection of endangered and threatened species

Environmental emergency preparedness and response activities

Environmental matters as they relate to economic development

The environmental implications of goods throughout their life cycles

Human resource training and development in the environmental field

The exchange of environmental scientists and officials

Approaches to environmental compliance and enforcement

Ecologically sensitive national accounts

Eco-labeling

Other matters as it may decide

Article 13. Investigations	Secretariat-initiated investigations of environmental problems of trinational relevance
Article 14. Citizen submissions of noncompliance complaints	Secretariat investigations of environmental law noncompliance complaints filed against a member government

Source: Secretariat of the Commission for Environmental Cooperation 1993.

The first of these, the 1992–94 Integrated Border Environmental Program (IBEP), was roundly criticized as less of a plan and more of a laundry list of then existing efforts already deployed in ad hoc fashion along the boundary. This program was replaced by the Border XXI Program (1995–2000). Border XXI benefited from the new NAFTA-inspired institutions and heightened national attention to the border's environmental woes. It also embraced the post-Rio idea of sustainable development as a guiding principle for binational environmental cooperation and prioritized public participation and input into policy implementation. And it incorporated a regional component for organizing policy effort around the distinct zones along the boundary: California–Baja California, Arizona-Sonora, New Mexico–Texas–Chihuahua, and Texas-Coahuila-Tamaulipas (EPA 1996).

A unique feature of Border XXI was its establishment of nine interagency and binational working groups that included conservation agencies within the scope of its binational activities. It also embraced policy decentralization, at least formally enlisting state and local agencies where possible in program implementation. Financially, the program adopted a pooled interagency funding model, seeking to harness the capabilities of federal agencies, the newly established NAFTA agencies, and those of subsidiary government entities at the state and municipal levels (GNEB 1998, 5). States and municipalities were required to contribute matching funds to access EPA, BECC, and NADB financing. Apart from the fund-sharing arrangements at the BECC and the NADB, there was no fixed financial commitment to the program. Under the policy mantel of Border XXI, for example, the EPA was able to justify investing heavily in the NADB's BEIF-based funding of water and wastewater treatment systems in the border region. While Border XXI was notable for engaging state and local governments in its cooperative programming, unfortunately, neither IBEP nor Border XXI thought to include tribal governments and communities in program planning, a defect remedied in later programs. A broader criticism levied by the Good Neighbor Environmental Board (GNEB) was "that the Program's goal is to promote sustainable development without having a parallel aspiration to achieve it" (GNEB 2000, 33). The GNEB also noted that "the Border XXI Program itself seems to be minimally funded, but the Program's existence has elevated awareness of the need for additional binational environmental infrastructure funding" (36).

Extended through 2002, the Border XXI Program was replaced by a ten-year binational interagency coordinating agreement, the Border 2012 Program. This new longer-term program, justified as building greater stakeholder involvement (see Table 6.3) and allowing more long-term planning, aimed to further decentralize the La Paz program planning and implementation effort by regionalizing and devolving greater policy responsibility to the border states and municipalities. It moved away from Border XXI's model of cooperation on nine border environmental problems (air, water,

TABLE 6.3 Guiding principles for Border 2012 and Border 2020 programs

Border 2012 guiding principles	Border 2020 guiding principles
Reduce the higher public health risks, and preserve and restore the natural environment	Same
Adopt a bottom-up approach for setting priorities and making decisions through partnerships with state, local, and U.S. tribal governments	Same
Address disproportionate environmental impacts in border communities	Same
Improve stakeholder participation and ensure broad-based representation from the environmental, public health, and other relevant sectors	Same
Foster transparency, public participation, and open dialogue through provision of accessible, accurate, and timely information	Same
Strengthen capacity of local community residents and other stakeholders to manage environmental and environmentally related public health issues	Same
The United States recognizes that U.S. tribes are separate sovereign governments, and that equity issues impacting tribal governments must be addressed in the United States on a government-to-government basis	Same
Mexico recognizes the historical debt it has with its indigenous communities; therefore, appropriate measures will be considered to address their specific concerns as well as to protect and preserve their cultural integrity within the broader environmental purposes of this program	Same
Achieve concrete, measurable results while maintaining a long-term vision	Same
Measure program progress through development of environmental and public health–based indicators	Same
	Promote sustainable communities by improving social, economic, and environmental systems in the border community

Sources: EPA 2003, 2012.

hazardous and solid waste, emergency contingency planning, pollution prevention, natural resources, environmental health, cooperation on enforcement and compliance, and environmental information resources), concentrating on just six goals: reducing water contamination, reducing air pollution, reducing land contamination, improving environmental health, enhancing emergency response readiness, and improving compliance with environmental regulations.[2] The program dropped its concern with natural resources and increased its emphasis on environmental health, collaborating and supporting the BHC's work from its inception. Operationally, it remained under EPA and SEMARNAT oversight but divided its effort into regional workgroups, border-wide workgroups, and general policy forums, each linking downward to specific regional- and community-level task forces charged with addressing regional and local concerns and implementing site-specific projects (EPA 2012, 21–23). The three policy forums centered on air, water, and wastes and toxics (EPA 2012, 22).

Handicapping the launch of Border 2012 was the stiff reduction in the EPA's BEIF funding, which dropped 50 percent in 2002, falling from US$100 million to US$50 million, severely impacting the BECC and NADB's financing for new border water and sanitation projects and indirectly diminishing funds for other BECC/NADB environmental projects along the border. BEIF funding would never recover, by 2008 falling to just US$10 million (GNEB 2012, 9). While it is difficult to plot a direct link to the new U.S. emphasis on border security in the post-9/11 era, the diminished funding for border environment projects and activities in the new hyper-security era does not appear to be just accidental. One important casualty that became evident by 2010 was reduced funding for participation in binational task forces within the five border regions, these billed by Border 2012 as a key element supporting the decentralizing thrust of the program (Siwik, Hebard, and Jacques 2012). Such funding is essential if residents of the many poor communities along the border are to have any voice in the planning and implementation of the La Paz programs, especially as heightened boundary security burdens all binational gatherings and transactions.

The Border 2012 Program was succeeded in 2014 with the launch of Border 2020, which is heavily modeled on Border 2012 (see the guiding principles comparison in Table 6.3). This latest program retains the organizational structure of its predecessor and its longer-term planning approach but adopts five basic goals and six distinct strategies for goal attainment (see Table 6.4). While these goals and strategies sustain foci found in the earlier agreements, a relatively new strategic concern is climate change and assisting communities in coping with greater climate variability. Operationally, Border 2020 has adopted biennial implementation plans built around objective performance indicators as well as a heightened emphasis on building program partnerships with state, local, and tribal governments along the border. Financing for Border 2020–supported programs, unfortunately, has not recovered and depends heavily on

TABLE 6.4   Border 2020 goals and strategies

Goals	Strategies
Reduce air pollution	Working to improve children's health
Improve access to clean and safe water	Building capacity toward climate change resiliency
Promote materials management and waste management, and clean sites	Protecting disadvantaged and underserved communities
Enhance joint preparedness for environmental response	Promoting environmental awareness
Enhance compliance assurance and environmental stewardship	Promoting environmental health
	Strengthening tribal, state, federal, and international communications and partnerships

Source: EPA 2012.
Note: Border 2020 strategies apply to programs as a whole and are not limited to specific goals.

variable, short-term commitments by participating governmental partners, particularly the federal partners (EPA, SEMARNAT, and NADB), occasionally bolstered by nongovernmental sources. The EPA's 2015 enacted budget allocation to border programs, which covers Border 2020, was US$2.97 million, a slight decline from its 2014 allocation (EPA 2016). SEMARNAT's contribution is not known but may reasonably be supposed to be less than the EPA's. Ominously, the current U.S. administration has proposed zeroing out the EPA's budget for border programs (EPA 2017, 55).

Trilateral Committee for Wildlife and Ecosystem Conservation and Management

The Trilateral Committee for Wildlife and Ecosystem Conservation and Management (hereafter Trilateral Committee) was established in 1995 by a joint Canada, U.S., and Mexico Memorandum of Understanding (MOU) to coordinate the work of national wildlife agencies in the North American region. It supersedes a couple of earlier agreements, the 1975 Mexico-U.S. Joint Committee on Wildlife and Plant Conservation and the 1988 Tripartite Committee for the Conservation of Migratory Birds and Their Habitat (MOU 1996). The Trilateral Committee's formal authority as it applies to the U.S.-Mexico border is grounded in the 1936 U.S.-Mexico Migratory Bird Treaty and the 1940 Western Hemisphere Treaty, as well as in the international conventions on biodiversity, endangered species, wetlands, and in the NAAEC. The committee, led by the heads of the Canadian Wildlife Service, U.S. Fish and Wildlife

Service, and the International Affairs division of Mexico's SEMARNAT, is charged "to facilitate and enhance coordination, cooperation, and development of partnerships among the wildlife agencies of the three countries" (MOU 1996) in matters related to wildlife and ecosystem conservation. It is obligated to meet annually.

The Trilateral Committee functions more as a program, or set of programs, like the La Paz programs with which it was loosely affiliated during the Border XXI period (1996–2000). Although its mandate is continental, like the CEC's, it supports a number of activities specific to the border region, including for a time several working tables focused on Borderlands, Wildlife Without Borders-Mexico, and the Border XXI Program. These working tables were discontinued in 2005 in favor of less regionally specific organizing frames. One casualty of this shift in focus may have been the U.S.-Mexico Border Field Coordinating Committee, which from 1994 to 2005 served as a U.S. federal coordinating umbrella for joint U.S.-Mexico conservation projects along the boundary (DOI 2005). A broad spectrum of conservation activities continued, however, under the mantle of other working tables, including the tables of Species of Common Concern, Migratory Birds, Ecosystem Conservation, and a table dedicated to implementing the Convention on Trade in Endangered Species of Wild Flora and Fauna (CITES) in the North American region.

Because the Trilateral Committee lacks a fixed (line-item) budget, with funding contributed by agencies of the three governments—in the U.S. case, for example, funds are contributed by the U.S. Fish and Wildlife Service—we have not been able to determine budgetary trends in support of conservation projects along the border. But at its twenty-second annual meeting in 2017, it was evident that many of the specific activities of its working tables were centered around the border region, focusing, for example, on northwestern jaguar recovery, bat conservation in Mexico's northwest, conservation in the Rio Sonoyta (a boundary river), aquatic conservation in the Rio Yaqui headwaters (a boundary river), Sonoran Pronghorn recovery, black-tailed prairie dog conservation in Sonora, and California Condor recovery (Trilateral Committee 2017). An important and continuing theme of the Trilateral Committee since 2005 is the adverse effect of the U.S. border fence and tactical security infrastructure in fragmenting habitats of at least nineteen species of wild fauna along the border (Trilateral Committee 2017).

The Challenge of Governance Along the Border

Our review of the binational agencies and programs contributing to environmental protection reveals a pattern of institutional development in which environmental protection has gained standing on the binational agenda, certainly since the mid-

1970s. If we take 1975 as a baseline, more than forty years of political and diplomatic effort have produced mandate expansion and strengthened environmental capacity at older institutions like the IBWC as well as generating new binational and trinational agencies and programs with mandates for environmental protection and sustainable development in the region. The array of boundary-spanning interactions and cooperative activities is impressive compared to those at the time the La Paz Agreement was signed in 1983. Seen strictly through an additive lens, there is now considerably greater capacity to address environmental conditions in the border region via the IBWC, the NADB/BECC, the BHC, the La Paz programs, and trilateral institutions like the CEC and the U.S.-Mexico Trilateral Committee.

And yet we agree with recent reports from the GNEB that argue these institutional gains have not kept pace with the environmental stresses that have accompanied the rapid urbanization and trade-led development of the border region since environmental awareness took hold along the border in the 1970s (GNEB 2003, 2004, 2007, 2008). As the GNEB notes, the suite of different institutions and efforts remains fragmented and falls well short of constituting a comprehensive and strategic approach to border-wide environmental protection and sustainable development. The accrual of agencies and programs in this issue area has certainly come to resemble a multilevel governance system of hierarchically structured federal and state institutions coupled with binational and subsidiary entities and programs, most with overlapping and complementary missions for environmental protection. The functional and geographic policy span of these institutions has amplified since the La Paz Agreement was signed. But the agencies and programs themselves resemble more of what Elinor Ostrom described when she discussed the idea of polyarchical governance systems (Ostrom 2010, 641), more a pastiche of institutions, programs, and policy commitments in which the parts exist in semiharmonious relationship, lacking any overall or common strategic direction, the La Paz programs' best efforts notwithstanding. This can be seen in a simple perusal of the basic elements associated with these programs (see Table 6.5).

While polycentric systems are potentially resilient by their decentralized but overlapping authority, we do not believe this is evident in many situations in border area environmental management. Legal authority for these programs is spread across several very different mechanisms. Only one agency, the IBWC, has strong treaty authority, though the La Paz Agreement has certainly stood the test of time and multiple presidential administrations in both countries and the NAFTA-based institutions have likewise endured, if altered in terms of their original mandate and missions. Financial support for key institutions, except for the IBWC, remains quite variable and fragile, this in an environment where federal help is needed to compensate for the burdens international trade and development impose on local communities and governments.

TABLE 6.5 Binational environmental agencies and programs along the U.S.-Mexico border

Agencies and programs	Authority	Mandate	Functions	Personnel	Geo-span	Sector coverage
USIBWC	Water Treaty, 1944	Administer all U.S./Mexico boundary and water treaties / resolve disputes	Diplomacy, operations, construction	50+	Immediate boundary	Water supply, water quality, groundwater
BECC/NADB	BECC/NADB Agreement as amended, 2004	Advance sustainable development through environmental project development in the border area	Certify and finance border area environmental infrastructure projects	18 directors + support staff at San Antonio and Ciudad Juárez offices	62 miles north; 186 miles south of the boundary	Water supply, water quality, air quality, solid wastes, toxic wastes and substances
BHC	BHC Agreement, 2000	Promote binational health in the border zone	Organizing, networking, educating, immunizations, vector management	N/A	62 miles north; 62 miles south of the boundary	Environmental health

CEC	NAAEC, 1993	Advance environmental cooperation at a North American scale	Scaling, spotlighting, investigations, citizen-initiated investigations of government noncompliance with environmental law	28	North American region	Ecosystem monitoring and conservation, pollution prevention, toxic release inventory, citizen complaints & factual investigations
Border 2020	La Paz Agreement, 1983	Promote and coordinate environmental cooperation in border zone	Air quality, water quality, solid waste and toxics, environmental health, environmental compliance with law	N/A	62 miles north; 62 miles south of the boundary	Environmental protection and health (air, water, solid and hazardous waste), environmental education, environmental compliance
Trilateral Committee	Trilateral Committee MOU, 1996	Promote transboundary cooperation on ecosystem conservation and management	Support protected areas, targeted conservation efforts for border wildlife	N/A	North American region; variable by ecosystem	Fauna and flora along and across the border with a focus on ecosystems

Sources: BECC/NADB 2004; EPA 2012; MOU 1996; NAAEC 1993; Treaty 1944.

Needed consensus on cost-sharing arrangements, particularly an acknowledgment of the need for subsidies that address the asymmetrical capacity to invest in border environmental infrastructure, has often eluded binational agencies and programs, complicating agreement on solutions to compelling environmental problems at the border. A strong focus on the need for greater public participation and voice in designing and implementing border-focused environmental programs has been a work in progress, gaining important ground in the 1990s and losing ground in recent years under the stresses imposed by limited budgets and border security operations.

In sum, the history and trend lines in binational environmental cooperation certainly play into an older narrative of boom and bust attention to the border region's priorities by national governments. Taken as a whole, the border has seen real gains in institutional capacity, but the lesson of the past decade is that national attention and priority given to border area environmental affairs continues to be subject to rather substantial swings of the policy pendulum. Despite the creation of and investment in border environmental agencies as NAFTA entered into force, there is no steady national priority attendant to these institutions for a region whose needs require substantial federal-level investment to cope with the hazards and stresses of international trade-driven manufacturing and commerce. After forty years, it is fair to say that the problems flagged by early analysts of the border environment, such as Howard Applegate (1979), or those flagged by the U.S.-Mexico Chamber of Commerce in 1990 or by the American Medical Association in 1990 are still alive and well and compelling in the border area.

Policy Recommendations

We conclude with suggestions for strengthening border environmental institutions, many of which have previously been placed on the table by various analysts, including ourselves, the GNEB, and other environmental advocacy organizations. Our policy recommendations fall into the categories of both institution-specific and generally needed reforms.

Agencies and Programs
- IBWC
  - Each national section should revise its strategic plan to stress sustainable development as part of its overall mission—and a new minute should be signed to this effect.
  - Building on recent progress in Minutes 319, 320, and 323, the IBWC should move to clearly incorporate ecological benefits in its treaty-based understanding of the beneficial uses of treaty-allocated water.

- Each national section should strengthen its citizen advisory process; the commission should adopt a new minute that recognizes the value of citizen advisory functions and establishes a mechanism by which citizen advisory groups may communicate and consult with each other on treaty-related issues in their respective regions along the border.
- For the Rio Grande River, the IBWC should move forward with its Minute 308 commitment to form a basin-wide advisory board to counsel the commission on watershed stewardship in the basin.
- The IBWC should build on recent cooperative measures to pursue agreements on groundwater management along the international boundary.
- Building on Minute 320 (Tijuana River), the commission should establish similar mechanisms of stakeholder engagement in addressing water quality and ecological management in other transboundary river basins under its jurisdiction.
- NADB (BECC)
  - Ensure that transparency and public participation in board decisions are sustained in its new charter.
  - Restore BEIF funding for water and sanitation infrastructure to 1998 levels.
  - Ensure that poor communities have access to available technical expertise and financing for project development.
  - Preserve and support the BECC's sustainable development criteria in project certification.
  - Prioritize grant funding for the La Paz Agreement–denominated border zone (62 miles north and 186 miles south of the boundary).
- BHC
  - Augment base funding for the BHC.
- CEC
  - Protect CEC citizen-initiated investigations process by limiting the ability of domestic governments to use legal challenges to delay or prevent the implementation of factual investigations.
  - Augment the CEC's budget to keep pace with inflation, which in 2017 means increasing the CEC's budget from US$9 million to US$15 million.
- La Paz programs (Border 2020)
  - Protect and augment funding for La Paz programs, including BEIF line item.
  - Restore BEIF funds for water and sanitation infrastructure to 1998 levels.
  - Allocate more funds to Border 2020 task forces, enabling citizens in both countries to actively participate in these activities.
- Trilateral Committee
  - Restore U.S.-Mexico border working tables.
  - Augment funding for border zone projects undertaken by the Trilateral Committee.

- Restore and strengthen collaboration between national wildlife agencies that compose the Trilateral Committee, the CEC, and environmental agencies in identifying problems and protecting habitats and ecosystems along the border.

General Recommendations

- Better utilize the La Paz Agreement annex process to negotiate binational solutions to particular environmental problems in the border region.
- Existing binational agencies and federal agencies participating in border environmental programs should routinely consult and periodically consider how their mission fits into a broader strategic vision for sustainable development along the border. Setting aside at least one meeting of the La Paz Agreement National Coordinators every five years for just this purpose would help bring greater coherence to the mixed assemblage of border programs for environmental protection in the border region.

Notes

1. A recent exception is the 2006 Transboundary Aquifer Assessment Program (TAAP) Act passed by the U.S. Congress and administered under the supervision of the U.S. Section of the IBWC. While TAAP is a U.S. initiative, it authorized the U.S. Department of the Interior (DOI) to cooperate with Mexican agencies in development studies of transboundary aquifers in Mexico that improve binational understanding of groundwater dynamics and availability in specific groundwater basins along the Texas, New Mexico, and Arizona boundaries with Mexico. See Public Law 109-448 (2006).

2. The first six focus areas of Border XXI were clearly authorized by the La Paz Agreement; the last three areas had less of a direct justification but were nonetheless adopted by the program (GNEB 2000, 27).

References

Abel, Andrea, and Marico Sayoc. 2006. "North American Development Bank: An Institution Worth Saving." IRC Americas, June 9, 1–6.

"Agreement to Establish a United States-Mexico Border Health Commission." 2000. U.S. Department of State, Washington, D.C., July 14.

Applegate, Howard. 1979. *Environmental Problems of the Borderlands*. El Paso: Texas Western Press.

Bennett, David. 1997. "Controversial Border Health Commission." *El Paso Times*, November 14.

Border Environment Cooperation Commission (BECC). 2012. "2012 Annual Report." Ciudad Juárez, Chihuahua, Mex.

Border Environment Cooperation Commission and North American Development Bank (BECC and NADB). 2000. "Joint Status Report." Ciudad Juárez, Chihuahua, Mex.

Border Environment Cooperation Commission and North American Development Bank (BECC and NADB). 2004. "Joint Status Report." Ciudad Juárez, Chihuahua, Mex., March 31.

Border Environment Cooperation Commission and North American Development Bank (BECC and NADB). 2014. "Institutional Integration of the Border Environment Cooperation Commission and the North American Development Bank." Ciudad Juárez, Chihuahua, Mex., July 15.

Border Environment Cooperation Commission and North American Development Bank (BECC and NADB). 2017. "Board of Directors Announces BECC/NADB Full Merger for 2017." July 21. http://www.becc.org/news/becc-news/board-of-directors-announces-becc-nadb-full-merger-for-2017#.WaCdFP6GNaR.

Border Health Commission (BHC). 2003. "Annual Report 2003." El Paso, Tex.

Border Health Commission (BHC). 2016. "U.S.-Mexico Border Health Commission: Goals, Actions, and Accomplishments." March. El Paso, Tex.

Border Health Commission (BHC). 2017. "U.S.-Mexico Border Health Commission (BHC): Initiatives and Activities." El Paso, Tex.

Chapa, Sergio. 2017. "NADBank to Merge with Border Environment Cooperation Commission." *San Antonio Business Journal*, June 15.

Coppege, Richard. 1978. *United States-Mexico Border Environmental Health Problems: Technical References*. El Paso, Tex.: Pan American Health Organization, Field Office.

Council on Scientific Affairs. 1990. "A Permanent U.S.-Mexico Border Environmental Health Commission." *JAMA* 264 (24): 3319–21.

Good Neighbor Environmental Board (GNEB). 1998. *Annual Report of the Good Neighbor Environmental Board*. Washington, D.C.: U.S. Environmental Protection Agency.

Good Neighbor Environmental Board (GNEB). 2000. *Fourth Report of the Good Neighbor Environmental Board to the President and Congress of the United States*. EPA 130-R-00-001. Washington, D.C.: U.S. Environmental Protection Agency.

Good Neighbor Environmental Board (GNEB). 2003. *Sixth Report of the Good Neighbor Environmental Board to the President and Congress of the United States*. EPA 130-R-03-001. Washington, D.C.: U.S. Environmental Protection Agency.

Good Neighbor Environmental Board (GNEB). 2004. *Children's Environmental Health: Spotlight on the U.S.-Mexico Border. Seventh Report of the Good Neighbor Environmental Board to the President and Congress of the United States*. EPA 130-R-04-001. Washington, D.C.: U.S. Environmental Protection Agency.

Good Neighbor Environmental Board (GNEB). 2007. *Natural Disasters and the Environment Along the U.S.-Mexico Border. Eleventh Report of the Good Neighbor Environmental Board to the President and Congress of the United States*. EPA 130-R-07-001. Washington, D.C.: U.S. Environmental Protection Agency.

Good Neighbor Environmental Board (GNEB). 2008. *Environment Protection and Border Security on the U.S.-Mexico Border. Tenth Report of the Good Neighbor Environmental Board to the President and Congress of the United States.* EPA 130-R-08-001. Washington, D.C.: U.S. Environmental Protection Agency.

Good Neighbor Environmental Board (GNEB). 2012. *Environmental, Economic and Health Status of Water Resources in the U.S.-Mexico Border Region.* EPA 130-R-12-001. Washington, D.C.: U.S. Environmental Protection Agency.

Hendricks, David. 2006. "Underserved Border May Well Lose Its Young Development Bank." *San Antonio News-Express*, March 9.

International Boundary and Water Commission (IBWC). 1979. "Minute 261, Recommendations for the Solution to the Border Sanitation Problems." El Paso, Tex., September 24.

International Boundary and Water Commission (IBWC). 1985. "Minute 270, Recommendations for the First Stage Treatment and Disposal Facilities for the Solution of the Border Sanitation Problem at San Diego, California/Tijuana, Baja California." Ciudad Júarez, Chihuahua, Mex., April 30.

International Boundary and Water Commission (IBWC). 1995. "Minute 294, Facilities Planning Program for the Solution of Border Sanitation Problems." El Paso, Tex., November 24.

International Boundary and Water Commission (IBWC). 1998. "Minute 299, Support to the Border Environment Cooperation Commission in Development of Projects for the Solution of Border Sanitation Problems." Ciudad Juárez, Chihuahua, Mex., December 3.

International Boundary and Water Commission (IBWC). 2002. "Minute 308, United States Allocation of Rio Grande Waters During the Last Year of the Current Cycle." Ciudad Juárez, Chihuahua, Mex., June 28.

International Boundary and Water Commission (IBWC). 2012. "Minute 319, Interim International Cooperative Measures in the Colorado River Basin through 2017 and Extension of Minute 318 Cooperative Measures to Address the Continued Effects of the April 2010 Earthquake in the Mexicali Valley, Baja California." Coronado, Calif., November 20.

International Boundary and Water Commission (IBWC). 2015. "Minute 320, General Framework for Binational Cooperation on Transboundary Issues in the Tijuana River Basin." Tijuana, Mex., October 5.

International Boundary and Water Commission (IBWC). 2017. "Minute 323, Extension of Cooperative Measures and Adoption of a Binational Water Scarcity Contingency Plan in the Colorado River Basin." Ciudad Juárez, Chihuahua, Mex., September 21.

Kelly, Mary, and Cyrus Reed. 2001. *The Border Environment Cooperation Commission (BECC) and North American Development Bank (NADB): Achieving Their Environmental Mandate.* Austin: Texas Center for Policy Studies.

Martin, Gary. 2006. "NADBank Execs Encouraged." *San Antonio News-Express*, March 24.

McKinney, Joseph A. 2000. *Created from NAFTA: The Structure, Function, and Significance of the Treaty's Related Institutions*. Armonk, N.Y.: M. E. Sharp.

Memorandum of Understanding (MOU). 1996. "Memorandum of Understanding Establishing the Canada/Mexico/United States Trilateral Committee for Wildlife and Ecosystem Conservation and Management." Oaxaca, Mex., April 9.

Mumme, Stephen, Donna Lybecker, Osiris Gaona, and Carlos Monterola. 2009. "The Commission for Environmental Cooperation and Transboundary Conservation Across the U.S.-Mexico Border." In *Conservation of Shared Environments: Learning from the United States and Mexico*, edited by L. Lopez-Hoffman, E. McGovern, R. Varady, and K. Flessa, 261–78. Tucson: University of Arizona Press.

North American Agreement on Environmental Cooperation (NAAEC). 1993. "Appendix III." Reprinted in *The Environment and NAFTA: Understanding and Implementing the New Continental Law*, edited by Pierre Marc Johnson and André Beaulieu, 1996, 331–61. Washington, D.C.: Island Press, 1996.

Ostrom, Elinor. 2010. "Beyond Markets and States: Polycentric Governance of Complex Economic Systems." *American Economic Review* 100 (3): 641–72.

Public Law 103-400. 1994. United States-Mexico Border Health Commission Act. 103rd U.S. Congress. https://www.hhs.gov/sites/default/files/res_2291.pdf.

Public Law 109-448. 2006. United States-Mexico Transboundary Aquifer Assessment Act. December 22. 109th U.S. Congress. 120 Stat. 3328. https://www.congress.gov/109/plaws/publ448/PLAW-109publ448.pdf.

Sanchez, Roberto. 1993. "Public Participation and the IBWC: Challenges and Options." *Natural Resources Journal* 33 (2): 283–98.

Secretariat of the Commission for Environmental Cooperation. 1993. "North American Agreement on Environmental Cooperation Between the Government of Canada, the Government of the United Mexican States and the Government of the United States of America." https://ustr.gov/sites/default/files/naaec.pdf.

Siwik, Allyson, Elaine Hebard, and Celso Jacques. 2012. "A Critical Review of Public Participation in Environmental Decision Making Along the U.S.-Mexican Border: Lessons from Border 2012 and Suggestions for Future Programs." In *The U.S.-Mexican Border Environment: Progress and Challenges for Sustainability*, edited by Erik Lee and Paul Ganster, 105–44. SCERP Monograph Series 16. San Diego: San Diego University Press.

Treaty Between the United States of America and Mexico. 1944. "Utilization of the Waters of the Colorado and Tijuana Rivers and of the Rio Grande." Washington, D.C., November 14.

Trilateral Committee for Wildlife and Ecosystem Conservation and Management (Trilateral Committee). 2017. XXII Annual Meeting, Ensenada, Baja California, May 15–19. https://www.trilat.org/index.php?option=com_content&view=article&id=1744&Itemid=291.

U.S. Department of the Interior (DOI). 2005. "Fact Sheet: U.S.-Mexico Border Field Coordinating Committee: FCC Goals, Purpose and Importance." Washington, D.C.

U.S. Department of State (DOS). 2014. "2014 IBWC Budget." https://www.state.gov/documents/organization/209003.pdf.

U.S. Environmental Protection Agency (EPA). 1991. *Integrated Border Environmental Plan for the U.S.-Mexico Border Area (First Stage Plan, 1992–1994)*. August. EPA A91-537. Washington, D.C.: EPA.

U.S. Environmental Protection Agency (EPA). 1996. *U.S.-Mexico Border XXI Framework Program: Framework Document*. October. EPA 160-R-96-003. Washington, D.C.: EPA.

U.S. Environmental Protection Agency (EPA). 2003. *Border 2012: U.S.-Mexico Environmental Program*. May. EPA 160-R-03-001. Washington, D.C.: EPA.

U.S. Environmental Protection Agency (EPA). 2012. *Border 2020: U.S.-Mexico Border Environmental Program*. EPA-160-R-12-001. Washington, D.C.: EPA.

U.S. Environmental Protection Agency (EPA). 2014. "Collaborative Agreement Between the U.S. Environmental Protection Agency, U.S.-Mexico Border 2020 Program and U.S. Section of the U.S.-Mexico Border Health Commission, U.S. Department of Health and Human Services." August 6.

U.S. Environmental Protection Agency (EPA). 2016. "2016 Annual Performance Plan and Congressional Justification." https://nepis.epa.gov.

U.S. Environmental Protection Agency (EPA). 2017. "EPA 2018 Budget in Brief."

U.S.-Mexico Border Health Association (USMBHA). 1993. "Establishment and Funding of the U.S.-Mexico Border Health Authority and the United States-Mexico Border Health Commission. Recommendations Generated at the January 8–9, 1993 Meeting of Representatives from the California, Arizona, and Texas Medical Associations, Tucson, Arizona." Manuscript in Stephen Mumme's possession.

U.S. Section, International Boundary and Water Commission (USIBWC). 2000. "Strategic Plan." El Paso, Tex.

Valdez, Lou. 1998. "U.S. Moves to Develop U.S.-Mexico Border Health Commission." *Closing the Gap*, October. Office of Minority Health Resource Center, HHS, Washington, D.C.

7

. . .

Health Institutions at the U.S.-Mexico Border

Eva M. Moya, Silvia M. Chavez-Baray, and Miriam S. Monroy

Despite barriers to interorganizational collaboration and cooperation, and cross-border inequities, the transnational nature of health on the U.S.-Mexico border has continued for more than seventy-eight years. The organizational history of the border health field is complex and demonstrates how macropolitics and interorganizational stratification shape public health priorities. Different formal and informal binational and bilateral collaboration attempts have been made to limit the spread of infectious diseases, control the traffic and use of (il)legal drugs, establish environmental controls, facilitate the adoption of healthy lifestyles, and improve communication and collaboration among the health-care systems and providers on both sides of the border. Residents at the border face opportunities as well as challenges to recover and enhance their health status. Proximity to Mexico and the possibility of using Mexican health-care providers and remedies is a safety net for the uninsured and underinsured and facilitates access to health services and medical tourism. At the same time, Mexican residents travel north to receive specialized care, and sexual and reproductive health services. While this cross-border utilization of services has been ongoing for centuries, the health systems of both countries continue to operate with limited formal interaction.

This chapter contextualizes how borderlanders adjust to health challenges along the U.S.-Mexico border, health insurance options on the U.S. side, formal and informal efforts that have been made to take advantage of the strategic location, and future challenges and opportunities for the region's health sector. Describing the health-care delivery and institutions in the United States and along the border is a daunting task. The main objective of this chapter is to provide a broad understanding of the health institutions on the U.S. side of the border. Examples of the historical collaboration and partnerships, health programming, and care in the borderlands are presented.

Health Care Systems in the United States

Effective, efficient, and equitable health care is associated with government-controlled universal primary coverage, comprehensive services, few or no copayments, and an even distribution of resources, not with the wealth of a country or the number of health-care personnel. Most developed countries have such national health-care programs, financed through general taxes, and nearly all their citizens are entitled to receive health-care services. This is not the case with the United States, where citizens are not covered by universal health insurance. In fact, the United States has a distinctively complex system of health care, different from other systems globally. Health care is referred to as an *industry* and not a *system* because its components, interactions, and services do not interact with one another. The health-care sector is characterized by a demand-of-services model, and care is delivered primarily through a fee-for-service approach (Shi and Singh 2017, 18). Health care in the United States includes educational and research institutions, medical suppliers, insurers, payers, claim processors, health- and mental-care professionals, practitioners, community health centers, private sectors/corporations, community-based organizations, community health workers, navigators, and community health representatives. Health and human services providers are involved in the delivery of preventive, primary, secondary, tertiary, acute, rehabilitative, and continuing care. Managed Care Organizations (MCOs) are integrated networks that provide a continuum of care. The industry is massive, with more than 16.4 million employees. Most health-care professionals work in ambulatory settings that offer short-term treatment facilities like urgent care clinics and outpatient surgical centers (5.7 million). A similar number (4.7 million) are employed by hospitals, nursing homes, and residential facilities (Shi and Singh 2019).

The health-care industry, a blend of public and private sources, is a highly profitable mosaic of loosely coordinated financing, insurance, delivery, and payment mechanisms. The U.S. market economy attracts a core of private entrepreneurs, who seek rents by performing key functions along the health-care delivery chain. Employers purchase health insurance coverage for their employees, who pay premiums and deductibles and receive services delivered primarily by nonprofit institutions and private entities (Rose 2018).

A 2015 Health Resources and Services Administration report indicated that about 1,375 Federally Qualified Health Center (FQHC) grantees, with the help of 188,851 employees, provided health-care services (primary and preventive) to more than 24.3 million individuals living in urban and rural areas (Heisler 2017). FQHCs included federally supported health centers (both grantees and look-alikes) as well as certain outpatient Indian Health Service health-care providers and health advocates for American Indians and Alaska Natives. Health centers are important safety net providers in both urban and rural areas. Of the more than twenty-two million Americans who receive health care, about one-third are rural residents. FQHCs provide primary care services in underserved areas. They are required to meet stringent requirements, including provision of a sliding-fee scale based on ability to pay. These centers may be Community Health Centers, Migrant Health Centers, Health Care for the Homeless, and Health Centers for Residents of Public Housing. American Indians receive services through the public Indian Health Service (IHS) (Rural Health Information Hub n.d. ["Federally Qualified Health Centers"]).

The government finances public health insurance programs through Medicaid, Medicare, and the Children's Health Insurance Program (CHIP). Medicare and Medicaid are social insurance programs that allow the financial burdens of illness to be shared among healthy and sick individuals and affluent and low-income families. Medicare is available to permanent legal U.S. residents aged sixty-five or older. Medicare also includes younger people who have received twenty-four consecutive months of Social Security disability benefits or any disability benefit from the Railroad Retirement Board. Those younger than sixty-five years of age can also qualify provided they have an end-stage renal disease or an amyotrophic lateral sclerosis health condition. Medicaid is a state and federal program intended for low-income individuals and families to help cover medical costs and any long-term custodial care. Medicaid might offer additional benefits that Medicare does not, such as dental, routine vision examinations, and hearing aids (Medicare n.d.). State and federal governments with the goal of providing coverage and expanding services to uninsured children who do not qualify for Medicaid and those who cannot afford private coverage fund the CHIP. Approximately 9.6 million children are enrolled, according to a 2018 Statistical Enrollment Report (Center for Medicare and Medicaid Services 2019). Undocumented migrants' children born in the United States are eligible for coverage under CHIP; however, increased immigration control and fear of giving out sensitive information—such as an address—leads parents to withdraw their children from the program or not apply (Bissonnette 2018).

The Patient Protection and Affordable Care Act of 2010 (PPACA), known as the Affordable Care Act (ACA) or Obamacare, is the most comprehensive health-care reform in recent history designed to reduce the number of uninsured. The primary objective is to expand health insurance coverage by requiring most persons to obtain coverage, expanding Medicaid to low-income adults, providing premium assistance for the purchase of private insurance, using tax credits and penalties to encourage employers to offer coverage, and increasing the regulation of the benefits of private coverage. The law also expanded standards to qualify people for Medicaid through states, although many states chose not to implement the Medicaid expansion based on the 2012 Supreme Court ruling. The PPACA includes a long list of health-care-related provisions, intended to lower health-care costs, improve efficiency, and eliminate injury practices that include rescission and denial of coverage due to preexisting conditions (Reininger et al. 2012). The impact of these provisions at the community level is influenced by size and characteristics of the populations eligible for coverage. Coverage projections by PPACA have not considered population growth and are limited to Medicaid coverage only ("Affordable Care Act" n.d.).

In sum, the U.S. health-care system is a combination of multiple financial arrangements, insurance agencies, or MCOs; multiple payers; a diverse array of settings; and numerous consulting firms that offer expertise in cost containment, quality, planning, and electronic systems. The United States consumes more health-care services as a proportion of the total economic output than any other country in the world. Although the United States has some of the best clinical care in the world, it falls short of delivering equitable health-care services to every individual, especially in terms of cost-efficient services, and displays a glaring failure to translate these costs into better health outcomes (Hathi and Kocher 2017; "Place Matters" 2009).

Mexican Health System

In Mexico, health care is a constitutional right and a system that includes the public and private sector. The origins of the modern Mexican health-care system date back to 1943, when the Secretaría de Salud (Secretary of Health) and the Instituto Mexicano del Seguro Social (IMSS, Mexican Institute for Social Security) were created. The IMSS would serve the workforce, while the Secretaría de Salud would establish a system to care for urban and rural populations. In 1960 a health-care system for government employees was created, the Instituto de Seguridad y Servicios Sociales de los Trabajadores del Estado (ISSSTE, Institute for Social Security and Services for Government Employees) (Frenk et al. 2003). To improve efficiency and quality of care, the Ley General de Salud (General Health Law) was passed in 1983 and included a constitutional amendment establishing the right to health care and services for the uninsured population, with decentralization to state governments following. In 2004 Mexico adopted the Seguro Popular (Popular Health Insurance), aimed to guarantee universal access to health services, especially for vulnerable populations. Seguro Popular provided health-care funding to families that were of low socioeconomic status, underprivileged, and previously excluded from health insurance. Seguro Popular purchased services for its affiliates from the Secretaría de Salud, Secretarías Estatales de Salud (SESA, State Health Services), and IMSS or private physicians at no cost to the user. Benefits in the public sector health-care system included reducing out-of-pocket payments, increasing coverage for vulnerable families, and mitigating health injustices and discrimination (Frenk, Gómez-Dantés, and Knaul 2009; Gómez-Dantés et al. 2011). Private sector benefits included facilities and providers offering services mostly on a for-profit basis financed through either insurance premiums or out-of-pocket payments. Thus, the Mexican state health-care system is a veritable mosaic of subsystems, composed of Secretaría de Salud, IMSS, and ISSSTE programs; social security institutions for oil workers (Petróleos Mexicanos [Pemex, Mexican Petroleum]), the armed forces (Secretaría de la Defensa Nacional [SEDENA, Secretary of National Defense]), and marine forces (Secretaría de Marina [SEMAR, Secretariat of the Navy]); and Seguro Popular, institutions offering services to the uninsured population, individual SESA, and the federal Programa IMSS Oportunidades (IMSS-O, IMSS Opportunities Program) (Gómez-Dantés et al. 2011). Each institution directed its own health-care facilities and providers. In 2019 President Andrés Manuel López Obrador scrapped the Seguro Popular health care program, replacing it with Instituto de Salud para el Bienestar (INSABI, Health Institute for Well-Being). This program promised to ensure comprehensive coverage for all Mexicans at any hospital, clinic, or public health system, at no cost to the patient (Agren 2020).

Mexico has made important progress and improvements in health care regarding illnesses controllable by vaccinations, with salient declines in pertussis, poliomyelitis, diphtheria, and measles. Some of the public health challenges include vector-transmitted conditions, raising efficiency, improving quality, securing greater public financing, and ensuring true universal coverage, especially in disadvantaged geographical areas (Aranda, Van Weel, and Goodyear-Smith 2017).

The U.S.-Mexico Border: Where Two Systems Meet

The U.S-Mexico border is among the world's most complex and dynamic regions. The region has substantial environmental challenges and unique demographic, social, cultural, economic, and policy forces created by increasing globalization (PAHO 2012). Concerns about U.S. national security have brought additional public issues for border residents, including excessive delays crossing the border and increasing surveillance, posing economic and social hardships on local communities. Fortunately, the capacity of health agencies to tackle these challenges has improved over time. That matters because it is widely agreed that the quality of health care for the fifteen million border residents needs improvement, as the population has limited access to health care, is exposed to communicable diseases, suffers from lack of proper sanitation, faces poor water and transportation infrastructure, and is subject to a growing incidence of chronic conditions such as diabetes, obesity, and cardiovascular diseases (Ganster and Lorey 2016). In addition, geographical areas within the border region are economically distressed and the entire region is medically underserved, which compounds health and environmental conditions (Moya, Loza, and Lusk 2012; Rosales, Carvajal, and Guernsey De Zapien 2016). Most of the border region is rural (Moya et al. 2013, 304). Of the U.S. border counties, 73 percent are Medically Underserved Areas (MUAs) and 63 percent are Health Professional Shortage Areas (HPSAs) for primary medical care. The uninsured population in the U.S. border states is higher than the national level (Rural Health Information Hub n.d. ["Rural Border Health"]).

Border and Binational Health Cooperation

In 1889 the International Boundary and Water Commission (IBWC) was given the mandate to manage water allocation between the United States and Mexico (IBWC n.d.). At the invitation of the U.S. Public Health Service, in 1942 the Pan American Health Organization (PAHO) established a Field Office in El Paso, Texas, as part of the World War II cooperative effort. This was the first Field Office of the World Health Organization (WHO). Through this agreement, the U.S. and Mexican governments' health authorities were instrumental in establishing local laboratories to conduct testing on sexually transmitted infections and train health personnel in detection and treatment practices (Collins-Dogrul 2006). PAHO's mission was to provide technical support to local and state health authorities on both sides of the border and assist with coordination through the Field Office. Health priorities included control of sexually transmitted infections and tuberculosis (TB) in the border population, which at that time included contingents of soldiers on rotation between World War II deployments. In subsequent years, the Field Office developed a comprehensive program of public health activities, facilitating binational collaboration, cooperation, and the development of partnerships and consensus among federal, state, and local organizations (PAHO 2012). Within the first year of PAHO's operations, health professionals and workers from Mexico and the United States collaborated to create a niche for health issues, which later was called "border health."

In 1943 the PAHO Field Office organized its first public health conference in Ciudad Juárez, Chihuahua, Mexico. It was during that convening that a physician from Mexico and a U.S. sanitation engineer proposed the creation of the first nongovernmental binational border membership group, the U.S.-Mexico Border Health Association (USMBHA) (Alvarez 1975). Julie Collins-Dogrul (2006) documented the organizational history of the U.S.-Mexico border health field and credits the

USMBHA for the development of the following salient effects: (1) transnational organizational structures, symbols, and practices; (2) the border health organizational field and transnational brokers; (3) long-term and temporary transnational voluntary groups like the Consejos Binacionales de Salud (COBINAS, Binational Health Councils) organized around specific health problems; and (4) broadening approaches to address health issues like tuberculosis, emergency response, substance abuse, maternal and child health, and communicable diseases. Through the USMBHA, border health was defined by the transborder geography. Resources for border health were scarce, and volunteer groups, organizational structures, and affiliated projects with the USMBHA and PAHO were prominent (Alvarez 1975; Collins-Dogrul 2006). In 1959 PAHO and the USMBHA established COBINAS to support health activities for health programs on both sides of the border. The mission of COBINAS was to unite local health efforts to gather and share information and combine resources to create healthy communities (Collins-Dogrul 2006). With the passage of the North America Free Trade Agreement (NAFTA) in 1994, governments and nongovernmental organizations (NGOs) began to fund border health programming, creating a new community of bureaucracies in the United States and changing the health organizational dynamics of the border. In the mid-1990s, U.S. Congress authorized the president to reach an agreement with Mexico to establish a binational border commission to address unique health problems, and in 1995 the USMBHA launched the first issue of the *Journal of Border Health*.

The U.S.-Mexico Border Health Commission (USMBHC, or the Commission) was created in 2000 through an agreement between the U.S. Secretary of Health and Human Services and the Secretary of Health of Mexico according to U.S Public Law 103-400 (1994). However, the Commission has been and continues to be inadequately funded by the two governments. Despite its limited funding, it brings the U.S. and Mexican federal authorities together with the state health departments from the ten border states and local entities to address health issues and establish priorities of the border region (Collins-Dogrul 2011).

For more than seven decades, PAHO and the USMBHA provided critical communication and promoted collaboration to address evolving health issues. In 2014, following two evaluations conducted by PAHO (1997 and 2013), both organizations ended their operations, based on a mutual agreement by the United States and Mexico. The 2013 evaluation included assessments of the cost-effectiveness and maintenance of a physical presence on the border. During this evaluation, about two hundred individuals, experts, and partner organizations were consulted. PAHO director Carissa F. Etienne stated, "The fact that our physical presence at this location is no longer necessary reflects the high level of success that both governments together with PAHO have jointly achieved" (PAHO 2014). However, health indicators and quality of life continue to be compromised by inequalities, disparities, and inadequate funding to support programming, services, and infrastructure (Moya, Loza, and Lusk 2012). Still, PAHO/WHO announced its commitment to maintain technical cooperation in the border area and to provide support for the Commission. Federal and state health authorities continue to devote attention to outbreaks of H1N1 influenza, disease-resistant tuberculosis, measles, and infectious and communicable diseases, especially because of the flow of people across the border (Cruz 2014). Presently, state departments of health are the authority to ensure health protection to populations in California, Arizona, New Mexico, and Texas. They focus primarily on licensing and regulation for health care, control of diseases, health promotion, immunizations, public health preparedness, service and medical emergencies, environmental health risks, laboratory services, epidemiology, and surveillance of public health. The state departments' programs are implemented in collaboration with local, state, federal, private, and community health partners. A significant portion of USMBHC resources are used to support the administration and programming of the state Offices of Border Health (see Table 7.1). The outreach offices offer technical support and opportunities for community partners to join together in addressing border health challenges (PAHO 2012).

The Commission is composed of U.S. and Mexico sections, each with its own budget, personnel, and strategic plan. Commission members (U.S. presidential appointments and appointments by the Secretaría de Salud de México [Secretary of Health of Mexico]) agree on health program priorities and jointly launch binational initiatives. Three of their primary structures include the Healthy Border Program, the Federal Interagency and Binational Working Group, and the establishment of the State Outreach Offices (USMBHC 2010). The California, Arizona, New Mexico, and Texas Departments of Health in the United States and the Baja California, Sonora, Chihuahua, Coahuila, Nuevo León, and Tamaulipas Departments of Health and Outreach Offices of Border Health in Mexico support the Commission's mission to provide leadership to optimize health and quality of life. The goals of the outreach offices are to institutionalize a domestic focus on border health that can transcend political changes and to create an effective venue for binational discussion to address public health issues affecting the border populations. The Commission established outreach offices in San Diego, California; Tucson, Arizona; Las Cruces, New Mexico; and Austin, Texas. In Mexico, outreach offices operate in Tijuana, Baja California; Hermosillo, Sonora; Ciudad Juárez, Chihuahua; Piedras Negras, Coahuila; Monterrey, Nuevo León; and Ciudad Victoria, Tamaulipas (Frenk, Gómez-Dantés, and Knaul 2009).

The Healthy Border Program, enacted in 2000, is a binational initiative composed of measurable and relevant goals focused on border health. It brings together key regional partners to develop and support policy change and evidenced-based interventions. The priorities include chronic degenerative conditions, infectious diseases, maternal and child health, mental health and addictions, injury prevention, and access

TABLE 7.1 U.S. public health departments and Offices of Border Health

Public health departments	Offices of Border Health. Established in 1990s by U.S. border state public health departments.	Website
California (Sacramento)	Office of Binational Border Health. Located in San Diego. Supports professionals in California and Mexico to facilitate communication, coordination, and collaboration between officials, professionals, and communities to optimize health.	https://www.cdph.ca.gov/Programs/CID/OBBH/Pages/OBBHhome.aspx
Arizona (Phoenix)	Office of Border Health. Located in Tucson. Promotes and protects the health of residents through public health practice. Coordinates and integrates public health programs to identify, monitor, control, and prevent adverse health events.	http://www.azdhs.gov/director/border-health/index.php
New Mexico (Santa Fe)	Office of Border Health. Located in Las Cruces. Aims to improve health status and services. Aligns local, state, border, and binational public health agencies in support of USMBHC priorities.	https://nmhealth.org/about/asd/ohc/obh/
Texas (Austin)	Office of Border Health. Located in Austin. The mission is to improve health and well-being along the Texas-Mexico border.	https://www.dshs.texas.gov/borderhealth/about_us.shtm

Source: Prepared by the authors in January 2018.

to health care. The program has been reiterated in 2015 through "Healthy Border 2020: A Prevention & Health Promotion Initiative" (Gómez 2014/15), but the Commission's Binational Technical Workgroup reduced the focus areas from the original eleven to five topics: chronic and degenerative disease, infectious disease, maternal and child health, injury prevention, and access to care. Furthermore, it identified social determinants of each of the health priorities as outlined in Table 7.2 (USMBHC 2010).

The Commission workgroup includes the U.S. Department of Health and Human Services (HHS), the Secretary of Health of Mexico, the state and county health departments, academic institutions, private sector organizations, nongovernmental health organizations, and the Commission, among others (HHS 2017a). The U.S. Section appropriations fall under the Office of Global Affairs (OGA) and funding is not broken down at the project level, so the funding allocated to the Commission is not publicly available.

The U.S. and Mexican health-care systems have various programs and projects in place to promote health services along the border. Examples include Border Binational Health Month (BBHM), a monthlong health promotion initiative that unites sister cities (cities on both sides) in support of border-wide partnerships addressing health challenges. The BBHM is sponsored by the Commission in partnership with the ten state Departments of Health, the Secretary of Health of Mexico, and the Health Initiative of the Americas. The initiative was initially established as Border Binational Health Week in 2004. Since then, more than 1.5 million residents have participated in events and benefited from resources provided (Gómez 2014/15). Another example is the Ventanillas de Salud (health stations) program, which provides on-site health advice and outreach at Mexican consulates in the United States to Mexican and Mexican-origin families unfamiliar with the U.S. health system. Since its inception in 2002, Ventanillas de Salud expanded to include all consular offices in the United States (Health Initiative of the Americas 2018).

Health-Care Access and Utilization

Similarities exist in health issues and priorities on both sides of the border, with eight of the ten leading causes of death being the same (HHS 2017a). This is not surprising; each day there are nearly 1.1 million crossings at the U.S.-Mexico border. The border population, estimated at fifteen million people, mostly Mexican and Mexican American, is expected to double to about thirty million by 2025 (HHS 2017b). The Commission reports that three of the ten poorest U.S. counties are located along the border, with twenty-one of twenty-four counties designated as economically distressed areas (Smith and Denali 2014). As the region continues to grow, residents living along the

TABLE 7.2 Healthy people priority areas and root causes

Categories	Priority health problems at the U.S.-Mexico border	Root causes and/or determinants
Chronic and degenerative disease	Obesity Diabetes Heart disease Asthma	Physical inactivity, poor diet (high caloric intake), low socioeconomic status, poverty, genes (nonmodifiable determinants), lack of breastfeeding, and education/access to information
Infectious disease	Tuberculosis HIV/AIDS/STIs Acute respiratory infections Acute diarrheal disease Vaccine Preventable diseases	Poverty, inadequate and poor nutrition, internal and external migration, poor living conditions, affordable housing, environmental health (water, sewer services), access to health and health-care delivery, and education/information
Injury prevention	Increase urgent care services Disability Mental health Mortality	Education on seat belt use / child car seats, built environment, lack of physical and social infrastructure, alcohol use, and substance abuse
Maternal and child health	Teen pregnancy Neural tube defects Maternal mortality Contraception	Access and quality of medical care, education on prenatal and postpartum care, poverty, unnecessary cesarean section / quality of care, personal hygiene, prenatal care, and lack of health education and counseling
Mental health disorders	Addiction Depression Violence (all types, including, and not limited, to intimate partner violence)	Poverty, genetic, biological, family dysfunction, addiction, disability, lack of social support, and education

Source: USMBHC 2010.

border may be adversely affected by the burdens placed on the existing natural and physical resources. Moreover, water is a limited resource in several areas of the border region. Access to drinking water and sanitation services is still one of the most significant physical environmental determinants of health in rural areas on both sides of the border (PAHO 2012).

Mental care is especially challenging for U.S. residents living along the border. Barriers to health-care access include economic deprivation, high rates of poverty, high costs, underemployment, high number of uninsured residents, and health professional shortages. Many residents have grown accustomed to accessing health services on both sides of the international boundary. Several studies have shown that individuals crossing the border northbound are U.S. citizens or residents who live near the border and are returning from medical treatment or purchasing medications at a pharmacy in Mexico (Byrd and Law 2009). Possible reasons for utilization of medical services in Mexico include affordability, different prescription requirements, and cultural and linguistic preferences. High costs of health care in the United States drive people south of the border in search of dental, visual, and pharmaceutical care at a fraction of their costs in the United States, along with other medical services, including primary care, cosmetic surgery, and other alternative therapies not available in U.S. border cities (Judkins 2007). While cross-border movements can help lessen the lack or difficulty of access to specific services on both sides of the border, women are particularly impacted by limited sexual and reproductive health services on both sides. While contraception is cheaper in Mexico, abortion is still illegal in most states—including border states. Therefore, clinics on the U.S. side serve both Mexican and U.S. populations. However, due to restrictive laws enacted in two of the four bordering states (Texas and Arizona), clinic closures have limited the resources available, increasing the distance that women must travel to the nearest clinic. Furthermore, increased immigration surveillance in the border region can burden some women who are targeted by racial profiling and subjected to more questions. While the border represents an opportunity for citizens of both countries regarding access to health services, for women, other political forces can limit that opportunity when it comes to reproductive health.

An alarming gap exists in health insurance coverage, with Texas-Mexico border counties having an estimated uninsured rate of 42 percent in 2002, compared with the national average of 15 percent (Su et al. 2010). Despite the economic, financial, and health-care access barriers, a sizable proportion of border residents resort to border cities in Mexico to meet their health-care needs (Bustamante et al. 2012; Homedes and Ugalde 2003). Pharmaceutical price differences between the United States and Mexico continue to be significant, with average medicine prices in the United States ranging from 50 to 100 percent higher than in Mexico (Rivera, Ortiz, and Cardenas 2009). Cross-border health-care utilization practices reflect unmet health-care needs in the United States. In addition, people with poorer health have greater health needs, which in turn results in increased health-care utilization in Mexico, if access to similar services on the U.S. side of the border is difficult, restricted, or cost-prohibitive (Pisani et al. 2012). Despite these findings, there are studies that show how middle- and upper-class populations use medical tourism in Mexico to meet their health-care needs too.

Cross-Border Health Access and Insurance

A large number of studies have found that the high cost of health care and the limited access to health professionals in the United States are two of the primary reasons why individuals cross the border to Mexico for their health care (Su et al. 2013). The vast majority of users of health services across the border pay for these services out of pocket even if they have U.S. health insurance coverage (Bergmark, Barr, and Garcia 2008). For U.S. retirees living in Mexico, lower health costs and increased accessibility provide an affordable alternative to the U.S. health-care system. Border cities such as Algodones in Baja California, Mexico, initiated dental services to winter residents in Imperial Valley and Yuma County. By 2000 these residents also known as snowbirds, often on fixed income, were able to find diverse services all advertised on English-language sources and signage (Bustamante, Ojeda, and Castañeda 2008). Mexican immigrants living in the United States also use Mexico's providers for health care. Research on one million adults from California using medical, dental, or prescription services in Mexico reported that about 500,000 of them are Mexican immigrants living in the United States (Wallace, Mendez-Luck, and Castañeda 2009).

Binational health insurance may be a venue to improve access to health and mental health-care services for residents of the border region. There are challenges and opportunities associated with binational insurance, and these need to be considered in determining the guidelines to improving the health status on both sides of border. For many Latinos and minorities, insurance is not an option, as they face higher rates of unemployment or underemployment, or work for small businesses that cannot afford health insurance (Su et al. 2013). Cross-border health insurance still relies on an employer-based principle and therefore does not address underserved populations. Those individuals who are employed are disproportionally in work settings that fail to provide affordable health insurance coverage. Even for individuals who qualify for health insurance, coverage is limited and often does not cover dependents, or it is too costly to cover them, and deductibles tend to be high (Bustamante, Ojeda, and Castañeda 2008).

Health insurance coverage regulations and licensing are also complex. They involve U.S. and Mexican federal and state laws and regulations. There are concerns over regulations, licensure requirements, liability, and jurisdiction. California began to recognize the need to legitimate cross-border health insurance in the mid-1990s and passed legislation allowing Mexican companies to sell cross-border insurance. Some plans were developed in California to provide coverage just for dependents in Mexico or to provide access to a network of providers in the United States and Mexico as part of a limited benefit medical insurance plan. New Mexico, Arizona, and Texas have not advanced as fully as California in allowing binational insurance due primarily to State

Medical Associations, or medical providers' concerns over the quality of health care and potential loss of patients due to more accessible and affordable services across the U.S.-Mexico border (Macias and Morales 2001). There are several health plans that cover health care in Mexico and a few hospitals that accept U.S. health insurance. Attempts in the Texas legislature to allow cross-border health insurance coverage similar to plans that exist in California have failed, and it is not legal in Texas to provide optional coverage in an insurance plan in which the insured could choose to receive their care exclusively in Mexico. Liability and legal recourse are problematic because there is no established mechanism to deal with such problems across countries (Bustamante et al. 2012).

Binational health insurance coverage has several advantages. One is the financial savings to the state, insured individuals, and hospitals because of reduced hospitalization costs. This is salient because with less primary and secondary care offered, catastrophic care, which is expensive, may be needed. Binational health insurance coverage allows for savings with out-of-pocket fees, and employers like it as they have healthy and productive employees with low turnover and higher satisfaction and health outcomes. Coverage to dependents regardless of location of residence is another benefit (Bergmark, Barr, and Garcia 2008; Macias and Morales 2001).

Medical Tourism

U.S. residents and citizens travel for health services to Mexico because of speed of care, quality, friendliness, cost, and faster relief of symptoms (Ramírez Cantú 2017). Studies have also found that easier prescriptions and a preference for Mexican care are reasons why patients obtain health services in Mexico (Sandberg 2017). Patients prefer care in Mexico because of the rapidity of both diagnostic tests and therapeutic treatment, while a patient may have to wait months to see a specialist in the United States. Language and culture are also important factors since many Mexicans living in the United States feel more comfortable speaking Spanish and receiving medical services in that language—or accessing a more holistic approach to health-care services (Macias and Morales 2001; Warner 2012).

Insurance companies are beginning to realize the benefits of medical tourism for themselves and their beneficiaries and have therefore started to introduce medical tourism plans for their clients as an option for their beneficiaries. The global tourism industry is estimated at US$3.1 trillion, and medical tourism is commanding US$50–60 billion of that (with an annual growth rate of 16–20 percent) (Majeed and Lu 2017). The industry is rapidly changing due to demographics. Approximately 10.8 percent of the global population will be sixty-five or older in 2019 and there will be seventy million aging Americans. The motivation of medical tourists to travel abroad for medical treatments is more diverse now. Some individuals are moving to avoid expensive health-care locally, including patients who are residents of both the United States and Mexico. Others are interested in quality or special services and are willing to travel to the comparatively well-developed medical infrastructure abroad. A third group is composed of members of young and old generations. This group is seeking cosmetic surgeries and health-related treatments for a better quality of life. They have the financial resources for elective surgery or high disposable capital, including some of the aging population, spending 130 percent more than normal tourists for medical treatment (Bolton and Skountridaki 2016).

Medical tourism has gained prominence in academic, policy, and practice settings because of the growth in the number of people traveling outside their home country to receive planned health and medical care and treatment, often combining pressing health concerns with a leisure trip (Jang 2017). Dental care along the northern Mexican border for American and Canadian tourists costs less than care domestically provided. This movement of patients across the Mexican border supports the practices of numerous dental clinics in Mexican border cities. The dental tourism industry relies heavily on border proximity and the mobility of people and medical equipment, much like the *maquiladoras* (twin plants) take advantage of the ability for goods to move quickly back and forth across the U.S.-Mexico border (Adams, Snyder, and Crooks 2017). This situation observed at the U.S.-Mexico border also has its counterpart at the northern border, with medical tourism between Canada and the United States.

Border Binational Programs and Initiatives

There is a mosaic of initiatives, programs, and projects that convene professionals and practitioners to engage in dialogue and launch health forums. Yet they lack an overarching strategic direction. Table 7.3 presents a synopsis of some of these initiatives and programs active at the time of publication.

Community Health Workers

The community health worker (CHW) is traditionally a member of the community and serves as a prominent outreach model throughout the country. CHWs increase access to health and human services in various arenas and have a unique role bridging communities with professionals (Kok et al. 2016; Sánchez et al. 2017). Their success in improving health outcomes is often attributed to the ways they are embedded in

TABLE 7.3 U.S.-Mexico border programs

Agency or program	Functions	Sector	Source
Agency for Healthcare Research and Quality	Collect data, chart book reports on the border, and provide comprehensive profile and implementation of public health programs and policies.	Serves as federal intra-agency advisor to USMBHC, U.S. Section.	http://www.ahrq.gov/research/findings/nhqrdr/2014chartbooks/hispanichealth/index.html
AIDS Education & Training Center Program	Regional centers on HIV/AIDS capacity building training for clinicians on HIV, tuberculosis, hepatitis C, and reproductive health.	U.S. border states.	https://www.aidsetc.org/border
Area Health Education Centers (AHECs)	Federal program to improve the supply, distribution, retention, and quality of primary care and health practitioners in medically underserved areas. Located in border counties where health care and health-care education needs are not adequately met.	San Diego Border AHEC. Southeast Arizona SEAHEC. Western Arizona WAHEC. New Mexico AHEC. West Texas AHEC.	www.nationalahec.org
Arizona-Mexico Commission	Public/private, membership-driven non-profit organization to formulate programs and actions impacting Arizona-Mexico.	Binational committees, Arizona-Mexico.	http://www.azmc.org/about/
Border Infectious Disease Surveillance (BIDS)	Binational network focused on surveillance protocols, training, establishment of serologic tests, creation of data sharing agreements, and notifications.	U.S.-Mexico border states.	https://wwwnc.cdc.gov/eid/article/9/1/02-0047_article

Organization	Description	Partners	URL
Border Reproductive Health Technical Work Group	Formed in 2014 to guide the USMBHC on evidence-based reproductive health practices, policies, and programs.	Public and academic partners. Border states based.	http://www.saludfronterizamx.org/iniciativas/cumbre-binacional-fronteriza-salud-reproductiva
Consejos Binacionales de Salud (COBINAS, Binational Health Councils)	Serve as a vehicle for the promotion of unity and collaboration between health officials in 16 neighboring cities to examine health needs and programs to promote joint actions in common benefit of the population of both sides of the border.	Border sister cities.	https://www.dshs.texas.gov/borderhealth/BHC.shtm https://nmhealth.org/about/asd/ohe/obh/#councils https://seahcc.org/home/programs/border-bi-national-health/arizona-border-communities-health-network/ https://www.cdph.ca.gov/Programs/CID/OBBH/Pages/OBBHHome.aspx#
Consorcio Fronterizo México-Estados Unidos en Tuberculosis (U.S.-Mexico Border Tuberculosis Consortium)	Respond to TB: continuity of care, multidrug-resistant, and legal issues that affect binational case management. New Mexico Office of Border Health conducts analysis and evaluation of existing TB programs.	Border states.	http://www.saludfronterizamx.org/iniciativas/consorcio-fronterizo-mex-eu-tuberculosis
Departments of Public Health / Offices of Border Health	California Department of Public Health, Office of Binational Border Health. Arizona Department of Health Services, Office of Border Health. New Mexico Department of Health, Office of Border Health. Texas Department of Health and Human Services, Office of Border Health.	State Departments of Health. Offices of Border Health.	https://www.cdph.ca.gov/Programs/CID/OBBH/Pages/OBBHhome.aspx http://www.azdhs.gov/director/border-health/index.php https://nmhealth.org/about/asd/ohe/obh/ https://www.dshs.texas.gov/borderhealth/about_us.shtm

(continued)

TABLE 7.3 (*continued*)

Agency or program	Functions	Sector	Source
Division of Global Migration and Quarantine	Quarantine stations.	El Paso, Texas, and San Diego, California, and ports of entry.	https://www.cdc.gov/quarantine /quarantinestations.html
Early Warning Infectious Disease Surveillance (EWIDS)	Program to improve cross-border activities in early detection, identification, and reporting of infectious diseases associated with bioterrorism agents or other public health threats.	Mexican border states, Secretary of Health. 20 U.S. states that share borders with Mexico & Canada.	https://azprc.arizona.edu/sites/default/files /pdf/CAB%20102904.%20Attachment%203 .Cecilia%20Rosales.pdf
Epidemiologic Surveillance and Information Exchange	Initiative to develop technical guidelines for U.S.-Mexico coordination on public health events of mutual interest.	U.S., Mexican federal and state public health officials.	https://www.cdc.gov/usmexicohealth/pdf/us -mexico-guidelines.pdf
Grupo de Trabajo Investigación en Salud Fronteriza	Identifies strategies for the development and implementation of a border health research agenda outlining actions for improving the border residents' life/ health.	Border technical experts, academicians, and scholars.	http://www.saludfronterizamx.org/iniciativas /grupo-trabajo-investigacion-salud-fronteriza
Health Initiative of the Americas, UC at Berkeley	Binational Health Month is a mobilization of community organizations, federal/ state agencies to improve the health and well-being of migrant population conducted annually in U.S.-Mexico border states.	SRE, Dept. of Health, Outreach offices, Ventanillas de Salud.	http://hia.berkeley.edu/

Program	Description	Scope	URL
Instituto de los Mexicanos en el Exterior (Institute of Mexicans Abroad), Secretaría de Relaciones Exteriores (SRE, Secretariat of Foreign Affairs)	Ventanillas de Salud in Mexican consulates to promote healthy lifestyles, refer to health services, increase access to primary health services and health insurance coverage, and promote a culture of prevention among Mexican families in the U.S.	50 consulates in the U.S.	http://www.gob.mx/ime/acciones-y-programas/ventanilla-de-salud
Laboratory Response Network	Diagnostic support for select pathogens; includes public health laboratories from Mexico & U.S.	U.S.-Mexico border states.	https://emergency.cdc.gov/lrn/pdf/lrn-overview-presentation.pdf
Leaders across Borders Program (LaB)	Eight-month leadership training program, designed to improve binational border communities.	Public, academic partners in the border.	http://www.saludfronterizamx.org/lideres-fronteras/
Office of National Drug Control Policy	Address substance use and mental health problems along the border through the Southwest Counternarcotic Strategy.	Federal, state communities working on substance abuse prevention.	https://obamawhitehouse.archives.gov/sites/default/files/ondcp/policy-and-research/southwest_strategy-3.pdf
TB Cross-Border Management and Referral Consortium	Facilitate health provider access to information on TB for patients traveling between U.S. and Mexico to ensure continuity of care.	U.S.-Mexico border states.	http://www.saludfronterizamx.org/iniciativas/consorcio-fronterizo-mex-eu-tuberculosis
U.S.-Mexico Border Health Commission (USMBHC, Commission) Comisión de Salud Fronteriza México-Estados Unidos	Provide international leadership to improve health and quality of life along the U.S.-Mexico border.	Binational Commission (62.5 miles or 100 km north and south of the border).	https://www.hhs.gov/about/agencies/oga/about-oga/what-we-do/international-relations-division/americas/border-health-commission http://www.saludfronterizamx.org

Source: Prepared by the authors in January 2018.

social, cultural, and linguistic contexts that expert medical professionals and practitioners may not know firsthand. In recent years, CHWs have proven to be an effective interface between public health initiatives and community education throughout the border. More policy and decision makers are convinced of the value of cost-saving preventive care and the role that CHWs play as frontline workers in promoting public health messaging, strengthening programs, and conducting services navigation with the expectation that they can better deliver culturally sensitive services and health messages (Fletcher and Price 2017).

CHWs traditionally canvas communities to offer education and motivation, going door to door as well as working in community venues. A significant portion of health promotion and protection is conducted by FQHCs, community health centers, community-based organizations, and CHWs. There are multiple CHW programs and projects along the border focusing on chronic conditions, self-care, sexual and reproductive health, and access to care. A crucial characteristic of CHW work is that it is genuinely holistic (Heredia et al. 2017; Sanchez-Bane and Moya Guzman 1999). In the Pasos Adelante program, implemented on the Arizona-Mexico border, CHWs demonstrated improvements in lifestyle behaviors with mixed effects on cardiovascular disease risk factors (Krantz et al. 2017). Health-care providers agree that CHWs are effective for the personal connection that helps them better bond with persons and the additional time they spend to better understand and individualize their health education (Brown et al. 2017).

Policy Recommendations

A review of health institutions, practices, and programs around health care on the U.S.-Mexico border reveals a pattern of development where cross-border health care has gained presence and momentum. Formally, there have been expanded legislative mandates, congressional appropriations from the United States and Mexico, increased political and diplomatic will, and efforts to dialogue and address public and environmental health priorities, and there is increased capacity to address public health conditions through the state departments of health, outreach offices, the USMBHC, binational initiatives, academic institutions, and community-based organizations. Market forces have also become very important.

All progress and achievements in health care, however, have been made possible by the collaboration, communication, and cooperation between health officials, decision makers, health-care workers, scholars, community leaders, educators, and researchers. This is truly a grassroots system. Yet these gains are not enough to keep up with the pace of population growth, health-care costs, and emerging needs. Infrastructure and resources remain behind demand and are fragmented and inadequate. Inequalities in access and outcomes are prominent.

To address the singular and complex realities of health care on the U.S.-Mexico border, it is essential to work on a binational framework to formalize and incentivize effective programs and models of collaborative practices in all areas of health care — portable insurance, bilingual access to health care, hedging price differentials, sharing information, promoting preventive care, and strengthening emergency preparedness and response to health outbreaks. This has been done successfully around the topic of communicable diseases. The partnership on this score can be a catalyst for using knowledge and innovation to come together to generate intellectual and physical resources to ensure health care and outcomes in the community at a lower cost. Transformative leadership models are required to create a lasting legacy of border collaboration with high-impact actions. Myths, structural violence, ignorance, ideologies, and antagonism on either side of the border continue to hamper the successful management of health conditions across the border and they must be politically dismantled.

To achieve an effective articulation of these efforts into a system, timely communication among decision makers, scientists, scholars, and professionals in a binational setting is necessary. The cross-training of health-care workers is needed so that students and scholars learn from each other and generate exchanges, internships, and mentoring opportunities. More funding by states and national and international partnerships for research, equipment, education, team practice, innovation, and dialogue with private and public sectors to improve health development are essential to create an effective cross-border system rather than the ersatz arrangement that exists today. Cross-border utilization of health care has been largely informal and unsupported by policy and health authorities on both sides of the border. Offering health insurance coverage for all health-care needs regardless of the country in which the services are offered is critical to establish a closer collaboration between the United States and Mexico to deal with health-care delivery, health outbreaks, and emergencies in the border area.

More effective exchange of health surveillance, data sharing, distribution of laboratory supplies, availability of highly trained technical staff, and ongoing training of public health personnel is also needed and can be coordinated even if the two health-care landscapes are not entirely compatible. Moreover, governments must allocate greater investment in physical and technological infrastructure in health and human services to improve availability and accessibility as well as emergency response to health outbreaks in rural and poorer urban areas. Increasing investments in physical and workforce infrastructure can help health services and outcomes. It is also necessary to strengthen base funding for the Community Health Centers, academic networks, health councils, and the USMBHC to support upstream practices that integrate research, education, and policy practices to fully engage partnerships at the community/local, state, and federal levels. Also important is developing, financing, and building sustainable projects that address behavioral and mental health on the border.

Binational protocols to respond to catastrophic events like mass shootings, pandemics, disease outbreaks, and environmental or ecological disasters to mitigate trauma and risk for future illness are indispensable. Emergency plans to coordinate communication responses and recovery between border cities are required. Projects to provide access to safe and sanitary water infrastructure, increased wastewater management efficiency, enhanced proper waste disposal, improved air quality, primary prevention, mental health first aid, and health promotion services are paramount. It is important to continue to support existing evidence-based practices and initiatives that demonstrate positive outcomes regardless of new administration or political preferences in both countries.

Timely information and data are crucial. To improve quality of life and border health, there is a need to institutionalize Healthy People and Healthy Border indicators as benchmarks to inform policy, research, practice, and services to improve health and address health inequalities. Development and implementation of evidence-based-practice approaches that contribute to strengthening health information, response systems, and improving health-care data are required, especially in rural communities. Health promotion and disease prevention, including the establishment of new mental health, behavioral health, social work, public health programs, and telehealth in the border area, will provide opportunities for young professionals and community health workers to serve and for underserved communities to receive care, especially if health outbreaks and epidemics emerge. Improving access to the medical, nursing, public health, social work, and mental health professions and workforce in the border region is important. This includes recruitment, retention, and ongoing training of health and human services professionals. Finding areas of agreement that could help surmount challenges and allow for improved access to health and wellness for all is vital.

References

Adams, Krystyna, Jeremy Snyder, and Valorie A. Crooks. 2017. "Narratives of a 'Dental Oasis': Examining Media Portrayals of Dental Tourism in the Border Town of Los Algodones, Mexico." *Journal of Borderlands Studies* 34 (3): 1–17.

"Affordable Care Act (ACA) Definition." n.d. Accessed February 5, 2018. https://www.health insurance.org/glossary/affordable-care-act/.

Agren, David. 2020. "Farewell Seguro Popular." *The Lancet* 395 (10224): 549–50.

Alvarez, Humberto Romero. 1975. *Health Without Boundaries: Notes for the History of the United States-Mexico Border Public Health Association, on the Celebration of Its 30 Years of Active Life, 1943–1973.* Mexico City: USMBHA.

Aranda, José Manuel Ramírez, Chris Van Weel, and Felicity Goodyear-Smith. 2017. "Strategies for Increasing the Role of Family Medicine in Mexican Health Care Reform." *Journal of the American Board of Family Medicine* 30 (6): 843–47.

Bergmark, Regan, Donald Barr, and Ronald Garcia. 2008. "Mexican Immigrants in the US Living Far from the Border May Return to Mexico for Health Services." *Journal of Immigrant and Minority Health* 12 (4): 610–14.

Bissonnette, Andréanne. 2018. "'Caged Women': Migration, mobilité et accès aux soins de santé au Texas et en Arizona." Master's thesis, University of Quebec, Montreal.

Bolton, Sharon, and Lila Skountridaki. 2016. "The Medical Tourist and a Political Economy of Care." *Antipode* 49 (2): 499–516.

Brown, Ariel, Garseng Wong, Radhika Gore, and Mark Schwartz. 2017. "Baseline Assessment of Providers' Perspectives on Integrating Community Health Workers into Primary Care Teams to Improve Diabetes Prevention." *CWIC Posters* 35. http://jdc.jefferson.edu /cwicposters/35.

Bustamante, Arturo Vargas, Miriam Laugesen, Mabel Caban, and Pauline Rosenau. 2012. "United States-Mexico Cross-Border Health Insurance Initiatives: Salud Migrante and Medicare in Mexico." *Revista Panamericana de Salud Pública* 31 (1): 74–80.

Bustamante, Arturo Vargas, Gilbert Ojeda, and Xóchitl Castañeda. 2008. "Willingness to Pay for Cross-Border Health Insurance Between the United States and Mexico." *Health Affairs* 27 (1): 169–78.

Byrd, Theresa L., and Jon G. Law. 2009. "Cross-Border Utilization of Health Care Services by United States Residents Living near the Mexican Border." *Revista Panamericana de Salud Pública* 26 (2): 95–100.

Center for Medicare and Medicaid Services. 2019. "Federal Fiscal Year (FFY) 2018 Statistical Enrollment Data System (SEDS) Reporting." https://www.medicaid.gov/sites/default/files /2019-12/fy-2018-childrens-enrollment-report.pdf.

Collins-Dogrul, Julie. 2006. "Managing US–Mexico 'Border Health': An Organizational Field Approach." *Social Science & Medicine* 63 (12): 3199–211.

Collins-Dogrul, Julie. 2011. "Governing Transnational Social Problems: Public Health Politics on the US-Mexico Border." *Global Networks* 12 (1): 109–28.

Cruz, Pamela Lizette. 2014. "Cross-Border Governance on the U.S.–Mexico Border: Institutional Challenges and Developments in Health Collaboration." *Regions and Cohesions* 4 (1): 53–71.

Fletcher, Erica Hua, and Daniel M. Price. 2017. "Capacity and Non-Compliance: Mental Wellness Modules in a Community Health Worker Certification Course." *Health Professions Education* 5 (1): 39–47.

Frenk, Julio, Octavio Gómez-Dantés, and Felicia Marie Knaul. 2009. "The Democratization of Health in Mexico: Financial Innovations for Universal Coverage." *Bulletin of the World Health Organization* 87 (7): 542–48.

Frenk, Julio, Jaime Sepúlveda, Octavio Gómez-Dantés, and Felicia Knaul. 2003. "Evidence-Based Health Policy: Three Generations of Reform in Mexico." *The Lancet* 362 (9396): 1667–71.

Ganster, Paul, and David E. Lorey. 2016. *The U.S.-Mexican Border Today: Conflict and Cooperation in Historical Perspective.* Lanham, Md.: Rowman & Littlefield.

Gómez, Gudelia Rangel. 2014/15. "Binational Health Initiatives on the Mexico-U.S. Border." *Voices of Mexico*, no. 98 (Autumn/Winter): 88–94.

Gómez-Dantés, Octavio, Sergio Sesma, Victor M. Becerril, Felicia M. Knaul, Héctor Arreola, and Julio Frenk. 2011. "Sistema de salud de México." *Salud Pública de México* 53 (2): S220–S232.

Hathi, Sejal, and Bob Kocher. 2017. "The Right Way to Reform Health Care to Cut Costs, Empower Patients." *Foreign Affairs*, July/August.

Health Initiative of the Americas. "2018 Activities Report." https://hiaucb.files.wordpress.com /2019/05/2018-activity-report.pdf.

Heisler, Elayne J. 2017. "Federal Health Centers: An Overview." Congressional Research Service, May 19. https://fas.org/sgp/crs/misc/R43937.pdf.

Heredia, Natalia I., Minjae Lee, Lisa Mitchell-Bennett, and Belinda M. Reininger. 2017. "Tu Salud ¡Sí Cuenta! Your Health Matters! A Community-Wide Campaign in a Hispanic Border Community in Texas." *Journal of Nutrition Education and Behavior* 49 (10).

Homedes, Núria, and Antonio Ugalde. 2003. "Globalization and Health at the United States–Mexico Border." *American Journal of Public Health* 93 (12): 2016–22.

International Boundary and Water Commission (IBWC). n.d. "The International Boundary and Water Commission — Its Mission, Organization and Procedures for Solution of Boundary and Water Problems." Accessed February 12, 2018. https://www.ibwc.gov/About_Us /About_Us.html.

Jang, Sou Hyun. 2017. "Here or There: Recent U.S. Immigrants' Medical and Dental Tourism and Associated Factors." *International Journal of Health Services* 48 (1): 148–65.

Judkins, Gabriel. 2007. "Persistence of the U. S.-Mexico Border: Expansion of Medical-Tourism amid Trade Liberalization." *Journal of Latin American Geography* 6 (2): 11–32.

Kok, Maryse C., Hermen Ormel, Jacqueline E. W. Broerse, Sumit Kane, Ireen Namakhoma, Lilian Otiso, Moshin Sidat, Aschenaki Z. Kea, Miriam Taegtmeyer, Sally Theobald, and Marjolein Dieleman. 2016. "Optimising the Benefits of Community Health Workers' Unique Position Between Communities and the Health Sector: A Comparative Analysis of Factors Shaping Relationships in Four Countries." *Global Public Health* 12 (11): 1404–32.

Krantz, Mori J., Brenda Beaty, Stephanie Coronel-Mockler, Bonnie Leeman-Castillo, Kelly Fletcher, and Raymond O. Estacio. 2017. "Reduction in Cardiovascular Risk Among Latino Participants in a Community-Based Intervention Linked with Clinical Care." *American Journal of Preventive Medicine* 53 (2).

Macias, Eduardo P., and Leo S. Morales. 2001. "Crossing the Border for Health Care." *Journal of Health Care for the Poor and Underserved* 12 (1): 77–87.

Majeed, Salman, and Changbao Lu. 2017. "Changing Preferences, Moving Places and Third Party Administrators: A Scoping Review of Medical Tourism Trends (1990–2016)." *Almatourism—Journal of Tourism, Culture and Territorial Development* 8 (15): 56–83.

Medicare. n.d. "The Difference Between Medicare and Medicaid." Accessed January 25, 2018. https://medicare.com/about-medicare/what-is-the-difference-between-medicare-and -medicaid/.

Moya, Eva M., Oralia Loza, and Mark Lusk. 2012. "Border Health: Inequities, Social Deter- minants, and Cases of Tuberculosis and HIV." In *Social Justice in the U.S.-Mexico Border Region*, edited by Mark Lusk, Kathleen Staudt, and Eva Moya, 161–78. New York: Springer.

Moya, Eva M., Guillermina Solis, Rebeca L. Ramos, Mark W. Lusk, and Carliene S. Quist. 2013. "U.S.–Mexico Border: Challenges and Opportunities in Rural and Border Health." In *Rural Nursing: Concepts, Theory, and Practice*, edited by Charlene A. Winters, 303–34. 4th ed. New York: Springer.

Pan American Health Organization (PAHO). 2012. *Health in the Americas*. Washington, D.C.: Pan American Health Organization. https://www.paho.org/salud-en-las-americas -2012/index.php?option=com_content&view=article&id=9:edicion-2012&Itemid=124 &lang=en.

Pan American Health Organization (PAHO). 2014. "PAHO/WHO's US-Mexico Border Field Office to Conclude Mission After Seven Decades of Service." January 27. http://www.paho .org/hq/index.php?option=com_content&view=article&id=9286%3A2014-paho-who -s-us-mexico-border-field-office-conclude-mission-after-seven-decades-service&Itemid= 1926&lang=en.

Pisani, Michael J., José A. Pagán, Nuha A. Lackan, and Chad Richardson. 2012. "Substitution of Formal Health Care Services by Latinos/Hispanics in the US-Mexico Border Region of South Texas." *Medical Care* 50 (10): 885–89.

"Place Matters." 2009. *Unnatural Causes*, episode 5. California Newsreel. https://www .unnaturalcauses.org/episode_descriptions.php?page=5.

Public Law 103-400. 1994. United States-Mexico Border Health Commission Act. 103rd U.S. Congress. https://www.hhs.gov/sites/default/files/res_2291.pdf.

Ramírez Cantú, Ana Luisa. 2017. "Is There Balance? Mexican Medical Practitioners' Work-Life Experiences and Emotion Management on the U.S.-Mexico Border." Master's thesis, Texas A&M University.

Reininger, Belinda M., Cristina S. Barroso, Lisa Mitchell-Bennett, Marge Chavez, Maria E. Fernandez, Ethel Cantu, Kirk L. Smith, and Susan P. Fisher-Hoch. 2012. "Socio-ecological Influences on Health-Care Access and Navigation Among Persons of Mexican Descent Living on the U.S./Mexico Border." *Journal of Immigrant and Minority Health* 16 (2): 218–28.

Rivera, José O., Melchor Ortiz, and Victor Cardenas. 2009. "Cross-Border Purchase of Med- ications and Health Care in a Sample of Residents of El Paso, Texas, and Ciudad Juarez, Mexico." *Journal of the National Medical Association* 101 (2): 167–73.

Rosales, Cecilia Ballesteros, Scott Carvajal, and Jill Eileen Guernsey De Zapien. 2016. "Editorial: Emergent Public Health Issues in the US–Mexico Border Region." *Frontiers in Public Health* 4:6–8.

Rose, Patti. 2018. *Health Disparities, Diversity, and Inclusion: Context, Controversies, and Solutions.* Burlington, Mass.: Jones & Bartlett Learning.

Rural Health Information Hub. n.d. "Federally Qualified Health Centers (FQHCs) and the Health Center Program." Accessed January 25, 2018. https://www.ruralhealthinfo.org /topics/federally-qualified-health-centers.

Rural Health Information Hub. n.d. "Rural Border Health." Accessed January 30, 2018. https:// www.ruralhealthinfo.org/topics/border-health.

Sánchez, Daisey, Stephanie Adamovich, Maia Ingram, Frances P. Harris, Jill De Zapien, Adriana Sánchez, Sonia Colina, and Nicole Marrone. 2017. "The Potential in Preparing Community Health Workers to Address Hearing Loss." *Journal of the American Academy of Audiology* 28 (6): 562–74.

Sanchez-Bane, Mary, and Eva M. Moya Guzman. 1999. "Community-Based Health Promotion and Community Health Advisors: Prevention Works When They Do It." In *Life, Death, and In-Between on the U.S.-Mexico Border: Así es la vida,* edited by Martha Oehmke Loustaunau and Mary Sanchez-Bane, 131–54. Westport, Conn.: Bergin & Garvey.

Sandberg, Debra S. 2017. "Medical Tourism: An Emerging Global Healthcare Industry." *International Journal of Healthcare Management* 10 (4): 281–88.

Shi, Leiyu, and Douglas A. Singh. 2017. *Essentials of the U.S. Health Care System.* 4th ed. Burlington, Mass.: Jones & Bartlett Learning.

Shi, Leiyu, and Douglas A. Singh. 2019. *Delivering Health Care in America: A Systems Approach.* 7th ed. Burlington, Mass.: Jones & Bartlett Learning.

Smith, Mary-Katherine, and David Line Denali. 2014. "Social Media in Health Education, Promotion, and Communication: Reaching Rural Hispanic Populations Along the USA/ Mexico Border Region." *Journal of Racial and Ethnic Health Disparities* 1 (3): 194–98.

Su, Dejun, William Pratt, Jim P. Stimpson, Rebeca Wong, and José A. Pagán. 2013. "Uninsurance, Underinsurance, and Health Care Utilization in Mexico by US Border Residents." *Journal of Immigrant and Minority Health* 16 (4): 607–12.

Su, Dejun, Chad Richardson, Ming Wen, and José A. Pagán. 2010. "Cross-Border Utilization of Health Care: Evidence from a Population-Based Study in South Texas." *Health Services Research* 46 (3): 859–76.

U.S. Department of Health and Human Services (HHS). 2017a. "U.S.-Mexico Border Health Commission Activities." Office of Global Affairs (OGA), December 13. https://www .hhs.gov/about/agencies/oga/about-oga/what-we-do/international-relations-division /americas/border-health-commission/activities/index.html.

U.S. Department of Health and Human Services (HHS). 2017b. "The US-Mexico Border Region." Office of Global Affairs (OGA), December 23. https://www.hhs.gov/about/agencies

/oga/about-oga/what-we-do/international-relations-division/americas/border-health
-commission/us-mexico-border-region/index.html.

U.S.-Mexico Border Health Commission (USMBHC). 2010. "Healthy Border 2020: A Prevention & Health Promotion Initiative." https://www.hhs.gov/sites/default/files/res
_2805.pdf.

Wallace, Steven P., Carolyn Mendez-Luck, and Xóchitl Castañeda. 2009. "Heading South."
Medical Care 47 (6): 662–69.

Warner, David C. 2012. "Access to Health Services for Immigrants in the USA: From the Great
Society to the 2010 Health Reform Act and After." *Ethnic and Racial Studies* 35 (1): 40–55.

8

From the Institutional to the Informal

Security Cooperation Between the
United States and Mexico

Octavio Rodríguez Ferreira

I t is never easy to discuss Mexico and the United States and their bilateral relations. There is a significant history and a profound sentiment, both positive and negative, toward each other. As a consequence, the relationship between the two nations concerning their common border has not become easier over time. Instead, it keeps changing due to political, economic, and even geographical reasons, always tainted by mistrust from either side.[1] After centuries of interaction, debate, and policy generation, it can be asked if there is still something to analyze and to discover in this "old couple's" relationship since "the nature of this critical binational relationship has been dissected and probed from every conceivable angle" (Olson, Shirk, and Selee 2010b, vii). As Eric L. Olson, David A. Shirk, and Andrew Selee explain, "The clichés describing United States-Mexico relations are well known and well worn. Given the enormity of the geographic, historical, cultural, and economic ties between both countries, it's now a commonplace to say Mexico is the United States' most important bilateral relationship, and vice-versa" (vii). Yet even if border dynamics between the United States and Mexico change frequently depending on the political climate in Mexico (Zagaris and Resnick 1997) and on political changes in the United States, there is still much to know about how Mexico and the United States can work together to jointly manage common threats (Olson, Shirk, and Selee 2010b).

This chapter seeks to show the significance of combined formal and informal mechanisms of cooperation. It compares high-level agreements and standardized institutional proceedings that have been largely effective to a much more diffuse series of organic, "on-the-ground" informal networks that enhance institutional mechanisms of cooperation between the United States and Mexico. It also highlights the importance of personal relations and trust in creating informal networks of collaboration and softening cumbersome standardized institutional procedures. Finally, this investigation explores how on-the-ground informal networks have become an effective facilitator of immediate binational collaboration. As organic networks build on mutual trust, these mechanisms have created channels of communication that go beyond politics and circumvent institutional bureaucracy.

Institutional Security Cooperation Between the United States and Mexico

Marked by their own historic and political contexts, the United States and Mexico have struggled with shared problems on both sides of the border for centuries. As José Z. García (2002) suggests, this cooperative relationship has been more focused on reducing tensions than on developing coordinated operations. Nevertheless, and despite different approaches, the United States and Mexico have found the means to collaborate, especially in recent decades. The framework of assistance and cooperation on security and law enforcement matters between the United States and Mexico has increased exponentially over the last fifty years. Despite countless tensions and disagreements, both countries have been putting together, piece by piece, a rather functional institutional framework that allows a certain degree of standardized cooperation. Yet this was not always the case.

In the early twentieth century, cooperation between the United States and Mexico focused primarily on arresting and prosecuting Mexican rebels fleeing to the United States. In the absence of formal procedures, U.S. authorities used informal mechanisms to detain and return those individuals to Mexico, including abductions, immigration charges, and deportations. As the Mexican Revolution erupted, U.S. concerns of a potential spillover of violence, or even of incursions into its territory, changed the situation, making the United States much more interested in its own security than in collaborating with its southern neighbor (Zagaris and Resnick 1997). After the end of the revolution and during the political stabilization of Mexico between the 1930s and 1940s, unilateral antismuggling and interdiction efforts in the United States caused tensions between the countries. This was perpetuated in part by repeated violations of territorial sovereignty by authorities who would cross the border without authorization to perform their duties. Simultaneously, however, the United States started assisting Mexico in crop eradications and targeting drug smugglers, including operations where U.S. agents operated directly on Mexican soil with consent from the Mexican government (Zagaris and Resnick 1997). Nonetheless, official cooperation between the United States and Mexico before the 1960s was still rare. Despite unilateral efforts to counter drug production and trafficking, both countries reached their first official cooperation agreement in 1969 with Operation Cooperation, which focused on joint border control efforts, followed by a collaboration of U.S. law enforcement agencies under Operation Condor, launched by Mexico in 1975 (Astorga and Shirk 2010, 46).

Washington's first significant effort to reevaluate its policy toward Mexico happened during the Jimmy Carter administration. In 1978 National Security Advisor Zbigniew Brzezinski presented a U.S. State Department initiative to improve coordination between more than a dozen U.S. agencies as well as with some of their Mexican counterparts. The proposal recommended the establishment of a coordinator of Mexican affairs and the creation of a binational commission. However, the efforts toward the consolidation of this framework were lacking and the plan vanished before the end of Carter's presidential term (IILSEN 2003). Perhaps the first landmark of binational security cooperation came later that year with the adoption of the U.S.-Mexican Extradition Treaty—a formal treaty that created opportunities for the two countries to work together in capturing, arresting, and extraditing individuals of mutual interest. It also enabled authorities to familiarize themselves with policies, laws, and institutions on each side of the border.

Additionally, through the 1970s and until the mid-1980s, the United States provided Mexico with equipment and training to eradicate marijuana and opium poppy fields. However, this initial effort of cooperation declined dramatically after the assassination of U.S. Drug Enforcement Administration (DEA) agent Enrique Camarena in 1985 and stalled until the late 1990s (Astorga and Shirk 2010, 46; Seelke, Wyler, and Beittel 2010). In the midst of the Camarena scandal—and the subsequent abduction of Mexican national Humberto Álvarez Machaín by U.S. authorities on Mexican soil in 1990—another landmark cooperation agreement was reached on December 9, 1987. This agreement, the Mutual Legal Assistance in Criminal Matters Treaty (MLAT), was initiated to investigate and prosecute cross-border crime (Zagaris and Resnick 1997). Nevertheless, the momentum for a more solid cooperation plateaued for several years following the Camarena scandal.

In the 1990s, drug abuse and trafficking were seen not only as a serious threat to the health of the population but also as a growing risk to the national security of the United States and Mexico. Both countries' governments were faced with the fact that their nations were producers, consumers, and transit points of illicit drugs. In response, Mexican president Ernesto Zedillo (1994–2000) and U.S. president Bill Clinton (1993–2001) agreed to the creation of the High Level Contact Group (HLCG) to design more effective bilateral policies and promote comprehensive cooperation (IILSEN 2003). Following the creation of the HLCG, cooperation efforts recovered and led to the adoption of the Binational Drug Control Strategy in 1998, through which the United States increased assistance to Mexico with programs focused on interdiction, combating production and trafficking of various illicit drugs, strengthening the rule of law, and countering money laundering. It is estimated that U.S. assistance to Mexico totaled US$397 million from 2000 to 2006 (Seelke, Wyler, and Beittel 2010).

Growing cooperation and new understanding between both governments at the beginning of the twenty-first century was overshadowed by the radical shift of the U.S. agenda following the terrorist attacks of September 11, 2001. A new bilateral framework being built by Mexican president Vicente Fox (2000–2006) and U.S. president George W. Bush (2000–2008), focused strongly on migration and on the consolidation of a more "transparent" border—with freer flow of persons and goods—dramatically changed. Bilateral relations were reoriented mostly toward strengthening border security (IILSEN 2003). Still, a new approach to borders emerged in the aftermath of 9/11 and borderlands were revaluated, though with a clear emphasis on national security (Benítez Manaut and Rodríguez Ulloa 2006). Indeed, the 9/11 terrorist attacks significantly impacted law enforcement and security challenges along the U.S.-Mexico border. Bilateral relations now had to deal with newly founded concerns on terrorism and tensions over the U.S. War on Terror. These tensions included the opposition by Mexico—as a nonpermanent member of the UN Security Council—to a military operation in Iraq, and the United States' reproaches for its opposition. Nevertheless, after the defeat of the Iraqi regime, the United States and Mexico reaffirmed their ties and developed a new security framework to address historic challenges while addressing concerns around terrorism (Shirk 2003).

Following an aggressive militarized countercrime strategy of Mexican president Felipe Calderón (2006–12), the United States and Mexico negotiated the Mérida Initiative, a landmark agreement that created a security and rule-of-law partnership. Under this agreement, the U.S. government agreed to allocate an original amount of more than US$2.6 billion to increase law enforcement and military cooperation, intelligence sharing, and extraditions. Prior to the Mérida Initiative, Mexico had never received such significant support in counterdrug assistance from the United States, partially due to concerns about U.S. involvement in Mexico's internal affairs (Seelke and Finklea 2017). Despite the progress, the future of bilateral security cooperation beyond the Mérida Initiative is uncertain. Mexican president Enrique Peña Nieto (2012–18) immediately reduced U.S. involvement in law enforcement and intelligence-gathering operations upon taking office and established a more centralized channel of communication with the "single-window" policy. However, the Peña Nieto administration later confirmed its commitment with the Mérida Initiative and Mexico allowed Mérida-funded projects to continue operating (Seelke and Finklea 2017).

Moreover, the election of Donald Trump as the president of the United States brought deep uncertainty, and diplomatic relations between both countries hit their lowest level in decades. Concurrently, the election of Mexican president Andrés Manuel López Obrador brought about a mandate for a transformation of Mexico, emphasizing greater opportunities for the poor, less corruption, and more prosperity (Wayne 2019). López Obrador has promised to change the logic of the War on Drugs "by focusing on the underlying economic drivers (poverty and inequality) that encourage ordinary Mexicans to participate in the illicit drug trade; . . . by offering amnesty to a segment of those involved; and . . . moving away from a heavy reliance on the military for internal security" (Olson 2018, 3). However, López Obrador's stance has brought skepticism over a sustained development of the bilateral agenda, especially with regard to security cooperation. This was made evident after López Obrador suggested an interest in diverting Mérida Initiative support from security and rule-of-law programs to investment in social programs (Sheridan 2019). However, after the initial turmoil caused by López Obrador's comments, the state of affairs seems not to have changed and Mérida-funded programs are still operating regularly. The bilateral relations seem to have gone back to the "new normal."

Current Challenges

As David Shirk (2003) points out, notwithstanding the accomplishment of different forms and levels of cross-border cooperation between law enforcement agencies, significant challenges and obstacles remain. Adding to running challenges that will always affect cooperation between both countries, such as the immense flow of people crossing the border back and forth or the trafficking of goods both legal and illegal, there are specific and current problems that compound the complicated task of understanding and coordinating with each other. Over the last decade, Mexico has suffered an unprecedented wave of crime and violence, the trajectory of which only continues to worsen. In fact, after an apparent decline in homicides from 2012 to 2014, security conditions have been steadily deteriorating since 2015 (see Figure 8.1). Beginning in 2017, every year has been breaking the record of the most violent year since there is reliable information publicly available; 2019 saw 29,406 cases of homicide and 34,588 victims, based on information published by the Sistema Nacional de Seguridad Pública (SNSP, National System of Public Security).[2]

The Mexican government's deployment of a kingpin strategy to crack down on major organized crime groups (OCGs) and the subsequent increase in extraditions of cartel bosses to the United States have had negative consequences and have significantly increased violence. Indeed, the efforts of U.S. and Mexican authorities to kill, detain, and/or extradite drug lords have helped dismantle larger drug trafficking networks. However, as a result, OCGs have fragmented into small organizations that

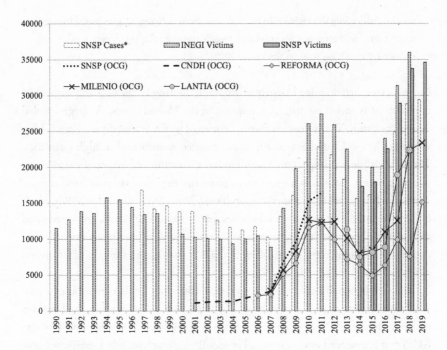

FIGURE 8.1 Comparison of homicide and organized crime, 1990–2019. *Source*: Calderón et al. 2019; SNSP n.d.

have infested Mexico with countless smaller and ruthless organizations. Yet these efforts also contributed to a more diffuse distribution of smaller organizations, and thus to a proliferation of internal conflicts and territorial disputes, all of which have contributed to an intense outbreak of violence and account for a considerable amount of the violence in the country, as Figure 8.1 also shows.

Though dialogue on the security of the common border focuses largely on crime and violence on the Mexican side, this illustrates only one side of the story. It does not acknowledge that while the illegal narcotics trade is most violently expressed in Mexico,

it is driven by U.S. consumers who spend billions of dollars a year on cocaine, marijuana, heroin, and synthetic drugs, many of which are produced in or pass through Mexico. While the U.S. has been somewhat successful at reducing the threat of drug trafficking to a local law enforcement matter and public health concern in this country, U.S. demand for illegal drugs has a very real impact in Mexico and Central America fueling the violence and exacerbating corruption south of the border. Furthermore, U.S. firearms supply much of the weaponry that these groups use to carry out their violent

attacks. Addressing the violence in Mexico, and the underlying dangers posed by organized crime, will require a binational approach and the acknowledgement of shared
responsibilities. (Olson, Shirk, and Selee 2010a, 1–2)

Mexico's violence is indeed largely attributable to drug trafficking and organized
crime, but it is fueled by drug consumption in the United States, the largest global
market for drugs. The violence is further worsened by the availability of high-caliber
weaponry in the United States, which is smuggled southbound in high quantities.
Therefore, while it is important to understand the nature and extent of the violence
affecting Mexico, it is also important to recognize that the "violence itself is more
symptom than cause" of an underlying problem (Olson, Shirk, and Selee 2010b, vii). It
is therefore important to focus on the issues that contribute to violence in Mexico and
to analyze policy areas "where reform and action by one or both governments could
contribute to a long term sustainable approach to weakening the grip of organized
crime and illegal drugs on both countries" (vii).

Violence is not the only obstacle to cooperation; the implementation of a new
accusatorial criminal justice system (ACJS) in Mexico could also be a challenge for
collaboration. In 2016 Mexico completed the nationwide implementation of the
ACJS that introduced oral, adversarial proceedings along with other significant provisions, including greater legal protections for criminal defendants, mechanisms for
alternative dispute resolution, plea bargaining, and a more central role of the victim in criminal proceedings. Certainly, some of the features of the ACJS in Mexico
are presumably more harmonious with the system in the United States. Therefore, it
could be argued that legal assistance and collaboration between both countries could
potentially work better in the future. Yet Mexico is still adapting to this new system,
oftentimes without a clear idea or plan and with a renewed opposition and criticism
from longtime antagonists and political opportunists, which could ultimately lead to
setbacks in the mechanisms of cooperation between the United States and Mexico
in this area.

Moreover, the political climate following the election of U.S. president Trump
in 2016 and of Mexican president López Obrador in 2018 altered the binational
discourse drastically. Indeed, security cooperation between both countries could be
severely affected by the politics and rhetoric from both presidents.

Trump's nationalistic, inflammatory narrative on immigration and border security, the continuous threats of border closures and trade war, the renegotiation of
NAFTA, and the increased pressure from Washington for Mexico to serve as a buffer
zone to the Central American diaspora have all contributed to increased tensions
(Wayne 2019). López Obrador's interest in fighting corruption and crime through
social, development, and infrastructure programs shifted the focus away from a bilat-

eral approach to security. His comments regarding the Mérida Initiative and the role of the United States have furthered skepticism.

Nonetheless, López Obrador's plan to reduce Central American migration and Mexico's acceptance to act more forcefully to stop migrants seeking to cross to the United States suggest a willingness to cooperate on some fronts. Mexico has resisted pressures from Washington to be considered as a "safe third country," which would force migrants to seek asylum in Mexico. Nonetheless, the country has unilaterally accepted thousands of asylum requests (Wayne 2019). This new dynamic has the potential to be followed by more dialogue concerning mutual economic benefit and strategies to address push factors that cause Central Americans to migrate (Wayne 2019).

The priority shift in binational relations to migration could potentially relegate other serious binational problems. At a time when both countries "urgently need to revitalize their partnership against cross-border crime" (Wayne et al. 2019), issues like drug and gun trafficking, public security and violence in Mexico, and the opioid epidemic in the United States should not be pushed to the background.

Mexico has become, probably unintentionally, the United States' number 1 trading partner, after Trump's struggles with China (Wayne 2019), and this should bring opportunities for greater cooperation. However, it is yet to be seen if the Trump and López Obrador presidencies will succeed in doing so or if binational security cooperation will end up deteriorating. Meanwhile, security challenges in and between the United States and Mexico will inevitably continue to increase and the existing cooperative framework will continue to be exacerbated by problems of violence, politics, and differing visions of how to address these challenges.

Dimensions of Security in the Binational Context

Historically, Washington has shown disinterest toward its southern neighbor. Mexico has never been a consistent priority in U.S. foreign policy, except during times of crises, epitomizing a persistent lack of coherence in U.S. policy toward Mexico (IILSEN 2003). This contradictory foreign policy has been especially observed in security issues, as priorities in the United States have switched dramatically over the last fifty years—from the polarized world of the Cold War to the War on Terror— changing the cornerstones of the U.S. security discourse and building a new narrative of international, binational, and border policy.

Similarly, Mexico has always kept an ambiguous agenda toward the United States. It has unwaveringly championed a noninterventionist foreign policy, reflecting obviously on the interventions on its sovereignty that caused, among other things, the loss to the United States of over half of its territory (Mares 1988). Simultaneously, Mexico has a strong dependence on U.S. trade, investment, refined oil, and other resources (Aguila et al. 2012).

Mexico has rarely been clear or consistent with regard to its own security priorities. Consequently, problems common to both countries are consistently seen through dissimilar lenses and sometimes through opposite frames of reference.

The United States and Mexico not only suffer from the already difficult relationship between a developed and a developing country; they also share the busiest border in the world. By nature, this creates a set of struggles that range from guaranteeing a free flow of persons and goods to much more complicated issues, such as the supply of illicit drugs to the world's largest consumption market, arms smuggling, a growing market in human trafficking for labor and sexual exploitation, and the persistent phenomenon of undocumented, northbound migration. All angles of the many issues that affect the relationship create different dimensions of common security challenges. Such asymmetry in the perspectives of the security problems develops a varying set of priorities and different understandings of challenges and risks that complicate potential solutions. The struggle between the United States and Mexico goes far beyond the problems generated by sharing a common border, and such a border has always symbolized a clash of understandings, challenges, and priorities.

Along the two thousand miles of shared border between the United States and Mexico, different visions collide among the dozens of closely operating law enforcement agencies (e.g., military units; drug enforcement agencies; customs and immigration authorities; federal and state investigators and prosecutors; state, county, and municipal police departments; interagency task forces). Not all of these agencies were designed, however, "to counter potential threats stemming from the actions of cross-border governments"; instead, they were meant to "monitor, regulate, deter, and sometimes punish the behavior of individuals and groups—often but not always—engaged in cross-border activities" (García 2002, 299). Although the U.S.-Mexico border region creates a "more complex and more intense set of security-related problems," it also creates "opportunities for cooperative solutions" (Bailey and Chabat 2002, 2). Moreover, while the United States and Mexico do not see eye to eye regarding challenges and priorities, a common agenda has been possible when both countries recognize and understand that such challenges are common and to accept their shared responsibility.

Despite the challenges noted, the United States and Mexico have been able to build an institutional framework that has proven effective in certain cases when bilateral interaction and cooperation from agencies across the border are needed. Such collaborative mechanisms and strategies used by both countries helped construct the notion of "shared responsibility," a binational framework that adds to a "larger engagement that cuts across a wide range of federal, state, and local agencies working to address the security challenges faced in both countries" (Olson, Shirk, and Seele

2010a, 2). In the end, while policies surrounding security at the national level often clash and challenges are viewed differently, many of the problems for communities living along both sides of the border are the same.

Layers of Cooperation Mechanisms

In an effort to describe the types of collaboration that the United States and Mexico have built with regard to law enforcement and security, Sigrid Arzt (2010) identified three mechanisms for cooperation between agencies on both sides of the border: institutional agreements, leadership and personal relationships, and standardized procedures. Building on Artz's classification, three layers of cooperation between Mexico and the United States can be identified, each with its own special characteristics and the levels of bureaucracy involved: (1) national-level collaboration agreements; (2) field-level interagency collaboration; and (3) organic *on-the-ground* informal networks.

The first layer is composed of agreements reached at the national level. This type of collaboration reaches the highest levels of both governments for negotiation and approval and constitutes the main guideline for the generation of bilateral mechanisms and policies in response to crime and violence. The second layer of cooperation is field-level interagency collaboration. It is a series of mechanisms established at the national level through institutional agreements. While this layer involves many agencies at different levels of government, the mechanisms become institutionalized as agencies adopt the capacity to apply them on a regular basis, establishing procedures and channels of communication with other agencies in their own countries and with their bilateral counterparts. A third layer of collaboration is composed of organic, on-the-ground informal networks. Such networks generate "organically" when officials in both countries establish interpersonal channels of communication and create or use extra-institutional frameworks to assist each other on a case-by-case basis. Each layer is examined in depth in the following sections.

National-Level Collaboration Agreements

The first level of cooperation between the United States and Mexico consists of agreements reached between the two governments, involving the highest levels of diplomacy and negotiation. This includes binational treaties and other Memoranda of Understanding (MOU), and aid and support programs. There are many examples of such landmark instruments that show the nature and characteristics of this layer of cooperation, such as the Extradition Treaty, the Mutual Legal Assistance in

Criminal Matters Treaty, the Hague Convention of October 25, 1980, on the Civil Aspects of International Child Abduction, and the Mérida Initiative.

Extradition Agreements

The first treaty between the United States and Mexico that involved extradition was signed in 1861 after years of tension over the issue of fugitive slaves crossing into Mexico. The document set forth twelve extraditable crimes, a prohibition to return fugitive slaves to the United States, and an agreement that neither state was bound to extradite its own citizens (Edmonds-Poli and Shirk 2018; Zagaris and Padierna Peratta 1997).

Domestic and foreign policies evolve over time, however, as do legal instruments. The 1861 Treaty was amended numerous times, for example, and other treaties were signed before ratification of the current extradition treaty of 1978 (Edmonds-Poli and Shirk 2018). The United States and Mexico signed an earlier extradition treaty in 1899, then went on to sign the Additional Conventions on Extradition in 1902, 1925, and 1939 (Zagaris and Padierna Peratta 1997).

The growing drug market in the United States and the increasing role of Mexican drug trafficking organizations (DTOs) by the 1960s drew the attention of Mexican president Gustavo Díaz Ordaz (1964–70) and U.S. president Richard Nixon (1969–74), though predictably with different understandings and approaches to the problem. While Nixon suggested that Mexico should impose stricter policies to combat DTOs, Díaz Ordaz argued that the main issue was to resolve the high demand for drugs in the United States. The difference in views and the inability to deter international drug trade between the two countries generated a unilateral response from Nixon with Operation Intercept, a part of his War on Drugs campaign (Doyle 2003). Díaz Ordaz publicly condemned the operation as discriminatory and insulting, forcing Nixon to apologize and promise a more cooperative approach. This led to an acceptance that any future campaign would have to be jointly conducted with Mexican personnel and under Mexican direction and supervision. In spite of this, the United States and Mexico were not able to reach any relevant security agreement during this period (Reich and Lebow 2014, 157–58). Nonetheless, in the hopes of combatting crime, strengthening border relations, reducing criminal activity, and upholding the law, the new Extradition Treaty between the United States and Mexico was drafted and signed on May 4, 1978. The treaty went into effect in January 1980, stating that the United States and Mexico agreed to fight crime and outlining a clearer bilateral extradition policy. This event marked the most important agreement on security matters at that time.

The 1978 Extradition Treaty consists of twenty-three articles that specify the requisite conditions for a suspect to be extradited from one country to the other. The treaty recognizes thirty-one extraditable offenses, establishes dual criminality, prevents double jeopardy, prohibits prosecution of cases in which the statute of limitations has run out in either country, excludes extradition for political or military crimes, recognizes that extradition may be refused in cases of capital punishment, and acknowledges that neither country is bound to surrender its own citizens (Edmonds-Poli and Shirk 2018).[3] Yet, despite having a treaty in effect, Mexico regularly refused to extradite its citizens for foreign prosecution until the 1990s. This changed after 1995, when Mexico realized it was in its own interest to concede on extraditing Mexican nationals when there was something to be gained. For example, in the mid-1990s, Mexico had an interest in financial support for economic purposes, and by the following decade, it had a stronger priority of combating criminal organizations (Edmonds-Poli and Shirk 2018).

Despite a lack of reliable data before 1995, Emily Edmonds-Poli and David Shirk (2018) found that Mexico extradited eight individuals to the United States. In comparison, the United States extradited thirty individuals to Mexico between 1980 and 1994. After 1995, based on available data from the Mexican government, the U.S. Marshals Service, and the Congressional Research Service (CRS), extraditions between the United States and Mexico increased noticeably, with sixty-one extraditions between 1995 and 2000 to the United States and eighty-six to Mexico. From 2001 to 2003, there were seventy-three extraditions to the United States and forty-six to Mexico. Beginning in 2006, there was a long surge in extraditions from Mexico to the United States. For example, with only forty-one in 2005, the number increased to sixty-four in 2006, eighty-three in 2007, and averaged ninety-eight between 2007 and 2012. In fact, between 2004 and 2006, the number of extraditions from Mexico jumped by 80 percent. Between 2013 and 2016, the numbers declined to an average of about fifty-eight, a significant drop from the previous period but still higher than before 2006. During this period, extraditions fell by nearly 29 percent in 2014 and by 20 percent in 2015. Although worldwide extraditions to the United States were in decline, there was a noticeable increase of 60 percent in extraditions from Mexico in 2016.

The surge of extraditions around 2001 became a larger trend starting in 2006, and marks a change in Mexico's traditional unwillingness to surrender its nationals to other jurisdictions, especially to the United States. According to Edmonds-Poli and Shirk (2018), this evident shift in Mexico's policy of extradition toward the United States can be explained by the development of stronger bilateral diplomacy and increased binational concern for shared problems, such as drug trafficking.

Mutual Legal Assistance in Criminal Matters (MLAT)

The mechanisms for law enforcement cooperation between the United States and Mexico did not keep pace with the celerity of crime, or the manipulation—to the criminal's personal advantage—of the legal, cultural, political, and economical differences between the two countries (Zagaris and Resnick 1997). In the aftermath of the Camarena scandal, tensions between the governments grew, affecting collaboration on security. However, the U.S. Department of Justice (DOJ) and the Procuraduría General de la República (PGR, Attorney General's Office) in Mexico still engaged in exchanges of information and mutual assistance as a response to the case.[4] Despite allegations of corruption and other misdeeds in the performance of Mexican law enforcement authorities, both countries were able to collaborate and build a solid case for U.S. courts in the Camarena case and other related cases being prosecuted in Mexican courts. Such collaborations served as a prelude to the Mutual Legal Assistance in Criminal Matters Treaty (MLAT) (Zagaris and Resnick 1997).

After years of negotiations, the MLAT was signed and ratified by both countries on December 9, 1987. The MLAT created mechanisms for cooperation on criminal matters, such as "(1) taking testimony or statements of witnesses; (2) providing documents, records, and evidence; (3) executing requests for searches and seizures; (4) serving documents; and (5) providing assistance in procedures regarding the immobilizing, securing and forfeiture of the proceeds, fruits, and instrumentalities of crime" (Zagaris and Resnick 1997, 6). As Bruce Zagaris and Julia Padierna Peratta (1997) suggest, bilateral enforcement mechanisms between the United States and Mexico, such as MLAT, are useful in helping to resolve controversies in extraditions, strengthening the operation of extradition cases, and, most importantly, reinforcing the operation of domestic prosecutions—according to Article 4, Mexican authorities can prosecute any Mexican national who has committed a crime in a foreign country. In general, MLAT has been regarded as successful by both Mexican and U.S. authorities (Guymon 2000; Zagaris and Resnick 1997).

The Mérida Initiative

After launching an aggressive counter organized-crime campaign, then Mexican president Felipe Calderón reached out to U.S. president George W. Bush for assistance in combatting drug and weapons smuggling. Both administrations then proposed a package of assistance to counter drugs and crime from the United States to Mexico and Central America, named the Mérida Initiative (Seelke and Finklea 2017). The first phase of the Mérida Initiative (2007–10) focused on (1) counternarcotics, border security, and counterterrorism; (2) public security and law enforcement; and (3) institution building and the rule of law (Seelke and Finklea 2017, 9). The total amount of funding allocated for this phase of the Mérida Initiative was more than US$1.5 billion (see Figure 8.2).

By 2011 the administrations of U.S. president Barack Obama (2008–16) and Mexican president Calderón revised the Mérida Initiative. They specifically agreed to shift

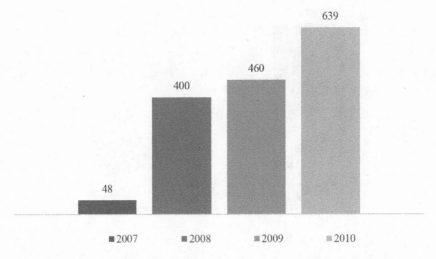

FIGURE 8.2 First phase of Mérida Initiative allocations (in millions of U.S. dollars), 2007–10. *Source*: Seelke and Finklea 2017.

and broaden the scope of binational cooperation to a four-pillar strategy focused on economic development, community-based social programs, institution building over technology transfers, and assistance for states and municipalities. As a result, the four pillars were identified as (1) combatting organized crime, (2) judicial sector reform, (3) improved border security, and (4) promoting community resilience (Heinle, Rodríguez Ferreira, and Shirk 2016, 48; Olson and Wilson 2010). Both countries decided to relocate the military cooperation under the Mérida Initiative to a different binational agreement (Seelke and Finklea 2017). For the second phase of the Mérida Initiative (2010–12), nearly US$500 million was allocated (see Figure 8.3).

Under President Obama, the initiative continued at a similar rate of funding with the new framework of four "pillars" of collaboration.

> Among other things, the program bolstered U.S.-Mexican intelligence sharing to dismantle organized crime groups, Mexican judicial and law enforcement capacity, southbound inspections to detect illicit bulk cash and arms shipments, and investments in crime prevention programs. Thanks to the program, U.S. officials regularly expressed great praise and admiration for President Calderón, frequently emphasizing his courage in the fight against organized crime. (Heinle, Rodríguez Ferreira, and Shirk 2016, 48)

However, a somewhat unexpected change occurred under Mexican president Enrique Peña Nieto, affecting the degree of continuity in the U.S.-Mexico security relationship

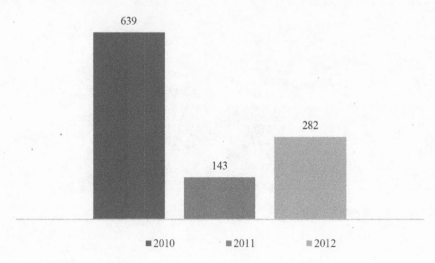

FIGURE 8.3 Mérida Initiative allocations (in millions of U.S. dollars), 2010–12. *Source*: Seelke and Finklea 2017.

across administrations. One of the main changes that Peña Nieto introduced early on was a more centrally managed relationship by means of a "single window" (*ventanilla única*) through Mexico's Secretaría de Gobernación (SEGOB, Secretariat of the Interior). This was a big switch from the Calderón administration, when "U.S. officials were able to interface directly with their Mexican counterparts at various Mexican agencies and at both the national and subnational level, without explicit approval from the President, which created a significant interdependence between U.S. and Mexican law enforcement agencies working toward common objectives" (Heinle, Rodríguez Ferreira, and Shirk 2016, 48). Still, while budget requests for the Mérida Initiative declined almost consistently throughout the Peña Nieto administration, as shown in Figure 8.4, cooperation on the operational side remained almost unchanged. Despite original setbacks by the Peña Nieto government, both countries reaffirmed a commitment to the Mérida Initiative and agreed to focus on justice sector reform, money laundering, police and corrections professionalization, and border security to address root causes of violence, opium production, and heroin trafficking (Seelke and Finklea 2017).

From 2007 to 2016, the Mérida Initiative allocated more than US$2.7 billion to efforts addressing Mexico's security challenges and strengthening the rule of law (see Figure 8.5). According to the U.S. Government Accountability Office (GAO 2019), the funding allocated for Mérida in 2017 slightly decreased from the previous year to US$125 million but increased again in 2018 to US$139 million.[5]

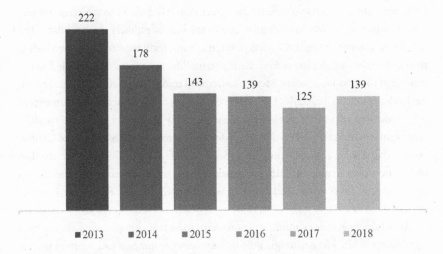

FIGURE 8.4 Mérida Initiative allocations during the Peña Nieto administration (in millions of U.S. dollars), 2013–18. *Source*: GAO 2019; Seelke and Finklea 2017.

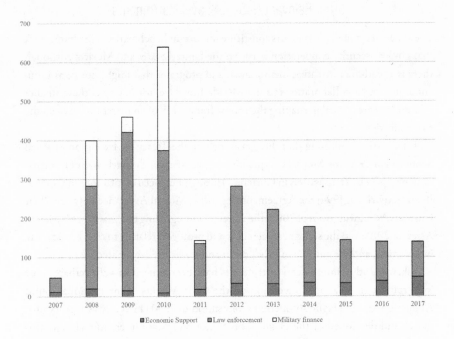

FIGURE 8.5 Total Mérida Initiative allocations, 2007–17. Data on 2017 are based on estimations by the authors of the source. *Source*: Seelke and Finklea 2017.

Despite the progress made under the agreement, it is difficult to ascertain the success or failure of the Mérida Initiative due to the lack of publicly available data. The U.S. Department of State (DOS) has pointed to some indicators of success, including the cooperation among law enforcement and intelligence officials that has led to the capture of top criminal leaders; Mexico's successful transition to an accusatorial criminal justice system in June 2016; increased extraditions from Mexico; improvements in infrastructure and policies that helped more than forty Mexican correctional facilities achieve international accreditation; and Mexico's increasing apprehension of Central American, African, and Asian migrants (Seelke and Finklea 2017). After the election of U.S. president Trump in 2016, prominent former officials encouraged the Trump administration to continue collaborating with Mexico (Heinle, Rodríguez Ferreira, and Shirk 2016).

Also, López Obrador's administration seems to be managing the challenges posed by a Trump White House, dodging the inflammatory comments and constant threats as well as scoring some points here and there (Wayne 2019). However, the constant tensions have raised questions about the sustainability of the current state of binational relations and the future of the long-term U.S.-Mexico security relationship.

Other Relevant National-Level Instruments

The abovementioned instruments constitute important benchmarks in the framework that governs security cooperation between the United States and Mexico. Although there is a plethora of treaties, memoranda, and programs that might not be as influential in regular collaborations as the Mérida Initiative, for example, these smaller instruments are critical in shaping the robust framework of cooperation between the two countries.

It is worth mentioning that these also include the Treaty on Execution of Penal Sentences of 1976; the Mutual Cooperation Agreement for the Exchange of Information in respect to Transactions in Currency Through Financial Institutions to Combat Illicit Activities of 1994; the Agreement Regarding Mutual Assistance Between Their Customs Administrations of 2000; the Agreement Regarding the Sharing of Forfeited Assets of 2001; and the series of agreements and protocols relating to crop eradication, interdiction, and the curbing of production and traffic of illegal narcotics.

Likewise, other multilateral instruments have been crucial as well. Perhaps most importantly, the Hague Convention on the Civil Aspects of International Child Abduction, or the Hague Abduction Convention of 1980 (HAC), was a treaty promoted and developed by the Hague Conference on Private International Law. This treaty created a faster process to return a child to another country when abducted by a parent and removed from their home across borders. With up to one hundred signatories, the HAC has become a widely accepted legal framework worldwide and has been extensively used between the United States and Mexico—especially in the border region—where agencies of both countries apply the treaty's protocols in close collaboration with their bilateral counterparts.

Such intergovernment accords are examples of another vast set of agreements reached by the United States and Mexico. More instruments, meetings, and summits also constitute diverse and alternative elements that contribute to the broader legal and institutional infrastructure that allows binational collaboration. For example, the High Level Contact Group encouraged the development of several expert groups to address the abuse of drugs, drug trafficking, and related crimes. The end goal was to reduce the illicit demand for drugs and to combat money laundering and arms trafficking, among others, in order to establish bilateral cooperation programs (IILSEN 2003). Another example of bilateral collaboration, now extinct, was the Security and Prosperity Partnership of North America (SPP) of 2005, which integrated matters of security and defense with economic and social elements (Benítez Manaut and Rodríguez Ulloa 2006). Additionally, the 2002 U.S.-Mexico Border Partnership Agreement and the 1999 Memorandum of Understanding on Cooperation Against Border Violence have directly or indirectly contributed to this vast corpus of legal instruments that focus, or at least address, binational and border security (Meyers 2003).

Measuring the Impact of National-Level Collaboration Agreements

While most high-level agreements have proven effective, they alone cannot entirely address binational security threats, mainly due to the general incapacity of top-down approaches to address everyday problems. High-level agreements tend to focus on the institutional and do not recognize or strengthen other efforts—like informal networks discussed below—and do not make attempts to address underlying issues that contribute to many shared problems. Despite being a good-faith partner, Mexico has also been unable to achieve some of the larger goals developed in the national-level collaboration agreements, given its own limited capability and capacity to address security issues, and its efforts remain too focused on U.S. interests (Meyers 2003, 21–22). Moreover, bilateral agreements face limitations when implemented in different regions, especially along the border, due to the decentralization of authority in the U.S. federal, state, and local agencies. These agreements tend to marginalize Mexican state and municipal governments, which do have some informal experience collaborating with U.S. agencies along the border (Ramos 2002, 336). Thus, top-down approaches can be effective in laying the ground for more structured collaboration; however, these strategies simply cannot address field-level problems of daily interactions, which need more layers of collaboration to have a real impact on security and the border region.

Indeed, agents in the field may or may not use the institutional framework to perform their everyday duties, but they certainly need channels of communication in order to respond to routine problems.

Field-Level Interagency Collaboration

Agreements reached at the national level create a series of standardized mechanisms, wherein agencies of different levels of government on both sides of the border interact on a regular basis. A second layer of collaboration comes into play when agencies from both countries need support from their counterparts across the border. These interactions benefit from the set of procedures and mechanisms set forth by the bilateral and multilateral collaboration agreements. Most cases of *actual* collaboration between the United States and Mexico fall under procedures set forth by a handful of instruments. The most important are extraditions, Article 4 prosecutions, intelligence sharing, training exchanges, and HAC cases.

Extraditions

The Extradition Treaty belongs to the first layer of national-level collaboration. However, extraditions belong to a second layer, as mechanisms have been established and agencies at various levels participate in different instances through official channels of collaboration. Extraditions can take place for various criminal offenses, excluding political and military matters, but the vast majority of extraditions from Mexico to the United States are for drug trafficking or organized crime–related offenses. This reflects the reality of the current binational security situation, where drug-related crime plays a central role in domestic and foreign issues for both countries. The Extradition Treaty, as a means of countering drug trafficking and other crimes, has succeeded in detaining, processing, and extraditing several of the biggest drug kingpins, leading to serious setbacks for the largest and the most influential Mexican DTOs.

The process of extradition between the United States and Mexico follows a series of steps. When the United States seeks to extradite a person in Mexico, the U.S. judge who is handling the case requests that the DOJ prepare the necessary paperwork for the extradition. The DOJ then passes the paperwork to the Mexican government first through the DOS and then through the U.S. Embassy in Mexico. The Secretaría de Relaciones Exteriores (SRE, Secretariat of Foreign Affairs) in Mexico receives the extradition request from the U.S. Embassy. If the request for extradition meets all criteria set forth by the Extradition Treaty, the SRE will review the paperwork. The SRE then sends the request to the PGR, which then sends it to a district judge, who will open a procedure to grant the person the possibility to fight the extradition. Mexican law grants any subject of extradition the possibility of appeal and an amparo—a figure similar to an injunction. If the request for extradition is granted by the federal judge, it returns through the same channels until the person is surrendered to law enforcement agencies stationed at the Mexican Embassy, who will then transfer the person to the requesting jurisdiction in the United States.[6] The extradition process from the United States to Mexico works almost exactly the same way, but it involves other institutions. The U.S. office charged with receiving extradition requests from the SRE is the Office of International Affairs within the Department of Justice. This office is the most knowledgeable involved in the process and arguably the one that has the better understanding of the whole process. After reviewing the case, the Office of International Affairs makes suggestions to federal and state prosecutors on whether a person should be extradited to the requesting country or not. Besides these minor differences, most other authorities involved and processes followed are similar in both countries.

The process for extraditions is arduous due to extensive bureaucratic and legal obstacles as well as the limits to the criminal offenses that are eligible for extradition. Nonetheless, the extradition policy has arguably been proven effective, with 936 out of the 998 individuals extradited from Mexico being rendered to the United States between 2000 and 2015, according to the SRE (Quiroz 2016).

Foreign Prosecution Units: Article 4 Prosecutions and HAC Cases

States on the U.S. side of the U.S.-Mexico border have created Foreign Prosecution Units (FPUs) to focus exclusively on crimes of a transnational nature and crimes with cross-border ramifications. FPUs are intended to assist local law enforcement in the investigations of such cases and to serve as liaisons with Mexican agencies at the municipal, state, and federal levels.

In California, for example, Section 11055 of the State Penal Code establishes the creation of the Foreign Prosecution and Law Enforcement Unit (FPLEU) under the California Department of Justice. It outlines its responsibility to assist state and local law enforcement agencies with Article 4 persecutions, deportation of fugitives wanted in California for any criminal violation, and HAC child abduction cases. The FPLEU also assists in formal requests under the MLAT as well as with informal requests for assistance between the two countries (California Department of Justice n.d. ["Foreign Prosecutions"]).[7] In Texas, the Criminal Law Enforcement Division of the Office of the Attorney General of Texas provides assistance to local law enforcement agencies in any Article 4 prosecutions, including reviewing cases, translating and drafting documents, acting as a liaison with Mexican authorities, making formal requests, and filing any document needed during the process (Attorney General of Texas 2017). On the Mexican side, the PGR has created special units to focus specifically on Article 4 prosecutions or HAC cases. However, despite being tasked by law to direct efforts of international collaboration, there is no legislation that bounds the government to create and maintain such kinds of units, and therefore, the existence of them tends to be intermittent. Different agencies at the state and local level, especially in the border region, have created their own liaison units to navigate through cases of cross-border collaboration. Most importantly, however, these units allow agencies to establish more immediate channels of communication without having to go through Mexico City and Washington in order to engage agencies just a few miles away from each other.

An alternative to extradition, Article 4 prosecutions have benefited U.S. agencies and FPUs, particularly with crimes committed in the border region in which the risk of a suspect fleeing across the border is higher. With such a tool, FPUs and prosecutors in the United States can request that Mexican authorities arrest and prosecute a suspect of a crime committed in the United States if the suspect—or the victim—is a Mexican national and is believed to be in Mexico. Article 4 of the Código Federal de Procedimientos Penales (CFPP, Federal Code of Penal Procedures) allows Mexican authorities to prosecute any Mexican national who has committed a crime in a foreign country or to prosecute anyone who has committed a crime against a Mexican national outside of the country, only if the suspect is on Mexican soil.

HAC cases have also been a common point of interaction between FPUs, prosecutors, and Mexican agencies when a child has been abducted by one parent and taken to Mexico. In HAC cases, as with Article 4 prosecutions, the channel usually follows the request from a U.S. local law enforcement agency to the PGR where an FPU or a designated prosecutor assists the local agency in generating all the necessary paperwork. The DOS will then issue an official request for collaboration to the SRE in Mexico, which will in turn ask for the PGR's and other local agencies' support in locating and securing the child.

Intelligence Sharing and Training Exchanges

Two topics that have always been a constant source of debate in the discussion of building a more effective and collaborative relationship between the United States and Mexico are training exchanges and intelligence sharing for criminal investigations. One of the first efforts to institutionalize and formalize intelligence sharing in the border region was the creation of the El Paso Intelligence Center (EPIC) in 1974, originally intended to improve coordination among U.S. agencies across the border and to coordinate bilateral cooperation with Mexico. Housing many U.S. federal agencies, EPIC also included Mexican nationals to support the tasks of U.S. law enforcement and to build personal relationships (Arzt 2010, 361). The Border Enforcement

Security Task Force (BEST) created in 2006 by the U.S. Department of Homeland Security (DHS) deployed several U.S. law enforcement teams across the border to coordinate with the Mexican agencies on smuggling cases. A big success of BEST, according to Arzt (2010, 361), has been the investigations into border-related arms and ammunition smuggling.

There are similar examples at the state level. For example, the California Department of Justice's Division of Law Enforcement created the California Anti-Money Laundering Alliance (CAMLA). The CAMLA is a specialized team of financial forensic investigators that brings together local, state, and federal law enforcement agencies to conduct financial investigations for prosecutions related to money laundering where the suspected transnational criminal organizations (TCOs) are engaged in the trafficking of humans, drugs, arms, and other counterfeit goods in the California border region with Mexico (California Department of Justice n.d. ["California Anti-Money Laundering Alliance"]). This unit regularly shares intelligence with its Mexican counterparts as part of their investigations.

In many of these mechanisms, there are also other concerted elements at play. Arzt points out that a clear characteristic of cooperation is the leadership of certain agencies and the commitment of those in charge. In those contexts, "trust remains a key component to bilateral cooperation." There are clear examples in which it is obvious that agreements and personal relations have developed standardized procedures of cooperation between the two countries at the agency level (Arzt 2010, 357–61).

Since the approval of the Mérida Initiative, the sharing of intelligence has been a hot topic in the actual collaboration between the United States and Mexico, leading to the arrest of major criminal figures in Mexico through real-time, binational, interagency collaboration. Such cooperation helped Mexico take down leaders of the Sinaloa Cartel, the Zetas, and the Gulf Cartel, among others (Heinle, Rodríguez Ferreira, and Shirk 2014). Indeed, the Mérida Initiative has prioritized "the establishment of a secure, cross-border telecommunications system between U.S. and Mexican border sister cities to provide public security forces on both sides of the border with the capability to request and exchange information on active criminal investigations" (DOS n.d.). Subsequently, the Mérida Initiative has invested in training federal, state, and local agencies in order to improve information sharing, increase the development of actionable intelligence, and foster greater coordination in law enforcement operations in general.

Training has become a key element by which to reach standardized means of communication and operation and, as such, has been one of the main outputs from the framework created by the Mérida Initiative. According to the DOS, under the Mérida partnership, many U.S. agencies have worked closely with their Mexican counterparts in training justice sector personnel. This includes the police, investigators, prosecutors, and defense counsel; correction systems development; judicial exchanges; and partnerships with Mexican law schools, all in support of Mexico's implementation of comprehensive justice sector reforms. U.S. agencies have also worked with Mexico in police capacity-building courses that focus on criminal investigations, criminal intelligence, professionalization, tactics and firearms, forensics, and strategic analysis. Police have also received specialized training in anticorruption, antigang, anti–human trafficking, anti–money laundering, and antikidnapping units. More broadly, police have also developed technical capacities in detection of narcotics, weapons, explosives, ammunition, currency, human remains, and beyond (DOS n.d.).

Other Instances of Field-Level Interagency Collaboration

As is the case with treaties, memoranda, and aid and support programs, there are many other MOUs, agreements, mechanisms, programs, initiatives, agencies, committees, associations, and organizations that compose the universe of institutions involved in security cooperation between the United States and Mexico, and particularly in the border region. These constitute just a few of the most common frameworks of field-level interagency cooperation, but there are many more that should be acknowledged. For example, DHS has signed MOUs with SEGOB, the SRE, and a variety of local offices under U.S. Customs and Border Protection (CBP), U.S. Immigration and Customs Enforcement (ICE), the Instituto Nacional de Migración (INM, National Migration Institute), and the Consulate Generals of Mexico in order to arrange the repatriation of Mexican nationals from the United States to Mexico (DHS 2008).

Through specific actions, such as Project Gunrunner and a series of MOUs with PGR and other law enforcement agencies in Mexico, the Southwest Border Initiative, a program of the Bureau of Alcohol, Tobacco, Firearms and Explosives (ATF) that seeks to reduce cross-border drug and firearms trafficking and the high level of violence associated with these activities on both sides of the border, has been able to increase the number of traced weapons seized in Mexico. As a result, the number of referred cases for the prosecution of firearms trafficking–related offenses has also increased (DOJ 2010).

Through the Mexico-U.S. Bilateral Security Cooperation Group meetings, both countries have joined forces to deepen and strengthen bilateral cooperation efforts in matters of security, law enforcement, and border collaboration (SRE 2017). Unilaterally, the United States has also created groups and centers in California, Arizona, New Mexico, and Texas to bring together federal representatives of both countries and to promote the exchange of experiences and resources (IILSEN 2003). At the state level, the State Attorney Generals of Arizona, California, New Mexico, and Texas; the director of the Arizona Department of Public Safety; the superintendent of the Arizona Department of Financial Institutions; and the chief of the Police Department of Phoenix govern the Southwest Border Anti-Money Laundering Alliance (SWBA). Based at the Office of the Arizona Attorney General, the SWBA coordinates investigations and prosecutions of money laundering, working regularly with the Comisión Nacional Bancaria y de Valores (CNBV, National Banking and Securities Commission) in Mexico (Arizona Attorney General n.d.).

Measuring the Impact of Field-Level Interagency Collaboration

Collaborations through the abovementioned mechanisms have become regular between agencies in the United States and Mexico and, in a way, can be considered a good performance indicator. Agencies in both countries have developed the capacity and knowledge to navigate through protocols and processes to achieve results while collaborating with their counterparts across the border. Extraditions, Article 4 prosecutions, HAC cases, intelligence sharing, and training programs are perhaps the best examples of a functioning collaboration. Nevertheless, recurrent problems in both countries make this process much more complicated than it already is. Since funding is not always secured for such efforts, it translates into a lack of sufficient qualified staff, and a lack of key training and support needed by some agencies, mainly on the Mexican side. Moreover, exchanging law enforcement and investigative information is cumbersome, and many internal problems within U.S. agencies responding to Mexican requests hinder coordination. Additionally, because Mexican agencies oftentimes do not have designated international liaisons or people responsible for international collaboration, coordination is inherently difficult. In almost every collaboration attempt, it is required that all pieces are coordinated and moving at the same pace. If a key actor is missing, or if one part does not move at the same speed, the whole process of collaboration can fall apart. States like California have an advantage in that the FPU has been legislated in the Penal Code and therefore these states have a regular stream of funding and permanent personnel to carry out such functions. The lack of similar legislation, mainly on the Mexican side, makes the existence of responsible units intermittent and leads to an irregular collaboration process.

Organic, on-the-Ground Informal Networks

The experience of the border region is certainly different from big-picture international relations and cooperation. As Emmanuel Brunet-Jailly puts it:

> The study of borders and borderlands allows us to study the complex mechanisms that produce and re-produce territorially defined cultures, economies and ultimately local

and central states. Borders are not hard territorial lines as assumed in the past in international relations; they are institutions and result from bordering policies. They are about people; and for most settled territories they are predominantly about inclusion and exclusion, as they are woven into varied cultural, economic and political fabrics. (2013, 29)

Thus, studying and defining borders tends to be an approach of top-down exercises of "implementation and management of border policies" and "processes of reproduction of borders as institutions" (Brunet-Jailly 2013, 29). However, the borderland region requires a bottom-up approach "where local and regional power and political clout, politics and cross-border governance are tightly woven into complex cultural, economic and political structures" (29). Hence, security cooperation in the border region faces the complexity of intertwined interaction between many fields and many levels. Notwithstanding, the borderland also creates opportunities for communication and interactions that cannot be reproduced at the national level since they belong and serve a specific regional context, a sort of "border community." While this is mostly evident in economic, social, and cultural contexts, it is also true at the security and law enforcement level.

Street-Level Bureaucracy and on-the-Ground Policy Making

Michael Lipsky calls public service workers "street-level bureaucrats," among whom we find police officers, law enforcement personnel, judges, and others "who interact directly with citizens in the course of their jobs and who have substantial discretion in the execution of their work" (1980, 3). According to Lipsky, the cumulative but individual decisions of these workers become or add up to agency policy (3). In addition, "the policy making roles of street level bureaucrats are built upon two interrelated facets of their positions: relatively high degrees of discretion and relative autonomy from organizational authority" (13). In this regard, these actors develop coping mechanisms, sometimes contrary to an agency's policy but actually basic to its survival (19). Though Lipsky's analysis focuses on the interaction between public service workers and citizens, the relevance of this approach is how such actors participate in the creation of policy beyond politics and law. Combining this with the "on-the-ground" approach that has been employed as a starting point for analyzing interactions at the micropolitical level, and in conjunction with macropolitical dynamics and conflicts (Hersant and Vigour 2017), this chapter builds on both ideas as a way to analyze the creation of policy from the bottom up.[8] The chapter further makes the case for the importance of a certain degree of informality wherein law enforcement personnel and security forces can generate organic networks to overcome politics and institutional bureaucracy, securing a more direct and expeditious way of dealing with cases, especially in a cross-border context.

The Formation of Organic Networks

There are instances of collaboration across the border that can be regarded as organic in the sense that they generate naturally from the environment and context. Based on qualitative and quantitative field-level research, interesting examples have been found of how networks organically generate and how trust among partners is built in the cross-border context.[9]

For instance, many law enforcement officers have family ties across the border and often cross frequently as private citizens.[10] At the professional level, many law enforcement agents have had the opportunity to attend training courses, conferences, symposiums, and meetings in their sister cities.[11] During such events, agents share contact information with their bilateral counterparts, sometimes leading to further contact and eventual exchange of information and assistance. While some law enforcement agencies have designated liaison officers in charge of communication with the other country's agencies, sometimes it is simply easier and faster to communicate directly with known and trusted agents across the border personally (Justice in Mexico 2011, 2015).[12]

Arguably, in such conditions, channels of communication can be easily established. While trust among institutional partners might not be as easy to build, interpersonal relations are strong, and peer-to-peer interaction creates the possibility of building networks, which, in turn, can lead to trust-based informal mechanisms of communication and collaboration. For example, once a trust-based channel of communication has been opened, it is not uncommon that agencies give each other "*pitazos*," meaning that they alert their counterparts about something that may help in an investigation, a case, or an operation across the border.

Moreover, informal networks create expedited alternative routes. For example, in HAC cases or when dealing with transnational fugitives, when authorities from one country apprehend a person who is wanted for any reason in the other country, authorities can simply drive them to the border and render them to the other agency without going through established institutional channels. Nevertheless, informal networks also need some sort of structure in order to be sustainable, especially because trust can be very hard to create and very easy to lose. While the idea of legislating informal organic networks is rather counterproductive, a framework that guarantees the existence of an organized structure to generate opportunities for informal communication could still be extremely beneficial.[13]

The Border Liaison Mechanism (BLM)

In 1993, a Border Liaison Mechanism (BLM) was created along the U.S.-Mexico border, chaired by U.S. and Mexican consuls in their "sister city" to deal with a variety of local issues, such as the accidental violation of sovereignty by law enforcement officials and the coordination of port security, among others (DOS 2011). The BLM is a joint governmental instrument to further regional bilateral dialogue; representatives from both sides of the border discuss issues of mutual interest, including public safety and law enforcement issues (Embassy of the United States in Mexico 2005). Indeed, the BLMs are a result of a bilateral agreement, which means that it technically could be considered a standardized interagency collaboration mechanism, thus belonging to the second and not to the third layer of collaboration. However, the BLMs started organically by agents without an ulterior agenda, seeking only to know their counterparts and to open a channel of dialogue. Eventually, this mechanism was officially supported, developing regular cross-border meetings of federal, state, and local authorities on both sides of the border. At the local level, BLMs continue to enhance cross-border communication organically by allowing authorities from different levels and from both countries to address local issues directly without intervention from the country capitals (Texas A&M International University n.d.).

Since their inception as informal networks, the BLMs have continued to operate along the U.S.-Mexico border as a common space for representatives of different agencies to discuss salient topics, create links and channels of communication, and build trust. In many cases, this has developed much wider informal, yet effective, networks that operate outside scheduled BLM meetings and that can address specific cases wherein there is a need for immediate support from counterparts across the border. Unfortunately, there cannot be data or indicators to measure the effectiveness of such networks. One thus relies on the opinions, comments, and stories from law enforcement agents to know this. Bearing in mind the limitations of such anecdotal information, the general sentiment is that BLMs, and the organic networks generated within, are the best method for immediate binational collaboration, avoiding the bureaucracy of both governments and its multiple agencies (Justice in Mexico 2011, 2015).

From the Institutional to the Informal

As Brunet-Jailly explains, "Government and politics retreat from equalization as they build on increasingly salient economic, social and political differences of places. Decentralization and downloading of policies progressively empower local and regional actors, and economic, social and political asymmetries develop" (2013, 31). He further suggests that this is visible to the extreme in borderland regions, "where economic, social and political asymmetries have either served, or come in conflict with, the recent security agenda of states" (31). Top-down—as opposed to bottom-up—analyses do not debate as effectively how local power and politics are transformed by structural changes. As such, borderland analysis should focus on the profound changes in states adapting to the works of agents. As institutional structures change, local participation becomes a determinant of power and local politics a determinant of policy, and the knowledge of the various linkages between multilevel governance become bottom-up channels of influence (31–42). This is more evident in regions "where culture and market forces cross the boundary lines and bring together communities that share a unique sense of belonging. Boundaries in such instances may well vanish, or bend, to adapt to the new political geography of those regions" (42).

Indeed, the U.S.-Mexico border not only divides two countries; it is also a line that crosses a broader economic, social, and cultural community. These divided communities have different jurisdictions with different regulations, practices, and systems, which respectively limit powers and control. Accordingly, authorities from both countries sometimes have to rely on their foreign counterparts as a last resort to perform their duties (Zagaris and Resnick 1997). Thus, despite being geographically situated in two different countries, agents share common problems, obstacles, and goals. Although this context creates inherent challenges, at the same time, it can facilitate certain arrangements that could lead to organic mechanisms of collaboration. This phenomenon has been referred to by García as border "security communities," a concept that he interprets as "the presence of binational operational cooperation in defining and containing a mutual security threat" (2002, 331). As he points out, the "security community" is said to "characterize the relations between two nations, where bellicose conflict between the national governments is so highly remote that it is not contemplated in the national plans of either country" (299). Therefore, instead of being a defense to any military threat, the whole apparatus of law enforcement along the border is designed to deter and prevent a threat that is shared by both countries but directly caused by neither.

As the shared and common threat is rooted in the community itself, it is important for communities to develop their own mechanisms to cope and prevent it. That is why collaborative networks are critical. Despite belonging to different agencies, cities, and even countries, agents who share an intertwined sociocultural and geographic context create a kind of regional community not explained by nationality or politics. In a way, they create their own specific culture, a common identity that generates a "security community," built upon leadership and trust.

Shirk (2003) explains "cooperative security" as key instances of collaboration and the existence of liaison mechanisms that facilitate problem solving along the border.

Likewise, Daniel Sabet (2005) explains that the role of liaisons focused exclusively on leading cross-border efforts have been an effective way to "build bridges" across the U.S.-Mexico border. Nonetheless, Sabet found that long-term, binational network actors with a reliable reputation serve as important bridges and, in those instances where organizations interact directly and without official intermediaries, those actors have developed a reputation that can be trusted through a long history of cross-border activity.[14] Trust then becomes a central aspect of building networks, and as Arzt (2010) suggests, law enforcement officials can build a sense of personal trust and cooperation with their counterparts across the border, which oftentimes translates into increased collaboration.

Building on what María Eugenia de Garay Suárez found among police cultures, individuals involved in law enforcement and security share certain characteristics, values, and rules; similar ways of thinking and feeling; and common practices in how they perform their activities regardless of their agency affiliation (2006, 25–27). Therefore, it can be acknowledged that agents share a certain work personality and develop a type of culture. This "culture" is not universal, meaning that it is not shared by all police or law enforcement officers per se; rather, it depends on the geographical and sociocultural context to which they belong (28). In the binational security cooperation context, and especially in the border region, personal relationships have been critical to create informal mechanisms of cooperation (Arzt 2010). Such informal mechanisms have helped navigate through interinstitutional bureaucracy and complicated collaboration procedures. Thus, in this case, "informal" does not have the negative connotation usually associated with a generalized border region context. In his work, Harlan Koff (2015) explains how "informality" in the border regions almost always is associated with either illegal markets and criminality or "unregulated" economies, to the extent of how they affect populations.[15] However, as he points out:

> Informal sectors are prominent in cross-border regions throughout the world. Borderlands have traditionally been places of opportunity and contact between people. For this reason, spontaneous exchanges have led to the development of cross-border economies and societies in all world regions, and often these exchanges take place outside the reach of government regulatory agencies. (Koff 2015, 461)

Thus, informality can acquire a different connotation in a cross-border context, from a negative economic phenomenon and deterrent to security to an understanding of the term *informal* as a cohesive concept that oftentimes benefits security cooperation: not as a "survival strategy" (Koff 2015) but as a means to build organic networks of support within a specific community—a "border security community."

There exists a border security community with a sense of "cooperative security," as explained by Shirk (2003). Such a community no longer falls into a traditional, multilateral approach but requires shared decision-making and consensual practices that are open to a broad array of actors that can address many of the urgent transnational problems (Payne 2012).[16]

Concluding Observations and Policy Recommendations

It would be naive to believe that the U.S.-Mexico border can be regarded as a single particular region. As José M. Ramos (2002, 340) says, regional and local actors' experiences vary based on the economic, political, and social contexts, characterizing the subregion in which they operate, meaning that the environment influences the roles and the kind of responses they face. While this chapter analyzes different perspectives at the local level, it does not propose a general diagnosis of security in and at the border region, which in fact is a series of different border subregions. As Ramos (2002, 340) also points out, generalized observations about U.S.-Mexico border issues lead to superficial diagnoses and limit the possibilities for finding solutions. Therefore, there are no easy policy solutions for the different subregions based on generalized assessments of particular practices. Instead, this chapter explores how bottom-up analysis could offer insights as to the potential benefits of organic, on-the-ground, informal initiatives, as they pollinize the institutional mechanisms of cooperation and high-level policy. Moreover, based on proven on-the-ground experiences, this chapter builds on larger legal and institutional frameworks already operating in the border region, which have proven effective and have, simultaneously, contributed to the generation of more organic ways of collaboration.

Instead of comparing the different layers of collaboration between agencies from the United States and Mexico, it is important to demonstrate how a combination of formal and informal factors interacts to compose a multilayer cooperative relationship, and yet these layers remain independent from each other. Most importantly, this chapter seeks to highlight the importance of personal relations and trust, not only in creating organic informal networks of collaboration but also in softening cumbersome, standardized, institutional procedures. As such, some conclusions can be drawn. First, high-level agreements have proven effective in setting the ground for a more institutionalized cooperation between the United States and Mexico. Also, continued financial support through the Mérida Initiative has facilitated contacts between two countries, which have been somewhat effective in supporting Mexico's efforts to reform its justice system.

Likewise, specific legal instruments, such as the extradition treaty, the MLAT, or the HAC, have eased the otherwise cumbersome and intricate process of international cooperation. The legal and institutional structure created by the Extradition Treaty has, for example, allowed the prosecution and sentencing of many high-profile criminals in the United States. Moreover, the MLAT has been helpful for law enforcement agencies to cooperate in a more standardized way. In addition, Article 4 prosecutions have proven effective when Mexican nationals commit crimes in the United States and flee to Mexico to avoid prosecutions. Likewise, the HAC has proven useful and effective in both solving cases of international child abduction and building trust among agencies, leading to the generation of informal networks of collaboration.

Most importantly, as Arzt (2010) suggests, personal relationships are critical informal mechanisms of cooperation. Personal trust and cooperation with a counterpart translate into better and increased cooperation. In the case of organic, on-the-ground, informal networks, it is hard to gauge their effectiveness, as there is no data to measure impact and performance and only anecdotal information from success stories. However, to determine the most important value of such networks, one would not look to the rate of success on solving cases or detaining suspects but to the capacity of building trust and channels of communication that go beyond the political framework and the institutional networks across borders, to reach a common goal. What is important is the cohesive effect that informality brings in building such networks. It is a space where a vibrant borderland community interacts to solve common problems, not as U.S. or Mexican citizens but as members of a border security community. Hence, the remainder of this chapter provides some basic policy recommendations that can be adopted to take advantage of existing mechanisms of cooperation in the binational context and to foster the formation of more organic channels and mechanisms of cooperation between law enforcement and security agencies across the border.

Maintain a Shared Responsibility Approach

Perhaps the most important lesson learned from all the attempts to build an efficient and mutually respectful security partnership between the United States and Mexico is to address common challenges as a shared responsibility and not only as one-sided problems. From the Clinton era to the Obama administration—and through the shaping of the Mérida Initiative—both countries have taken steps toward this direction, however precarious, and have laid the ground for more coordinated efforts. Nevertheless, the change of rhetoric under the Trump administration can seriously harm a collaborative partnership that, despite its successes, still has significant room for improvement. The position of López Obrador toward the United States and the bilateral cooperation relationship is not yet clear. Without any real change so far, there is still the possibility of a drastic shift should the new Mexican president's agenda be somehow affected by the White House.

As Guillermo Valdés, former director of Mexico's intelligence agency, Centro de Investigación y Seguridad Nacional (CISEN, Center for Research and National Security), suggested, it would be useful to conduct a binational joint security assessment where the most important threats and challenges are identified cooperatively. Consequently, the set of priorities developed by both countries derived from such an assessment would recognize mutual problems and subsequent ramifications across the border, helping to strengthen a "shared responsibility" approach. Acknowledgment of the shared responsibility by both will address the complicated binational collaboration, focusing on challenges that both nations identify as priorities and that have cross-border ramifications. After all, common challenges, especially in the border region, are just two sides of the same coin.

Strengthen the National-Level Legal Infrastructure

It would be ideal to have an overarching bilateral treaty on security collaboration that would consolidate beyond the Mérida Initiative, stress shared challenges, and encompass the vast set of mechanisms currently in place while fostering the generation of informal networks. The reality, however, is that it is more efficient to use the already working and somewhat effective mechanisms to keep fostering field-level collaboration rather than seeking a national-level command to do so. Yet even without such an overarching treaty, the current binational legal infrastructure allows both countries to address specific cases wherein binational collaboration is needed. However, neither country has taken steps to create a solid national structure to respond to this need institutionally. Therefore, it would be useful to incorporate more regulations and mechanisms that have contributed to develop a formal and informal set of networks and procedures and that could facilitate exchanges and communication in a much broader local, state, or federal legislation. Dispositions like Section 11055 of the California Penal Code and Article 4 of the Mexican CFPP, for instance, could be incorporated into every border state's penal legislation.

An interesting approach could be the inclusion of dispositions into a model legislation that states and federal agencies could adopt on both sides of the border. This would create and maintain permanent FPUs, international and border liaisons, and other necessity-based taskforces that could build on regulating or contemplating more specific, formal procedures of collaboration. This could address cases of certain jurisdictions that depend on the binational collaboration and assist other nonborder states with their collaboration channels, mechanisms, and expertise, when needed. Granting a certain degree of autonomy for such units in the legislation could ease the process of creating organic cooperative networks in the field, as is already the case in California.

Create Specialized Coordinated Field-Level Units

The legal framework built by the United States and Mexico has achieved various accomplishments, creating instances for collaboration with clear procedures and protocols to be followed by agencies from both countries. Along with other multilateral treaties, memoranda, programs, and meetings, there are now identified channels to address specific cases. An agency can now expect a response from its counterpart on the other side of the border, or at the very least to have someone with whom to communicate. Even without further legislation, the current legal framework favors the creation of FPUs, and thus there should be units with such specific attribution in every single border state. Along with or as an alternative to FPUs, there should also be an international or border liaison in the field at all times representing all local, state, and federal agencies in the border region. This agent ought to have sufficient knowledge of the current protocols and procedures of collaboration to ensure that every request for collaboration runs smoothly.

Another interesting idea would be the formation of "multinational, multidisciplinary task-force-style operations" by prosecutors and law enforcement officers from both countries that can bring "jointly investigated cases" to U.S. and Mexican courts (Da Silva 2018). Anthony Da Silva follows Cameron Holmes's assessment that "joint multinational, multidisciplinary task-force style operations would focus on specific border criminal economic activities . . . such as kidnapping, corruption, extortion, counterfeit goods, cargo theft, import-export fraud, theft of petroleum products and opioids" (Holmes 2014, 3–4). In this scenario, task-force-style operations "would identify key components and vulnerabilities in their respective areas of criminal and economic activity and focus accordingly in view of prosecuting" (Da Silva 2018).

Foster the Generation of Organic Networks

Organic informal networks generated on the ground have, according to hundreds of law enforcement and security personnel, eased the binational cooperation process and have been effective in solving cases. Thus, according to anecdotal information, informal trust and leadership-based networks have become one of the most important means of solving cases through transnational connections. However, trust building can only be achieved by constant interaction, and such interaction is only possible under the right conditions. Therefore, both countries need to foster opportunities for interaction—for example, by encouraging regular- and institutionalized-basis interagency exchanges, trainings, conferences, and meetings. Such opportunities, including those regulated by treaties, agreements, and MOUs, should be maintained and fostered, while other types of informal interactions, such as parades, picnics, sports tournaments, or even social events, should be encouraged. These opportunities for interaction can create an environment favorable to the generation of organic networks of collaboration. Although it is true that the context and environment can, per se, naturally generate organic networks, it is also true that developing collaboration channels takes time and these networks are very fragile by themselves. Therefore, both countries should work to maintain a structure that fosters such on-the-ground relationships.

A good approach would be to foster already existing, structured, yet somewhat informal BLMs. At the BLM formal meetings, law enforcement personnel from the United States and Mexico have a forum to interact regularly, which aides in building trust. As has been the case, a more formal infrastructure does not inhibit the formation of organic networks; rather, it provides the ground for its formation and the support for its sustainability. As the border is built from the bottom up, efforts to address border region problems should include bottom-up strategies. Organic on-the-ground informal networks serve this purpose by constructing a field policy that pollinizes the daily discourse of binational security cooperation in the border region. In the end, *informal* should not necessarily have a negative connotation. As law enforcement and security personnel, border region officials have a duty to represent an agency, but as peers, they share and follow a set of written and unwritten rules, or a sort of shared identity and culture. In many cases, informality leads to building a community with common concerns and goals. On the ground, law enforcement and security personnel know and agree that the set of problems affecting the border region is a shared responsibility, requiring joint cooperation to successfully identify, address, and avoid conflict.

Notes

I acknowledge and thank Anthony Da Silva and Elias Estrada for their input, comments, and suggestions, and especially for sharing their field-level knowledge regarding cooperation within formal and informal networks and processes. Likewise, I am grateful for the invaluable assistance of Ashley Ahrens-Víquez, Kimberly Heinle, and Lucy La Rosa in the revision and editing of this chapter; and David Shirk, Emily Edmonds-Poli, and Valeria Loayza for their direct contributions to this research. Additionally, I thank Laura Calderón, Rita Kuckertz, Diana Sánchez, and Mauricio Villaseñor for their support in the research process, and also acknowledge the help of all the Justice in Mexico program team. I also thank Tony Payan, Pamela Cruz, and all the team of the Center for the United States and Mexico at Rice University's Baker Institute for Public Policy for the invitation to participate in this project, their patience, and their valuable input. Finally, I thank my fellow writers who contributed to this work, for their comments and the excellent analyses they developed.

1.   As Luis Astorga and David A. Shirk (2010, 46) mention, the unilateral and un-negotiated Operation Intercept launched by the Richard Nixon administration in 1969 to reduce

drug flows northbound slowed traffic at the border dramatically and was regarded by Mexican authorities as a serious breach of trust. Clare Seelke, Liana Wyler, and June Beittel (2010) point out that mutual mistrust came largely from concerns from the U.S. government about Mexico somehow protecting criminals, while Mexico largely opposed drug certifications and was concerned about its sovereignty due to the history of U.S. interventions in Mexico.

2. SNSP modified its methodology for recording cases of homicide beginning 2015. Figure 8.1 combines the numbers of the old and new methodologies before and after 2015, respectively.

3. According to Emily Edmonds-Poli and David Shirk (2018), dispositions about capital punishment and the question of surrendering its own citizens contemplated in Articles 8 and 9 have created the most serious obstacles to cooperation on extradition cases.

4. According to Bruce Zagaris and Jessica Resnick (1997), the cooperation was the result of the decision of Mexican attorney general Sergio Garcia Ramirez to treat the U.S. request for evidence as though a mutual assistance treaty were in effect.

5. There are some variances from the data reported by the GAO (2019) and by Clare Seelke and Kristin Finklea (2017). GAO reports US$1 million less in 2015 and US$200,000 less in 2016 than Seelke and Finklea.

6. A detailed description of the extradition process can be found in Zagaris and Padierna Peratta 1997.

7. Cases of child abductions from California when the suspect crosses the border into Mexico are common. In such cases, the FPLEU was designated by the Child Abduction Unit, under the California Department of Justice, as the law enforcement point of contact for all such cases that are governed by the Hague Convention on the Civil Aspects of International Child Abduction, which are known as the Hague Cases (California Department of Justice n.d. ["Foreign Prosecutions"]).

8. It should be acknowledged that this "on-the-ground" approach focuses not on police and law enforcement but on judicial actors (Hersant and Vigour 2017). However, this chapter tries to find a common line on the construction of policy at the street level with other public service workers.

9. Most of the information included in this section that is credited to the Justiciabarómetro studies came from the qualitative assessments conducted in Ciudad Juárez in 2011 and in Tijuana in 2015. While this information was not included in the final reports for each study, it was compiled through focus groups and targeted interviews that helped shape the analysis.

10. Some Mexican police agents with decades of experience in the force recall a time when they did not have to have a visa to cross to the United States, and they were able to do it even with the patrol car. As the years went by, the contexts have changed, bringing stronger border security measures, and some original channels of communication and networks of trust have disappeared or changed (Justice in Mexico 2011, 2015).

11. The most common trainings mentioned in the course of the quantitative and qualitative research cited, where agencies from the United States and Mexico interact, include home and vehicle searches, conducting arrests, evidence gathering, police administration, gangs, and investigation techniques.

12. Agents have shared experiences of many operations that became joint operations, as suspects fled to the other side of the border during an ongoing operation in one country. In Tijuana, municipal police reported that at some point the tourist police used to have a frequency radio that communicated directly with the authorities in San Diego. However, it is a general feeling that the relation with law enforcement agencies was more direct and personal in the past years. Over the last decade, the relations have been more centralized, making it harder to interact directly with agents across the border (Justice in Mexico 2011, 2015).

13. In San Diego, for example, the predecessor of the current border liaison mechanism was a series of regular meetings promoted by law enforcement agents themselves, to get to know and trust their Mexican counterparts. Eventually, such meetings became more "formal" when the agencies and consular authorities legalized the benefits of open transborder communication. Currently the mechanism depends on these regular and formal meetings but remains a space where organic networks generate.

14. Sabet's (2005) analysis focuses mainly on civil society organizations and not on law enforcement agencies.

15. Koff (2015) cites Sabet (2005) as to how informal sectors along the U.S.-Mexico border have grown because they are more lucrative, and how criminal organizations have been participating and establishing resource-intensive activities.

16. As Rodger A. Payne (2012, 609) suggests, in traditional policy, "cooperative security" has been typically employed somewhat narrowly, as collective actions by states in international institutions to counter aggression and as a shared strong interest in world peace where the community of states should work together as much as possible to preserve peace and avoid war. Until more recently, "cooperative security" commonly implies an understanding about the world community's behavior in response to a wide variety of problems and threats.

References

Aguila, Emma, Alisher Akhmedjonov, Ricardo Basurto Davil, Krishna Kumar, Sarah Kups, and Howard Shatz. 2012. *United States and Mexico: Ties That Bind, Issues That Divide.* Santa Monica, Calif.: RAND.

Arizona Attorney General. n.d. "Southwest Border Anti-Money Laundering Alliance." Accessed February 16, 2018. https://www.azag.gov/criminal/borders-security/swbamla.

Arzt, Sigrid. 2010. "U.S.-Mexico Security Collaboration: Intelligence Sharing and Law Enforcement Cooperation." In *Shared Responsibility: U.S.-Mexico Policy Options for Confronting Organized Crime*, edited by Eric L. Olson, David A. Shirk, and Andrew Selee, 351–70.

Washington, D.C.: Woodrow Wilson International Center for Scholars; San Diego: Trans-Border Institute, University of San Diego.

Astorga, Luis, and David A. Shirk. 2010. "Drug Trafficking Organizations and Counter-Drug Strategies in the U.S.-Mexican Context." In *Shared Responsibility: U.S.-Mexico Policy Options for Confronting Organized Crime*, edited by Eric L. Olson, David A. Shirk, and Andrew Selee, 31–62. Washington, D.C.: Woodrow Wilson International Center for Scholars; San Diego: Trans-Border Institute, University of San Diego.

Attorney General of Texas. 2017. "Criminal Prosecutions Under Article 4 of the Mexican Federal Penal Code." Accessed November 12. https://www2.texasattorneygeneral.gov/files/cj/article4.pdf.

Bailey, John, and Jorge Chabat. 2002. "Transnational Crime and Public Security: Trends and Issues." In *Transnational Crime and Public Security*, edited by John Bailey and Jorge Chabat, 1–50. San Diego: Center for U.S.-Mexican Studies, University of California, San Diego.

Benítez Manaut, Raúl, and Carlos Rodríguez Ulloa. 2006. "Seguridad y fronteras en Norteamérica: Del TLCAN a la ASPAN." *Frontera Norte* 18 (35).

Brunet-Jailly, Emmanuel. 2013. "Power, Politics and Governance of Borderlands." In *Theorizing Borders Through Analysis of Power Relationships*, edited by Peter Gilles, Harlan Koff, Carmen Maganda, and Christian Schulz, 29–45. Brussels: P.I.E. Peter Lang.

Calderón, Laura Y., Kimberly Heinle, Octavio Rodríguez Ferreira, and David A. Shirk. 2019. *Organized Crime and Violence in Mexico*. San Diego: Justice in Mexico, University of San Diego.

California Department of Justice. n.d. "California Anti-Money Laundering Alliance." Accessed May 7, 2020. https://oag.ca.gov/bi/.

California Department of Justice. n.d. "Foreign Prosecutions and Law Enforcement Unit (FPLEU)." Accessed May 7, 2020. https://oag.ca.gov/bi/fpleu.

Da Silva, Anthony. 2018. "Reducing Crime and Violence in Tijuana: Challenges and Strategies." Paper presented at Rethinking the War on Drugs and U.S.-Mexico Security Cooperation, Center for U.S.-Mexican Studies at the University of California, San Diego, February 9.

Doyle, Kate. 2003. "La Operación Intercepción: Los peligros del unilateralismo." *Proceso*, April 13.

Edmonds-Poli, Emily, and David Shirk. 2018. "Extradition as a Tool for International Cooperation: Lessons from the U.S.-Mexico Relationship." *Maryland Journal of International Law* 33 (1): 215–43.

Embassy of the United States in Mexico. 2005. "Meeting of Border Liaison Mechanism." Press release, Ciudad Juárez, Chihuahua, Mex., August 24.

García, José Z. 2002. "Security Regimes on the U.S.-Mexico Border." In *Trasnational Crime and Public Security*, edited by John Bailey and Jorge Chabat, 299–334. San Diego: Center for U.S.-Mexican Studies, University of California, San Diego.

Guymon, CarrieLyn Donigan. 2000. "International Legal Mechanisms for Combating Transnational Organized Crime: The Need for a Multilateral Convention." *Berkeley Journal of International Law* 18 (1): 53–101.

Heinle, Kimberly, Octavio Rodríguez Ferreira, and David Shirk. 2014. *Drug Violence in Mexico.* San Diego: Justice in Mexico, University of San Diego.

Heinle, Kimberly, Octavio Rodríguez Ferreira, and David Shirk. 2016. *Drug Violence in Mexico.* San Diego: Justice in Mexico, University of San Diego.

Hersant, Jeanne, and Cécile Vigour. 2017. "Judicial Politics on the Ground." *Law & Social Inquiry* 42 (2): 292–97.

Holmes, Cameron. 2014. *Organized Crime in Mexico: Assessing the Threat to North American Economies.* Lincoln: University of Nebraska Press.

Instituto de Investigaciones Legislativas del Senado de la República (IILSEN). 2003. *Agenda Bilateral México–Estados Unidos: Avances y temas pendientes.* Mexico City: Instituto de Investigaciones Legislativas del Senado de la República.

Justice in Mexico. 2011. "Justiciabarómetro: Policía Municipal de Ciudad Juárez."

Justice in Mexico. 2015. "Justiciabarómetro: Policía Municipal de Tijuana."

Koff, Harlan. 2015. "Survival Strategy, Victimless Crime or Challenge to Nation-States? Exploring Informality in Cross-Border Regions." *Journal of Borderlands Studies* 30 (4): 461–67.

Lipsky, Michael. 1980. *Street Level Bureaucracy: Dilemmas of the Individual in Public Services.* New York: Russell Sage Foundation.

Mares, David R. 1988. "Mexico's Foreign Policy as a Middle Power: The Nicaragua Connection, 1884–1986." *Latin American Research Review* 23 (3): 81–107.

Meyers, Deborah W. 2003. "Does 'Smarter' Lead to Safer? An Assessment of the US Border Accords with Canada and Mexico." *International Migration* 41 (4): 5–44.

Olson, Eric L. 2018. *Where Do We Go from Here? Merida 2.0 and the Future of Mexico-United States Security Cooperation.* Washington, D.C.: Mexico Institute, Wilson Center.

Olson, Eric L., David A. Shirk, and Andrew Selee. 2010a. "Introduction." In *Shared Responsibility: U.S.-Mexico Policy Options for Confronting Organized Crime,* edited by Eric L. Olson, David A. Shirk, and Andrew Selee, 1–30. Washington, D.C.: Mexico Institute, Wilson Center.

Olson, Eric L., David A. Shirk, and Andrew Selee. 2010b. "Preface." In *Shared Responsibility: U.S.-Mexico Policy Options for Confronting Organized Crime,* edited by Eric L. Olson, David A. Shirk, and Andrew Selee, vii–viii. Washington, D.C.: Mexico Institute, Wilson Center.

Olson, Eric L., and Christopher E. Wilson. 2010. "Beyond Merida: The Evolving Approach to Security Cooperation." Working Paper Series on U.S.-Mexico Security Cooperation. Washington, D.C.: Mexico Institute, Wilson Center; San Diego: Trans-Border Institute, University of San Diego.

Payne, Rodger A. 2012. "Cooperative Security: Grand Strategy Meets Critical Theory?" *Millennium: Journal of International Studies* 40 (3): 605–24.

Quiroz, Carlos. 2016. "Se ha extraditado a casi mil personas de México para EU." *Excelsior,* June 9. http://www.excelsior.com.mx/nacional/2016/06/09/1097694.

Ramos, José M. 2002. "Cooperation on Narco-Trafficking and Public Security on the U.S.-Mexico Border." In *Transnational Crime and Public Security,* edited by John Bailey and Jorge

Chabat, 335–68. San Diego: Center for U.S.-Mexican Studies, University of California, San Diego.

Reich, Simon, and Richard Lebow. 2014. *America and Security Sponsorship*. Princeton, N.J.: Princeton University Press.

Sabet, Daniel. 2005. "Building Bridges: Binational Civil Society Cooperation and Water-Related Policy Problems." *Journal of Environment & Development* 14 (4): 463–85.

Secretaría de Relaciones Exteriores (SRE). 2017. "Fifth Meeting of Mexico-U.S. Bilateral Security Cooperation Group." https://www.gob.mx/sre/en/prensa/fifth-meeting-of-mexico-u-s-bilateral-security-cooperation-group?idiom=en.

Seelke, Clare, and Kristin Finklea. 2017. *U.S.-Mexican Security Cooperation: The Mérida Initiative and Beyond*. Washington, D.C.: Congressional Research Service.

Seelke, Clare, Liana Wyler, and June Beittel. 2010. *Latin America and the Caribbean: Illicit Drug Trafficking and U.S. Counterdrug Programs*. Washington, D.C.: Congressional Research Service.

Sheridan, Mary Beth. 2019. "Mexico's President Just Says No to U.S. Cash to Fight Drug Crime." *Washington Post*, May 9.

Shirk, David. 2003. "Law Enforcement and Security Challenges in the U.S.-Mexican Border Region." *Journal of Borderlands Studies* 18 (2): 1–24.

Sistema Nacional de Seguridad Pública (SNSP). n.d. "Datos Abiertos de Incidencia Delictiva." Accessed February 19, 2020. https://www.gob.mx/sesnsp/acciones-y-programas/datos-abiertos-de-incidencia-delictiva.

Suárez de Garay, María Eugenia. 2006. *Los policías: Una averiguación antropológica*. Guadalajara: Universidad de Guadalajara and ITESO.

Texas A&M International University. n.d. "Laredo / Nuevo Laredo Border Liaison Mechanism." Accessed September 11, 2017. http://www.tamiu.edu/binationalcenter/BLM.shtml.

U.S. Department of Homeland Security (DHS). 2008. "Local Arrangement for Repatriation of Mexican Nationals." San Diego, Calif.

U.S. Department of Justice (DOJ). 2010. "Review of ATF's Project Gunrunner." Edited by Office of the Inspector General, Evaluation and Inspections Division. Washington, D.C.

U.S. Department of State (DOS). 2011. "Background Notes: Mexico." https://2009-2017.state.gov/outofdate/bgn/mexico/1838.htm.

U.S. Department of State (DOS). n.d. "Merida Initiative." Accessed May 7, 2020. https://2009-2017.state.gov/j/inl/merida//index.htm.

U.S. Government Accountability Office (GAO). 2019. *U.S. Assistance to Mexico*. Report to Congressional Requesters GAO-19-647. Washington, D.C.: U.S. Government Accountability Office.

Wayne, Earl Anthony. 2019. "Mexico, the Leading US Trade Partner, Seeks to Fortify Relations." *The Hill*, September 9. https://thehill.com/opinion/finance/460529-mexico-the-leading-us-trade-partner-seeks-to-fortify-relations.

Wayne, Earl Anthony, Cecilia Farfan-Mendez, Vanda Felbab-Brown, and Rafael Fernandez de Castro. 2019. "Tariffs Won't Solve U.S.-Mexico Drug Crime—We Must Work Together." *Dallas Morning News*, April 26.

Zagaris, Bruce, and Julia Padierna Peratta. 1997. "Mexico-United States Extradition and Alternatives: From Fugitive Slaves to Drug Traffickers—150 Years and Beyond the Rio Grande's Winding Courses." *American University International Law Review* 12 (4): 519–627.

Zagaris, Bruce, and Jessica Resnick. 1997. "The Mexico-U.S. Mutual Legal Assistance in Criminal Matters Treaty: Another Step Toward the Harmonization of International Law Enforcement." *Arizona Journal of International and Comparative Law* 14 (1): 1–96.

9

U.S.-Mexico Law Enforcement and Border Security Cooperation

An Institutional-Historical Perspective

Guadalupe Correa-Cabrera and Evan D. McCormick

O n July 7, 2017, then U.S. secretary of homeland security and currently White House chief of staff John F. Kelly and then Mexico's Secretaría de Gobernación (Secretary of the Interior) Miguel Ángel Osorio Chong met in Mexico City. In his prepared remarks, Kelly portrayed U.S.-Mexico security cooperation as "natural."

> We recognize that our prosperity and security are intertwined, and that criminal networks grow in influence and power when our two countries do not work together. As a practical matter, that means looking towards new agreements where we can share information, training, infrastructure, and planning resources. We will accomplish this with mutual trust and support. (Kelly 2017)

But the U.S.-Mexico partnership did not seem like a given in political terms. Earlier in 2017, just after his inauguration, U.S. president Donald Trump dismissed a cooperative approach to border security and signed an executive order authorizing the construction of a formidable 1,900-mile-long wall on the U.S.-Mexico border. He then repeatedly insisted that Mexico would pay for the wall, a claim that led then Mexican president Enrique Peña Nieto to twice cancel planned visits to Washington to meet with Trump (Rucker, Partlow, and Miroff 2018).

Notwithstanding Trump's posturing, cooperation in terms of trade and security has not stopped, and mounting evidence suggests that elites in both countries see the institutional relationship as vital. Kelly and then U.S. secretary of state Rex Tillerson visited Mexico in summer 2017 and communicated the U.S. president's desire for his country to work with its neighbor on many of their "shared issues," as well as his attempt to create "stronger, durable bonds" between the two nations. Indeed, in his inscrutable way, Trump seems to have arrived at the idea that Mexico is instrumental to his goal of using the border as a nationalistic and political device. When Trump recently put the issue in typically offensive and obtuse terms, claiming, "I'm using Mexico to protect our border because the Democrats won't change loopholes and asylum" (White House 2019), Mexican president Andrés Manuel López Obrador tellingly responded by saying Mexico had "nothing to be ashamed of.... We protect Mexico's sovereignty. At the same time, we try to avoid confrontation" (Ramos 2019).

These comments reveal a latent paradox between the Trump administration's initial nationalistic approach to border control and the reality of U.S.-Mexico relations on the border as they have developed over the last thirty years. Threats and efforts to unilaterally control the border and limit cooperation have been regular political ploys in the United States, but no ploy has succeeded in interrupting broader shifts toward cooperation between the two countries. Consider, for example, attempts by U.S. customs commissioner William von Raab to shut down the U.S.-Mexico border after the murder of Drug Enforcement Administration (DEA) agent Enrique "Kiki" Camarena in 1985, or the George W. Bush administration's immediate reaction after the attacks of September 11, 2001. Trump's bombastic threats to end the North American Free Trade Agreement (NAFTA)—which led to a follow-on free trade agreement, the United States-Mexico-Canada Agreement (USMCA)—were simply the latest in a stream of challenges to cooperation with Mexico. And yet, in each instance, the development of a solid, binational approach to law enforcement on the border has preempted populist tendencies, including the Trump administration's, from wrecking the relationship. A key question is: How has this binational relationship evolved so that cross-border collaboration has proven durable enough to survive even Trump's hostile rhetoric?

Objectives and Methods

Drawing on interviews with principal officials and secondary research, this chapter analyzes the history of U.S.-Mexico border security cooperation and transnational law enforcement from an institutional perspective.[1] Focusing on the period after 1993, we trace the emergence of a binational border security regime—one in which the U.S. and Mexican governments began to view border security as a shared responsibility. The emergence of this cooperative framework was made possible by two broad transformations in approaches to the border. The first was a shift in the way borders were viewed by both sides: away from the notion of lines differentiating sovereignties and toward the conception of flows of goods and people between economies and labor markets.

The second was the erosion of the long-held belief that securing the border and facilitating transport across it were exclusive motivations, replaced by a paradigm in which security and trade were seen as complementary dimensions of border management.

The arrival at a binational border security framework has been accompanied by political, economic, and technological changes in both countries that have made progress on border security halting at times. In this chapter, we trace the key stages in that transformation. In the first section, we examine the geopolitical power asymmetries that led the countries to act for much of the twentieth century as, in Alan Riding's (1989) famous expression, "distant neighbors." In the second phase, which stretched from 1993 to 2000, we draw on the framework formulated by Alan Bersin to show how Bill Clinton and Ernesto Zedillo discovered "*el Tercer País*," or "the Third Country," establishing for the first time a common framework that allowed for cooperation between law enforcement agencies. The terrorist attacks of 9/11 interrupted this process, ushering in a third phase, during which the politics of security interfered with the impetus to create "smart borders" among North American partners. The creation of the U.S. Department of Homeland Security (DHS) turned security and prosperity into exclusive goals. But the consolidation of law enforcement agencies focused on the border allowed the Bush administration, by the end of its second term, to renew collaboration with Mexico through the Mérida Initiative. During the fourth phase, the Barack Obama administration built upon the earlier institutional foundations to establish a framework in which trade facilitation and security were seen as integrated and complementary—rather than mutually exclusive—goals.

Phase 1 (Pre-1994): "Distant Neighbors" (*Vecinos Distantes*)—Different Perspectives

Prior to the signing of NAFTA, official relations between the United States and Mexico were marked by a history of cool tolerance at best, and outright antagonism at worst. Dating to the Mexican-American War (1846–48)—considered an "invasion" by Mexico—the two countries have behaved as "distant neighbors" (Riding 1989). For much of Mexico's history after it lost more than half of its territory (including Texas) to the United States in the Treaty of Guadalupe Hidalgo, the two countries managed civil relations but essentially no meaningful institutional cooperation on border affairs occurred until the 1990s.

Rugged geography and limited means of communication among Mexico's central, plateau, and northern regions traditionally weakened national approaches to law enforcement at the border. As one analyst has characterized it, the U.S.-Mexico border region was long considered a zone of "little economic value, and it was inherently difficult to police due to the terrain. It separated the two countries, but it became a low-level friction point throughout history, in which economies of smuggling and banditry flourished at various times on both sides" (Friedman 2012, 2).

The border was a specific point of friction in a broader bilateral relationship defined by territorial disputes and power asymmetries. Most notable in this regard was the "Punitive Expedition" by the U.S. Army—led by Brigadier General John J. Pershing—to capture rebel leader Francisco "Pancho" Villa in Mexican territory after his cross-border raid into Columbus, New Mexico. This history of U.S. intervention lent a distinctly anti-American hue to the nationalism that emerged from the Mexican Revolution (1910–20). The Mexican Constitution of 1917, which asserted subsoil mineral rights and justified subsequent nationalization of foreign oil concerns, codified this revolutionary nationalism and would serve as the guiding ideology of the Partido Revolucionario Institucional (PRI, Institutional Revolutionary Party) for much of the twentieth century.[2]

Notwithstanding this antagonism, the two countries succeeded in creating a peaceful but distant modus vivendi. Mexican political elites often rhetorically opposed the United States to shore up legitimacy and security of the PRI regime at home but resisted taking steps to substantially oppose U.S. foreign policies. For its part, the United States acquiesced to Mexico's frequent antagonism on various policy matters while enjoying the reassurance of a stable neighbor to the south (McCormick and Bersin 2017, 6). With the exception of immigration enforcement meant to control the flow of cheap labor across the border (Heer 2016; Henderson 2011, 213–14), "security" as such was largely absent from bilateral concerns until the 1980s, when increasing drug-related violence in Mexico intersected with the Ronald Reagan administration's focus on the War on Drugs. Although Mexico had been engaged in its own war on drugs since the 1960s, the murder of Camarena, a DEA agent, in 1985 highlighted the need for cooperative responses to what had become a transnational issue. In response to this incident, U.S. customs commissioner von Raab attempted to shut down the border. Although his efforts proved to be contrary to U.S. interests and were summarily reversed, the episode highlighted the absence of formal institutions for formal law enforcement and border security cooperation.

Phase 2 (1993–2000): Discovering "*el Tercer País*"— Developing a Common Framework During the Clinton-Zedillo Years

Political, social, and economic changes in both Mexico and the United States during the 1990s led to a mutual discovery of *el Tercer País* (the Third Country), or lands physically adjacent to the roughly two-thousand-mile shared border. Although this region was traditionally treated as a no-man's land by both countries, the benefits of free trade, along with the ambiguities of migration and drug trafficking, increasingly turned the border region into "a thermostat for bilateral relations" (Bersin 1996, 1413). During this period, which roughly coincided with the presidencies of Ernesto Zedillo (1994–2000) and Bill Clinton (1993–2000), public and media attention on the movement of goods and people across the U.S.-Mexico border led to an increasing emphasis on security. While border initiatives during these years were primarily political in nature, they nonetheless proved pivotal in allowing the two countries for the first time to develop a common framework to tackle security issues related to immigration, trade, and organized crime.

NAFTA was the engine of this transformation. Negotiations for the free trade pact, which was signed on December 17, 1992, and came into force on January 1, 1994, ushered in a period of unprecedented high-level cooperation on trade issues that in turn facilitated bilateral collaboration in other areas, namely security and law enforcement (Bersin 1996, 1413). The political opposition to a sweeping free trade agreement—led by labor organizations in all three countries—along with a fear of increased Mexican immigration in the United States, required the two nations to establish a more organized regime for regulating the flow of goods and restricting the flow of people across the border. The economic model established under NAFTA, which allowed for the free mobility of goods but not of labor, would concentrate development in the *maquila* industries along Mexico's northern border, allowing U.S. transnational companies to access cheaper labor while keeping jobs in Mexico.

In Mexico, NAFTA came during a moment of political upheaval that—although it threatened elite support of the PRI in the short term—was part of a broader democratic opening that played out through the 1990s and ultimately strengthened the bilateral approach to law enforcement. A series of events between 1993 and 1995 heightened a perception among Mexicans that malfeasance and corruption in the PRI had made it incapable of governing. During the 1994 presidential campaign, Mexico witnessed a series of high-profile political murders that claimed the lives of, among others, PRI presidential candidate Luis Donaldo Colosio. The May 1993 assassination of Cardinal Juan Jesús Posadas Ocampo, believed to have been caught in a shootout between rival cartels in Guadalajara, increased suspicion that the rising tide of political violence was related to the burgeoning narcotics trade. A second factor was the peso crisis of 1994, which struck weeks after the Zedillo administration took office. With confidence wavering in the strength of the Mexican economy at the end of Carlos Salinas de Gortari's term, Mexico's central bank devalued the peso in December 1994. The decision resulted in a massive run on the peso and skyrocketing inflation. The following year, the United States offered a US$20 million bailout package that, although politically controversial in both the United States and Mexico, had the effect of binding the Clinton administration tightly to the economic fortunes of Zedillo's Mexico.

The northern border became an increasing priority for Mexican elites who were simultaneously seeking to stimulate industrial trade and attract investment, on the one hand, and to fight perceptions of corruption and instability, on the other. Luis Herrera Lasso, former Mexican consul in San Diego and a key actor who favored bilateral cooperation on border issues in the San Diego–Tijuana sector in the 1990s, points out that in the previous decades, "illegality, lack of control, and lack of effective border management to regulate immigration and assure safety then severely affected border communities, border people, as well as the safety and human rights of migrants." Hence, "something effective needed to be done to gain control of the border, and bilateral cooperation was a key element for achieving this task" (Luis Herrera Lasso, Skype interview, October 10, 2017).

NAFTA had similarly highlighted the importance of border issues in the United States, but there the fixation on security came from nativist concerns over Mexican immigration and the persistent cultural fears associated with the narcotics trade. California's 1994 gubernatorial race resulted not only in the reelection of incumbent Republican Pete Wilson, who campaigned on an anti-immigration platform, but also the approval of the controversial anti-immigrant Proposition 187 by California voters.[3] This election made clear that significant segments of the U.S. population had developed fundamental concerns about evident changes resulting from Mexican immigration to the United States. The use of the subject of illegal/undocumented immigration as a political/electoral tool by the Republican Party forced the Clinton administration to turn to strategies for addressing immigration, which explicitly linked the issue to law enforcement. Under the Clinton administration, the United States adopted a national border policy of "prevention through deterrence," which sought to use physical barriers, electronic surveillance, and the prospect of interception by law enforcement to limit attempts at crossing (Cornelius 2001). This policy was first outlined in a study commissioned by the Office of National Drug Control Policy (ONDCP) in 1993 but took shape in a series of operations overseen by the U.S. Border Patrol (USBP), at that time part of Immigration and Naturalization Services (INS), concentrated at specific points along the border.[4] The first of these was Operation Hold-the-Line, engineered by Silvestre Reyes, a regional USBP supervisor in El Paso, Texas, in 1993–94. Reyes's strategy entailed continuously positioning law enforcement vehicles at border-crossing points to deter potential illegal border crossings. Following dramatic short-term results in El Paso, the INS sought to replicate Operation Hold-the-Line by concentrating agents and technologies at other major crossing points. In October 1994, the INS began Operation Gatekeeper in San Diego, gradually expanding the deployment of concentrated border enforcement east to Yuma, Arizona. Later in 1994, the INS launched Operation Safeguard in its Tucson sector, aiming to increase control of the border in Arizona. In 1997, the INS focused its attention on Southeast Texas with Operation Rio Grande in the McAllen sector (Cornelius 2001; Krouse 1997). While each of these initiatives was tailored to specific geographic and demographic challenges, they shared an underlying logic, as character- ized by Peter Andreas, to disrupt the most concentrated entry points, forcing human traffic to areas that are either more remote or easier for the USBP to regulate (Andreas 1998, 346–47; 2009; see also Bersin 1995).

Were the initiatives successful? Andreas (1998) argues that deterrence was success- ful in political terms but a failure in policy terms. In the short term, the operations resulted in a dramatic drop-off in the number of apprehensions by border enforcement officials. In El Paso, the drop was roughly 76 percent during the first fiscal year of Gate- keeper (Cornelius 2001, 662). By FY1997, INS statistics showed a decrease in appre- hensions of roughly 9 percent compared to FY1994 levels (CRS 1997, 3). However, by FY2000, apprehensions had shown a net increase of 68 percent, suggesting that the long-term deterrent effect had not prevented the flow of illegal immigrants. While some critics pointed out the unreliability of apprehensions as a statistical measure, others pointed to the lack of predicted effects on the labor market to show that the INS deterrence strategy had not decreased the availability of cheap immigrant labor. Crit- ics also noted the humanitarian cost, suggesting that concentrated enforcement was increasing the reliance on human smugglers and pushing border crossers to more dan- gerous and inhospitable areas, resulting in an increase in fatalities (Cornelius 2001).

Andreas (1998) argues that the political success of Clinton's deterrence-based bor- der security initiatives lay in creating, for the first time, a sense of an orderly physical presence at the border. This is accurate, but the distinction underestimates just how significant—in policy terms—the bilateral border cooperation of the 1990s was. For the first time, Mexican and U.S. officials had ceased treating the border simply as a line demarcating contentious sovereignties. Sovereignty still mattered, of course, but both governments were now acknowledging the shared responsibility and benefits of ensur- ing the transit of goods—even if not people, as Mexico would prefer. Thus, while there was a political effect to the establishment of order at the physical borderline, the coop- erative approach had much deeper effects on the policy level. Gone was the recrimi- nation that had marked law enforcement interaction in previous decades, replaced by a common framework between officials at the highest levels that established a basis for what was later achieved concretely during the Bush and Obama administrations.

David V. Aguilar—who served in various leadership positions within the USBP and later became national chief of the USBP under George W. Bush—was one archi- tect who shared this positive assessment. As the person in charge of Operation Rio Grande, Aguilar explains how "this was the start of a deterrence-type strategy that would later become the prevailing strategy across the entire southern border." Aguilar calls this the "gain, maintain, and expand" effort that would later characterize overall Border Patrol operational objectives: provide sufficient resources to *gain* control of an area, continue providing resources to support and *maintain* control, and then *expand* operations linearly across the border (David V. Aguilar, phone interview, July 6, 2017). In Aguilar's view, rather than dedicating resources "to apprehend individuals crossing the border, transport them to the station, process and feed them, and then return them across the border (all the while drawing personnel and resources from the border), it was much more efficient and effective to prevent them from entering in the first place by having a visible and prominent presence at key border areas."

The implementation at the national level of the "prevention through deterrence strategy" greatly transformed U.S. institutions of border enforcement and their logic of operation. This process would ultimately lead to a US$18 billion annual budget dedicated to border control under Clinton, Bush, and Obama and a substantial increase in the number of agents from three thousand to twenty-two thousand in a period of some ten years (Alan D. Bersin, personal interview, Washington, D.C., July 21, 2017). As part of the efforts to make the border a more meaningful deterrent, the United States also significantly toughened the penalties for alien smugglers and document forgers, and has dramatically increased the number of inspectors at the ports of entry (POEs).

Clinton emphasized the importance of border matters in his 1996 State of the Union address, highlighting his border enforcement record and noting that "after years and years of neglect," his administration was taking a series of measures to control undocumented immigration and increase protection along the U.S. borders. Between 1993 and 1996, the Clinton administration augmented the size of the USBP by 45 percent. At the same time, Attorney General Janet Reno appointed Alan Bersin, then U.S. Attorney for the Southern District of California, as the first "border czar." Bersin was responsible for coordinating all southwest border enforcement initiatives both internally and with the Mexican government, propelling him to the frontlines of bilateral institution building that would occur over the next three decades (Alan D. Bersin, personal interview, July 21, 2017).

Seeking to beef up enforcement on the U.S. side, Clinton signed the Illegal Immigration Reform and Immigration Responsibility Act (IIRIRA) on September 30, 1996, authorizing a near doubling of the Border Patrol by the year 2001. Clinton also called for a controversial triple fence along fourteen miles south of San Diego and increased penalties for migrant smuggling. At the same time, crimes related to undocumented migration/migrant smuggling were reviewed and reclassified, leading "to a restructuring of the caseload in a manner which [altered] decisively the emphasis from misdemeanor to felony prosecutions." Overall, the Clinton administration "sought to mesh—coordinate and reinforce—administrative and criminal sanctioning systems into an integrated system of deterrence and punishment" (Bersin and Feigin 1998, 285).

The Beginning of U.S.-Mexico Cooperation

Most important, the new U.S. strategy of "prevention through deterrence," combined with national attention to free trade issues, ushered in the first era in which the United States and Mexico would share "responsibility and authority for the costs and outcomes of illegal immigration and related crime" (McDonald 1997, 2). This partnership allowed for law enforcement agencies to delineate between the missions of crime control and immigration control, which would become a crucial pillar of border security enforcement in later years.

Historically, the Mexican government would always defend the right of freedom of movement of individuals, while its U.S. counterpart would complain that a significant number of Mexicans were moving illegally into U.S. territory. To overcome this enduring impasse, the governments of both nations decided that the best way to move forward was to work toward a common goal, which emphasized the safety of migrants as well as the safety of the communities through which migrants passed. By implementing appropriately coordinated policies, the two sides hoped to make progress without finger pointing or disagreements about legality, both conscious of a spate of attacks and crimes committed against migrants in the San Diego–Tijuana border region during the preceding years. As Luis Herrera Lasso stated, "The two countries were well aware of this situation and wanted to do something about it" (Luis Herrera Lasso, Skype interview, October 10, 2017).

With these ideas in mind, in their 1997 summit in Mexico City, Presidents Clinton and Zedillo affirmed a mutual "political will to strive to fulfill a vision of [a] shared border in the twenty-first century as a place that supports and depends on building communities of cooperation rather than conflict" (Zedillo and Clinton 1997b, 1). Hence, on May 7, 1997, Zedillo and Clinton signed the "Declaration of the Mexican/US Alliance Against Drugs." Here the two heads of state recognized that "drug abuse and drug trafficking are a danger to [their] societies, an affront to [their] sovereignty and a threat to [their] national security." They declared their "nations united in an alliance to combat this menace" (Zedillo and Clinton 1997a). The two governments took important steps in this direction, and the collaborative effort quickly yielded significant results, particularly in the San Diego–Tijuana and El Paso–Ciudad Juárez border regions. Overall, the primary goal was "to build a binational region"—in other words, "one that works satisfactorily from the two sides of its single shared border which itself was created in war and fixed by treaty" (Bersin 1998, 719–20).

The results of the new partnership in border affairs were first visible on the western U.S.-Mexico border. Informal links between law enforcement agencies in San Diego and Tijuana that had grown in the previous half decade were "made permanent in the form of a binational council" (Gross 1997, B1). In this new context, on June 20, 1997, U.S. attorney general Janet Reno and Mexico's secretary of foreign relations José Ángel Gurría announced the creation of three new border groups on public safety, ports of entry, and migration. These three groups fell under the Border Liaison Mechanism (BLM) formed by the United States and Mexico in 1992 "as a bilateral means of tackling issues of mutual concern" (Gross 1997, B1). This model was based on the Tijuana–San Diego BLM, for which Bersin and Herrera Lasso had established coordinating groups to address specific issues of concern between those border cities, where the cooperation on border affairs began to be very significant (Gurría 1997; Office of the U.S. Attorney 1997; Reno 1997). Under the auspices of the BLM—then supervised by the consuls general in San Diego and Tijuana—regional authorities established a Border Public Safety Working Group, a Migrant Protection Working Group, and a Border Port Council for the California–Baja California border region. In addition, a Binational Committee on Education and Culture was created. This institutionalization reflected "the determination by both private and public sector organizations in the region to sustain the cooperation that was achieved here and to maintain forward progress in areas of mutual concern in which concerted action [benefited] both sides" (Bersin 1998, 725).

As Bersin explains, this transformation in the bilateral relationship was "immense from the vantage point of law enforcement, as well as from other perspectives." For the first time in U.S. and Mexican history, the two countries moved "decisively toward a border that functions effectively, one that is a lawful and orderly gateway, and one that promises and routinely delivers handsome dividends from an investment in regional integration" (Bersin 1998, 725). This cooperation expanded to other parts of the border and the results were quite positive. According to Peter Andreas, "A much greater sense of order [had] been created along the most visible and contested sections of the border" (1998, 352). For the first time in its history, "security" for Mexican elites entailed looking outward to its border rather than to the security of the regime itself (Herrera and Santa Cruz 2011, 359).

Phase 3 (2001–10): Security, 9/11, and the Long Road to "Smart" Borders

The administrations of George W. Bush (2001–9) and Vicente Fox (2000–2006) came to office poised to capitalize on the cooperation achieved during the Clinton–

Zedillo years. Bush, a native Texan and former governor of a border state with deep personal affection for Mexico, made improved bilateral relations the cornerstone of his foreign policy in the Western Hemisphere. Vicente Fox, of the Partido Acción Nacional (PAN, National Action Party), Mexico's first non-PRI president since the revolution, made clear he wanted to improve relations with the United States, seeking an equal status for Mexico within the North American framework created by NAFTA. Fox's election contributed to the initial optimism for further institutionalized cooperation in migration affairs, in what came to be known as the "Whole Enchilada" (La Enchilada Completa). During Bush's first foreign trip, a visit to San Cristóbal Ranch in the state of Guanajuato, the new presidents discussed the possibility of signing a migration agreement (*acuerdo migratorio*) that would involve the two nations in the discussions for the United States to open its borders to a greater flow of Mexican workers. In other words, both countries would sit at the negotiating table to discuss a bilateral agreement that would characterize them as "equal partners."

Presidential diplomacy initially led to cooperation on technical issues. For the first part of 2001, U.S. attorney general John Ashcroft worked with his Mexican counterpart, General Macedo de la Concha, on a range of border security issues. The thrust of this cooperation was to expand the scope of shared responsibilities on technical law enforcement matters—for example, an agreement to share assets seized from criminal apprehensions, signed in 2001. The cooperation also entailed issues of human rights related to immigration enforcement. The Border Patrol Search, Trauma, and Rescue Unit (BORSTAR) teams were established for search and rescue of undocumented immigrants in Arizona, and Ashcroft reiterated that cooperation meant "making sure that we respect the dignity and humanity of individuals that are involved on our borders" (White House 2001). In short, for the first nine months of the Bush administration, U.S.-Mexico cooperation on border security continued the foundation that had developed since the signing of NAFTA, where—as Bush put it in a speech on September 5, 2001—the two countries would work "together to extend the benefits of free trade throughout our hemisphere and throughout the world" (Bush and Fox 2001).

Days later, terrorist attacks in New York City; Washington, D.C.; and Pennsylvania completely altered the security regime of the United States and, in turn, North America. Facing the unimaginable political challenge of making Americans feel safe after the largest foreign attack against the continental United States, the Bush administration responded by emphasizing public security as its overriding goal, a decision that led the country to implement full inspections at the border, resulting in massive delays that virtually halted cross-border traffic (Wilson 2015). As border crossings reopened, stringent vehicle inspection and identification procedures led to unprecedented wait times; gridlock slowed the transport of supplies for many companies relying on transborder shipments of goods and parts. It was not long before the administration recognized that "the costs of 'hunker down security,' i.e. the impact of closing the borders, would deliver an unacceptable, catastrophically self-defeating blow to [the U.S.] economy" (Bersin and Huston 2015, 2).

In the months following the attacks, Bush gradually began to emphasize the importance of maintaining free trade. Completely closing the border, in effect, would have meant "Al Qaeda would have won" (Bersin and Huston 2015, 2). The administration thus encountered a political dilemma between security and trade facilitation. Previous border security frameworks were insufficient to deal with the new urgency of controlling who or what crossed the border. In this context, policy makers in the United States "were compelled to formulate new theories of action and respond to a dramatically altered threat environment. Specifically, policymakers grappled with the challenge of how to secure the homeland in a world that was increasingly borderless" (2).

Thus, U.S.-Mexico cooperation was not abandoned after the attacks, but now border efforts were refracted through the urgent context of national security, which re-emphasized the importance of physical borders as a demarcation of nationality and sovereignty. As Aguilar recognizes, "there was a much more intense focus on the border, and more resources and intelligence efforts were placed there." But, out of necessity, the "pendulum had swung heavily towards security" (David V. Aguilar, phone interview, July 31, 2017). As Alfredo Corchado wrote, "Just as the budding friendship took off, it seemed to fall apart in the uncertainty after the 9/11 attacks." Immediately after this incident, "Bush turned away from Fox's immigration overhaul ideas, citing the need for stronger U.S. border security" (Corchado 2013).

During a visit in March 2002, Bush and Fox jointly announced the adoption of a plan for creating a "Smart Border," modeled on a similar set of agreements with Canada the previous year. The Smart Border framework laid out thirty components in four areas: securing the flow of goods, securing the flow of people, securing border infrastructure, and improving information sharing to meet these objectives. While building upon some programs already in place at the U.S.-Mexico border, the plan represented an attempt to leverage technologies that would shift the border security paradigm to one of risk management—targeting flows that might be related to contraband, narcotics, or terrorism without hampering legitimate trade and travel. To secure the flow of people, for example, the plan called for increased information sharing between the United States and Mexico, coordinating immigration systems and sharing no-fly lists and databases with information on visa applicants.

For trade, the plan envisioned a completely "harmonized" commercial processing system that also allowed for preclearing truck and rail cargo away from the border. For the United States, the plan required a major increase in border security spending. In its FY2003 budget, the Bush administration called for US$11 billion (an increase on the previous year's budget of US$8.8 billion) in spending on border security, with a focus on Smart Border initiatives on the southern and northern borders. The spending would rapidly expand the number of customs inspectors and Border Patrol agents while also funding new technologies and the implementation of an entry-exit visa system (White House 2002).

The most significant post-9/11 institutional shift vis-à-vis border security was the creation of the U.S. Department of Homeland Security (DHS) in November 2002, which represented a political innovation as much as a bureaucratic one. In bureaucratic terms, the DHS brought together all agencies previously responsible for border management, creating as component organizations U.S. Customs and Border Protection (CBP), U.S. Immigration and Customs Enforcement (ICE), and U.S. Citizenship and Immigration Services (USCIS). Importantly, the creation of DHS for the first time gave the United States not only an agency that could coordinate strategies of border security and enforcement but one that could more coherently engage with international partners on the strategic and technical aspects of border management. In political terms, the creation of DHS was problematic. It guaranteed that policies designed to address the balance between security and trade facilitation on the southwest border would be made by an agency for which the mandate and political context was heavily skewed toward security.

Initially, and in technical terms, the Mexican government was fully cooperative with the Bush administration's energetic emphasis on security at the border. In the wake of the 9/11 attacks, the Fox administration carried out law enforcement operations against Mexican citizens suspected of links to global terrorist organizations and restricted entry from countries considered high risk by U.S. officials (Andreas 2003, 12). In addition to expanded information sharing, the two countries undertook a series of collaborative efforts to train and enhance border enforcement, particularly on Mexico's southern border with Guatemala. In 2001–2, for example, the Mexican government established a border patrol force of Mexican Federal Police personnel who worked closely with the USBP and the Mexican intelligence agency Centro de Investigación y Seguridad Nacional (CISEN, Center for Research and National Security). The project, called Una Frontera, Una Meta: Seguridad (One Border, One Goal: Security), also entailed U.S.-Mexico training of local Mexican police. The USBP also started to work with and train Grupos Beta, Mexican teams in Sonora that were part of the Instituto Nacional de Migración (INM, National Institute of Migration) but—modeled on the earlier BORSTAR program—designed to provide aid to migrants in need.

In terms of cargo security, the CBP developed programs and processes to "push the border out." Efforts were made to streamline the process at the POEs, with inspections occurring at the "earliest point possible in the supply chain." For example, the Customs Trade Partnership Against Terrorism (CTPAT) program was created in November 2001 to ease the pressure on the POEs by allowing companies down the supply chain—"importers, carriers, consolidators, licensed customs brokers, and manufacturers"—in Mexico and Canada to voluntarily opt in as partners to the CBP supply chain security measures (CBP n.d. ["CTPAT"], par. 1).[5]

Despite the early promise of U.S.-Mexico efforts within the context of Smart Borders, overall cooperation proved halting and unsatisfactory. A number of the programs developed under the Smart Borders framework did not materialize or were slow to come to fruition on the southwestern border (David V. Aguilar, phone interview, July 31, 2017). Why was this the case? The first reason was the overbearing effect that the politics of security in the wake of 9/11 had on the U.S.-Mexico relationship. The partnership with Mexico that had been so central to Bush's foreign policy during the first year—built upon the intertwined benefits of free trade and political democracy—suffered as the administration's War on Terror inevitably recast borders as points of vulnerability. During the Clinton–Zedillo years, the two countries had arrived at a common deterrence framework that, as Peter Andreas has argued, "projected an image of heightened security, while making sure not to slow legitimate cross-border flows" (2003, 11). In the aftermath of 9/11, the "political tolerance" for a deterrence strategy was diminished (11). This placed previously unforeseen pressure on other aspects of cooperation, namely immigration policy, as was seen during Bush's attempt at immigration reform. In short, the American political environment after 9/11 turned security and prosperity into exclusive objectives (Flynn 2003, 123).

The second and related reason for plodding process on border security after 9/11 was the politics of security in Mexico. Fox had eagerly accepted the U.S. emphasis on security, framing terrorism as a mutual concern. But this enthusiasm had also come in part from Fox asserting to Bush the Mexican interest in finding a way to regularize the status of 3.5 million Mexican workers residing in the United States—a political gambit that reflected Mexican power to shape the agenda that was truly unprecedented in the U.S.-Mexico relationship. As security emerged as the primary concern and Bush was forced to put immigration issues on the backburner, cooperating with the United States became an increasingly hard political sell for Fox. The Fox administration's opposition at the United Nations to the U.S. war in Iraq can be seen as a tentative return to the "distant neighbors" framework predating NAFTA.

The two countries, along with Canada, sought to "reset" the focus of relations with the Security and Prosperity Partnership of North America (SPP) that began in March 2005. The SPP was a nonbinding initiative in which the three countries agreed to improve information cooperation with the goal of furthering North American security and prosperity—in essence, a recommitment to the objectives that had initially guided NAFTA. Under the SPP, the three nations created trilateral working groups in a number of areas, one of which was the creation of smart and secure borders. While the SPP re-energized bilateral efforts on border security, in large part it was symptomatic of—and not ameliorative to—the turbulence that securitization of the border had caused.

The Mérida Initiative: Unprecedented Cooperation to Fight Organized Crime

Political change in Mexico was the impetus that allowed the United States and Mexico to overcome these hurdles and begin to deliver on the promises of the Smart Border plan and the SPP during the final years of the Bush administration. There were growing concerns in the Bush administration over Mexico's ability to control the scale of violence resulting from transnational criminal organizations (TCOs, commonly known as "drug cartels") operating on the border.[6] In 2005 U.S. ambassador Tony Garza sent a note to then minister of foreign relations Luis Ernesto Derbez and attorney general Rafael Macedo de la Concha expressing concern over Mexico's "incapacity" to deal with violence associated with drug trafficking (Herrera and Santa Cruz 2011, 401). The Mexican government bristled at what it saw as an intervention in its internal affairs.

Nonetheless, Felipe Calderón's election and inauguration in December 2006 placed law enforcement against organized crime at the center of the Mexican political agenda. Ten days after taking office, Calderón declared a war against drugs and in 2007 deployed federal forces to a number of northern Mexican states (including Baja California, Michoacán, and Sinaloa) to deal with the issue. He also created a Cruzada Nacional contra la Delincuencia (National Crusade Against Crime). With organized crime activity intensifying in Mexico's northern border region, Calderón called for a sweeping effort to bring military power to bear on TCOs while also reforming Mexico's law enforcement system. Bucking decades of refusal to acknowledge U.S. cooperation in law enforcement matters, Calderón called on the United States to provide aid, training, and development to overhaul Mexico's internal security apparatus. This strategy was welcomed by the United States, which complemented and supported Calderón through the Iniciativa Mérida (Mérida Initiative), a bilateral program designed to combat organized crime and violence.[7]

Since the launch of the Mérida Initiative in 2007, the U.S. Congress has appropriated almost US$2.5 billion. The program—inspired on the one hand by Plan Colombia and, on the other, by the U.S.-Canada Smart Borders Accord signed in 2001 by Governor Tom Ridge and Deputy Prime Minister John Manley—established several pillars related directly or indirectly to border security: "(1) disrupting organized criminal groups, (2) institutionalizing the rule of law, (3) creating a 21st-century border, and (4) building strong and resilient communities" (Seelke and Finklea 2017, 2).

The more than US$1.6 billion of Mérida funding disbursed by March 2017 had also provided the initiative for the two countries to expand security on Mexico's border with Guatemala and to address the production and trafficking of heroin and fentanyl (Seelke and Finklea 2017). The amount of money and technology transfer was marginal compared to the cost of Mexico's overall counterdrug operations but was nonetheless seen as symbolically important by U.S. officials, like assistant secretary of state for Western Hemisphere affairs and later deputy secretary Tom Shannon (Herrera and Santa Cruz 2011, 402). Again, perhaps the greatest policy achievement within Mérida was the bilateral cooperation that it entailed, as the State Department description makes clear.

> The Merida Initiative is an unprecedented partnership between the United States and Mexico to fight organized crime and associated violence while furthering respect for human rights and the rule of law. Based on principles of common and shared responsibility, mutual trust, and respect for sovereign independence, the two countries' efforts have built confidence that is transforming the bilateral relationship. (DOS n.d.)

The agreement marked the first time that Mexico ever accepted overt foreign aid to fight organized crime. Mexican leaders knew that since 9/11 changed the priorities of the United States, cooperation on law enforcement and security priorities would help keep the border open to trade (DHS 2009).

The Mérida Institutions

In previous decades, there had been close regional cooperation at the border among law enforcement agencies of the two countries. However, relevant actions performed during these years had not been institutionalized or considered as long-term measures at the agencies' headquarters. Regional cooperation had never been translated into formal mechanisms within the U.S. and Mexican governments. Through the Mérida Initiative, binational cooperation in border security matters was formalized. As one former DHS and National Security official put it, "the Mérida Initiative effectively changed the way the U.S. and Mexico thought about border management."

Officials on the U.S. side sought a way to make Mérida more effective and less of a "shopping list" for the Mexican government. There was a sense that drug violence was increasing and that there was a need to recognize shared responsibility to address the issue properly and effectively. In such a context, "there was an urge to be more strategic and develop an institutional framework" (Ben Rohrbaugh, phone interview, May 19, 2017). By the end of the Bush administration, complementary changes in the way the two countries viewed the border were allowing cooperation to be translated into integration at the operational level. For much of the twentieth century, "security" had been managed at the Foreign Ministry level—that is, between the U.S. Department of State (DOS) and the Secretaría de Relaciones Exteriores (SRE, Secretariat of Foreign Affairs).

Law enforcement at the border was previously seen as marginal to diplomacy. When the United States created the DHS, however, the action led Mexico to create equivalent law enforcement counterparts within Mexico's Secretaría de Hacienda y Crédito (SHCP, Ministry of Finance and Public Credit) and SEGOB. In 2007 both countries created the Bilateral Strategic Plan, a cooperation initiative between the DHS and Mexico's Servicio de Administración Tributaria (SAT, Tax Administration Service), part of the SHCP. It focused on customs, trusted traveler programs, processing goods faster, and coordinating operations at the border. The plan was an immediate success and led U.S. and Mexican officials to push for increased institutional cooperation along the same lines. It provided the CBP and ICE a venue for close collaboration with their Mexican partners (SHCP and SEGOB) within the Mérida framework.

Phase 4 (2008–16): The New Alliance—Trust and Collaboration

The presidential transition from George W. Bush to Barack Obama occurred during a pivotal moment for bilateral security collaboration. Although the Bush administration had steadfastly backed Calderón's efforts to confront organized crime, the perception of lawlessness along the border was beginning to manifest itself in a political backlash on the U.S. side. Weeks before Obama took office, outgoing CIA chief Michael Hayden told reporters that lawlessness in Mexico would pose as much of a challenge for the incoming administration as would Iran. Shortly afterward, U.S. Joint Forces Command published an intelligence report warning of the possibility of failed states in Mexico and Pakistan (Debusmann 2009). The Mexican government bristled at these characterizations, with Interior Secretary Fernando Gomez-Mont deeming it "inappropriate" to "call Mexico a security risk" (Carl 2009). At the same time, from Obama's left came calls to revisit the NAFTA agreement, particularly labor and environmental aspects, and to roll back the border enforcement policies of the preceding Republican administration.

Nonetheless, during Barack Obama's two terms (2009–16), coinciding with the administrations of Mexican presidents Felipe Calderón (PAN, 2006–12) and Enrique Peña Nieto (PRI, 2012–18), the two countries continued to expand and institutionalize collaboration on border security issues in spite of increasing politicization of specific bilateral issues in the United States. This collaboration reflected the culmination of a binational approach to the border—not one in which the border was seen as a site of contentious sovereignties but instead one in which both the United States and Mexico would work together to expedite economic flows while taking joint responsibility for the security issues arising from those connections. Security and prosperity had long been treated as contradictory objectives, but during the Obama years, a consensus emerged in Washington, D.C., and Mexico City on the importance of free trade, together with modernization and technological advances that would allow the two countries to apply a risk management approach to border security. During the Obama years, regular high-level cooperation between law enforcement and security officials facilitated data cooperation on both bilateral infrastructure improvement and information sharing.

Building a Twenty-First-Century Border

Obama's commitment to pursue a binational border strategy began with the selection of Janet Napolitano as secretary of homeland security. Previously serving as the governor of Arizona (2003–9), Napolitano came to the position with a keen focus on the southwest border. She quickly selected Alan Bersin as her special border representative (also known as the border czar), a role he had played earlier during the Clinton administration when he had worked with Napolitano in Janet Reno's Attorney General's Advisory Committee. Bersin went on to serve during the Obama administration as US commissioner of Customs and Border Protection (2010–11) and then DHS assistant secretary for policy and international affairs and chief diplomatic officer (2012–17). In each of these roles during the eight years, under the successive leadership of Secretaries Napolitano and Jeh Johnson, Bersin played a principal role in shaping U.S. border security policy and significantly improving U.S.-Mexico bilateral security and the cross-border trade relationship.

In April 2009, the Obama administration launched the Southwest Border Initiative (SBI), a concerted effort by U.S. law enforcement and security agencies to redouble manpower, technology, and attention on security issues at the southern border. In addition to deploying new inspection teams to U.S. POEs, the CBP also deployed six Mobile Response Team special operations units, as well as other assets designed specifically to target drug trafficking organizations. As part of the initiative, the CBP also expanded and integrated the uses of new technology, including inspection imaging systems used on vehicles and unmanned aerial systems deployed along the border between California and Texas. Although the SBI was an interagency U.S. effort, it was implemented in coordination with Mexican authorities. ICE increased the number of attachés assigned to Mexico City and increased Border Liaison Officers responsible for working with their Mexican counterparts. The U.S. Department of Justice (DOJ) greatly expanded its extradition of criminals from Mexico (a total of ninety-four in 2010) and trained more than 5,400 Mexican prosecutors and investigators.

The Southwest Border Initiative and further actions taken in 2009 and 2010 were noteworthy for the way they responded to Mexico's foreign policy demands: an insistence that the United States take responsibility for its part of border management, specifically the southward flow of illegal guns and cash that Mexican officials were highlighting as major accelerants in the growth of organized crime. The goals of the initiative—most notably the goal of 100 percent screening of southbound rail traffic—were designed to respond to these concerns (DHS 2011). ICE also worked with its Mexican counterparts on Operation Armas Cruzadas (Crossed Arms), which brought U.S. and Mexican intelligence together to target criminal networks responsible for transiting arms across the border.

The Mérida Initiative served as the funding vehicle and framework for further cooperation by U.S. and Mexican law enforcement agencies, but the Obama administration set out to "make Mérida more strategic" (Alan D. Bersin, personal interview, July 21, 2017). The primary means for doing this was the Bilateral Strategic Plan, signed in December 2009 between Napolitano and Agustín Carstens, Mexico's secretary of finance. The Bilateral Strategic Plan would "create a framework for increased, intensified interaction and engagement between our nations"—an approach that went beyond the traditional law enforcement view of "fighting the cartels" and was referred to by some in the U.S. government as Mérida 2.0 (Alan D. Bersin, personal interview, July 21, 2017). One of the components of this extended version of the Mérida Initiative was the creation of a "21st Century Border," an institutionalized bilateral mechanism for border security cooperation. It included the May 19, 2010, "Joint Statement on 21st Century Border Management," issued by Obama and Calderón, which set forth the full range of border issues that the United States and Mexico would work on together. The 21st Century Border framework contributed presidential endorsement to further progress in bilateral affairs, becoming the basis for deep cooperation over the following years. During this period, the character of U.S.-Mexico border security policy began its transformation from "bilateral" to "binational." This process was gradual, marked initially by a number of infrastructure projects and the joint management at the POEs (Alan D. Bersin, personal interview, July 21, 2017). Alan Bersin and Michael D. Huston describe this pillar of the Mérida Initiative as a series of bilateral arrangements entered into by the DHS and SEGOB and SHCP.

> These arrangements provide for concrete plans, programs and initiatives that implement the overall vision and the significant policy changes it requires. Sustained by regular engagement at senior levels of government and a framework for reporting and account-

ability, the reinvented bilateral relationship includes: coordinated patrolling of the U.S./ Mexico border; the development of mutually recognized "trusted trader and traveler" programs; information sharing and the conduct of joint targeting against airline and (much) cargo manifest data; the conduct of joint investigations to interdict and disrupt and dismantle transnational criminal organizations; the integration and harmonization of manifest data requirements; cooperation regarding repatriation and migration management; consultation regarding law enforcement use of force at the border; and the development of shared priorities and common public private partnership approaches to border infrastructure development. The support of the *Secretaría de Relaciones Exteriores* (Secretariat of External Relations or SRE) and the U.S. Department of State has mediated the transformation. (2015, 9)

One successful U.S. program in this effort to facilitate commercial flows while enhancing security was Global Entry, which was extended in 2009 to include Mexicans. Global Entry was a CBP program that aimed to expedite clearance for "pre-approved, low-risk travelers" arriving in the United States (CBP n.d. ["Global Entry"]). Mexico has also made substantial advancement to strengthen bilateral collaboration within this new framework, including, for example, Operadores Económicos Autorizados (OEA, Authorized Economic Operators), formerly known as Nuevo Esquema de Empresas Certificadas (NEEC, New Scheme of Certified Companies). As Mexico's equivalent of CTPAT, OEA certification is available to companies complying with international standards on supply chain security (CTPAT Security Services 2017).

These programs represented the new paradigm of "co-responsibility" (*corresponsabilidad*) in border management, an acknowledgment that applying law enforcement to a modern border required close binational collaboration that would challenge traditional boundaries of sovereignty. One example of this co-responsibility was the sharing of flight manifests, allowing law enforcement authorities in both countries to know the names and criminal backgrounds of all passengers before every plane lands. In 2016 U.S. authorities began working for the first time in Mexican territory to inspect trucks as part of an "enforcement program intended to reduce congestion and speed cargo" across the nations' busiest border crossings (Spagat 2016). Joint inspections of this kind "were launched after Mexican lawmakers approved changes to the country's firearms law to permit foreign customs and immigration officials to be armed on the job" (Spagat 2016).

For the Obama administration, this deliberate, intense interest in law enforcement cooperation was seen as part of a political tradeoff. By adopting the binational approach to border security and stressing cooperation with Mexico on shared security goals, the administration sought to improve its chances for achieving comprehensive immigration reform in the U.S. Congress. One example of this approach was the

Secure Communities Initiative, by which DHS sought to prioritize the apprehension and deportation of serious criminals (as opposed to law-abiding immigrants) by promoting information sharing between state and local law enforcement and federal agencies. Although the Obama administration was criticized from the left for its aggressive approach to deportations and border security, Obama himself routinely touted co-responsibility for security as a building block for long-term immigration reform. This approach was on display in a May 2010 speech at the border in El Paso, in which Obama touted the administration's record on border security—including the construction of 652 miles of fencing along the southwest border, the increase of Border Patrol agents, and seizures of contraband—as a tradeoff for comprehensive immigration reform (Paulson 2010).

The Obama administration initially found a willing partner in Calderón's PAN party. Mexican ambassador in the United States Arturo Sarukhán called the United States and Mexico "co-stakeholders" in tackling the issues of illicit narcotics and weapons trafficking across the border, and he repeatedly emphasized that the two countries would "fail together or succeed together" ("Arturo Sarukhán" 2009; DOS 2009). The election of the PRI candidate Enrique Peña Nieto (EPN) in 2012, however, threatened to limit cooperation. He promised during the campaign to limit the direct access enjoyed by U.S. security agencies to Mexican police in the so-called drug war. In effect, EPN's approach harkened back to Mexico's traditional approach to border issues, dominated by considerations of nationalism and sovereignty. This stress was worsened by the "unaccompanied minor crisis" of 2014, which highlighted the disparity in the way that U.S. political institutions treated migration as a security issue.

Nonetheless, it was most telling that the United States and Mexico responded to these challenges by further deepening collaboration. In a visit to Mexico City in 2013 and later during EPN's visit to Washington in 2015, Obama stressed the way that institutional cooperation did not represent an infringement on Mexican sovereignty. The unaccompanied minor crisis, for example, triggered the implementation of Plan Frontera Sur (Southern Border Plan), an ambitious migration control effort on Mexico's southern border. Plan Frontera Sur has included interagency cooperation, Federal Police checkpoints, and the use of the military to enforce border control. The U.S. government has complemented these efforts by providing training and material resources to Mexico's immigration authorities. Additionally, there has been enhanced cooperation and better communication concerning deportations on the U.S.-Mexico border.[8]

While the broader Mexican strategy underlying Plan Frontera Sur remains vague, its implementation was perhaps the most obvious example of Mexico operating according to the logic of co-responsibility for a shared North American security. It must also be noted that in the issue of undocumented migration, Mexico is no longer a "sending country" but has become a "destination country," especially for Central

American migrants. Thus, it was possible for the two countries to develop common doctrines in migration management and cooperate to enforce immigration laws, creating and maintaining an enforcement deterrent when necessary while still providing humanitarian treatment wherever possible. In order to formalize this cooperation, in 2010 the Obama administration created the 21st Century Border Initiative, consisting of a series of committees and working groups specializing in key areas of border enforcement. Alan Bersin, who was at the time serving as commissioner of CBP, joined the Executive Steering Committee along with the head of ICE and senior officials from the DOS, the Department of Agriculture, and the DOJ, as well as the DEA. A similar counterpart group was formed in Mexico. In the United States, the initiative was chaired by a senior director of the National Security Council (NSC), and in Mexico it was chaired by the undersecretary for North America of the SRE.

This mechanism included the formation of three smaller committees, each dedicated to specific law enforcement issue areas with their cross-border counterparts. One committee coordinated border infrastructure. Another committee, dubbed Secure Flows, focused on operations at the POEs and was chaired by the CBP and the SAT. The Secure Flows committee worked on projects such as trusted traveler, trusted shipper, and pre-inspection programs. The third committee was Corridors, Security, and Human Change, which focused on law enforcement between the POEs. Its major accomplishment was the creation of border violence prevention protocols. Through this effort, a structure was set in place where the regional leaders of Mexican and U.S. law enforcement agencies would meet quarterly to develop joint programs to identify risks and potential for violence (Ben Rohrbaugh, phone interview, May 19, 2017).[9]

Despite these developments, improvements remained to be made to the current institutional framework of U.S.-Mexico border security cooperation by the end of the Obama years. Both countries recognized a need to improve border infrastructure and transportation in both countries, and to produce "streamline[d] IT capacities into all major elements of the manufacturing process" along the border, according to Gustavo Mohar, former undersecretary for migration, population, and religious affairs at the Ministry of the Interior. Mohar believes that Mexico and the United States should also promote and expand enrollment in trusted traveler programs. To help reduce the costs of trade, the customs administrations of the two countries should "continue the implementation of single cargo manifests in the rail, air, and maritime modes of transportation and initiate the development and implementation of the truck single manifest." Overall, the two countries should strengthen their binational coordinating processes to collaborate better on priority projects and policy issues (Mexico's Embassy in the United States 2016). Mohar believes that "there is still much needed in terms of customs operation and infrastructure, because both countries want a safe and efficient border." He suggests that there needs to be a binational agreement that establishes and institutionalizes the sharing of information through a binational intelligence center (Gustavo Mohar, phone interview, July 31, 2017).

Challenges to the New Framework

In the United States, expanded border security cooperation during the Obama administration did not go unchallenged, as the wave of national populism and anti-immigrant sentiments in the 2016 U.S. election made clear. During the Obama years, the fruitful cooperation that took root at the border was threatened regularly by political developments at the national level that portrayed law enforcement as an adversarial endeavor. One particularly tense episode was the passage of Senate Bill 1070 (SB-1070) in Arizona—titled Support Our Law Enforcement and Safe Neighborhoods Act.[10] SB-1070, in its original format, would have required local police officers to question people about their immigration status if there was a reason to suspect they were residing in the United States illegally. Bersin reflected later that "this was not the first time that law enforcement was used to separate the two countries, but finally this legislation was rejected by the courts and the two countries ended up cooperating even more" (Alan D. Bersin, personal interview, July 21, 2017).[11]

Likewise, a series of incidents involving the use of force at the border created new protocols for the use of force, even if this process of protocol creation proved challenging in the short term. In late 2012, three separate incidents where Border Patrol agents shot individuals at the border created serious diplomatic crises. According to one U.S. official, "The mechanisms used for cooperation and communication after these events allowed for the creation of a bilateral council on the use of force, which effectively integrated law enforcement and diplomatic concerns going forward" (phone interview, July 8, 2017).

The outcome was the implementation of coordinated patrols on both sides of the border, in which law enforcement agents in the two countries could deter and prevent problems before they escalated. In the United States, officers are much freer to use their discretion in the application of force; therefore, it was in the best interest of both nations to work on schemes of violence prevention. The U.S. official previously quoted explains, "Initially, Mexico allocated approximately 120 INM officers (including members of the Grupos Beta) to patrol the border, and added some members of the *gendarmerie*"—a division of the Federal Police. Many of these officers received some training by the USBP. According to this official, "These actions were not designed to prevent migration but to respond more adequately to emergencies, with the main function to prevent violence."

Conclusion: Binational Partners and the Logic of North America

Most scholarly assessments of U.S.-Mexico bilateral cooperation have tended to see cooperation, through the Mérida Initiative and institutionalized by the 21st Century Border Management Initiative, in political or strategic terms. That interpretation holds that Mexican leaders succumbed to the U.S. infatuation with law enforcement—and, after 9/11, national security—sacrificing Mexico's traditional aversion to U.S. power in exchange for U.S. funding that allowed them to strengthen the state's security apparatus in ways that were quite conservative. This analysis ignores the way in which cooperation has changed the approach to the border on both sides, "recast[ing] the partnership," in the words of Bersin and Huston, as "one based on the assumption of shared responsibility and the joint management of common issues" (2015, 9). The main objectives became to secure and expedite "lawful flows of persons and goods across the common border, to mitigate threats that could disrupt the system and to confront illicit markets that use and exploit the system" (9). The transformation was initially made possible by NAFTA, which began to recenter attention on cross-border flows and not simply on the physical borders (the "lines") differentiating sovereignties and power.

Although political circumstances have periodically jeopardized this consensus, by the start of 2017, institutional cooperation had essentially become a functioning regime. No longer "distant neighbors," Mexico and the United States were working to secure and expedite "lawful flows of persons and goods across the common border, to mitigate threats that could disrupt the system and to confront illicit markets that use and exploit the system" (Bersin and Huston 2015, 9). This new paradigm of borders reconfigured the notion of border security. Owing to the United States' and Mexico's approach to bilateral relations, both countries had traditionally defined security in reference to the border as a line of separation. Under NAFTA, the border came to link "jurisdictional lines to the flows of people, goods, ideas . . . toward and across them, rendering the border multi-dimensional" (5). According to this new logic, as Bersin and Huston have written, "the task of securing the flows of goods and people toward the homeland . . . must begin abroad" (5).

It was no mere coincidence that this paradigm shift to focus on flows occurred during a period of economic integration between the United States and Mexico. Moving away from cultural notions of trade as a zero-sum game, elites in Mexico and the United States increasingly acknowledged that free trade permitted a "shared production platform." Bersin and Huston described the system and outlined its security implications as follows:

Half of all trade between the two [countries] is intraindustry, involving multiple border crossings prior to final assembly and sale. This economic and fiscal reality in turn has highlighted fragmented border management as an artifact of history that regionalization/globalization requires transcending. Networks are acknowledged as the organizational route to effective and efficient operation. Collaboration is key. The relevant partnerships reside within the government, with the private (stakeholder) sector and with cross-border authorities in Mexico and the United States. A premium is placed on operational coordination to reduce transaction costs in order to enhance overall regional economic competitiveness; on data harmonization to facilitate information sharing and common risk assessments; on consultation to build a more coherent and efficient border crossing infrastructure; and on coordinated enforcement at and between the ports of entry. (2015, 6)

This new perspective of viewing borders as both "lines" and "flows" brought dramatic changes in border security policies and border security cooperation. For the first time in U.S.-Mexico bilateral history, "borders are viewed primarily as opportunities for coordination and cooperation rather than defensive perimeters and occasions for conflict" (Bersin and Huston 2015, 8). Indeed, the past few years have witnessed movement from merely bilateral border relations toward genuinely transnational relationships across those borders. Paradoxically, however, the increasing prevalence of the "intermestic" approach to border favored by elites in the United States and Mexico has come under increasing pressure from political forces, which reject the concept of bargaining national sovereignty. This has played out most explicitly on the U.S. side in the surge of nativist populism that helped bring Donald Trump to office, Trump's subsequent threat to unilaterally abandon NAFTA, and the now-familiar "wall" refrain. In Mexico, too, however, flagging confidence in the PRI government (which ended in decisive defeat in the 2018 elections) and ongoing concerns about human rights abuses by security forces have turned border cooperation into a contentious concept. Not for nothing did Andrés Manuel López Obrador (AMLO) unveil his National Peace and Security Plan 2018–2024, which abandons the joint focus on TCOs in favor of addressing anticorruption, human rights, and social reform in Mexico (Felbab-Brown 2019). Although it is too early to judge the results of AMLO's turn away from cooperation, the common thread is that, as the distinction between domestic and international issues recedes, politicians can appeal to their publics by painting this kind of cooperation as out-of-touch technocrats sacrificing national interest—in the economic or security realm—for narrow gains.

The staying power of the paradigm of law enforcement cooperation at the border relies, to a certain extent, on how well politicians are able to show that binationalism works to the public good of security and prosperity without compromising other domestic priorities and basic human rights principles. Doing so will require integrating the opinions of those who best understand the dynamics of *el Tercer País*—the people who actually live and work at the border, the *fronterizos*. Perceptions of border security and assessments of the impact of recent border security policies also differ, depending on the side of the border where people are located. The views of critics, human rights advocates, analysts, and inhabitants of border communities in both the United States and Mexico are crucial in evaluating implemented actions, including their possible reform in the search for better results and improved cooperation.[12] In addition to economic, commercial, and cultural advantages for those who live and work on the border, locally led integration actually provides the best opportunity to manage border relations in ways that respond to wishes of two separate publics whose futures are very much intertwined. In some regions of the border, immigration agents and officers view cooperation with human rights advocates and other civil society organizations as an effective tool in building trust between institutions and communities, better informing migrants of the risks of crossing the border without official documents.[13]

The Trump administration's insistence on treating Mexico as an adversary, its past threats to unilaterally withdraw from NAFTA (now the USMCA), and its framing of immigration issues in xenophobic terms threaten to undo the binational approach to law enforcement that has developed over the last thirty years (Alvarez 2017). At the same time, however, the institutional changes of the post-NAFTA cooperation in North America may prove harder to undo, as Trump's conciliatory stance toward AMLO seems to suggest.

The value of integration to national economies is readily apparent. The U.S. and Mexican border states have emerged as an economic powerhouse, consisting of a half-billion people and approximately 25 percent of global gross domestic product (GDP) (Bersin and Huston 2015, 10). Notwithstanding Trump's vilification of the trade agreement, it now appears more likely that his fixation on security might have the muted effect of updating aspects of the trade agreement rather than discarding them (Bersin 2017).

With regard to U.S.-Mexico tensions under Trump, it is worth keeping them in the perspective of diplomatic history that has seen routine patterns of conflict and cooperation in response to U.S. power (McCormick and Bersin 2017, 2). Indeed, even during the last three decades, in which cooperation has become more prevalent, the unilateralism underlying the U.S. approach to certain border issues has rankled Mexican policy makers. Consider, for example, that the Bush and Obama administrations' overriding emphasis on drug trafficking, terrorism, and overall security has entailed very little cooperation with Mexico on a broader reform of migration policy. Gustavo Mohar notes that "even under Obama with the Dream Act and immigration reform, immigration initiatives did not involve any input from Mexico. Obama also deported many people, and there was no explicit dialogue in this area that involved Mexico." Mohar perceives the situation today as even worse, and states that there have been major steps backward under the Trump administration, since "it now seems that actions related to border security cooperation, trade, and immigration have become completely unilateral" (Gustavo Mohar, phone interview, July 31, 2017).

Nonetheless, according to Ben Rohrbaugh, former White House director for enforcement and border security at the National Security Council, "it is concerning that we may remove the cooperation structures that have been set in place without any beneficial alternative to replace them." In his view, "most Americans who talk about extreme unilateral measures of border security do not know that the number of Mexican nationals crossing into the United States has decreased enormously. For example, the number of apprehended Mexicans in 2016 was 88 percent lower than it was in 2000." The single most important factor that Rohrbaugh credits for increased border security "is having good cooperation with the Mexican counterparts, and having a physical presence of Mexican counterparts at the border." He also states that "when Mexico deployed the Federal Police to the border, working in cooperation with the U.S. Border Patrol, the numbers of assaults on agents, illegal crossings, and drugs trafficked decreased enormously." Hence, "if the United States refuses to work with Mexico, border security will sharply deteriorate. It will be an unnecessary self-inflicted wound" (Ben Rohrbaugh, phone interview, May 19, 2017).

Even as political negotiations over immigration, border security, and law enforcement prove contentious, large segments of the populations in both countries agree with Rohrbaugh (Wilson, Parás, and Enríquez, 2017, 12, 15). The dramatic uptick in distrust of the United States among Mexicans since 2017 suggests skepticism over how easily such cooperation can be turned to self-interested ends, as Trump's recent comments about "using" Mexico suggest. Nevertheless, bilateral cooperation and collaboration on law enforcement have demonstrated that binational approaches are not historically impossible but "required hard work, and a self-conscious recognition by policymakers on both sides that the countries are more valuable as friends than foes" (McCormick and Bersin 2017, 2). As former national chief of the USBP David Aguilar says, "The relationship with Mexico is much better now than it was before." Aguilar mentions that when he started at the Border Patrol, "the last people anyone would trust would be the Mexicans. But now, the relationship has grown so much that Mexican immigration authorities are the first people the Border Patrol calls" (David V. Aguilar, phone interview, July 31, 2017). This remarkable transformation in law enforcement cooperation reflects a broader paradigm shift in the way the two countries treat sovereignty at the border.[14] The deep and ongoing history of bilateral institutional development will continue to be written beyond the era of nationalism wrought by Donald Trump.

Notes

The authors thank José Alfaro, Kurt Birson, and Arthur Sanders Montandon, who contributed to this article as research assistants. They also express enormous gratitude to Alan Bersin, for his guidance, and for sharing his time and expertise on the subject.

1. This work is based on structured interviews conducted with the key architects of the U.S.-Mexico border security cooperation framework on both sides of the border, to include the following: Luis Herrera Lasso, former Mexican consul in San Diego and a longtime official of the Mexican intelligence agency CISEN; David Aguilar, former acting commissioner of U.S. Customs and Border Protection (CBP) and national chief of the U.S. Border Patrol; Ben Rohrbaugh, former White House director for enforcement and border security at the National Security Council; Gustavo Mohar, former undersecretary for migration, population, and religious affairs at the Secretaría de Gobernación (SEGOB, Secretariat of the Interior), veteran official of SRE, and executive at CISEN in Mexico; and Alan Bersin, who served (at various times) as assistant secretary for policy and international affairs and chief diplomatic officer in the U.S. Department of Homeland Security (DHS), commissioner of CBP (2010–11), and DHS assistant secretary and special representative for border affairs (2009).

2. For more on the troubled history of the US-Mexico borderlands, see Truett 2008.

3. Proposition 187 was a ballot measure to deny public services, such as public education and health care, to undocumented migrants. Most of its provisions were struck down in court.

4. The INS used to be part of the U.S. Department of Justice (DOJ). In 2003 the agency disappeared and most of its functions were transferred to three entities of the then newly created U.S. Department of Homeland Security (DHS): U.S. Citizenship and Immigration Services (USCIS), U.S. Immigration and Customs Enforcement (ICE), and U.S. Customs and Border Protection (CBP).

5. The Security and Accountability for Every Port Act of 2006 provided a statutory framework for the CTPAT program and imposed strict program oversight requirements (CBP n.d. ["CTPAT"]).

6. For a critique of the usage of the term *drug cartels* when referring to Mexican organized crime groups, see Correa-Cabrera 2017, 9–10.

7. On the security situation in Mexico at the time, see Schaefer, Bahney, and Riley 2009.

8. CBP officers interact with their Mexican counterparts on a daily basis. For example, when the CBP returns individuals to Mexico, it works jointly with the INM. Returns occur at certain agreed POEs and at certain times. Actually, the DHS and SEGOB formed a group to make sure that the Mexican government is ready to receive returned individuals. The DHS has also provided support and advice to Mexican migration authorities in the framework of Plan Frontera Sur.

9. Each of the three committees had a co-chair. The infrastructure committee was co-chaired by the CBP and the DOS on the U.S. side and by the SRE on the Mexican side. The secure flows committee was co-chaired by the CBP on the U.S. side and the SAT and SEGOB on the Mexican side. The law enforcement committee was co-chaired jointly by the DHS and the DOJ on the U.S. side and SEGOB on the Mexican side. The PGR also co-chaired the law enforcement committee for a while. Ben Rohrbaugh, phone interview, May 19, 2017.

10. It was signed into law on April 23, 2010, by then governor Janice K. Brewer.

11. A U.S. Supreme Court ruling in 2012 and a settlement with plaintiffs in 2016 collectively gutted the law.

12. Critical perspectives on U.S.-Mexico border security policy can be found in Correa-Cabrera, Garrett, and Keck 2014; Dunn 1995; and Payan 2016. The views of inhabitants of border communities were captured by José Antonio Alfaro, who traveled along the entire U.S.-Mexico border in the summer of 2017. He shared his perspectives with us; we are grateful for his collaboration in the present work.

13. One example is José Antonio Alfaro's Border Studies Project, a collection of fifty-three interviews with law enforcement agents, local politicians, human rights advocates, experts, entrepreneurs, journalists, and other *fronterizos* in the summer of 2017.

14. It is worth noting that the aim of the present chapter is not to qualify nor to analyze in depth the state of U.S.-Mexico border security cooperation (and migration enforcement) in the Trump era. That is material for a separate piece. We focus here exclusively on the history of binational institutional development in the area of border security cooperation. We are not evaluating U.S.-Mexico border policy today.

References

Alvarez, Priscilla. 2017. "How Trump Is Changing Immigration Enforcement." *The Atlantic*, February 3.

Andreas, Peter. 1998. "The US Immigration Control Offensive: Constructing an Image of Order on the Southwest Border." In *Crossings: Mexican Immigration in Interdisciplinary Perspectives*, edited by Marcelo M. Suárez-Orozco, 343–56. Cambridge, Mass.: Harvard University Press.

Andreas, Peter. 2003. "A Tale of Two Borders." In *The Rebordering of North America*, edited by Peter Andreas and Thomas J. Biersteker, 1–23. New York: Routledge.

Andreas, Peter. 2009. *Border Games: Policing the US-Mexico Divide*. Ithaca, N.Y.: Cornell University Press.

"Arturo Sarukhán on the Evolving U.S.-Mexico Relationship." 2009. *Zócalo Public Square* (blog), June 29. https://www.zocalopublicsquare.org/2009/06/29/last-night-mexican-ambassador-arturo-sarukhn/events/the-takeaway/.

Bersin, Alan. 1995. "Deterring Illegal Immigration and Drug Smuggling at Land Border Ports of Entry." Memorandum to Jamie S. Gorelick, Deputy Attorney General, U.S. Department of Justice, Washington, D.C., July 28. Transcript.

Bersin, Alan. 1996. "El Tercer País: Reinventing the US/Mexico Border." *Stanford Law Review* 48 (5): 1413–20.

Bersin, Alan. 1998. "Threshold Order: Bilateral Law Enforcement and Regional Public Safety on the US/Mexico Border." *San Diego Law Review* 35 (3): 715–26.

Bersin, Alan. 2012. "Lines and Flows: The Beginning and End of Borders." *Brooklyn Journal of International Law* 37 (2): 389–406.

Bersin, Alan. 2017. "Trump Just Might be Giving Us the Opportunity to Make NAFTA Even Stronger." *Dallas Morning News*, June 7.

Bersin, Alan, and Judith S. Feigin. 1998. "The Rule of Law at the Margin: Reinventing Prosecution Policy in the Southern District of California." *Georgetown Immigration Law Journal* 12 (2): 285–310.

Bersin, Alan, and Michael D. Huston. 2015. "Homeland Security as a Theory of Action: The Impact on US/Mexico Border Management." In *The Anatomy of a Relationship: A Collection of Essays on the Evolution of US-Mexico Cooperation on Border Management*, edited by Christopher Wilson, 2–11. Washington, D.C.: Mexico Institute, Wilson Center.

Bush, George W., and Vicente Fox. 2001. "Remarks by President George Bush and President Vicente Fox of Mexico at Arrival Ceremony." White House Office of the Press Secretary, September 5. https://georgewbush-whitehouse.archives.gov/news/releases/2001/09/20010905 -2.html.

Carl, Traci. 2009. "Mexico's Increasing Lawlessness Poses Unexpected Challenge." Associated Press, January 19.

Corchado, Alfredo. 2013. "Once Solid, the George W. Bush-Vicente Fox Partnership Faded After 9/11." *Dallas Morning News*, April 26.

Cornelius, Wayne A. 2001. "Death at the Border: Efficacy and Unintended Consequences of US Immigration Control Policy." *Population and Development Review* 27 (4): 661–85.

Correa-Cabrera, Guadalupe. 2017. *Los Zetas Inc.: Criminal Corporations, Energy, and Civil War in Mexico*. Austin: University of Texas Press.

Correa-Cabrera, Guadalupe, Terence Garrett, and Michelle Keck. 2014. "Administrative Surveillance and Fear: Implications for US-Mexico Border Relations and Governance." *European Review of Latin American and Caribbean Studies*, no. 96 (April): 35–53.

CTPAT Security Services. 2017. "Mexico OEA Certifications (Authorized Economic Operators)." October 18. https://ctpatsecurity.com/neec-benefits/.

Debusmann, Bernd. 2009. "Among Top US Fears: A Failed Mexican State." *New York Times*, January 9.

Dunn, Timothy J. 1995. *The Militarization of the US-Mexico Border, 1978–1992: Low-Intensity Conflict Doctrine Comes Home*. Austin: University of Texas Press.

Felbab-Brown, Vanda. 2019. "AMLO's Security Policy: Creative Ideas, Tough Reality." Brookings Institution, March. https://www.brookings.edu/wp-content/uploads/2019/03/FP_20190325_mexico_anti-crime.pdf.

Flynn, Stephen E. 2003. "The False Conundrum: Continental Immigration Versus Homeland Security." In *The Rebordering of North America*, edited by Peter Andreas and Thomas J. Biersteker, 110–27. New York: Routledge.

Friedman, George. 2012. "Mexico's Strategy." *Stratfor*, August 21.

Gross, Gregory. 1997. "Mexico, US Forge Police Ties." *San Diego Union-Tribune*, June 21, B1.

Gurría, Ángel. 1997. "Palabras del Secretario de Relaciones Exteriores de México, Ángel Gurría, en el Foro Fronterizo." Speech, San Diego, Calif., June 20. Transcript.

Heer, Jeet. 2016. "Operation Wetback Revisited." *New Republic*, April 25.

Henderson, Timothy J. 2011. "Bracero Blacklists: Mexican Migration and the Unraveling of the Good Neighbor Policy." *Latin Americanist* 55 (4): 199–217.

Herrera, Octavio, and Arturo Santa Cruz, eds. 2011. *Historia de las relaciones internacionales de México, 1821–2010*. Vol. 1, *America del Norte*. Mexico City: Dirección General del Acervo Histórico Diplomático.

Kelly, John F. 2017. "Statement by Secretary John F. Kelly on Mexican Partnership." July 7. https://www.dhs.gov/news/2017/07/07/statement-secretary-john-f-kelly-mexican-partnership.

Krouse, William J. *U.S. Border Patrol Operations*. Washington, D.C.: Congressional Research Service, 1997.

McCormick, Evan D., and Alan Bersin. 2017. "Adversarial Partners: Patterns of Contention and Cooperation in US-Mexican Diplomatic History." September 30. Manuscript in author's possession.

McDonald, William F. 1997. "Crime and Illegal Immigration: Emerging Local, State, and Federal Partnerships." *National Institute of Justice Journal*, no. 232 (June): 2–10.

Mexico's Embassy in the United States. 2016. "Joint Statement: 2016 US-Mexico High-Level Economic Dialogue." February 25. https://embamex.sre.gob.mx/eua/index.php/en/press-releases/press-releases-2016/1140-joint-statement-2016-u-s-mexico-high-level-economic-dialogue.

Office of the U.S. Attorney. 1997. "Reno and Gurría Announce Creation of Three Border Groups on Public Safety, Ports of Entry and Migration." Southern District of California, San Diego, June 20. Transcript.

Paulson, Amanda. 2010. "Obama to Lay Out New Immigration Reform Blueprint in El Paso." *Christian Science Monitor*, May 11.

Payan, Tony. 2016. *The Three US-Mexico Border Wars: Drugs, Immigration, and Homeland Security*. 2nd ed. Santa Barbara, Calif.: ABC-CLIO.

Ramos, Jorge. 2019. "Trump: 'I'm Using Mexico.'" *New York Times*, October 7.

Reno, Janet. 1997. "Towards Borders that Work: Reinventing the US/Mexico Border; Law Enforcement Challenges to Cross/Border Region Building." Speech, San Diego, Calif., June 20. Transcript.

Riding Alan. 1989. *Distant Neighbors: A Portrayal of the Mexicans*. New York: Vintage Books.

Rucker, Philip, Joshua Partlow, and Nick Miroff. 2018. "After Testy Call with Trump over Border Wall, Mexican President Shelves Plan to Visit White House." *Washington Post*, February 24.

Schaefer, Agnes, Benjamin Bahney, and K. Jack Riley. 2009. *Security in Mexico: Implications for US Policy Options*. Arlington, Va.: RAND Corporation.

Seelke, Clare Ribando. 2009. *Mérida Initiative for Mexico and Central America: Funding and Policy Issues*. Washington, D.C.: Congressional Research Service.

Seelke, Clare Ribando, and Kristin Finklea. 2017. *US-Mexican Security Cooperation: The Mérida Initiative and Beyond*. Washington, D.C.: Congressional Research Service.

Spagat, Elliot. 2016. "US Border Agents Begin Inspecting US-Bound Trucks in Mexico." *San Diego Union-Tribune*, January 12.

Truett, Samuel. 2008. *Fugitive Landscapes: The Forgotten History of the US-Mexico Borderlands*. New Haven, Conn.: Yale University Press.

U.S. Customs and Border Protection (CBP). n.d. "CTPAT: Customs Trade Partnership Against Terrorism." Accessed October 10, 2017. https://www.cbp.gov/border-security/ports-entry/cargo-security/ctpat.

U.S. Customs and Border Protection (CBP). n.d. "Global Entry." Accessed October 15, 2017. https://www.cbp.gov/travel/trusted-traveler-programs/global-entry.

U.S. Department of Homeland Security (DHS). 2009. "Secretary Napolitano Highlights Illegal Immigration Enforcement, Appoints Alan Bersin as Assistant Secretary for International Affairs and Special Representative for Border Affairs." April 15. https://www.dhs.gov/news/2009/04/15/secretary-napolitano-highlights-illegal-immigration-enforcement-appoints-bersin.

U.S. Department of Homeland Security (DHS). 2011. "Senior Administration Officials Release Southwest Border Counternarcotics Strategy." Press release, July 7. https://www.dhs.gov/news/2011/07/07/senior-administration-officials-release-southwest-border-counternarcotics-strategy.

U.S. Department of State (DOS). 2002. "US-Canada Smart Border/30 Point Action Plan Update." December 2. https://2001-2009.state.gov/p/wha/rls/fs/18128.htm.

U.S. Department of State (DOS). 2009. "U.S. Ambassador to Mexico Carlos Pascual and Mexican Ambassador to the United States Arturo Sarukhan." https://2009-2017.state.gov/r/pa/prs/ps/2009/sept/129672.htm.

U.S. Department of State (DOS). n.d. "Merida Initiative." Accessed October 16, 2017. https://2009-2017.state.gov/j/inl/merida//index.htm.

White House. 2001. "US-Mexican Cabinet Officials Hold Press Conference." Office of the Press Secretary. September 5. https://georgewbush-whitehouse.archives.gov/news/releases/2001/09/20010905-6.html.

White House. 2002. "Securing America's Borders Fact Sheet: Border Security." January 25. https://georgewbush-whitehouse.archives.gov/homeland/01.html.

White House. 2019. "Remarks by President Trump upon Air Force One Arrival, Prince George's County, MD." September 26. https://www.whitehouse.gov/briefings-statements/remarks-president-trump-upon-air-force-one-arrival-prince-georges-county-md/.

Wilson, Christopher. 2015. "The Lessons of Post-9/11 Border Management." Wilson Center, November 18. https://www.wilsoncenter.org/article/the-lessons-post-911-border-management.

Wilson, Christopher, Pablo Parás, and Enrique Enríquez. 2017. *A Critical Juncture: Public Opinion in U.S.-Mexico Relations*. Washington, D.C.: Mexico Institute, Wilson Center.

Zedillo, Ernesto, and William F. Clinton. 1997a. "Declaration of the Mexican/US Alliance Against Drugs." Mexico City, May 6. Transcript.

Zedillo, Ernesto, and William F. Clinton. 1997b. "Joint Statement on Migration Adopted by the President of the United States and the President of Mexico." Mexico City, May 6. Transcript.

10

. . .

Transportation Institutions Along the U.S.-Mexico Border

Kimberly Collins

The transportation sector is currently undergoing a major transition with new technology development that is surely going to disrupt how people move in cities, through rural areas, and, for the purposes of this chapter, across borders. Alternative fuels, more efficient and effective batteries for electrical storage, and new road engineering and construction materials to integrate the human and artificial intelligence into one seamless system are all on the horizon (Ili and Basedow 2018; McGrath 2018). Important models for autonomous transportation systems are being tested and deployed around the world. With this as a backdrop, it is crucial to remember that transportation linkages and networks are the spine of any community—urban, rural, or cross-border. If the traffic does not flow effectively or efficiently, the economy does not move and the quality of life is impaired for all residents. Moreover, operational transportation infrastructure is related to the security, environmental quality, mobility, and public health in a community. Because of these interrelated issues, there is generally political will at all levels of government, and between governments in border contexts, to work on transportation infrastructure buildout and operations. This is true for any region, in any place in the world, with the one caveat of resource availability—financial, human capacity, and institutions. Even these obstacles, however, are often overcome upon the realization that without transportation, many aspects of well-being in a community, along with its security and prosperity, are threatened. Based on the assumption of the centrality of transportation as the backbone of society, this chapter will review the current transportation networks and institutions in the U.S.-Mexico borderlands and look a bit toward the future on what will be needed to prepare for the next generation of transportation technologies.

Transportation in Context Along the Border

The U.S.-Mexico border is approximately two thousand miles long. Jurisdictions cover two federal governments, four U.S. and six Mexican states, twenty-six U.S counties, thirty-eight Mexican municipalities, forty-seven shared land crossings / ports of entry (POEs), and seven rail crossings. In 2014 there were also approximately fifteen million people living in counties and municipalities along the border and one hundred million in all ten border states (INEGI 2015; U.S. Census Bureau n.d.). To manage this region and all its complex issues, a network of agencies at the national, state, and local levels exists. These agencies assist people living, working, doing business, and studying in the region. This includes millions of people who cross on a regular basis and the visitors who cross occasionally as well as those who do not have the documents to cross the borderline but are part of the borderlands community. In all, hundreds of millions of individuals travel within and through the region, and billions of dollars in goods move back and forth as part of a global supply chain network.

The agencies in charge of monitoring this traffic are part of and help create the formal and informal institutions working on transportation-related issues. Formal networks and institutions include meetings among national and state transportation authorities, port of entry and international bridge management entities, and governmental joint committees coordinating the construction and management of cross-border infrastructure. Examples of informal networks and institutions include academic research, business transactions in the local economies, environmental and human rights networks, and even cultural and educational exchanges, among others. Governance of cross-border infrastructure occurs in the day-to-day interaction of all these different actors and interests.

The governing institutions (legal and political) and the agencies that manage a society are part of a strong social order—the same is true with infrastructure in complex environments such as borders. Looking at good governance in such conditions is essential to understand what the future of border infrastructure is likely to be. As John Dewey notes, good governance leads to good social order (Bertman 2007). With a policy issue such as transportation, there needs to be good communication, institutions, and networks to keep the flow of goods and people at the most efficient and effective levels possible.

To help provide a picture of the complexity of the border transportation network, a bit of data is provided to help tell the story. In 2016 a total of 75.6 million personal vehicles crossed the border, carrying 140.7 million people. Many of these trips are day shopping, or going to work or school, and consist of crossing back and forth between cities in the region. In that same year, 181,000 buses, carrying 2.3 million people, crossed between the United States and Mexico, primarily on trips further into the interior of both countries (DOT n.d. ["Border Planning Fact Sheet"]). Moreover, there are a variety of supply chain models to move goods across the North American trading region, and much depends on the product, commodity, and/or manufacturing process. One example outlined by Anne G. Robinson and James H. Bookbinder (2007) shows the manufacturing of components in Canada, trucked to Mexico for assembly, finished in the United States, and sent to distribution centers in the United States and Canada for release into the market. Another model looks at the movement of bulk freight (such as chemicals and automobiles/components) by rail. For these types of goods, intermodal rail and truck transport systems are marketed as an improved method to move goods more effectively. Additionally, new technologies to speed up communication, manifests, and custom paperwork are being used (Hamilton 2010; Nunez 2016). In 2016 a total of 5.8 million trucks carrying approximately 20.8 million tons of freight crossed the U.S.-Mexico border, with a total trade value of US$526 billion. Of this trade, 86 percent was moved by surface transportation modes, either truck, rail, or pipeline (BTS n.d.; DOT n.d. ["Border Planning Fact Sheet"]). The majority of the highways carry more than 40,000 trucks annually. Managing the infrastructure to support and accommodate this volume of traffic is clearly a huge endeavor.

The sheer volume and mix of cross-border transportation are but one dimension to consider. There are a number of other challenges to the transportation network. For example, economic costs of border wait times for people and goods to get across have been estimated to be up to US$7.2 billion and impacted more than 62,000 jobs in the San Diego and Baja California border region (HDR/HLB Decision Economics Inc. 2006). In addition, in August 2017, state officials from Arizona and Sonora met to work together to reduce the wait time for truck traffic at the border to four and a half hours (Gobierno del Estado de Sonora n.d.)—which is still a long time and just a bit improved upon a full-day wait. For a border that sees many agricultural products cross, the costs in wasted produce if delays are too long can pile up quickly. The problem of wait times has become nearly intractable all along the border, and it is getting worse as border agencies assert themselves in border governance with a security-focused primary mission—largely leaving aside their obligation to also facilitate cross-border traffic.

Along the same line of the delays at the border crossings, there are other issues that stand out in the buildout and management of the infrastructure that serves the binational border. There is a need for infrastructure development on the highways that run through both counties toward the border, for example. Roberto Durán-Fernández provides an extensive review of the Mexican and U.S. highway systems and the reasons for delays in the movement of freight. His article is based on a review of the recommendations from the 2007 Border Governor's Conference report, titled "Competitiveness and Areas of Opportunity in the Border Region" (Protego-Evercore Partners

2007). The report states, "Deficient infrastructure is a major cause of bottlenecks at the international border ports" (Durán-Fernández 2014, 81). Another major problem is the inefficiencies of the inspection process, which can be conducted for multiple reasons by one or more participating agencies in the state and federal governments—and sometimes on the basis of sheer arbitrariness by border agents. A third problem has to do with the delays that occur with the use of the drayage firms, in cases where Mexican trucks are unable to cross the border and different cabins drop, hitch, and haul containers across the POEs. Such drayage arrangements survived NAFTA and continue to be a part of the system, as there is still no U.S. domestic political consensus on integrating transportation of goods by companies all across the continent as mandated by the treaty (Gerald 2014). Even so, conclusions from Durán-Fernández's calculations show that infrastructure investment in neighboring border states, on both sides, generates positive economic spillovers. He also points to the need for a better system for checking traffic at the border; changes to the current system of fiscal federalism in Mexico to enhance the role of states and municipalities; and more coordination of infrastructure plans between Mexico and the United States, which would improve important synergies to the benefit of both countries. Such reports hint at the importance of solid cross-border infrastructure systems for the region and for the economic integration that both countries have pursued since the 1990s.

Interestingly, although when thinking about transportation across the border, cars, trucks, and sometimes public systems come to mind—trains are an increasingly important component of the binational network. And they appear to share the same problems. Delays in crossing, for example, are not just found in the movement of trucks and people; they are also problems related to the movement of cargo by rail. Movement by rail is slowed at the border by security checks from U.S. Customs and Border Protection (CBP) and by safety regulations by the U.S. Federal Railroad Administration that mandate crew changes (GAO 2016). These rail crossings block highways and streets in border cities and towns and contribute to congestion at the border POEs. This is due partially to poor planning and a lack of updates to local infrastructure at the border. When rail infrastructure problems occur, train backups can go on for hundreds of miles, stopping local traffic from crossing one side of the city to the other. In these cases, both commerce and local livability lose.

Clearly, putting the entire picture of cross-border transportation in perspective, with all its positive effects and its challenges of construction and management, gives a picture of the need for viewing the entire system as crucial for the prosperity of both countries. The best method to overcome its challenges, however, is through a planning process based in strong institutions and collaboration between both countries and among all authorities with varying jurisdictions over parts of the overall system. This chapter provides a descriptive meta-review of the transportation-related institutions and planning documents for the U.S.-Mexico border region. It begins with a discussion of governance and institutions and then provides an overview of the federal institutions and the mechanisms for collaboration and coordination. Within these federal agreements, the joint transportation plans for the border are reviewed. From here, a review of the local transportation planning organizations and related stakeholders in communities is conducted. This involved an extensive search of the border planning documents and organization websites, with a specific focus on the "about us" page, the board of directors, and annual reports. Finally, a number of interviews with transportation officials and related organizations were conducted in 2014 in the California–Baja California border region to provide a ground truth to the document review. From this framework of current institutions, the possible implications in the implementation of future technologies and the movement of goods and people across the border are discussed.

Governance and Institutions of the Cross-Border Transportation System

Most people, except maybe the most hard-core anarchists, believe that a system of good governance and effective administration is needed to maintain order and to improve the human condition. The great debate over the centuries has been: How should this be organized and what is the role of the different actors in society? How these decisions are made and who makes the decisions determines and shapes the types of the governance and administration institutions, both formal and informal, in a particular society. What is true is that when formal institutions are not created, alternative mechanisms emerge to fulfill governance requirements. Generally, working in the U.S.-Mexico border area provides a good example of instances of when there is a lack of formal institutions to help manage society. Border communities have seen numerous informal agreements and interactions arise to accomplish projects and local goals (Collins 2006). So a key question addressed in this chapter becomes: Given the difficult institutional conditions for infrastructure buildout and management at the border, how do we develop the institutions that can improve our lives and those of others? The American pragmatists during the Progressive Era provide a strong theoretical standing to build on this discussion.

American pragmatic thinkers, such as John Dewey and Jane Addams, lived, worked, and wrote during the late nineteenth and early twentieth centuries. This was a time very similar to what we are experiencing today in the world. The end of the nineteenth century was an era of industrialization and described as the first period of globalization in the modern era, with fast technological advancements and high numbers of people migrating from rural areas to cities to find jobs. This dynamic created societal tensions with new migrants competing with workers from rural parts of the county in cities that lacked sufficient infrastructure, and the necessary political and legal institutions to support the needs of residents. Domestic populations often blamed their economic and social problems on the migrant communities. In confronting the kind of change that comes to society with the rapid movement of people, ideas, commerce, and finances, the American pragmatists saw the need for strong institutions to address issues of social equity and fairness while supporting the development of the individual and overall community. This was not easy to accomplish, but the development of new laws and political structures along with an urban infrastructure, such as transportation, social services, and education, fit very well into the pragmatic construct that focused on science and the strength of the individual (Bertman 2007; Lacey 2008). It is important to note that pragmatists believed the strength of the individual did not come from within but from the constructs of society (Lacey 2008). To achieve this, governments at all levels, the nonprofit sector, and the business community need to work together to build and back societal institutions that support individuals to become the best that they can be. In observing the current affairs in the United States, we are living in a similar age and therefore can look toward the Progressive Era and the ideas of the pragmatists once more to move society forward. The present age of globalization and raising inequality has stressed that twentieth-century institutions and people are searching for new solutions for cities, rural areas, and the nation's borders.

The current state of transportation infrastructure and planning along the U.S.-Mexico border is based on the "can-do" society of the pragmatists (Bertman 2007). If you are unable to move people and goods effectively and efficiently not only within the country but also across borders, you impact the overall quality of life in the nation as the economy will struggle with unmet market demands. From this perspective, the movement of goods and people efficiently and effectively supports a strong economic system.

To build a quality transportation system, science and engineering principles are obviously critical, but this system also needs to include planning, economics, public finance, environmental review, security, and social factors. The process needs to be democratic as well, listening to those who are directly impacted by projects or by negative externalities of transportation systems, such as pollution. Local governments and the private sector have much to gain or lose depending on the quality and efficiency of the transportation system, but the people living in the communities should not be ignored either. Even so, because transportation is truly local, there are limits to participation as this depends on local stakeholders' resources and the political will to interact. At the border region in particular, the venues for consultation with local communities are fairly limited. These limitations include the lack of resources and political will as noted, along with difficult social conditions in the region, and the inadequacy of binational institutions in the region (Collins 2017). The forums where these issues are discussed, for example, are not well attended by the local residents. Now, as Dewey notes, democracy is based in the ability of individuals to fully exercise their free will, and many borderlanders do not know or cannot exercise that free will for multiple reasons. As those who study the border know, free will is limited by the public space at the border and at the national level (Collins 2017). This is not to say there are not any local institutions to support transportation infrastructure development. There are a number of formal and informal institutions, but as usual, more could be done to bolster the system to develop more efficient and effective transportation flows, and to do so more democratically. To review the border institutions dedicated to the issue of cross-border infrastructure, the next section is a review of the pertinent legislation and laws in both countries, all of which provide the legal institutional framework to connect highways and regional planning in the border.

Federal and State Transportation Institutions in the Border Region

Since the mid-1990s, the North American Free Trade Agreement (NAFTA) has been the overarching legal framework by which trade moves through the region. The binational manufacturing and logistics industries have undoubtedly been very successful, as has agricultural trade, but this success has also increased exponentially the level of traffic flowing through the region. With the passage of this treaty, more companies began maximizing their manufacturing processes for goods by using the strengths of both sides of the border (Cedillo-Campos et al. 2014; Robinson and Bookbinder 2007). If there is one way to measure binational economic integration, it has to be by observing and measuring traffic flows over the transportation infrastructure. Yet it is important to note that although the primary purpose of NAFTA was to reduce tariffs on specific goods, nothing in the agreement addresses issues of transportation infrastructure, the movement of people, or security protocols. This gap is in fact one of the major deficiencies of the agreement. Indeed, it can be said confidently that the treaty does not provide any governance solutions to the traffic it created and no institutions were built up to manage this burden on existing infrastructure, explore the need to expand it, or manage what exists better. Instead, transportation infrastructure continues to be developed and managed through a system of laws and agencies that operate independently in both countries and are poorly articulated. To be sure, there are structures for planning, investment, operations, and security, but they continue to be part of the *national* and *state* systems, and their *binational* interface remains reedy. Worse yet, transportation planning, investment, and operations are inherently a local issue, with the need for local buy-in through regional planning mechanisms. Federal and state governments have not, however, devolved any of these mechanisms to the local governments, perhaps in part because transportation building and managing requires the kind of capital that only federal and state governments can muster. This leads us to a short but important conversation on federalism in both countries—how power and fiscal authority establish the means for project development.

United States

For the United States, intergovernmental management has become a part of the governance process in many different ambits, including infrastructure. There is a mix of federal, state, local, and private sector involvement in infrastructure development. This is seen in the interaction of the U.S. Department of Transportation (DOT) with the individual states, and with local and regional governments and entities, such as the Metropolitan Planning Organizations (MPOs), where many of the discussions on infrastructure take place. Regional plans in the United States are governed by acts approved by Congress, which allocates funding and sets the priorities for the planning process, and by various agencies, which regulate infrastructure standards and use, ensure public safety, and keep statistics to help set priorities. Currently, agencies are working under the framework of TEA-21, SAFETEA-LU, MAP-21, and the FAST Act.[1] Thus, in the United States, according to Gian-Claudia Sciara (2017, 265), the standards for regional transportation planning include the following:

1. Economic vitality of the metro region under observation
2. System safety for motorized and nonmotorized users
3. Accessibility and mobility of people and for freight
4. Enhance environment, energy conservation, quality of life, and transportation and land use consistency
5. Integration and connectivity of modes for people and freight
6. Efficient system management and operation
7. Preservation of the existing transportation system
8. Transportation system resiliency and reliability, reduction/mitigation of surface transport storm water impacts
9. Enhance travel and tourism

These standards are mandates given to state governments, which implement them through state departments of transportation, MPOs, and county-based transportation authorities. All these agencies have to work together, which they do by holding regular meetings to address transportation issues at the local level and communicate them to the state and federal levels. In effect, to facilitate that interface between the local, state, and federal levels, in the United States, the 1962 Highway Act established the Metropolitan Planning Organizations and "aimed to increase urban participation in regional transportation decisions over federal highway funds, largely directed by state highway departments" (Sciara 2017, 263). Furthermore, the National Environmental Policy Act (NEPA) leads "MPOs to invest in projects likely to win environmental approval and match the region's budget" (264). Clearly, very early on in the 1960s, the U.S. government recognized the need to create structures and institutions that could coordinate vertically between governments. This act, however, is silent on cross-border infrastructure issues. Those remain largely, and awkwardly, in the hands of the federal government, where foreign policy agencies still assert strong influence.

Interestingly, MPOs ended up having a central role in coordinating all institutions on transportation but are limited on land use decisions. As Sciara (2017) notes, MPOs promote regional planning and approve regional plans and investments, yet land use decisions are done by the local governments and private land ownership—both important components of the U.S. system. The conclusion from her comprehensive article is that MPOs do not have the appropriate authority or at times ability to effectively impact transportation planning. This limits the strategic planning process and regional investment plans. And this is certainly felt when it comes to cross-border infrastructure, where MPOs have almost no impact beyond pointing out specific needs. Even so, this does not stop MPOs from working regionally and supporting projects, as will be seen in the discussion of local groups working on binational issues. The point is that local planning organizations are limited in their impact on land use decisions, economic development projects, and ultimately transportation projects.

Sciara's (2017) review of the transportation planning process provides an overview of how lengthy and hard it is to develop the institutions that provide the needed structure to the system. The system that currently exists was developed over decades with hard-won legal battles in the United States. There have been focused leadership and allocated resources to work toward comprehensive transportation planning systems, and the political will existed as it was absolutely necessary for communities to grow and for the government to respond to increasing congestion in U.S. cities.

The U.S. federal government provides support through program development and research, and especially through funding. Many of the financial resources for infrastructure are in fact allocated by Congress and trickle down to the states and local governments. Additionally, there are state laws such as AB32 (Global Warming Solutions Act) and SB375 (Sustainable Communities and Climate Protection Act), passed in California, that mandate that MPOs develop plans to mitigate traffic congestion and reach specific goals in the reduction of greenhouse gas (GHG) emissions by implementing more smart growth techniques. The goal of this legislation in California is to better plan communities, land use, and the transportation networks to alleviate congestion, and to improve sustainability and environmental quality in the state. This shows that in the United States, with all its institutional interface limitations, the states have a strong voice in the development of transportation networks and infrastructure in their jurisdictions and often advocate for cross-border networks as well. Again, they do so with the consultation of local governments, but ultimately, the states make the decisions.

States are becoming even stronger actors with the decrease in federal funds and the political will at the national level to raise the necessary funds to pay for needed improvements. In 2017 California passed SB1 (Road Repair and Accountability Act of 2017), a transportation funding bill to provide US$50 billion in revenues over the next ten years. The other three border states have not passed any tax increases to pay for needed infrastructure for twenty-four years or more (Institute on Taxation and Economic Policy 2017)—and certainly not for cross-border infrastructure. Texas, however, did pass a bill to enable counties and cities to finance, acquire, design, construct, operate, maintain, expand, and extend transportation projects, primarily through various funding mechanisms such as bonds, special tax zones, and so on (Texas Department of Transportation 2014). Interestingly, the law allows border counties and cities to fund cross-border infrastructure, if it is satisfactorily demonstrated that it benefits the U.S. local communities. No such projects have yet taken place, but four Regional Mobility Authorities (RMAs) have been created along the U.S.-Mexico border: Camino Real in El Paso, Texas; Webb County–Laredo in Laredo, Texas; and Hidalgo County and Cameron County in South Texas. This is meant to provide more control to local authorities over transportation projects and help finance such projects.

Overall, conversations are being held as transportation infrastructure spending is at deficit levels throughout the United States. And state governments are looking for ways to make up for this deficit along with many initiatives at the local level. Self-help counties are able to raise funds for local transportation projects through sales tax measures passed by the counties' voters. These are found in California and in the new RMAs in Texas. Though this helps deal with the lack of funding from the federal government, the expenditure of local funds on projects related to Mexico can be a difficult sell for some communities—as evidenced by the operations of the various border RMAs in the state of Texas. Infrastructure needs are great at the border and local funding is limited, meaning the driving factor for funding decisions is based on the greatest impact on those seen as local residents.

Mexico

The Mexican federalist experience is a bit different from that of the United States, though both nations have federal, state, and local governments. The main difference is that Mexico historically has had a centralized system of governance with planning and investment coming from the national government, including national transportation networks and infrastructure. Mexico has also exerted strong control on cross-border infrastructure at the federal level, with little say from local communities. This has been evolving with the opening of the Mexican economy since the 1980s, which culminated with the passage of NAFTA in 1994 and the modernization of the public system to meet the systems in the United States and Canada (Cabrero Mendoza 2013; Huerta and Lujambio 1994). But even with this liberalization process, local governments have not developed the necessary institutions, resources, or information to help with the planning process at the local level (Cabrero Mendoza 2013). State and local governments remain largely disengaged from cross-border infrastructure and the country remains highly centralized in the collection of revenues, with the federal government collecting the majority of taxes (94 percent) and maintaining control over a centralized expenditure system. This financial centralization continues the lack of development of administrative systems at the state and local levels (Cabrero Mendoza 2013). This is reflected on infrastructure development in the states, at the local level, and of course on cross-border issues, where infrastructure needs are great but low levels of assessment and investment are the norm.

Under the political and legal institutions in Mexico, transportation plans are generated at the federal level and generally coincide with the presidential term of six years. The program under review for this chapter was set for the term of President Enrique Peña Nieto (2013–18)—Programa Sectorial de Comunicaciones y Transportes 2013–2018. This plan was developed as mandated by Articles 9, 16, 23, 26, and 29 of the national constitution (Constitución Política de los Estados Unidos Mexicanos). It is also provided for under Article 36 of the federal law on public administration (Ley Orgánica de la Administración Pública Federal [APF, Organic Law for Federal Public Administration]). As part of Article 36 of the APF, the Secretaría de Comunicaciones y Transportes (SCT, Secretariat of Communications and Transportation) is assigned the following activities:

1. Formulate and conduct the policies and programs for the development of transport and communications according to the needs of the country
2. Regulate, inspect, and monitor the public postal services and telegraph and its various services
3. Grant concessions and permits for establishing and operating air services in the national territory; the provision of motor transport services on federal highways; establishing and operating services for communication related to water issues and to construct the public works projects to be executed
4. Regulate and monitor the administration of the national airports

5. Manage the operation of traffic control services, as well as air navigation and information safety
6. Regulate and monitor the administration of the railway system
7. Regulate the communication on and transport of water
8. Manage and coordinate the central ports that are state owned
9. Build and maintain federal roads and bridges
10. Build and maintain roads and bridges in cooperation with the state and municipal governments and individuals
11. Construct federal airports (Gobierno de la República 2013, 17–18)

Moreover, the SCT's plans need to be aligned to the Plan Nacional de Desarrollo (PND, National Development Plan)—a much broader roadmap for the priorities of the central government on economic development, of which transportation projects are only a portion. The main goals and objectives of the PDN are as follows:

1. Communicate to the stakeholder and create safe movement
2. Permit access in communities to services and markets
3. Connect public sites such as schools and universities
4. Improve the productivity with competitive costs for communication and transportation services
5. Position Mexico as a logistics platform at the international level (Gobierno de la República 2013, 20)

To be exact, the PDN does include transportation issues—it must, as effective and efficient transportation is part of economic development. But these goals tend to be very general and allow a lot of space for the president of Mexico to determine which projects can go and which projects can be postponed. Even so, it is sufficiently broad that, if the president sets it as a priority, cross-border infrastructure projects could bubble to the top. The specific transportation areas of focus in the 2013–18 plan are as follows:

1. Costs of the transportation services
2. Connectivity
3. Security
4. Regional development
5. Level of service for the user
6. Capacity to meet the demands on the system
7. Environment
8. Urban development (Gobierno de la República 2013, 27)

It is very likely that Mexican president Andrés Manuel López Obrador will publish his own infrastructure program—as the law requires it—and the priorities in planning and funding will go to his preferred projects. It is unclear if there will be a separate and clear rubric for cross-border infrastructure. This is something that is needed, especially if trade is increased under the new NAFTA agreement—the United States-Mexico-Canada Agreement (USMCA). The administration of López Obrador must find a way to work with local and state governments, including those on the border, as the 1983 constitutional reform mandated that development plans include the participation of all levels of government (Mendez and Dussauge-Laguna 2017). Along the border, this change has led to the states being strong actors within the planning process. But at the local level, not all municipalities have established planning and infrastructure agencies, and generally only the larger municipalities have the resources to do so (Mendez and Dussauge-Laguna 2017). This leads to inconsistencies and uneven institutional development of local voices in the process of infrastructure buildup and maintenance. Additionally, term limits at the local level limit continuity of the regional plans, although this may change given that the most recent political reform in Mexico will allow for mayors to be re-elected—a first since the 1920s. Prior to this possibility, each new administration modified local plans to fit the goals of the new leaders (Mendez and Dussauge-Laguna 2017), usually lasting three years—an insufficient time for infrastructure to really develop, given the length of time these types of projects take. Where municipal institutes for planning and infrastructure do exist along the border, the leadership appointments generally do not coincide with municipal elections, but obviously there will still be influences from the new local administrators.

From this brief review of the planning institutions and federalist system within Mexico, the process emanates from political- rather than data-based decision-making. This has resulted in a lack of information on the best practices for planning or regional development in Mexico. The federal government is still central to the process, with the states playing a stronger role in the planning process, but not quite as strong as it should be, and the local governments are largely absent. Democratically, the interaction and discussion with locals exists, but this is very much dependent on the local human and financial resources, which unfortunately are not given the necessary support and backing to fully flourish.

Binational Coordination

These two separate governance systems coordinate on regional transportation planning projects for border infrastructure and have management arrangements. All the border states, for example, have developed Border Master Plans as part of the

U.S.-Mexico Joint Working Committee on Transportation Planning (JWC). The goals of the JWC are "to cooperate on land transportation planning and the facilitation of efficient, safe, and economical cross-border transportation movements" (FHWA 2015). The voting members are the Federal Highway Administration (FHWA), SCT, the U.S. states' departments of transportation and related organizations, and the Mexican border states' offices working on some aspect of cross-border transportation infrastructure buildup and management. Other federal agencies that attend the meetings include the U.S. Department of State (DOS) and the Secretaría de Relaciones Exteriores (SRE, Secretariat of Foreign Affairs); U.S. General Services Administration (GSA) and its counterpart in Mexico, the Instituto de Administración y Avalúos de Bienes Nacionales (INDAABIN, Institute for Administration and Appraisal of National Property); U.S. Customs and Border Protection (CBP) and Mexico's Aduana (Customs); and the U.S. Environmental Protection Agency (EPA) and Mexico's Secretaría de Medio Ambiente y Recursos Naturales (SEMARNAT, Secretariat of Environment and Natural Resources).

The JWC remains the forum to coordinate much of this binational work on border transportation infrastructure. It is working on a number of initiatives and special studies to improve the flow of traffic in the border region. This includes working with wait-time data, transportation modeling, financing workshops, data sharing and analysis, and traffic incident management programs. Important components to all this are the Border Master Plans. The first to be completed and updated was in the California–Baja California region (2008 and 2014). The second was the Laredo District in Texas-Tamaulipas / Nuevo León / Coahuila in 2012. In 2013 the Arizona-Sonora border region, West Texas–New Mexico and Chihuahua region, and the Lower Rio Grande Valley–Tamaulipas region all completed their plans. The Master Plans were developed by the JWC (U.S. DOT n.d. ["Joint Working Committee"]) to meet the following goals:

1. Create an inventory of transportation and ports-of-entry (POE) infrastructure
2. Prioritize through a comprehensive planning process with federal, state, and local input
3. Allocate funding
4. Maintain dialogue between the different actors and stakeholders engaged in the process

As part of the Border Master Plans development process, municipalities, counties, and MPOs were part of the discussion and given a chance to provide input. They did not have voting rights but had a voice, which can be seen as progress. The private sector was another important actor, especially railroad companies, and although they also were consulted, they did not have the right to vote on projects. Largely absent were representatives of the local communities. The overall goal of these plans was to ensure good communication and cooperation among all levels of government on both sides of the border to make certain that the transportation infrastructure projects support the needs of businesses and residents alike.

There are additional binational stakeholders and groups that have been important to maintaining a strong relationship between the states and local governments. These include the U.S.-Mexico Border Governors Association, the Border Legislative Conference as part of the Council of State Governments, and the Border Mayors Association.[2] These associations have all struggled over the past few years to maintain a large binational attendance at their meetings, and they have met infrequently. Although they remain a weak voice, they play an important role in keeping communication open between the state and local governments. Another regional group includes the Binational Bridges and Border Crossing Group based in the Texas–New Mexico border region. This is an official interagency group coordinated by the U.S. and Mexican federal governments, out of the DOS and the SRE. Again, the U.S. and Mexican border states are active participants in the negotiation of ports-of-entry agreements, both new and existing. In all, put together, these efforts constitute an important institutional scaffolding to build, maintain, and operate infrastructure at the border.

Local Institutions and Interaction

In communities along the border, there are Metropolitan Planning Organizations (MPOs) and Councils of Governments (COGs) on the U.S. side and the INDAABIN and the Instituto Municipal de Investigaciones y Planeación (IMIP, Municipal Institute for Research and Planning) in Mexico. These autonomous coordinating agencies interact and do much of the transportation planning at the local level and serve as important articulators of local voices to higher levels of government. Table 10.1 provides a listing of all the MPOs, COGs, and IMIPs along with key community stakeholders engaged to work on infrastructure issues along the border. These regional organizations are important, as they are tasked with having a broader yet localized view of transportation issues—an obvious need in transportation infrastructure development, maintenance, and operations. The IMIPs in Mexico are also key to providing planning professionals who work somewhat independently of the local political machine. Additionally, the IMIPs provide continuity to projects, are reservoirs of expert information, and are technical bodies that advise local authorities. Obviously, the largest inhibitor for a border-wide response is the variance in institutional support and capacity at the local level.

TABLE 10.1 Local transportation stakeholders

	Metropolitan Planning Organizations [U.S.] / Municipal Planning Organizations [Mex.]	Councils of Governments located in border counties	Other transportation-related organizations—NGOs and private sector	Stability of relationship for the other organizations
California–Baja California				
San Diego	San Diego Association of Governments (SANDAG)	SANDAG–Borders Committee	Smart Border Coalition; Mexico Business Center in San Diego Regional Chamber of Commerce; Tijuana Innovadora; Cali-Baja Megaregion; Tijuana A.L. Rodriguez Airports–Otay Tijuana Venture	Strong: meet consistently throughout the year
Tijuana	Tijuana Metropolitan Institute of Planning (IMPLAN)	—	—	—
Imperial	Southern California Association of Governments (SCAG) (based in Los Angeles)	Imperial County Transportation Commission	Imperial-Mexicali Binational Alliance	Yes: bimonthly meetings
Mexicali	Municipal Institute for Research and Planning (IMIP)	—	Imperial-Mexicali Binational Alliance	Yes: bimonthly meetings
Arizona–Sonora				
Yuma	Yuma MPO	Western Arizona COG (WACOG) (does not do transportation in Yuma)	—	—
San Luis Rio Colorado	—	—	—	—

Pima	Pima Association of Governments (PAG)	—		—
Cochise	Sierra Vista MPO (SVMPO)	Southeastern Arizona Governments Organization (SEAGO)	Nogales Economic Development Foundation	—
Nogales	Municipal Institute for Research and Planning (IMIP)	—		—
Santa Cruz	Sierra Vista MPO (SVMPO)	Southeastern Arizona Governments Organization (SEAGO)		—
Agua Prieta	—	—		—
New Mexico–Chihuahua				
Hidalgo	—	Southwest New Mexico Council of Governments		—
Luna	—	Southwest New Mexico Council of Governments		—
Dona Ana	Mesilla Valley MPO; El Paso MPO	South Central Council of Governments; Rio Grande Council of Governments	Border Industrial Association; Borderplex Alliance	Yes: regular meetings
Texas–Chihuahua–Coahuila–Nuevo León–Tamaulipas				
El Paso	El Paso MPO	Rio Grande Council of Governments	Borderplex Alliance; Greater El Paso Chamber of Commerce; Hispanic Chamber of Commerce; BNSF Railway Company; Ferromex	Yes: regular meetings
Ciudad Juárez	Municipal Institute for Research and Planning (IMIP)	—	Borderplex Alliance; BNSF Railway Company; Ferromex	Yes: regular meetings

(continued)

TABLE 10.1 (*continued*)

	Metropolitan Planning Organizations (U.S.) / Municipal Planning Organizations (Mex.)	Councils of Governments located in border counties	Other transportation-related organizations—NGOs and private sector	Stability of relationship for the other organizations
Hudspeth	–	Rio Grande Council of Governments	–	–
Jeff Davis	–	Rio Grande Council of Governments	–	–
Presidio	–	Rio Grande Council of Governments	–	–
Ojinaga	–	–	–	–
Brewster	–	Rio Grande Council of Governments	–	–
Terrell	–	Perminian Basin Regional Planning Commission	–	–
Val Verde	–	Middle Rio Grande Development Council	–	–
Ciudad Acuña	–	–		
Kinney	–	Middle Rio Grande Development Council	–	–
Maverick	–	Middle Rio Grande Development Council	–	–

Piedras Negras	—	—	—	—	—
Webb	Laredo MPO	South Texas Development Council	—	BNSF Railway Company; Union Pacific Railroad; Kansas City Southern de Mexico S.A. de C.V.; Kansas City Southern Railway Company; Ferrocarril Mexicano S.A. de C.V.	n/a
Nuevo Laredo	Municipal Institute of Research, Planning, and Urban Development (IMPLADU)	—	—	BNSF Railway Company; Union Pacific Railroad; Kansas City Southern de Mexico S.A. de C.V.; Kansas City Southern Railway Company; Ferrocarril Mexicano S.A. de C.V.	—
Zapata	—	South Texas Development Council	—	—	—
Starr	—	South Texas Development Council	—	—	—
Hidalgo	Hidalgo County MPO	Lower Rio Grande Valley Development Council	—	—	—
Reynosa	—	—	—	—	—
Cameron	Brownsville MPO; Harlingen / San Benito MPO	Lower Rio Grande Valley Development Council	Brownsville Economic Development Council	—	—
Matamoros	Municipal Institute for Research and Planning (IMIP)	—	—	—	—

Sources: Data compiled from the organizations' websites.

There is quite a bit of variation from one region of the border to the next, as the states and local governments deal with border infrastructure differently. Along the California–Baja California border, there are a number of local actors and stakeholders working to increase efficiency and flows across the border. This comes primarily from the strength of the business community in San Diego and Tijuana. The San Diego Association of Governments (SANDAG), the regional MPO and COG for the San Diego region, has representation from all the cities in the region and the county government. Additionally, Tijuana, the sister city in Mexico, has an ex-officio membership to hear of the plans and activities. In Imperial County in southeastern California, there is a regional transportation authority that derived from the COG. This group is led by a former state transportation official, works with actors throughout the region, and is a leader within a binational committee working on transportation, economic development, and environmental challenges facing the binational region.

In addition to planning and the formal institutions, another important component to getting things done along the border can be found in personal relationships of those working in the region. In San Diego and Tijuana, the groups and stakeholders working on border issues have strong relationships. This is supported by interviews conducted of stakeholders in the region. From these relationships, other organizations arise. For example, in San Diego–Tijuana, there is a Passenger Forward Working Group—an off-the-record session of stakeholders from the mayors' offices, the economic development corporations, CBP, and the Smart Border Coalition. The Smart Border Coalition is a nonprofit organization formed out of the Mexico Business Center that was part of the Greater San Diego Chamber of Commerce. It has connections to both mayors' offices, the consulate generals, and business leaders from throughout the region (interview with the executive director of the Smart Border Coalition, 2015). Topics include reducing border wait times and improving regional infrastructure through a multimodal approach.

Trust and mutually established goals are important components of getting things done in any network (Walker and Hills 2012). Looking at the port working group, they have been able to maintain a fifteen-minute wait in the Sentri lines at the San Diego–Tijuana POEs, even on Sundays, a day that can have five-hour waits in the regular and ready lanes (interview with a San Diego nonprofit leader, 2015). Additional organizations and programs that support informal institutions include Tijuana Innovadora; the Binational Airport Terminal for Rodriquez Airport in Tijuana; the California–Baja California megaregion; the Borders Committee at SANDAG; and a Memorandum of Understanding (MOU) between the cities of San Diego and Tijuana.

Tijuana Innovadora is a business organization that holds a ten-day binational event to promote the business activity in Tijuana and the importance of the border region.

This is an effort based in Tijuana but supported by both sides of the border. The cross-border terminal located in Otay Mesa, California, with a bridge to the Tijuana A.L. Rodriquez Airport was built by a private, for-profit enterprise owned by Otay Tijuana Venture. This is a great example of a public-private partnership operating in the region. It is officially called the Cross Border Xpress—to cross the border here, passengers pay a fee, which pays for the CBP and for Mexican Aduana officers.

The California–Baja California border (CaliBaja) megaregion is not directly a transportation program but is related to supporting the improvement of networks and institutions that ease the flow of goods. The Borders Committee at SANDAG is a formal, locally based committee that has a membership of local governments from the San Diego and Tijuana regions. The Mexican representatives do not pay dues to SANDAG and serve in an ex-officio position, but they are part of the committee that makes decisions (interview with representative from local planning agency, 2015). The cities of San Diego and Tijuana also have an MOU that sets goals and work groups for collaboration between local governments. As with CaliBaja, transportation is not specifically listed as one of the projects, but they do agree to collaborate on municipal and regional planning.

As noted, the majority of these local networks and institutions are supported by the private sector, with only one project supported fully by the local governments. Therefore, a review of the institutions in the region provides some insight. The formal institutions are developed as governance tools as discussed by Dewey, to do what government is charged to do—improve the public good. More informal networks and institutions are supported by the business sector or government working with business in public-private partnerships.

In Arizona-Sonora, we see remarkably fewer organizations than in California but still more than in the New Mexico–Chihuahua region. In the communities along the Arizona-Sonora border, there are a number of special initiatives, and collaboration happens with organizations on the other side, but these are more project-based than a set of standing institutions. For the New Mexico–Chihuahua border, as many observers of the border know, few people live in the northern Mexico Chihuahua desert. This creates its own dynamic on the U.S. side of the border, with little local organizational development in the area of transportation—and other aspects of economic expansion. Of course, there are businesses and nonprofits working in the region. The focus is on quality of life, health, education, and economic growth. Transportation discussions are led by the state government's Office of International Programs within the DOT and the New Mexico Border Authority.

In Texas, the border is a mix of rural and urban areas. In the larger urban areas, there are MPOs, but the regional Councils of Governments are engaged in many different activities, although only a few are related to transportation issues. COGs in Texas primarily work on coordinated planning for community and economic development, emergency response, and health and human services. Transportation planning in the smaller, rural areas along the border is led by the Texas Department of Transportation. There are a few nonprofit groups along the New Mexico–Texas border with Mexico. These include the Border Industrial Association in Dona Ana County; the Borderplex Alliance in the El Paso–Ciudad Juárez region; and the Brownsville Economic Development Council. On the Mexican side of the border, not surprisingly, there are municipal planning institutes in only the larger, more metropolitan municipalities. Looking comparatively at the number of organizations in the San Diego–Tijuana region to other parts of the border, additional work can be done to build up local capacity. Interestingly, the private sector appears to play a much larger role in Texas, as industry associations are very active in promoting infrastructure projects—and protecting commercial relationships in places like El Paso, Laredo, McAllen, and Brownsville. These do not necessary provide for a solid voice for civil society, but they do seek ways to interact and interface with higher authorities in state capitals and even in Washington, D.C., and Mexico City. Clearly, because Texas is the origin, destination, and transit point for two-thirds of U.S.-Mexico trade, the stakes are much higher and the benefits quite concentrated in certain cities and municipalities, which might explain why they actively seek to have their voice heard in various forums and committees and before representatives in Austin and Washington, D.C.

There is also a border-wide organization that supports transportation and economic development—the Border Trade Alliance (BTA). Members include businesses, cities, universities, and nonprofits primarily from the border region. Its work is based in advocacy for infrastructure-related issues in the northern and southern border regions of the United States. In the alliance's own words, "The BTA's vision is to be the recognized leader in authority for the facilitation of international trade and commerce in the Americas. Its core values include a commitment to improving the quality of life in border communities throughout trade and commerce, and a commitment to work as a community-based grassroots organization" (BTA n.d.). Its role as an advocate of the border is highlighted by the fact that the current president of the organization is the founding principal of a "government affairs and strategic consulting firm" based in Washington, D.C. (BTA n.d.). Overall, there are a variety of different local actors— government and private sector led—working along the border. As noted, the strength of these stakeholders comes from the centers of population and business, and the capacity within regions is based on these stakeholders.

It is interesting to note the strength of institutions around the issue of transportation infrastructure, as it is tied directly to the economic development goals of each state and local community. In fact, the business community has the ability to move governments to build mechanisms to address their needs—even when the general community may not have the resources or the political will to do so. Partly based on this voice, the public sector at the local level—cities, counties, and municipalities—generally has planning and transportation agencies and pushes for specific projects. A more in-depth study should examine the overall effectiveness of these agencies to understand the capacity of local governments in the border region to effect change. In many cases, there is not a human resource capacity or funding to improve the local quality of life (Collins 2006), but a more comprehensive analysis of local governments' transportation departments and agencies border-wide is needed.

The federal and state governments lead transportation planning and funding within the border region. While local governments are part of these forums and coordinating mechanisms and the business community exerts some influence, general populations are largely absent. The Border Master Plans are a strong part of the transportation institutions, which manage the connections and the flow of traffic. An argument can be made, however, for more local institutional development and increasing the local capacity to address current and future transportation matters. A final consideration touched upon earlier is the availability of funding for infrastructure development. This is a critical issue across the United States, and the budgeting for large border projects is different in both countries. At the federal level, the United States has historically set aside funding in the president's budget or monies come from federal grant programs for transportation projects. This process is time consuming and long. In response, states have begun to piece together their own transportation funding or funding mechanisms, as discussed with the passage of SB1 in California and the RMAs in Texas. Discussions in other border states are currently ongoing, but the bulk of the funding still comes from the federal government, particularly for POEs and their management.

Many public sources of transportation funds in the United States have waned over the past few years, with higher vehicle mileage efficiencies and without a raise of the federal gas tax in more than twenty years. Many areas are now looking to access private funding to complete transportation projects. This is the case in a number of bridges along the Texas-Mexico border and is how the Tijuana Airport cross-border terminal was built and is supported operationally. This raises an important question: If federal officials are paid by private dollars, where does the loyalty sit? Public-private partnerships (PPPs) are great opportunities but must be managed with transparency and with specific guidelines to prevent corruption from entering the system.

In Mexico, the budgeting process is more fluid, with financial needs coming more quickly, but timing can be an issue. There does need to be a more profound analysis of funding resources available for transportation projects in the border beyond this simple description. This is key to understanding transportation networks and institutions along the border. The hope here is to begin the conversation on a very complex issue.

Connected Transportation and the Future of Cross-Border Travel

Anyone who studies governance knows that strong institutions, whether formal or informal, are crucial to planning, implementing, financing, or operating a public policy, program, or project. This is particularly true for transportation infrastructure, which takes a tremendous amount of resources, time, and planning to successfully keep people and trade moving. If a community is unable to do this effectively or efficiently, the overall quality of life in a region is impacted as the overall economy, natural environment, jobs market, education, and health of the people suffer. Dewey and the American pragmatists advocated for institutions to provide a strong structure in society that works for the best society possible to help the individual succeed. These institutions are going to be needed more than ever as technological advances in the transportation sector disrupt how society functions. There will be new jobs created and old ones removed from the system, as the sharing economy increases with smart phones and new applications development. With new electric technologies for vehicles, most importantly as battery storage becomes more efficient, the need for vehicle charging stations will increase. What will this mean for those living and working in the border region? How will charging stations, for example, be coordinated between the two countries? As vehicle automation moves forward, for both passenger and freight vehicles, what will this mean for port-of-entry infrastructure and driving in both countries? Finally, there is a strong need for regulations and structure to manage the use of drones, hyperloop, and other new technologies as they become more part of the mainstream.

As we move into a new century of transportation technologies, public-private partnerships, and the management of the border system, the need for a strong, interconnected network of institutions that embrace border flows needs to be further developed and maintained. As we look at how the current system works, it thrives where there are organizations and institutions as theorized by Dewey. A network of people collaborating under good governance, with laws and regulations to guide the decision-making, can be quite effective. We see from the Border Master Plans and the other specific transportation plans for the region that it is possible to develop a good set of institutions to support needed development. What is missing from other areas of institutional development is the political will to invest in and build out the network further. As a community, the border needs to come together and to build the capacity to adequately respond. Only time will tell if they are successful, and hopefully a proactive approach will be taken in order to improve the quality of life in the region.

Notes

All translations are mine unless otherwise indicated.

1. TEA-21 is the Transportation Equity Act for the 21st Century (1998); SAFETEA-LU is the Safe, Accountable, Flexible, Efficient Transportation Equity Act: A Legacy for Users (2005); MAP-21 is the Moving Ahead for Progress in the 21st Century Act (2012); and FAST Act is the Fixing America's Surface Transportation Act (2015).

2. See the website of the Council of State Governments, https://www.csg.org/.

References

Bertman, Martin A. 2007. *Classical American Pragmatism*. Philosophy Insights. Tirril, UK: Humanities-Ebooks.

Border Trade Alliance (BTA). n.d. "About Us." Accessed May 9, 2020. https://thebta.org/about-us.

Bureau of Transportation Statistics (BTS). n.d. "Transborder Freight Data." Accessed September 17, 2017. https://www.bts.gov/transborder.

Cabrero Mendoza, Enrique. 2013. "Fiscal Federalism in Mexico: Distortions and Structural Traps." *Urban Public Economics Review*, no. 18: 13–37.

Cedillo-Campos, Miguel Gastón, Cuauhtémoc Sanchez-Ramirez, Sharada Vadali, Juan Carlos Villa, and Mozart B. C. Menezes. 2014. "Supply Chain Dynamics and the 'Cross-Border Effect': The U.S.-Mexican Border's Case." *Computers & Industrial Engineering* 72 (June): 261–73.

Collins, Kimberly. 2006. "Local Government Capacity and Quality of Life in the U.S.-Mexican Border: The Case of Calexico and Mexicali." PhD diss., El Colegio de la Frontera Norte, Tijuana, Mexico.

Collins, Kimberly. 2017. "Globalization, Democracy, and Public Space: The Case of the U.S.-Mexican Border Region." *Journal of Public Management and Social Policy* 24 (1): 53–70.

Duran-Fernandez, Roberto. 2014. "Infrastructure Policy in the USA-Mexico Border: Evaluation and Policy Perspectives." *Research in Transportation Economics* 46 (October): 70–102.

Federal Highway Administration (FHWA). 2015. "U.S. Mexico Joint Working Committee on Transportation Planning." Accessed September 16, 2017. https://www.fhwa.dot.gov/planning/border_planning/us_mexico/.

Gerald, Rossano V. 2014. "NAFTA-Transportation Challenges: Case Study U.S.-Mexico." *Journal of International Business and Economics* 2 (1): 1–9.

Gobierno de la República. 2013. "Plan Nacional de Desarrollo, 2013–2018: Program Sectoral de Comunicaciones y Transportes." Accessed September 18, 2017. http://www.sct.gob.mx.

Gobierno del Estado de Sonora. n.d. "Capacitan autoridades de Sonora y Arizona a transportistas de carga en cruce fronterizo." Accessed September 3, 2017. http://sidur.gob.mx.

Hamilton, Stephen. 2010. "Railway to Mexico." *ICIS Chemical Business*, May 24–30.

HDR/HLB Decision Economics Inc. 2006. "Economic Impacts of Wait Times at the San Diego–Baja California Border." Final Report, January 19. https://www.sandag.org/programs/borders/binational/projects/2006_border_wait_impacts_report.pdf.

Huerta, Carla, and Alonso Lugambio. 1994. "NAFTA: Recent Constitutional Amendments, Sovereignty Today, and the Future of Federalism in Mexico." *Constitutional Forum Constitutionnel* 5 (1–4): 63–67.

Ili, Serhan, and Gustav M. Basedow, eds. 2018. *Mobility of the Future: #DigitalOrDead #ConstructiveDisruption*. Karlsruhe, Germany: Ili Consulting LG.

Institute on Taxation and Economic Policy. 2017. "How Long Has It Been Since Your State Raised Its Gas Tax?" July. https://itep.org/wp-content/uploads/gastaxincreases0717.pdf.

Instituto Nacional de Estadística y Geografía (INEGI). 2015. "México en Cifras: Información Nacional por Entidad Federativa y Municipios." https://www.inegi.org.mx/app/areasgeograficas/.

Lacey, Robert J. 2008. *American Pragmatism and Democratic Faith*. Dekalb: Northern Illinois University Press.

McGrath, Michael E. 2018. *Autonomous Vehicles: Opportunities, Strategies, and Disruptions*. n.p.: independently published.

Mendez, Jose Luis, and Mauricio I. Dussauge-Laguna, eds. 2017. *Policy Analysis in Mexico*. Bristol, UK: Policy Press.

Nunez, Jenifer. 2016. "Agreement Reached to Reconstruct the U.S.-Mexico Desert Line Railroad." *Railway Track & Structures*, July 10. https://www.rtands.com/freight/shortline-regional/agreement-reached-to-reconstruct-the-us-mexico-desert-line-railroad/.

Protego-Evercore Partners. 2007. "Competitiveness and Areas of Opportunity in the Border Region." Report for the 35th Border Governors Conference. Mexico City, Mex.

Robinson, Anne G., and James H. Bookfinder. 2007. "NAFTA Supply Chains: Facilities Location and Logistics." *International Transactions in Operational Research* 14 (2): 179–99.

Sciara, Gian-Claudia. 2017. "Metropolitan Transportation Planning: Lessons from the Past, Institutions for the Future." *Journal of the American Planning Association* 83 (3): 262–76.

Texas Department of Transportation. 2014. "Regional Mobility Authorities: A Partnership for Progress." November. http://ftp.dot.state.tx.us/pub/txdot-info/tpp/rma/report.pdf.

U.S. Census Bureau. n.d. "QuickFacts." Accessed September 8, 2017. http://www.census.gov/quickfacts.

U.S. Department of Transportation (DOT). n.d. "U.S.-Mexico Border Planning Fact Sheet." Federal Highway Administration. Accessed May 9, 2020. https://www.fhwa.dot.gov/planning/border_planning/factsheets/mexico_fact_sheet.cfm.

U.S. Department of Transportation (DOT). n.d. "U.S.-Mexico Joint Working Committee on Transportation Planning." Federal Highway Administration. Accessed May 9, 2020. https://www.fhwa.dot.gov/planning/border_planning/us_mexico/master_plans/.

U.S. Government Accountability Office (GAO). 2016. "U.S. Border Communities: Ongoing DOT Efforts Could Help Address Impacts of International Freight Rail." January. https://www.gao.gov/assets/680/674851.pdf.

Walker, Richard M., and Peter Hills. 2012. "Partnership Characteristics, Network Behavior, and Publicness: Evidence on the Performance of Sustainable Development Projects." *International Public Management Journal* 15 (4): 479–99.

11

Human Mobility at the U.S.-Mexico Border

Tony Payan, Pamela L. Cruz, and Carla Pederzini Villarreal

The U.S.-Mexico border is a complex region. The geography itself is a good indicator of this complexity. For example, the *borderline* between the two countries runs nearly two thousand miles from San Diego and Tijuana on the Pacific coastline of the continent to Brownsville and Matamoros on the Gulf of Mexico. The *border region* reflects that complexity even more so—whether it is defined as a territorial band along the borderline or the counties and *municipios* (municipalities) that lie adjacent to it or even as the ten states that border each other (see chapter 2 by Payan and Cruz). Beyond the geographical dimension, the aboveground activity is staggering. There is in fact little doubt that the U.S.-Mexico border region is one of the most economically and demographically dynamic areas in the world, even if, and perhaps because, it has one of the largest gaps in terms of average real income between neighboring territories (Clemens 2016; Moré 2011). Indeed, the *cross-border* activity that takes place in the region includes one of the highest levels of human and vehicle mobility on the planet—including documented mobility (Bureau of Transportation Statistics n.d.) *and* undocumented migration. Regulating and managing human mobility across the border is one of the most cumbersome parts of governing the border. It involves extensive collaboration among federal, state, and local authorities and many different agencies and civil society groups, all of which must necessarily, and sometimes unwillingly, cooperate to ensure that cross-border mobility is both legal and legitimate and undocumented mobility is both reduced to a minimum and prevented from affecting the binational relationship. The U.S. and Mexican governments have not always seen eye to eye on the issue of human mobility, but over time they have had to find ways to collaborate to attempt to balance security and prosperity when dealing with the desire and aspirations of borderlanders (and those who come from beyond) to have access to one side or the other.

If we focus on the dimensions of human cross-border movement—the object of this chapter—it is easy to see the kind of organizational, budgetary, and normative investment effort that has to go into regulating border crossing on a day-to-day basis. Each year, more than 250 million northbound pedestrian and passenger entries pass through the United States land border ports of entry (POEs), including individual visitors, tourists, shoppers, students, workers, and so on, and millions of vehicles, trains, and trucks carrying hundreds of millions of dollars' worth of trade—nearly US$721 billion in trade in 2017 (GAO 2019a). This is of course mirrored by the southbound traffic. Viewed this way, it is then evident that individual border crossings in both directions surpass the populations of both countries combined. This cross-border dynamism is not new. During the entire twentieth century, the region became a magnet for people from all over Mexico and beyond, as they reconceived the borderline as a resource and the place as a land of opportunity (Sohn 2013). American corporations also viewed the border as a resource and relocated much of their economic activities to border towns such as Tijuana, Ciudad Juárez, Nuevo Laredo, and Reynosa. They also sent thousands of American managers, engineers, and workers to labor in those factories, and many of them cross the border, often several times a day. Many U.S. businesses practically survive thanks to the economic activities of Mexican citizens shopping on the U.S. side of the borderline. At the same time, given the evident attractiveness of the border region, for several decades beginning in the 1960s, the population on the Mexican side of the border grew more rapidly than any other region in the country, although the border region now has roughly 7.5 million people on each side thanks largely to the San Diego metropolitan region's nearly three million residents. On the Mexican side, demographic growth was clearly directly related to proximity to the United States and the population is largely concentrated in a few municipios, including Tijuana, Juárez, Reynosa, and Matamoros (Ybáñez Zepeda 2008). On the U.S. side, population growth was largely a gradual phenomenon, partly driven by population drift from the interior of the United States but especially by Mexican migration to the borderlands—most residents on the U.S. side of the border, for example, are of Mexican origin. All this raises important questions regarding cross-border human mobility and the way it has come to be governed over time, including the nature and character of the institutional scaffolding that is currently in place to do so. To be sure, we do not want to solely focus on undocumented migration, although it is an important part of the chapter. There are many books and articles that have explored that issue (Cornelius and Lewis 2006; Heyman 2014; LeMay 2007; Nevins 2010; Payan 2016). We want to focus on the whole experience of human mobility at the U.S.-Mexico border, how it is currently governed, and what institutions participate in that governance.

Thus, in this chapter, we first focus on providing a historical overview of the way the border has been seen in terms of it being a place where people want to be and the kind of access they want to have across the border for numerous reasons, and of the main regulations and policies that have affected human mobility across the line. In that sense, we want to focus on how it went from a labor issue to a law enforcement issue, and how it has shifted to a national security issue—each stage with important implications for borderlanders and for the way bureaucrats charged with managing human mobility have behaved. We then move to explore the main institutions—including the bureaucracies or organizations themselves—tasked with regulating cross-border mobility, and discuss their progression, challenges, and opportunities for deeper collaboration in an increasingly mobilized world. We assume here that the intensity of human mobility is not the problem. The problem, we hypothesize, is the fact that the system has not provided for legal and legitimate mechanisms for human mobility more in tune with the needs of borderlanders and the needs of both countries in terms of their relationship. Restriction has in fact made the border, we argue, less governable rather than more, and it has increased the cost of the border as a transaction, when it could have been a much better-run place with high-efficiency gains for everyone involved. Finally, it is important to note that the chapter examines both documented and undocumented flows of people and ends with a discussion on the growing interconnectedness of the United States and Mexico; it focuses on the undocumented migrants not specifically as a problem but as a result of the inability of both countries to facilitate mobility along integrative lines rather than punitive lines. We also assume that the future of human mobility governance must accommodate a modern and just cross-border paradigm that strengthens border security but also facilitates trade and travel for the twenty-first-century border. We argue that criminalizing human mobility is counterproductive, costly, and very likely unnecessary.

Measuring the dynamics of human mobility at the border is a challenging task, given the hundreds of millions of persons, vehicles, trucks, trains, and planes that cross the border every year. One of the main limitations we face in measuring this kind of human activity—all of which must be done at least in theory securely and efficiently—relates to the uneven gathering of data, which limits the analysis of the back-and-forth flows of the border region. This does not mean, however, that attempts to measure cross-border movement at the U.S.-Mexico border have not been attempted.

The majority of Mexican visitors arriving to the United States come to shop, and several studies have focused on measuring the economic impact of Mexican visitors and their cross-border shopping activities (Cañas, Coronado, and Phillips 2006; Ghaddar and Brown 2005). Some studies at the regional and local level have used survey data and personal interviews to determine cross-border spending characteristics of Mexican shoppers and the economic impact of wait times at POEs (Nivin 2013; Pavlakovich-Kochi and Charney 2008; Roberts et al. 2014; SANDAG 2006; Sharma et al. 2018). Also, since 1995, the Bureau of Transportation Statistics (BTS) has maintained "Border Crossing/Entry Data" (BTS n.d.), which provides summary statistics for inbound crossings with data provided by the U.S. Customs and Border Protection (CBP). Data collected is available for trucks, trains, containers, buses, personal vehicles, passengers, and pedestrians. On the Mexican side, however, the Instituto Nacional de Migración (INM, National Migration Institute), which provides data on registered entries into Mexico, has not yet implemented a comprehensive system to count the number of crossings. This is evident when one crosses into Mexico, which does not require a passport or ID check, unless one is to travel beyond border towns. It is simply assumed that southbound traffic mirrors northbound traffic, and that the difference is not significant enough to require replicating the northbound data collection system. Thus, even though actions like the North American Free Trade Agreement (NAFTA) brought about a more closely monitored border when it comes to mobility, due to shortage of infrastructure, technology, and human and budgetary resources, a high percentage of entries into Mexico are still not registered—and very often the data may exist, but it is not made publicly available in the same interactive way in which the U.S. government makes the data available through the BTS system.

It is also important to note that each entry recorded by BTS does not represent a unique traveler, and a single traveler may cross multiple times (GAO 2019a). This is the case for many people in the borderlands, who cross up to multiple times *per day* to live, work, attend school, visit family, shop across the border, and conduct business on both sides of the border. With the lack of harmonized data on entries from both governments, we are left to assume that the southbound traffic mirrors the northbound traffic, with the assumption that most border crossers are routine travelers and whoever travels one way is likely to travel the other way. That may be fine, but it still lacks precision in the sense that many who travel one way may simply not return or may use a different means of returning—someone traveling to Mexico City from Tijuana but who came to Tijuana from San Diego, for example, may travel back to the United States from Mexico City to another U.S. airport. Consequently, all these methodologies have serious problems—even if they are probably good enough to understand the general dimensions of cross-border human mobility. These two approximations or estimates (border resident population sampling and northbound-southbound mirroring) of cross-border mobility are more closely related to the territorial definition of the border than the simple but easier count of whom and what crosses the borderline measured by document checks and technological devices—which the United States does collect, with the complication of not being able to count accurately those who cross without documents, between POEs, and go undetected.

Regardless of the problem of territorial and demographic definitions and the accuracy of the statistics, or the method employed, the numbers are staggering. The U.S.-Mexico border is evidently the busiest border in the world in terms of sheer individual crossings. That in and of itself merits a good understanding of the institutional scaffolding that currently governs cross-border human mobility, especially if we are to propose public policies that can manage that traffic more efficiently, in a less costly fashion, and more facilitating of the aspirations of all borderlanders and the needs of both countries.

In other words, there are several reasons why a solid understanding of human mobility and its governance at the U.S.-Mexico border is important. First, policies that regulate human mobility at the border shape the intense relation between two countries. It is along the border that these policies governing trade flows, foreign investment, migration enforcement, antiterrorism, and security controls materialize (Gerber, Lara-Valencia, and de la Parra 2010). It is, so to speak, where the rubber meets the road. Thus, understanding how these hundreds of millions of individual crossings are managed is important to ensure that the right policies are in place to make the border work for the prosperity and security of both countries. Second, more than a billion dollars of commercial activity a day crosses the border between the United States and Mexico, and the economic well-being of millions of people now depends on the seamless movement of these flows (Murphy 2019). The institutions that govern these exchanges bear the burden of monitoring these flows but also facilitating them to reduce the transaction costs at the border—for example, wait times at POEs for people, vehicles, and goods. This is more pressing because Mexico and the United States do not just sell goods to each other. Through a process known as production sharing, companies on both sides of the border work together to manufacture goods with materials crossing back and forth between factories on both sides of the border, sometimes several times. NAFTA—which led to a follow-on free trade agreement, the United States-Mexico-Canada Agreement (USMCA)—has spurred the creation of a continent-wide production chain whose disruption would be economically catastrophic to both countries. These chains now depend on legal and orderly governance of all traffic, including human mobility. Finally, it is important to understand the historical evolution of the institutions that normalize and regulate cross-border mobility in order to prevent the border from becoming a hostage to policies that are less than helpful and guide the border to become a prosperous and secure region for both countries. The latest rhetoric around immigration is an example of how the border can sometimes become the focus of political profiteering. A big-picture understanding of what works and what does not work can shield the border and protect the interests of borderlanders.

A Historical Overview of Human Mobility Regulation at the U.S.-Mexico Border

Although the U.S.-Mexico border has a long history of territorial changes, the near-final settlement of the borderline occurred soon after the Mexican-American War of 1846–48 and the Gadsden Purchase of 1853. The rest of the land exchanges have been minor and obey mostly riverine shifts along the Texas-Mexico border (Wilson 1980). The Treaty of Guadalupe Hidalgo, which settled the war and largely laid out the borderline, stipulated that Mexicans living in what is now the southwestern United States would be able to choose to stay and become U.S. citizens or migrate to Mexico. For the next six decades, however, Mexicans were able to move largely unimpeded across the border, although the vast migration of European Americans slowly marginalized them and consolidated their hold on land and resources in the region. This was not an era free of problems for Mexican Americans, as there were periods of lynchings and expulsions and the increasing enforcement of land confiscations.

It was in the early twentieth century, however, that Mexicans began arriving in greater numbers into the United States, especially into Texas and California. After the Mexican Revolution began at the end of 1910, as many as one million Mexicans may have sought refuge in the United States (Johnson 2018). This is an important first wave of Mexican migration to the United States, one that would leave an important mark in the southwestern United States. Moreover, during the 1920s, Mexicans were also excluded from national quotas in U.S. immigration laws and regulations. This further incentivized crossing the border freely—to work and to live. The anti-immigration sentiments of the early twentieth century, however, would eventually reach Mexican migration and provoked the United States to attempt to control cross-border human mobility more strictly. Several measures were slowly implemented to control it. First, the Texas Rangers, who patrolled the border between that state and Mexico, primarily to stop alcohol smuggling, began to enforce rules precluding entry between checkpoints much more strictly. By 1924 the United States Border Patrol (USBP) was created to effectively enforce all traffic between ports of entry (Payan 2016, 128). It is in that decade that it became illegal to cross the border between POE. Finally, in 1929 Mexicans needed a visa to enter the United States. This would not stop Mexicans from moving across the border relatively freely, but it did become more complicated to do so. By the early 1930s, under pressure from the Great Depression and increasing unemployment and economic hardship, half a million of these migrants and refugees were returned to Mexico—many of them forcibly and others voluntarily, but hundreds of thousands stayed behind and became the vibrant Mexican American communities that Texas, New Mexico, and California have today. This ebb and flow would characterize cross-border mobility throughout the twentieth century.

World War II, however, brought a considerable labor shortage to U.S. factories and agricultural fields. This fact would reverse the migration flow again, formalizing it under the guest worker program known as the Bracero Program of 1942—a guest worker program that was to last through 1964. As many as five million Mexican citizens participated in it—many of them eventually settling in the United States and adding to the Mexican American population in the United States. Further cementing the idea that Mexican migration has followed economic up- and downturns in the United States, the 1950s rise in unemployment saw massive deportations to Mexico, even as the Bracero Program continued. This massive repatriation project, known as Operation Wetback, sent as many as one million Mexicans across the border. Paradoxically, the end of the Bracero Program in 1964 only encouraged Mexicans to continue to cross without documents, and the undocumented population of Mexican origin in the United States grew enormously (Espenshade 1995). At this point, however, immigration law enforcement was not yet what it is today, and the many relations that Mexican laborers had developed with their employers under the Bracero Program continued, but without papers (Massey and Pren 2012). This further demonstrated two key issues with Mexican cross-border mobility. First, despite new laws, regulations, and agencies—institutions—enforcing immigration and cross-border human mobility, the phenomenon more closely followed U.S. economic performance than the creation of the institutions themselves. The economic incentives to move across the border simply proved to be a more formidable channel shaping human mobility across the border. And many of these Mexican laborers, additionally, stayed in the United States after a while or had U.S.-born children, many of whom still live in the Southwest and beyond. Second, institutions regulating human mobility seem to have created flows that became criminalized over time, even when they served the economic interest of the United States. The increasing law enforcement character of the immigration institutional scaffolding clashed with the economic dynamism of the country, creating a conflict in governance paradigms.

The end of the Bracero Program corresponded exactly with a rise of undocumented migration as avenues for legal entry diminished (Massey and Pren 2012). Other actions, such as amendments enacted by Congress to the Immigration and Nationality Act—annual and hemispheric caps and country quotas—left temporary migrants with little to no legal avenues to enter and work in the United States (Massey and Pren 2012; Orrenius and Zavodny 2012). President Ronald Reagan responded to popular anger around undocumented migration by signing immigration legislation into law, the Immigration Reform and Control Act (IRCA), which granted permanent residency to around 2.8 million undocumented residents, increased border enforcement funding, imposed civil criminal penalties on employers who hired undocumented workers, and established the H2A-H2B programs for temporary agriculture workers and other temporary seasonal workers (Chishti, Meissner, and Bergeron 2011). Circular migration, however, was a reality on the ground. Institutional weakness and lax law enforcement allowed people to enter the United States, work without authorization, and return to Mexico. But the number of people settling in the United States between 1964 and 1986 did tick up. It further accelerated in the 1980s and even more so in the 1990s because of severe economic dislocations caused by NAFTA in Mexico and more draconian enforcement after the mid-1990s. By the 1990s, the United States had increased immigration enforcement between POEs and began to deploy additional technology at POEs as well. But borderlanders and other arrivals did not stop crossing the border. If they succeeded, given stiffer law enforcement, many simply stayed. Thus, the increasingly restrictive nature of U.S. cross-border mobility was largely responsible for a considerable increase in the undocumented population within the United States. This further shows that Mexican cross-border migration kept a close but complicated relationship with both economic performance and policy and law enforcement along the borderline. It also shows that criminalizing migration, instead of building institutions that index it to the economic dynamism of both countries and crafting smart policies that enable legal and orderly mobility, is likely to produce more problems than it solves.

The September 11, 2001, terrorist attacks on the United States gave rise to growing border control and militarization and association between terror and immigration, which would have enormous repercussions for cross-border governance. The result of linking these two was a new impetus in the reinforcement of the institutions dedicated to restricting cross-border mobility, despite the fact the terrorist attacks happened far away from the southwest border. Yet it spurred a massive border security industrial complex—interweaved with dozens of agencies, partnerships, investments, multinational corporations and industries, partnerships, funding, binational/international agreements—to militarize and "secure" and "control" the border (Payan 2016). It is noteworthy, however, to point out that as the United States increased immigration enforcement, human smugglers became more organized and charged additional fees to guide undocumented migrants across the border—presumably the premium charged for the higher risk of being caught. This in turn incentivized new entrants into human smuggling. Thus, the increasingly punitive system appeared to have simply added to the hardship of migrant workers but also to have incentivized more rapacious activity around undocumented migration. This is a lesson that cannot be lost in any future migration/human mobility reform. Government punitive approaches sometimes create additional conditions that incentivize entry into the business of illegality. Unfortunately, this approach would get even worse after September 11.

On March 1, 2003, the Homeland Security Act of 2002 created the U.S. Department of Homeland Security (DHS)—which consolidated the two main border agencies, U.S. Customs Service and the Immigration and Naturalization Service (INS)—along with twenty other separate federal agencies into a unified agency (DHS n.d.). The DHS assumed immigration responsibilities, with functions under three agencies: U.S. Citizenship and Immigration Services (USCIS), U.S. Customs and Border Protection (CBP), and U.S. Immigration and Customs Enforcement (ICE). New rules on admissibility and inadmissibility were put into place; more agents were hired to guard the border; new technology was deployed to monitor the borderline and the POEs; and new barriers were erected and reinforced, starting with the Secure Fence Act of 2006, which funded the 650 miles of barriers that exist today. Anti-immigration sentiments continued to grow, and a new restrictionism force has overtaken the debate on immigration, making it impossible to pass immigration reform despite many efforts and, more recently, with the election of Donald J. Trump to the presidency, refocusing all political attention on building a wall between Mexico and the United States. Lately Mexico has agreed to sign the harshly questioned Migrant Protection Protocols (MPP), a one-sided U.S. policy that states that asylum seekers must wait in Mexico for a U.S. court to decide whether their request proceeds. Mexico's ability to provide safe and dignified conditions for applicants has been singled out by border lawyers and activists as part of Washington's deterrent against the growing number of applications from Central America. The result is that for nearly a century, the U.S. government has built a governance regime whose objective has been to restrict human mobility at the border and to stem immigration from Mexico and increasingly from Central America as more people from that region try to make their way north. Many of the demographic and economic anxieties the country has experienced over the last decades have become focalized on the border, affecting the ability of borderlanders to take advantage of the border as a resource and the opportunities that cross-border differentials offer in shopping, working, tourism, and even trade. The U.S. government has not been able to distinguish among different types of human mobility and create a nuanced system to be able to facilitate cross-border mobility—although there are some programs that point the way, and which will be discussed later.

Interestingly, throughout the increasing barriers to northbound mobility, Mexico has remained a relatively open border. Americans, Mexicans, and Mexican Americans continue to visit Mexico with few or no restrictions to the south side of the borderline. Mexico continues to be a place where many borderlanders from both sides find entertainment, health care, and even schooling with few restrictions. Passports now required to cross the border are not a Mexican requirement for cross-border mobility. They are needed instead to return to the United States.

Institutions Governing Human Mobility at the U.S.-Mexico Border

The previous discussion makes two things evident. The first is that the single most powerful actor governing cross-border human mobility is the government of the United States. All laws, norms, regulations, technological deployment, document requirements, and so forth governing human mobility are those introduced by the United States. Mexico's requirements for cross-border mobility remain relatively low—and minimal in the case of those who travel within the immediate border area (approximately twenty kilometers [12.4 miles] into Mexico) without the need to obtain a visitor's permit (Forma Migratoria Múltiple [FMM, Multiple Migratory Form]). Second, the organizing principle that underlies U.S. governance of cross-border mobility is the criminalization of mobility—it relies primarily on law enforcement and a punitive approach to even minor violations of human mobility. It has, in fact, historically moved from viewing cross-border mobility as a largely economic phenomenon to a problem of law enforcement and today to a problem of national security. Without delinking these concepts, governing human mobility across the border will likely continue to make the border a difficult place to live and a costly transaction for all involved. If one examines the institutions that govern cross-border human mobility, it is clear that they are increasingly castigatory institutions, with very few considerations for the facilitation of such human mobility and increasingly without a thought to the idea that the border is a resource and could be run differently. Having said this, it is worth looking at the more specific institutional norms that govern the ability to cross the border freely.

This is further reinforced by the sheer number of institutions that participate in the governance of cross-border mobility. The institutions, understood as laws, norms, regulations, practices, and organizations that oversee a field of action, in this case human mobility, and which encompass all flows between and through nations' POEs—air, land, and sea—are numerous. The bureaucrats who participate in their enforcement are in the tens of thousands—a veritable small army. Some have to do with persons crossing, while others focus on merchandise, capital, strategic goods and services, and so on. In the end, these institutions govern all flows between the U.S.-Mexico border. Moreover, this myriad of institutions that directly oversee cross-border people and services and goods crossing the borderline are at the federal, state, and local levels, and the number of policies crisscross many different issue areas—infrastructure, migration, tourism and shopping, labor markets, security, and so forth. When someone crosses the border, for example, toward the United States, some of the major institutions that intervene or may have intervened are the U.S. Department of State (DOS) and the DHS, both of which handle the bulk responsibility for human mobility issues—the first issuing the right documentation and the second ensuring that no U.S. laws are violated in the act of border crossing. But there are many other federal institutions and agencies with responsibilities to immigration aspects and movement of people, such as the U.S. Department of Justice (DOJ), the Transportation Security Administration (TSA), the U.S. Department of Labor (DOL), the Federal Bureau of Investigation (FBI), the U.S. Social Security Administration (SSA), the U.S. Department of Health and Human Services (HHS), and the International Revenue Service (IRS), to name a few. Local governments may also have a say on infrastructure building and management, along with the General Services Administration (GSA). State authorities may also participate inasmuch as they must ensure that individuals and vehicles that cross the border comply with state laws. Even private contractors may participate, as they offer different services for maintenance, monitoring, and so on. And even then, cross-border activity is not deterred. It is massive, and it is difficult for all these agencies to monitor a substantive part of what crosses the border. At most a smaller percentage of all individuals and especially of all cargo are fully inspected.

A key consequence of the many institutional mechanisms and the many agencies involved at all levels is that the border has become nearly all about law enforcement. Even when the actors governing border crossings are well coordinated, their focus has been on ensuring that all laws and regulations are complied with, ultimately paying little mind to the costs to borderlanders and any other border users. The result is a system that is run primarily through law enforcement at the expense of efficiency, convenience, and a reduction of costs. But even so, the resources would never be enough to balance these two kinds of interests. At the end of the day, the border is choked but illegal drugs and undocumented migrants—the two major issues that are often cited as the justification for authoritarian and punitive border management—still make it through (Payan 2016). So far, in fact, there is no sign that drugs have been prevented from making it to the U.S. markets, although it has become more difficult to cross the border without documents.

The next two sections are divided to explore the coordinated complexity of managing the U.S.-Mexico border to handle cross-border flows of goods and people both *at* and *between* border ports of entry. Major agencies, agreements, initiatives, enforcement actions, policies, challenges, and opportunities are discussed.

Legal and Legitimate Mobility at the Ports of Entry

Undocumented immigration at the U.S.-Mexico border has taken over the headlines in the last couple of years, has monopolized the largest portions of border management budgets, and has drawn most of the political attention. It is imperative to remember and acknowledge that the overwhelming majority of cross-border flows are legal, legitimate, and duly documented. Through the ports of entry (POE), hundreds of millions of persons and vehicles cross every year, all in compliance with the requirements imposed by the U.S. government. The number of undocumented entries is in fact a small number when compared to documented entries. Most entries take place through the legal POEs at the U.S.-Mexico border, not between them, and if the number of undocumented entries is divided by the number of legal and legitimate traffic, the problem of illegality is in fact less than a quarter of a percentage point of all border crossings. This is true everywhere, all along the border. For example, the busiest land border crossing in the Western Hemisphere is the San Ysidro Land Port of Entry (LPOE), which processes an average of seventy thousand northbound vehicle passengers and twenty thousand northbound pedestrians *per day* (GSA 2019) and sees only a few thousand attempts at border crossing without documents per year. That scenario is reproduced at almost every region of the two-thousand-mile border.

The lead inspection agency at the border is U.S. Customs and Border Protection (CBP), within the Department of Homeland Security. The CBP is the federal agency responsible for the complex dual mission of protecting the borders of the United States and facilitating legitimate trade and travel. The CBP houses three operational components—the Office of Field Operations (OFO), the U.S. Border Patrol (USBP), and the Air and Marine Operations (AMO)—and works *at* and *between* U.S. borders and certain overseas locations (GAO 2019c). The Office of Field Operations, however, is the largest component in the CBP, and it manages all lawful trade and travel at the U.S. border POEs. The USBP is responsible for securing the U.S. border areas between POEs. The CBP employs more than forty-five thousand law enforcement agents across its three operational components, yet it faces many challenges in recruiting, hiring, and retaining its personnel (GAO 2019c).

On the Mexican side, where the primary goal is tax collection, the CBP's counterparts are primarily the Servicio de Administración Tributaria (SAT, Tax Administration Service) and the Aduanas de México (Mexican Customs Authority) as well as the Instituto Nacional de Migración (INM, National Migration Institute), which grants permits to those who wish to travel further south into the country. These are the agencies seen operating at every POE, and they are sometimes indistinguishable from each other until the border crosser must engage one of them in a particular transaction—a tax payment, a travel permit, or some other action. Interestingly, the Mexican government has installed equipment at the POEs, much of which consists of vehicle barriers and cameras, but vehicles and individuals are checked only occasionally and under the complete discretionary authority of the agent who may want to perform an inspection. It has been estimated that Mexican customs officials inspect only 8 percent of traffic crossing into Mexico (Binational Task Force on the United States–Mexico Border 2011, 14). Much of the attention of Mexican border agents tends to go toward vehicles or individuals carrying obvious loads of merchandise from the United States to Mexico—further making evident the tax collection purposes of the Mexican authorities. This lax attitude toward individuals traveling in vehicles and on foot is what often facilitates U.S. criminals and fugitives crossing into Mexico to find haven from law enforcement. It may also facilitate gun and cash smuggling.

However, it was not until 2001, after the terrorist attacks on the U.S. East Coast, that Mexico began changing its border control, responding particularly to pressure from the United States and the potential threat of shutting down borders for national security purposes (Marchand 2017). This led to a greater partnership between Mexico and the United States to address key issues at the southwest border. In 2002, the U.S. and Mexican governments announced a joint action plan called the U.S.-Mexico Border Partnership Agreement (also known as the Smart Border Plan) with the purpose of addressing border security issues through investments in infrastructure and plans to ensure the efficient flow of goods and people (CRS 2006).

The issue of efficiency is not lost in the American bureaucracy, of course. The United States began efforts to invest and expand Trusted Traveler Programs to expedite the flow of preapproved travelers and cargo. Risk-based programs such as the Secure Electronic Network for Travelers Rapid Inspection (SENTRI), Free and Secure Trade (FAST), Global Entry, and NEXUS (only Canada) were designed and implemented for U.S. citizens and foreign nationals (GAO 2014). For example, the SENTRI program allows those enrolled to cross the border via designated commuter lanes (DCLs). The crossing of the border is relatively easy, and the number of inspections is considerably fewer, although the penalties for violating this government-given trust are higher if this privilege is abused. The DCL program consists of paying for the FBI to conduct a full background check on the program user and, if the individual is deemed trustworthy, he or she is issued a special identification, which can be used to cross at designated lanes at certain POEs. It is indeed a privilege but made possible only through heavy lobbying by certain communities and by the ability of the U.S. government to separate certain individuals from the bulk of the cross-border traffic. Of course, such privilege is not easily accessible to many other individuals because the Mexican government charges heavily for the privilege of using the lane itself. An individual who has been "cleared" by the United States to use that lane must disburse around US$300 per year to the Mexican government to be allowed to use this privilege. That is prohibitive to many border users, most of whom must use the regular lanes and wait sometimes several hours to be able to enter the United States. In the end, the DCL program is an important lens for understanding priorities. Whereas the United States allows only individuals who have passed a strict background check to use those lanes, Mexico allows any individual who can pay the annual fee to use it. This program marries American security interests with Mexican tax collection interests. In the end, however, it works, but it reinforces the privileges created by the borderline itself.

To be sure, there have been some recent attempts at coordinating cross-border mobility in relation to trade. The goal is to maintain a strict security regime in place but to eke out efficiencies from a better-coordinated border trade management system—which of course includes hundreds of thousands of truck drivers (Jones and Seghetti 2015). Although the United States and Mexico have not systematically sought effectively to manage the border jointly, particularly because of historical distrust and U.S. suspicions of corruption by Mexican border authorities, there are nascent efforts in places like Tijuana and San Diego to establish joint mechanisms for the management of cross-border flows, including those composed of persons. Additionally, the Tijuana international airport, which lies right along the borderline, now has a bridge specifically dedicated to individuals from San Diego, whose airport is too small and is unable to expand to accommodate international travel, and who want to travel from Tijuana to other parts of Mexico or even Asia by using the Tijuana airport. This effort has resulted in the Cross Border Xpress mechanism, an investment of some US$120 million USD that has yet to become profitable.[1] Similarly, both states, California and Baja California, have recently tried innovative mechanisms to jointly inspect cross-border cargo—joint customs inspections—although they have yet to find ways to facilitate crossings by persons. At the Otay Mesa, a new port of entry between San Diego and Tijuana, joint inspections are already taking place (Dibble 2017). This requires that all drivers be registered and cleared in advance, taking them off the regular trade lines and expediting their cross-border activities. These mechanisms, which are clearly collaborative efforts for border management, are few and far between. Some of them are experimental but over time can possibly evolve into more sophisticated mechanisms to manage the border jointly—as functionalist theories would predict. Even so, any such mechanism will be done on U.S. terms, prioritizing security above all.

The law enforcement and more punitive focus of U.S. border management when it comes to individuals who use the border is not entirely void of efforts to facilitate and make border crossings more efficient. The United States has gradually moved the documentation required for border crossing to more sophisticated technologies that, presumably, permit easy identification of the individuals approaching the border and, in theory, facilitate agents' ability to detect problem persons before they reach the inspection booth. New passports and other documents include radio frequency identification (RFID) technologies, for example. Such documents are relatively good at detecting potential problems and, ideally, moving those individuals who raise red flags to secondary inspection without interfering with the rest of the traffic (GAO 2019b). Part of the problem with border management of persons crossing is that there is little trust between U.S. and Mexican agencies. The transgovernmental networks that have developed around the issue of drug trafficking are far from developing in the area of human mobility management.

An important concession made by the United States has been the establishment of programs created to separate trusted travelers and trade from those that might need to be double-checked or even barred from access to the United States, according to the Department of Homeland Security. The SENTRI and FAST programs, among others, are designed to collect data on individuals who apply to those programs and use that data to screen threats, although it might also serve to expedite the crossing of participants (GAO 2019b). However, although there are trusted traveler and safe cargo programs for travelers and shippers that permit low-risk crossings of people and shipments, there are still long lines to cross the border in both directions—and more so as the United States checks every traveler as they enter back through the POEs.

Even so, cross-border traffic has not decreased, and there is, for example, a long list of visa types that borderlanders are making use of to accomplish their individual goals. The visa system is quite complex and involves the visas given in Table 11.1 among the most used (see DOS n.d. for a complete list of nonimmigrant and immigrant visa categories).

It is worth reiterating that nearly all border crossers do so legitimately and legally, most using one of the visas or documents shown in Table 11.1. However, possessing one of these visas or passports does not save one from waiting to cross the POE northbound to the United States or southbound to Mexico. The border region has a population of around fifteen million, and it is expected to double in size by 2025 (HHS n.d.). This population growth, however, points to additional problems. If the resident population at the border is projected to increase, why is it taking longer and longer to cross the border? Inspection times have become lengthier and border authorities have not figured out how to sort out the admissible population from the nonadmissible population in a way that facilitates border crossing by those who can exercise that right. The U.S. Government Accountability Office (GAO) has reported several challenges and actions necessary for CBP to improve in this regard—infrastructure and staffing needs, better data collection methodologies, outcome-oriented performance measures to determine the extent of trade, and travel facilitation, to name a few (GAO 2013, 2019a). Increased wait times may also point to the fact that the system itself is becoming less efficient. This inefficiency, in the long run, is unsustainable. But the political environment does not allow for additional experimentation with innovative organizational and technological devices to facilitate human mobility—or to allow residents to flow freely back and forth unencumbered, at least within a certain territorial band along the borderline. This idea is something that will likely have to wait many more decades. The focus today appears to be on the border wall and adding barriers— something that is not likely to change, at least not under the Trump administration.

TABLE 11.1 Most common visa types (and documents) used by border residents

Visa type	Purpose
B1-B2 and Border Crossing Card (BCC): both a BCC and a B1/B2 visitor's visa (also referred to as a DSP-150)	Border resident, tourism, shopping business (visa category B-1), tourism (visa category B-2), or a combination of both purposes (B-1/B-2)
J	Exchange visitor
F and M	Student
H1B	Professional or specialized worker
TN/TD	NAFTA-originated visa for professional and specialized workers
H2A and H2B	Temporary agricultural workers or temporary seasonal workers
E	Treaty trader (E-1) and treaty investor (E-2)
Green Card	Legal permanent resident
Passport	U.S. citizen

Source: DOS n.d.

Illegal and Illegitimate Cross-Border Human Flows

During the second decade of this century, Mexican irregular migration—undocumented border crossers—to the United States has slowed considerably, and since 2016, there have been more apprehensions of non-Mexicans at the southwest border (Gonzalez-Barrera and Krogstad 2019). At the same time, the resources in terms of budget, personnel, technology, and barriers have increased exponentially. The CBP's second operation component, the USBP, is charged with dealing with this population. Agents are deployed all along the border and their ability to control the borderline, mile by mile, has increased considerably. It is fair to say that the border is now under almost full operational control. It is increasingly difficult to cross the border without papers between ports of entry. The USBP now has an array of technological devices that have allowed it to detect more of these border jumpers and apprehend them (GAO 2018). This operational control has also expanded well into the United States, where ICE is charged with interior enforcement. In all, these two agencies have made it more difficult not only to cross the border without documents but also to live and work in the United States without papers. The activities of these two agencies, along with the CBP's activities at the POEs, however, continue to prop up the law enforcement and national security orientation of the overall human mobility policy space at the U.S.-Mexico border. Other potentially useful approaches, such as labor market integration, have been excluded for the most part. Even minor violations often draw the most draconian of punishments by border management agents.

This is not to say that the border is under full control just yet. Even if most undocumented border crossers are caught, some issues remain—especially and probably because the United States and Mexico have not sought to figure out how to manage human mobility under a different logic, one that appeals to a bilateral rather than a unilateral framework and one that appeals to economic integration rather than law enforcement and national security. An important part of the problem today is that migration to the United States from other countries—which transits through Mexico, mainly from Guatemala, Honduras, and El Salvador—has increased (Pederzini et al. 2015). This has renewed the call for further restrictions in cross-border human mobility—including keeping Central American asylum seekers in Mexico while their cases are processed in the United States. In this regard, it is important to note that the case of "apprehensions" of asylum seekers—a crisis that we have seen in the last five years at the border, beginning in 2014 and ebbing and flowing continuously—is different from the case of undocumented border crossers (DHS 2017, 17). These asylum seekers are not primarily trying to breach the border barriers or fences between ports of entry and cross undetected. They are mostly turning themselves in to CBP agents, both OFO officers and Border Patrol agents (Human Rights First 2017, 2018). It is important to keep these categories separate because these crises often create public panic, and bureaucrats on the U.S. side overreact and affect the ability of the legitimate and legal travel to use the border efficiently.

President Donald Trump has used the increase in Central American asylum seekers to his political advantage, and the recent incursion of the so-called migrant caravan from these countries during recent months only provides additional political reasons for the Trump administration to keep calling for a border wall, additional border security, and so forth, including expanding the Border Patrol. The Trump administration adopted a zero-tolerance policy toward undocumented border crossings, which sparked outrage and media coverage as it led to thousands of family separations at the border. More recently, Trump declared a national emergency at the border to be able to reallocate funding from some national projects to the construction of the border wall (Levine and Arkin 2019). Furthermore, in January 2019, the United States announced the Migrant Protection Protocols (MPP, also known as Remain in Mexico) to allow the DHS to return non-Mexican migrants in immigration court proceedings to await their court decisions in Mexico (DHS 2019). The MPP is currently facing legal challenges, and as of February 2020, the DHS has confirmed that fifty-nine thousand migrants have been returned to Mexico under this policy (CRS n.d.). Even at ports of entry, asylum seekers are regularly turned away by CBP officers (also referred to as metering), and limits are set to restrict the number of asylum seekers who can be processed. A special review of the zero-tolerance policy conducted by the DHS's Office of the Inspector General (OIG) concluded that metering has led to an increase in illegal border crossings (OIG 2018). All this, however, points to political opportunism rather than smart ways to expand and manage the rights of borderlanders to move freely across. The border continues to be, in fact, prey to political impulses of those who profit from portraying it as a fundamentally lawless and chaotic region. This is even more evident if we consider that largely absent in Mr. Trump's discourse is the desire to modernize POEs to facilitate legal and legitimate trade and travel. Even so, what is clear is that the border between the United States and Mexico has been and will continue to be an area of attraction for migrants, not only because of its economic development and work supply but also because its adjacency to the United States allows for the possibility of working, studying, and visiting in the neighboring country (Ybáñez Zepeda 2008). And many border residents, present and future, are likely to continue to see the border as a resource (Sohn 2013).

Another important issue affecting the border is the number of deportations from the United States. These, not unlike the massive deportations of the 1930s and 1950s, are putting additional pressure on border communities, which must provide housing, educational, health services, and added public safety and security as well as economic opportunities. As deportations increased in the United States, Mexican urban localities at the border became the main reception areas for returned migrants (Passel, Cohn, and González 2012), and even if these populations are not mobile across the border because they are barred from ever entering the United States again, they increase economic activity along the border and add to the population that might in the future demand cross-border access. This is even more so because so many deportees have spent years and even decades in the United States that return to their hometowns is not an option. They no longer have family in their hometowns or there is a lack of employment opportunities or their social networks have all but disappeared. Hence, return migrants are drawn to the same cities where internal migrants are moving to— for example, border cities (Masferrer and Roberts 2012). Moreover, for families with members of mixed nationalities—for example, families whose parents were deported but brought their U.S.-born children along so as not to separate the family—the border constitutes a strategic option that helps them take advantage of labor markets and school opportunities in the United States for their U.S.-born children who might have come with them to the border and have the right of return now and in the future (Vargas Valle 2015). In the end, the border is a place of change and dynamism; it is a place in motion (Konrad 2015). Providing for these new arrivals, as well as regulating their demand for cross-border mobility, is likely to place additional pressure on the system that regulates it. Thus, the border region will still need good governance institutions to continue to be an asset to both countries and to those who choose to make the borderlands their home. This need will also demand that increasingly both countries will have to address cross-border mobility as a binational issue—something that is hard to conceive, as each country considers cross-border mobility largely a national issue, when in reality its character is binational and its ability to contribute to prosperity in the entire region is vital for both countries.

Twenty-First-Century Cross-Border Mobility

The last thirty years at the U.S.-Mexico border have seen the construction and contestation of an increasingly complicated region, where border agencies in charge have built an institutional scaffolding that relies increasingly on surveillance, control, and punishment to manage the borderline and to "secure" and "facilitate" cross-border activity. Clearly, however, securitization has prevailed over any possibility of facilitation. Even those mechanisms designed to facilitate cross-border mobility have, in the end, resulted in additional costs in terms of human hours, energy, resources, and time for all involved. It is quite possible that border agencies prefer it that way because portraying and managing the border—that is, giving border crises maintenance rather than resolution—helps them maintain their vested interests, primarily in terms of influence, prestige, budget, and so forth. This chapter has provided a brief historical overview and some highlights of the agencies and agreements that have shaped human mobility at the U.S.-Mexico border, but it is not an exhaustive and in-depth view on the issue of human mobility, which merits its own book to accomplish. Yet the issue of human mobility is deeply embedded to the notion of defense and security, and one cannot discard the potential vested interests created over time in maintaining the security apparatus. But for any student of the U.S.-Mexico border, it is evident that the region is not a great source of danger to U.S. national security, nor does the illegality component surpass the overwhelming legal and legitimate trade and travel. Unfortunately, the national security and law enforcement concerns that dominate the logic of border management today when it comes to border users is not about to change.

Even so, the border is in dire need of a new paradigm for human mobility. The use of technology is certainly an important element, but as we have already seen, technology has proven to cut both ways, and current technology, as used, has in fact made the border worse off. It has helped criminalize more border users than ever and increased the costs of border use. Beyond technology, what is clear is that a new paradigm has to be a renewed emphasis on orderly and legal labor market integration, the use of free zones with smarter regional enforcement of illicit or unpermitted activities, and the construction of interests from the perspective of those who reside in the borderlands. For that, in turn, political will to reconceive the border is needed, along with creativity and innovation in public policy and institutional design. In an interconnected world, it is important to consider ways to balance security and prosperity in practice, not only in rhetoric. It is also important to ensure that borderlanders have a say in institutional design and the ability to verify that border management agencies do not develop vested interests that run directly against the interest of all border residents. The Otay Mesa binational inspection station and the Cross Border Xpress experiment in San Diego–Tijuana are clear examples of how ingenuity and political will can go a long way in expediting solutions for the border of the future, balancing the more restrictive policies that prevail today, and neutralizing agencies from hijacking border management for their own organizational interests.

Note

1. On the Cross Border Xpress, see https://www.crossborderxpress.com/en/.

References

Binational Task Force on the United States–Mexico Border. 2011. "Managing the United States–Mexico Border: Cooperative Solutions to Common Challenges." Coordinated by the Pacific Council for International Policy (PCIP) and the Mexican Council on Foreign Relations (COMEXI). http://consejomexicano.org/multimedia/1520449700-930.pdf.

Bureau of Transportation Statistics. n.d. "Border Crossing/Entry Data." Accessed May 5, 2020. https://www.bts.gov/content/border-crossingentry-data.

Cañas, Jesus, Roberto Coronado, and Keith Phillips. 2006. "Border Benefits from Mexican Shoppers." *Southwest Economy*, May/June, 11–13.

Chishti, Muzaffar, Doris Meissner, Claire Bergeron. "At Its 25th Anniversary, IRCA's Legacy Lives On." Migration Policy Institute, November 16. https://www.migrationpolicy.org/article/its-25th-anniversary-ircas-legacy-lives.

Clemens, Michael A. 2016. *Una frontera común, un futuro común*. Washington, D.C.: Center for Global Development.

Congressional Research Service (CRS). 2006. "Mexico-United States Dialogue on Migration and Border Issues, 2001–2006." February 16. https://www.everycrsreport.com/files/20060216_RL32735_d9023aff22d3f7eded6c179f9d1a82d180c7dc76.pdf.

Congressional Research Service (CRS). n.d. "Mexico's Immigration Control Efforts." Accessed May 5, 2020. https://fas.org/sgp/crs/row/IF10215.pdf.

Cornelius, Wayne A., and Jessa M. Lewis, eds. 2006. *Impacts of Border Enforcement on Mexican Migration: The View from Sending Communities*. La Jolla, Calif.: Center for Comparative Immigration Studies, University of California, San Diego.

Dibble, Sandra. 2017. "Joint U.S.-Mexico Cargo Inspections Launch at Otay Mesa Port of Entry." *San Diego Union-Tribune*, December 22.

Espenshade, Thomas J. 1995. "Unauthorized Immigration to the United States." *Annual Review of Sociology* 21:195–216.

Gerber, James, Francisco Lara-Valencia, and Carlos de la Parra. 2010. "Re-imagining the U.S.-Mexico Border: Policies Toward a More Competitive and Sustainable Transborder Region." *Global Economy Journal* 10 (4): 1–17.

Ghaddar, Suad F., and Cynthia J. Brown. 2005. "The Economic Impact of Mexican Visitors Along the U.S.-Mexico Border: A Research Synthesis." International Council of Shopping Centers Working Paper Series.

Gonzalez-Barrera, Ana, and Jens Manuel Krogstad. 2019. "What We Know About Illegal Immigration from Mexico." Pew Research Center, June 28. https://www.pewresearch.org/fact-tank/2019/06/28/what-we-know-about-illegal-immigration-from-mexico/.

Heyman, Josiah. 2014. "'Illegality' and the U.S.-Mexico Border: How It Is Produced and Resisted." In *Constructing Illegality in America: Immigrant Experiences, Critiques, and Resistance*, edited by Cecilia Menjívar and Daniel Kanstroom, 111–35. New York: Cambridge University Press.

Human Rights First. 2017. "Crossing the Line: U.S. Border Agents Illegally Reject Asylum Seekers." May. https://www.humanrightsfirst.org/sites/default/files/hrf-crossing-the-line-report.pdf.

Human Rights First. 2018. "Refugee Blockade: The Trump Administration's Obstruction of Asylum Claims at the Border." December. https://www.humanrightsfirst.org/sites/default/files/December_Border_Report.pdf.

Johnson, Benjamin H. 2018. "The Mexican Revolution." *Oxford Research Encyclopedia of American History*. December. https://oxfordre.com/americanhistory.

Jones, Vivian C., and Lisa Seghetti. 2015. "U.S. Customs and Border Protection: Trade Facilitation, Enforcement, and Security." Congressional Research Service, May 18. https://fas.org/sgp/crs/homesec/R43014.pdf.

Konrad, Victor. 2015. "Toward a Theory of Borders in Motion." *Journal of Borderlands Studies* 30 (1): 1–17.

LeMay, Michael C. 2007. *Illegal Immigration*. Santa Barbara, Calif.: ABC-CLIO.

Levine, Marianne, and James Arkin. 2019. "Republicans Support Trump's Wall Even After He Grabs Military Funds from Their States." Politico, September 11. https://www.politico.com/story/2019/09/11/republicans-border-wall-military-funding-1488818.

Marchand, Marianne H. 2017. "Crossing Borders: Mexican State Practices, Managing Migration, and the Construction of 'Unsafe' Travelers." *Latin American Policy* 8 (1): 5–26.

Masferrer, Claudia, and Bryan Roberts. 2012. "Going Back Home? Changing Demography and Geography of Mexican Return Migration." *Population Research and Policy Review* 31 (4): 465–96.

Massey, Douglas S., and Karen A. Pren. 2012. "Unintended Consequences of US Immigration Policy: Explaining the Post-1965 Surge from Latin America." *Population and Development Review* 38 (1): 1–29.

Moré, Íñigo. 2011. *The Borders of Inequality*. Tucson: University of Arizona Press.

Murphy, John. 2019. "How Closing the Southern Border Would Slam the U.S. Economy." U.S. Chamber of Commerce, April 4. https://www.uschamber.com/series/above-the-fold/how -closing-the-southern-border-would-slam-the-us-economy.

Nevins, Joseph. 2010. *Operation Gatekeeper and Beyond: The War on "Illegals" and the Remaking of the U.S.-Mexico Boundary*. New York: Routledge.

Nivin, Steve. 2013. *The Spending Patterns and Economic Impacts of Mexican Nationals in a Twenty-County Region of South and Central Texas*. San Antonio, Tex.: SABÉR Research Institute. ·

Office of the Inspector General (OIG). 2018. "Special Review—Initial Observations Regarding Family Separation Issues Under the Zero Tolerance Policy." September 27. OIG-18-84. https://www.oig.dhs.gov/sites/default/files/assets/2018-10/OIG-18-84-Sep18.pdf.

Orrenius, Pia M., and Madeline Zavodny. 2012. "The Economic Consequences of Amnesty for Unauthorized Immigrants." *Cato Journal* 32 (1): 85–106.

Passel, Jeffrey, D'Vera Cohn, and Ana Gonzalez-Barrera. 2012. *Net Migration from Mexico Falls to Zero and Perhaps Less*. Washington, D.C.: Pew Research Center.

Pavlakovich-Kochi, Vera, and Alberta H. Charney. 2008. "Mexican Visitors to Arizona: Visitor Characteristics and Economic Impacts, 2007–08." Economic and Business Research Center, University of Arizona, December.

Payan, Tony. 2016. *Three U.S.-Mexico Border Wars: Drugs, Immigration, and Homeland Security*. 2nd ed. Santa Barbara, Calif.: Praeger Security International.

Pederzini, Carla, Fernando Riosmena, Claudia Masferrer, and Noemy Molina. 2015. *Tres décadas de migración desde el triángulo norte centroamericano: Un panorama histórico y demográfico*. Guadalajara, Mex.: CIESAS Divulgación.

Roberts, Bryan, Adam Rose, Nathaniel Heatwole, Dan Wei, Misak Avetisyan, Oswin Chan, and Isaac Maya. 2014. "The Impact on the US Economy of Changes in Wait Times at Ports of Entry." *Transport Policy* 35:162–75.

San Diego Association of Governments (SANDAG). 2006. "Economic Impacts of Wait Times at the San Diego–Baja California Border." January 19. https://www.sandag.org/programs /borders/binational/projects/2006_border_wait_impacts_report.pdf.

Sharma, Sushant, Dong Hun Kang, Abhisek Mudgal, Jose Rivera Montes de Oca, Swapnil Samant, and Gabriel A. Valdez. 2018. "Developing Adaptive Border Crossing Mobility Measures and Short-Term Travel Time Prediction Model Using Multiple Data Sets." Center for

International Intelligent Transportation Research, report number 185917-00015. https://static.tti.tamu.edu/tti.tamu.edu/documents/185917-00015.pdf.

Sohn, Christophe. 2013. "The Border as a Resource in the Global Urban Space: A Contribution to the Cross-Border Metropolis Hypothesis." *International Journal of Urban and Regional Research* 38 (5): 1697–1711.

U.S. Department of Health and Human Services (HHS). n.d. "The U.S.-Mexico Border Region." Accessed November 19, 2019. https://www.hhs.gov/about/agencies/oga/about-oga/what-we-do/international-relations-division/americas/border-health-commission/us-mexico-border-region/index.html.

U.S. Department of Homeland Security (DHS). 2017. "Efforts by DHS to Estimate Southwest Border Security Between Ports of Entry." Office of Immigration Statistics, September. https://www.dhs.gov/sites/default/files/publications/17_0914_estimates-of-border-security.pdf.

U.S. Department of Homeland Security (DHS). 2019. "Migrant Protection Protocols." January 24. https://www.dhs.gov/news/2019/01/24/migrant-protection-protocols.

U.S. Department of Homeland Security (DHS). n.d. "Who Joined DHS." Accessed May 5, 2020. https://www.dhs.gov/who-joined-dhs.

U.S. Department of State (DOS). n.d. "Directory of Visa Categories." Accessed November 19, 2019. https://travel.state.gov/content/travel/en/us-visas/visa-information-resources/all-visa-categories.html.

U.S. General Services Administration (GSA). 2019. "San Ysidro Land Port of Entry Fact Sheet." July 24.

U.S. Government Accountability Office (GAO). 2013. "U.S.-Mexico Border: CBP Action Needed to Improve Wait Time Data and Measure Outcomes of Trade Facilitation Efforts." July. https://www.gao.gov/assets/660/656140.pdf.

U.S. Government Accountability Office (GAO). 2014. "Trusted Travellers: Programs Provide Benefits, but Enrollment Processes Could Be Strengthened." May. https://www.gao.gov/assets/670/663724.pdf.

U.S. Government Accountability Office (GAO). 2018. "Border Security: Progress and Challenges with the Use of Technology, Tactical Infrastructure, and Personnel to Secure the Southwest Border." March 15. https://www.gao.gov/assets/700/690679.pdf.

U.S. Government Accountability Office (GAO). 2019a. "Border Infrastructure: Actions Needed to Improve Information on Facilities and Capital Planning at Land Border Crossings." July. https://www.gao.gov/assets/710/700221.pdf.

U.S. Government Accountability Office (GAO). 2019b. "Land Ports of Entry: CBP Should Update Policies and Enhance Analysis of Inspections." August. https://www.gao.gov/assets/710/700758.pdf.

U.S. Government Accountability Office (GAO). 2019c. "U.S. Customs and Border Protection: Progress and Challenges in Recruiting, Hiring, and Retaining Law Enforcement Personnel." March 7. https://www.gao.gov/assets/700/697349.pdf.

Vargas Valle, Eunice Danitza. 2015. "Una década de cambios: Educación formal y nexos trans-fronterizos de los jóvenes en áreas muy urbanas de la frontera norte." *Estudios fronterizos, nueva época* 6 (32): 129–61.

Wilson, Larman C. 1980. "The Settlement of Boundary Disputes: Mexico, the United States, and the International Boundary Commission." *International and Comparative Law Quarterly* 29 (1): 38–53.

Ybáñez Zepeda, Elmyra. 2008. "La estructura por edad y sexo en los principales municipios y condados de la frontera entre México y Estados Unidos." *Frontera norte* 21 (42): 31–52.

12

Governance and Energy Trade on the U.S.-Mexico Border

Adrián Duhalt

More than two and a half decades since the North American Free Trade Agreement (NAFTA) came into force, two disparate economic and social realities rub elbows along the U.S.-Mexico border. In other words, the development gap between the two countries joined by a two-thousand-mile border continues to grow and now appears to have affected the way the U.S. government and the public view Mexico—this is especially true since the election of Donald Trump to the presidency of the United States. The relationship at the border, however, looks more complicated than ever. Despite a failed promise of convergence in income and wealth, which was supposed to be the result of NAFTA, a close look at the border space reveals the growing degree of economic interdependence and integration the two countries have forged in the last quarter century. Border states and local communities along the borderline have built entwined families, economies, livelihoods, and even deeply linked productive structures, all connected to one another through vertical value chains that NAFTA has helped facilitate. There is a leading indicator for this, a rise in cross-border trade that is valued at more than one billion dollars daily.[1]

In this regard, manufacturing and trade in goods and services has received much attention in the scholarly literature, the public policy community, and certainly in the political narrative in both countries. One economic sector, which has also integrated steadily, has received less attention—energy trade. The extent of cross-border interdependence and integration on energy—from crude oil and natural gas to gasoline and petrochemicals—is undeniable and is being further deepened by crucial structural changes in the energy sector in both the United States and Mexico. In the United States, production of hydrocarbons has soared due to technological developments and deregulation and the so-called shale revolution. These factors have produced a boom of exports of natural gas, gasoline, and other refined products to its southern neighbor. Closer to the border, these exports have spun the construction of multiple pipelines that now seamlessly cross the borderline.

In Mexico too, there have been important structural changes in the energy sector. In 2013 and 2014, Mexico passed constitutional amendments and changed its enabling legislation to allow for greater participation of private firms in energy production, distribution, and retail, partly forced by its own energy production declines. Although such a structural change coincided with a sharp increase in imports of energy commodities from the United States as a response to a persistent fall in domestic production and robust demand, energy integration, including infrastructure building along and through the borderlines, was already quietly happening. The structural reforms in Mexico were meant to deregulate and accelerate energy integration. But energy imports from the United States to Mexico were already growing and were expected to continue to grow even more. The Mexican structural reforms only acknowledged legally the fact that energy markets in both countries have established much closer linkages against the backdrop of this evolving landscape (Morales 2016). And necessarily much of this energy trade crosses the borderline. This suggests that the binational border must increasingly be viewed as a strategic geographical space not only from the perspective of investment and the cross-national flow of general trade in goods and services but also from the perspective of energy commodities trade, energy security issues, and access to markets.

Thus, to subjects such as manufacturing, trade, security, and migration, which have habitually permeated the U.S.-Mexico agenda, the U.S.-Mexico binational relationship and the border must also be described and examined in terms of energy flows. Indeed, the extent of cross-border energy-related connections reveals that energy is a feature that policy makers must now ponder in terms of cross-border governance. This argument is exemplified by the fact that various stakeholders aware of the growth in the cross-border energy markets have already expressed their desire and have prepared to participate in, regulate, foster, and even oppose energy activities such as production, trade, and investment not only in Mexico but also along the border. This quieter struggle, however, may have had an effect on the Mexican elections of 2018, as the winner, Andrés Manuel López Obrador, explicitly ran against the energy reform. Even so, the importance of the energy industry gathered momentum during the negotiations to revamp NAFTA (currently known as the United States-Mexico-Canada Agreement [USMCA]). The final draft of the USMCA includes a chapter on energy, something that NAFTA did not—even if, in the end, it was watered down upon the request of López Obrador. As this chapter is being finalized, the USMCA is expected to enter into force on July 1, 2020, indicating that the certainty that may well come with it is likely to lift cross-border trade and investment going forward all around, including investment in the energy trade and investment in energy-related infrastructure (Office of the United States Trade Representative n.d.).[2] The border is likely to be an important piece of that new scenario. Considering these trends over the next years, it must be acknowledged that institutional coordination and cooperation between Mexico and the United States concerning border energy issues deserves more attention and can no longer be postponed.

In terms of cross-border energy trade, the discussion centers on crude oil, natural gas, and petroleum products and does not deal with electricity. While the former commodities represent most of the value and volume being exchanged and are the main determinants behind the changing pattern of trade between Mexico and the United States in recent years, the role of the latter in that sense is not significant. The case of natural gas is relevant in particular because, thanks to production and regulatory dynamics, the construction of pipelines along the border has boomed since 2013. And this is a topic that has seldom been explored in scholarly works.

This chapter focuses on several critical factors that help shape energy border governance, paying attention to market conditions of the energy industry in Mexico and the United States and assessing the institutions that govern energy trade at the border and the participation of local communities in it. The first section offers a concise contextualization of what shapes energy governance at the border. The second part describes the recent developments in the energy sector in Mexico and the United States and the structure of trade in energy commodities, with a focus on cross-national flows and crucial infrastructure projects. The third section discusses how access to information, the binational dialogue among institutions, and the role of federal regulatory bodies and subnational initiatives influence the extent of cooperation and coordination among stakeholders. The issue of local community participation is examined throughout.

Contextualizing Energy Governance on the U.S.-Mexico Border

Governance around energy issues in border states is embedded in a much broader context that cannot be delinked from Mexico's 2013 constitutional reforms and the notable expansion in the production of hydrocarbons in the United States. These two developments are dissimilar in the sense that the former relates to a regulatory and institutional framework seeking to lure investment and generate a more competitive energy environment south of the border, while the latter is mostly associated with the shale industry that has boomed in states such as Texas and New Mexico, turning the United States into an energy power house. As Mexico's production of crude oil, natural gas, and refined products has declined, the United States has risen to make up for that decline. Hence, understanding the impact that such context is having on both flanks of the border involves looking beyond local dynamics. This chapter contends that the transformation of the energy sector in Mexico and the United States in recent years—each in their own way and in opposite directions—constitutes the leading factor remaking border governance around energy matters. This is a key point as these are the essential determinants that can help explain the mounting and shifting pattern of U.S.-Mexico energy trade, which has boosted investment linked to infrastructure and production projects not only within each country but in between—that is, at the border—and the influence of regulations and institutions over energy-related activities (see Figure 12.1).

As already stated, energy trade between Mexico and the United States has experienced a profound transformation in recent years. The value and volume of energy commodities trade are not only growing rapidly but are also changing their pattern. Since 2015 the value of U.S. exports to Mexico exceeds that of imports, a balance that used to favor Mexico. The crucial point to carry from an examination of this volume flow reversal is that energy commodities across the border deserve additional attention for their importance in terms of border governance—at least as much attention as other aspects of border governance have received among academics and policy makers. This is particularly true as infrastructure across the border should experience substantial growth in the future.

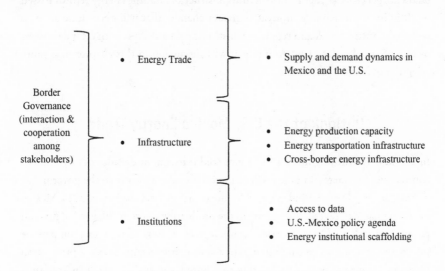

FIGURE 12.1 Border energy governance.

Interestingly, few students and scholars focusing on the U.S.-Mexico border have fully realized that, as a result of the considerable increase in energy trade, the infrastructure to produce and transport commodities in the border region has expanded, with natural gas pipelines being the most important example, as they have undergone significant expansion in the last decade to fifteen years. The importance of understanding this infrastructure expansion is yet to be examined under the various theories of border governance, including the different factors that connect stakeholders such as producers, marketers, and consumers but also borderlanders, especially as the additional infrastructure that runs across the borderline affects local communities in various ways. This clearly indicates that there is an additional need to create both formal and informal institutional arrangements that facilitate the interaction and cooperation among energy stakeholders and borderlanders, who should be made aware how energy infrastructure affects or could affect their lives and their communities. In fact, it is the absence of local participation and formal institutions providing opportunities for borderlanders to participate in decision-making on energy infrastructure at the border that characterizes energy trade along the binational borderline. When one examines the roles of the different stakeholders and energy-related activities, what becomes apparent is the paucity of border institutional scaffolding on energy, something much more evident in Mexico's case. This is surprising, given that energy crossing the border has grown exponentially and fuels Mexican manufacturing competitiveness. A cast into the future also crystalizes the importance of building cross-border institutions focused on energy. Not only did the shale boom in the United States propel cross-border infrastructure construction, but the energy reform passed in 2013/14 in Mexico also motivated greater changes that will necessitate an even more solid institutional and regulatory institutional landscape, with clear awareness of the role the border plays. And that is why discussion in this chapter pays more attention to Mexico's experience.

Outlook of the U.S.-Mexico Energy Trade

In Mexico, overturning inefficiencies gathered throughout decades of government control over the energy industry will undoubtedly take longer than the government of Enrique Peña Nieto vowed at first. Despite constitutional changes in 2013, Mexico has been unable to reverse the decline in the production of crude oil, natural gas, and petroleum products. On the flip side, technological progress, along with a competitive private sector and a market-oriented policy setting, has recently boosted production of hydrocarbons and refined products in the United States. The consequences of such a divergent trajectory of production go beyond issues of interdependence and market integration. This increase in production affects the energy flows across the border. In fact, largely driven by this trend, U.S.-Mexico energy trade is not only increasing in volume and value; it is also shifting in pattern. What goes south is changing as much as what goes north. The border region embodies some of the implications of such shifts in energy trade and exchange in the form of infrastructure investment and production activities, and highlights the need to address issues of institutional governance.

Drivers of Energy Trade

Mexico's energy trade with the United States used to register annual surpluses, as it was characterized by exports of heavy crude oil at relatively high prices and lesser imports of petroleum products.[3] This trend has virtually disappeared during the last three years. A swift plunge in crude oil production starting in 2005 and a decline in oil prices, accompanied by lower yields of natural gas and petroleum products such as gasoline (see Figure 12.2), have led to Mexico's energy exports being outpaced since 2015 by greater imports from the United States. As the U.S. Energy Information Administration (EIA) puts it:

> In each of the past three years (2015–2017), the value of U.S. energy exports to Mexico has exceeded the value of U.S. energy imports from Mexico. Energy trade between Mexico and the United States has historically been driven by Mexico's sales of crude oil to the United States and by U.S. exports of refined petroleum products to Mexico. As the United States has reduced crude oil imports from Mexico, the trade balance has shifted. (EIA 2018b)

And as for 2018, the trade balance has widened further, to the point that "the value of U.S. exports of petroleum products nearly tripled from $10.4 billion in 2008 to a record high of $30.5 billion in 2018, while the value of U.S. energy imports from Mexico remained at a near record low of $15.8 billion in 2018 for a second year in a row" (EIA 2019). The end of this trend is nowhere in sight.

For Mexico, the main determinant behind its energy trade deficit is the fall in crude oil production, which has been steady since 2005. More recently, production sank from 2.55 million barrels per day (MMb/d) in 2012 to 1.67 MMb/d in 2019, leading to a drop in exports from 0.975 MMb/d to 0.600 MMb/d in the same years (EIA n.d. ["US Imports from Mexico of Crude Oil"]). Unfortunately for Mexico's sagging production, international crude oil prices retreated during these years owing to demand and supply imbalances, so the price per barrel dispatched to U.S. refiners tumbled from an average of US$101.84 in 2012 to US$56.72 in 2019.[4] The value of U.S crude oil imports from Mexico dwindled from US$37.55 billion to US$12.25 billion

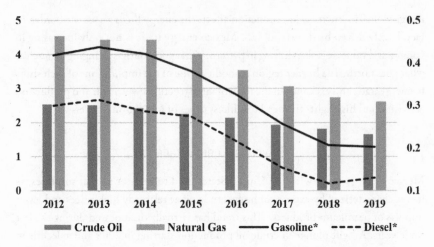

FIGURE 12.2 Mexico's production of selected energy commodities, 2012–19. Crude oil, gasoline, and diesel are given in million barrels per day; natural gas is in billion cubic feet per day. *Sources*: CNH n.d. ("Tablero de producción"); Pemex n.d.; SIE n.d.
*shown on secondary axis

through the same period (UN Comtrade Database n.d. ["U.S. Imports of Crude Oil from Mexico"]).

On the part of the United States, exports predominantly consist of natural gas and petroleum products, both of which have seen volumes and values go through the roof recently. Due to abundant supply at competitive prices (see Figure 12.3), natural gas is finding its way to Mexico, where both demand from the power sector and greater cross-border pipeline capacity have helped turn the United States into a net exporter (EIA 2017a). Since production of dry gas plummeted in Mexico by 43 percent between 2012 and 2019, or from 4.6 billion cubic feet per day (Bcf/d) to 2.62 Bcf/d, as exhibited in Figure 12.2, the volume of natural gas the United States pipes across its southern border grew by 171 percent, namely from 1.70 Bcf/d in 2012 to 5.1 Bcf/d in 2019.[5] The value of U.S. natural gas exports to Mexico surged from US$1.677 billion to US$5.3 billion over the referred period.[6]

Moreover, it must be pointed out that demand south of the border is not the only force behind rising U.S. exports of (dry) natural gas. With U.S. production expanding by 81.9 percent between 2006 and 2019, the subsequent domestic glut has made spot prices at Henry Hub fall from a peak of US$8.89 per one million British Thermal Units (MMBtu) in 2008 to an average of US$2.56 per MMBtu in 2019. At first sight, access to abundant supply of natural gas at inexpensive prices may look like advantageous circumstances for any country, but for Mexico it has generated incentives to

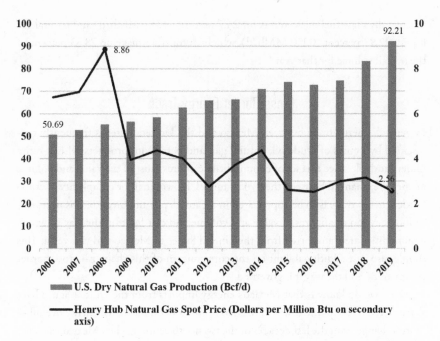

FIGURE 12.3 U.S. dry natural gas production and spot price, 2006–19. *Source*: EIA n.d. ["U.S. Dry Natural Gas Production"].

encourage imports instead of developing its own resources. As of January–September 2019, Mexico's imports accounted for 67.9 percent of all natural gas available domestically, although once Pemex requirements are not considered, import dependency stood at 89.7 percent of domestic supply (CNH n.d. ["Mexico's Natural Gas Balance"]). This, without a doubt, is viewed as the most pressing issue for Mexico in terms of energy security—even ahead of petroleum products—and the border plays a critical role in that respect.

In the same way, U.S. exports to Mexico of petroleum products such as gasoline, diesel, and natural gas liquids are thriving, and again, this is not wholly attributed to favorable production conditions in states like Texas. The main determinant is the low utilization rates of Mexico's refineries in recent years, which as a result has left a significant gap in the domestic market that has been fulfilled by imports.[7] In 2019 Mexico bought an average of 1.16 MMb/d of petroleum products from U.S. refiners, a volume that is almost twice as large as the 0.565 MMb/d imported in 2012. And if U.S. exports of petroleum products to Mexico in 2018 are broken down, it is noted that gasoline tops the list, constituting 40.7 percent of the overall volume (0.472 MMb/d), whereas distillate fuel oil accounts for 24.7 percent (0.287 MMb/d) and natural gas liquids 12.93 percent (0.150 MMb/d), which all together make up 78.33 percent of the overall volume for that year.[8]

Cross-Border Energy Trade

In general, energy trade between Mexico and the United States is frequently represented by figures of crude oil, natural gas, and petroleum products. This is quite understandable since this set of commodities captures most of the value and volume of energy exchanged between the two countries. However, if the complexity of cross-border energy trade is to be appreciated in greater depth and breadth, it is necessary to look beyond the figures of value and volume and cast light on the way in which commodities are transported from the United States to Mexico and vice versa. This should also cast additional light on the core concern of this chapter—cross-border energy trade and the way it is governed.

What we do know is that Mexico's energy imports from the United States have skyrocketed to the point at which Mexico is now a net importer of energy overall—quite a change from the last decades of the twentieth century, when Mexico was a net exporter of energy. Based on the evidence provided by the Center for Transportation Analysis (CTA), it is possible to corroborate and to measure the extent of Mexico's energy trade deficit first in terms of volume by mode of transport in 2018.[9] Looking at Figure 12.4, it is possible to see the energy flows and appreciate the difference between U.S. imports of energy from Mexico and the imports of Mexico from the United States. This too allows us to draw important conclusions on border infrastructure. It is evident, for example, that the bulk of energy commodities flowing southward is transported via pipelines, followed by rail and trucks (CTA n.d.). All three of these transports of energy cross the borderline, evidently, but pipelines are now favored because they handle enormous volumes very efficiently. That clearly means that the border energy infrastructure is becoming increasingly important.

What appears to be less evident is which commodity is the most important in any of the three modes of transport depicted. Here, it must be underscored that CTA data are not detailed, as products are grouped into categories, or codes, and each of these codes is made up of several commodities.[10] For example, U.S. energy exports traveling down by pipelines are for the most part constituted by products categorized under codes 17 and 19, where each of these is presumed to be gasoline and natural gas, respectively—both of which are the most representative of the total energy trade. But it is not always possible to know precisely if the code matches the load pushed through the pipelines. As for U.S. exports through rail and trucks, the Department of Transportation (DOT 2011) reports that the volume principally refers to twelve

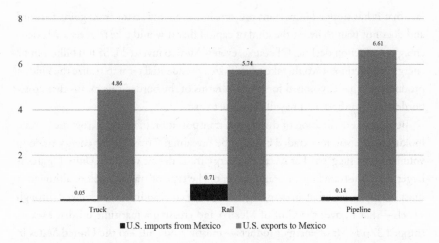

FIGURE 12.4 U.S.-Mexico cross-border trade of selected energy commodities by mode of transport, 2018, in millions of tons. *Source*: CTA n.d.

energy commodities categorized under code 19 but does not specify the most important among these. Even if we cannot always know exactly what is being transported, the central point remains unchanged: cross-border energy exchanges are growing and becoming more diverse. This is what should not be lost. Neither should the fact that these exchanges deserve commensurate well-institutionalized cross-border governance and border communities deserve to know what is crossing through their communities and the potential risks that this could bring if an accident were to occur.

Regardless of the restriction of data to examine the composition of energy trade, what is also certain is that the volume of energy products crossing the border on both directions reveals two important points in the North American context: the growing production and export capabilities of the United States, reflected not only in increased energy independence but also in the fast-growing exports toward its southern neighbor; and the extent of Mexico's dependence on energy imports from the United States. To be precise, the United States delivered across the border 17.21 million tons (MMt) of energy commodities to Mexico and imported only 0.91 MMt from its southern neighbor in 2018 (CTA n.d.). This imbalance is expected to grow for the foreseeable future. The Mexican government has shown signs that it is worried about this dependence on U.S. energy markets—something inconceivable just a few years ago—and has tried to deal with it, but for now, Mexico's dependence on American energy is expected to continue its rapid growth. Even if the López Obrador administration in Mexico seeks to diversify energy sources for Mexico, it will take years to do so. Its statements on increasing production within Mexico are also contradicted by the fact that it has stopped important projects in the energy sector from going forward and does not plan to invest the kind of capital that it would take to reverse Mexico's energy production decline. Of course, even if Mexico invested US$100 billion in its energy production, it would take more than a presidential term to realize the kind of production it has envisioned for itself. In terms of the border, this means that cross-border energy infrastructure will continue to expand.

Besides an examination of the type of transportation of energy across the border, looking at the volumes traded can also be revealing. Cross-border energy trade in volume terms suggests that Mexico's energy trade deficit with the United States is larger than illustrated by an examination of the type of transportation, although it must be emphasized that an even larger volume of commodities is exchanged through vessels—that is, over the Gulf of Mexico and crossing a maritime border. Mexico shipped 37.6 MMt of energy products—mostly crude oil—to the United States in 2018, while importing 46.16 MMt of refined products such as gasoline and diesel, mainly, and that brings the 2018 total volume of U.S. exports to Mexico to 63.37 MMt and Mexico's exports to the United States to 38.57 MMt.[11] But how much is this trade worth? Concerning cross-border energy trade through pipelines, rail, and trucks, the numbers favor the United States by a significant margin, as exports to Mexico in 2018 accounted for US$10.46 billion and imports amounted to US$0.29 billion (see Figure 12.5). In relation to trade via vessels, the gap slightly narrows though the United States continues to stand out since exports were estimated at US$23.27 billion and imports from Mexico at US$15.16 billion. And again, that brings the 2018 overall value of U.S. exports to Mexico to US$33.73 billion and Mexico's exports to the United States to US$15.45 billion (CTA n.d.).

Nonetheless, the actual challenge relating to cross-border energy trade lies ahead, in the sense that volumes are projected to continue rising, predominantly from U.S. suppliers to Mexican buyers. The CTA forecasts that by 2030, the volume of energy commodities being exported by the United States over its southern border will be considerably larger than the 17.21 MMt registered in 2018—that is, 65.02 MMt.[12] In relation to U.S. imports from Mexico, the CTA forecasts that by 2030, imports are set to grow from 0.91 MMt in 2018 to 4.59 MMt, or just one-fourteenth of what the United States is anticipated to export (CTA n.d.).

Overall, the volume of energy goods crossing the U.S.-Mexico border is expected to grow from 18.12 MMt in 2018 to 69.61 MMt in 2030, something that in turn indicates that the border region will experience additional infrastructure construction to transport a much larger volume of commodities. This will require that all stakeholders and the border communities examine and regulate effectively all the potential impacts of energy-related activities—land use and right of way, resources, pollution, and even potential accidents. At the same time, this is indicative that good border governance

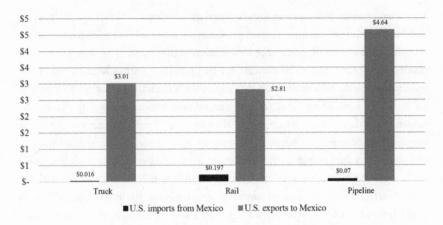

FIGURE 12.5 U.S.-Mexico cross-border trade of selected energy commodities by mode of transport, 2018, in millions of U.S. dollars. *Source*: CTA n.d.

and the institutions that produce it need to be stronger and will be of greater consequence going forward. The mode of transport that is expected to lead cross-border trade all the way to 2030 is pipelines, whose handling capacity is anticipated to carry almost 80 percent of the overall volume of energy commodities being exchanged by then.[13]

Cross-Border Energy Infrastructure

Even though most of the cross-border trade between Mexico and the United States is transported via trucks and rail, when it comes to the energy trade, both modes of transport have not experienced considerable expansion in terms of capacity—since at least 2012—as in the case of natural gas pipelines (BTS n.d.).[14] With the objective to deliver natural gas to a larger number of users and regions, the 2013–14 energy reform in Mexico contemplated the upgrading of transport capabilities. Besides projects within the country, the strategy also involved enhancement of infrastructure connectivity along the northern border and thus the capacity to source natural gas from U.S. basins such as Eagle Ford and the Permian in Texas. The number of cross-border connections is projected to increase from sixteen in 2012 to twenty-four in 2019, which corresponds to an overall capacity to carry more than 11,000 million cubic feet per day (MMcf/d), up from 2,758 MMcf/d in 2012 (see Map 12.1). Such a growth indicates that in a seven-year period, Mexico will have put in place infrastructure to import a volume of natural gas four times the capacity registered prior to the 2013 energy reform (SENER 2019).

Contrary to the information about natural gas pipelines, which is relatively accessible, infrastructure to move refined products such as gasoline and diesel is more complex to understand, given that information is presented in an overgeneralized manner, and that seems to be the case for fuel pipelines within Mexico and at the border. Access to information on fuel pipelines is difficult to come by since it is viewed as an issue of national security and what is available may differ from one source to another (CartoCrítica 2017). Therefore, building a broader picture of the pipeline interconnections between the two countries requires conferring with several sources. A fuel transport infrastructure map prepared by Mexico's Secretaría de Energía (SENER, Secretariat of Energy) exhibits three crossing points at the U.S.-Mexico border, but data on handling capacity is not straightforward (SENER 2015). Instead, the figure is found in a report prepared by the Congressional Research Service (CRS), which states that cross-border transport capacity amounts to 0.11 MMb/d (Parfomak et al. 2017). The same report also informs that an additional pipeline to move petroleum products (gasoline, diesel, and jet fuel) from Texas to northeastern Mexico is awaiting a presidential permit and that it would add 0.15 MMb/d of capacity (DOS 2016).

It is necessary to place these numbers in context to corroborate that cross-border trade of petroleum products via pipelines is not as significant as that of natural gas, whose infrastructure is much larger (see Map 12.1), or that of sea vessels over the Gulf of Mexico. The existing cross-border capacity of 0.11 MMb/d is just a fraction of the 1.08 MMb/d Mexico imported in 2017, most of which was moved through maritime routes. And if 2018 numbers are comparable through years, Figure 12.4 shows that both rail and trucks are less important in volume terms than pipelines, not to mention vessels. However, overall, the eight rail and dozens of truck crossings are part of the collection of cross-border infrastructure that as such are also part of what outlines governance of energy trade. Under some considerations, the limited information on petroleum product pipelines may have governance implications in the sense that, if relevant government agencies are left in the dark, the planning process around the safety of communities could be put into question, and in the end, it also hinders the participation of other stakeholders in addressing the risks associated with such infrastructure.

Border Energy Governance

If the border region is to deal with its energy trade and infrastructure challenges and materialize investment opportunities but also successfully regulate potential risks posed by the exponential growth of cross-border energy infrastructure, enhancing the

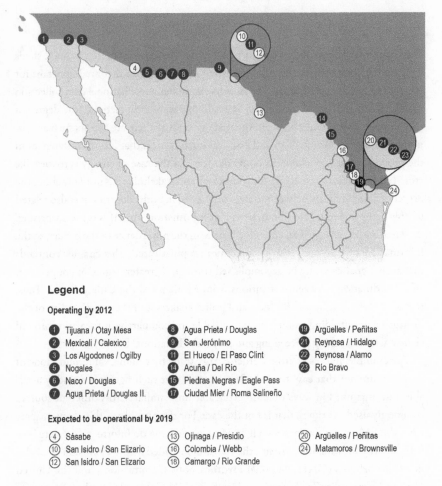

Legend

Operating by 2012

① Tijuana / Otay Mesa
② Mexicali / Calexico
③ Los Algodones / Ogilby
⑤ Nogales
⑥ Naco / Douglas
⑦ Agua Prieta / Douglas II.

⑧ Agua Prieta / Douglas
⑨ San Jerónimo
⑪ El Hueco / El Paso Clint
⑭ Acuña / Del Río
⑮ Piedras Negras / Eagle Pass
⑰ Ciudad Mier / Roma Salineño

⑲ Argüelles / Peñitas
㉑ Reynosa / Hidalgo
㉒ Reynosa / Alamo
㉓ Río Bravo

Expected to be operational by 2019

④ Sásabe
⑩ San Isidro / San Elizario
⑫ San Isidro / San Elizario

⑬ Ojinaga / Presidio
⑯ Colombia / Webb
⑱ Camargo / Rio Grande

⑳ Argüelles / Peñitas
㉔ Matamoros / Brownsville

MAP 12.1 Natural gas pipeline connectivity at the U.S.-Mexico border.

quality of governance is fundamental. The need for solid institutions, with participation from the energy sector stakeholders but also from border communities, is even more important. This is part of creating more democratic governance of all the issues that affect border communities. This section claims that access to reliable information, the involvement of borderland communities, the effectiveness of the dialogue among U.S. and Mexican institutions, and the influence of institutions over energy border issues are important and should be further systematized in the future. Compared with the kind of institutionalization that other issue areas along the border have undergone over time, energy is barely on the radar of borderland communities, and it is seldom mentioned.

Gaps in Energy Data

The chapter by James Gerber and Jorge Eduardo Mendoza Cota in this book sheds light on the complexities around the existing sources of data that are important for scholars researching the border. The authors claim that while national data collection programs in Mexico and the United States follow standard practices, "the degree of comparability should not be overestimated," given that there are factors such as economic conditions (inequality) and political organization that lead to differences in the process of data collection in both countries. In the case of energy activities like cross-border trade, the challenge for researchers and stakeholders is not only about the degree of comparability between sources originated in both countries; it is also related to how complicated it is to obtain pertinent information. And this is not surprising. As stated earlier, energy is an emerging feature in the governance of the border, so the information systems are yet to become more sophisticated. This chapter contends that such a goal can only be accomplished through a greater degree of cooperation and coordination between institutions from Mexico and the United States. Thus, the decisions taken by stakeholders and policy makers and the functionality of the institutional scaffolding require access to reliable and comparable information around energy activities taking place along and across the binational border.

For example, figures of cross-border energy trade by volume, value, and mode of transport are not that easy to find. One assumes that such figures are readily available and organized in ways that are explicable and similar across different sources commonly used. At times, that is not the case. For the purpose of this chapter, apart from the EIA, other databases such as Mexico's Sistema de Información Energética (SIE, Energy Information System), the statistics provided by the Comisión Nacional de Hidrocarburos (CNH, National Hydrocarbons Commission), and the United Nations Commodity Trade Statistics Database (UN Comtrade Database) comprise the pillars for gathering quantitative information. Although these sources help grasp the broader picture of the U.S.-Mexico energy trade, it is fair to claim that existing sources appear to be insufficient when it comes to detailed and specific figures of cross-border trade. This shortcoming, however, varies from one case to another. It is comparatively simpler to know the volume of natural gas being piped across the border or via specialized maritime transport than finding consistent and comparable data on volumes of gasoline and/or diesel crossing the border or being shipped via vessels. Another example identified is when Mexico and the United States report figures of natural gas being imported and exported, respectively, to the same source, as in the case of the UN Comtrade Database, where figures for the same year and commodity are dissimilar. The United States informs that exports of natural gas to Mexico in 2019 amounted to US$3.668 billion, whereas Mexico reports that the value of imports of natural gas from the United States in the same year accounted for US$5.293 billion, a discrepancy that was similarly found in other years as well as in liquefied natural gas (LNG) numbers. What is more, even within Mexico, sources present data in a different way. Mexico's Central Bank estimates that imports of natural gas reached US$6.288 billion in 2019, and even if it includes LNG, it does not match the number found in the UN database, while SIE just echoes values reported by Pemex. Here, the argument to emphasize is that information of this nature may be helpful for firms, regulators, local institutions, and communities to make informed decisions in terms of policies, investments, and managing risks associated with energy activities, which in the end contributes to building a more efficient border governance (Banxico 2019).

It was shown in the previous section that the CTA oversees the gathering of statistics related to modes of transport used in cross-border energy trade. The information obtained from various sources such as the EIA and the Census Bureau feeds a platform branded as the "Freight Analysis Framework Data Tabulation Tool" (FAF4), which also provides users with records as to volume and value of goods flowing across the U.S.-Mexico border.[15] Nevertheless, the tool has its own limitations. Several energy commodities are cataloged under a single code, and in that way, users do not have access to numbers for a single product. That problematizes the level of analysis. Is there a Mexican source to acquire the same information? There is, but again, facts are dispersed and presented in a way that fails to facilitate comparisons. SENER's map of transport infrastructure shows that there are three border pipelines to import oil products, but no specific information is provided as to which products are transported (Parfomak et al. 2017). This inconsistency from one source to another is just an example revealing that the quality of information, at least from the Mexican side, is a pending issue that can benefit from a closer binational dialogue.

Aware of how markets are increasingly interconnected, the energy secretaries of Mexico, the United States, and Canada, who assembled on the sidelines of the North American Leaders Summit, held in Toluca, Mexico, in February 2014, signed a memorandum of understanding (MOU) in December of that year related to cooperation on energy information. The aim of the MOU was to "create an institutional framework for consultation and cooperation on sharing publicly available energy information among the participants, with the purpose of setting the stage for dialogue, comparison and deliverables on each of the participant's energy outlooks and information" (NACEI 2014). The trilateral initiative led to the launch on November 14, 2017, of the North America Cooperation on Energy Information (NACEI) online platform, which merges in one place information supplied by a broad range of institutions from the three countries.[16]

From an institutional standpoint, NACEI looks like a step forward in terms of the quality of information concerning trade, energy infrastructure, projections of cross-border flows, and the harmonization of terminology and concepts (EIA 2017b). However, it has become evident that there is space for improvement. The sources feeding NACEI exhibit the sort of discrepancies mentioned previously. For example, in revising the 2017 U.S.-Mexico natural gas trade, numbers provided by Mexico's SENER do not match those of the EIA. Likewise, NACEI is yet to broaden its scope beyond crude oil, electricity, and natural gas to present detailed information of cross-border trade of specific commodities such as fuels.

Managing Cross-Border Energy Issues

The complex reality of the U.S.-Mexico border has led to the establishment of binational mechanisms to discuss and tackle common challenges such as migration and security, which are topics commonly associated with such a dialogue. But in the case of energy, it is recognized that its role within the sphere of border issues became more relevant, considering the opening of the Mexican energy sector in 2013–14 and the shale boom the United States has experienced recently. Both developments exposed the potential and alleged benefits that integrating energy markets could bring about and swayed policy makers and other stakeholders such as firms and industry associations from both countries to step up institutional channels to discuss and manage cross-border energy issues. But before proceeding to discuss recent initiatives in that respect, it is necessary to review an example that illustrates how cross-border engagement has evolved.

In the early 1990s, the construction of a coal plant in the Mexican state of Coahuila and the proposition to establish disposal facilities for dangerous toxic waste near El Paso, Texas, raised concerns among communities on both sides of the border. Until then, it was understood that binational collaboration around this sort of topic, at least at the border level, was missing. It quickly became apparent for stakeholders in both countries that it was necessary to establish avenues to discuss energy issues. In 1994 the Texas General Land Office (TGLO) began organizing what came to be branded as the Border Energy Forum (BEF), an event that eventually grew into (probably) the most comprehensive assembly for government officials, energy firms, academics, and environmental groups to get acquainted. The BEF became a platform to discuss the energy challenges of the border region concerning supply, demand, and infrastructure and helped the private sector and government community identify business opportunities and regulatory loopholes, respectively. Currently, the BEF is no longer organized by the TGLO, as the San Antonio–headquartered North American Development Bank (NADBANK) has recently taken over this task.

The argument to emphasize is that in terms of border governance, energy was a sort of secondary topic that failed to be among the priorities of the U.S.-Mexico policy agenda—which usually corresponded to trade, migration, and security. This is helpful to understand why cooperation on energy issues mostly took place locally and failed to engage high-ranking decision/policy makers from both countries. The changes that the energy industry in Mexico and the United States has experienced over the course of the present decade mean that the topic of energy is now at the center of the binational dialogue at a much higher government level.

In that respect, one scheme that must be reviewed is the U.S.-Mexico High Level Economic Dialogue (HLED), which was launched by U.S. president Barack Obama and Mexican president Enrique Peña Nieto in 2013 and whose objective was to turn North America into one of the most competitive regions of the world. The HLED, led at the cabinet level, first convened in Mexico City on September 20, 2013, and set the stage for the tasks to be carried out by both governments. By the second meeting of the HLED in Washington, D.C., on January 6, 2015, the working group determined that energy and the border must be part of the strategic priorities set to guide future cooperation (White House 2016).

Here, it is important to make a parenthesis and highlight that the election of Donald Trump as president of the United States meant that the last meeting of the HLED took place under the Obama presidency on February 25, 2016, in Mexico City (White House 2016). However, the well-known antagonism of President Trump toward Mexico did not prevent government agencies from both countries from cooperating and pursuing some of the targets set out by the HLED. Four years after the last summit, the efforts continue.

The HLED established that both governments will seek to enhance cooperation between energy agencies, facilitate the cross-border flow of energy-related equipment, improve information on U.S.-Mexico energy flows, create a binational business-to-business energy council, increase regulatory cooperation, and share best practices with Mexican regulators to support the energy reform, among other initiatives. Since 2015, progress has been made on several fronts, one of which is the previously mentioned North America Cooperation on Energy Information (NACEI).

Another outcome of the HLED is the U.S.-Mexico Energy Business Council, an initiative that has prevailed over the absence of HLED meetings and is thought of as an advisory body composed of private sector representatives and high-ranking officials from both countries (DOS 2019). The council, which has met five times since its inception in 2016, with the last meeting taking place on November 7, 2018, is tasked with identifying those areas where the governments of the United States and Mexico can boost cooperation and coordination to strengthen cross-border energy trade and investment in the energy sector (DOC 2018b). In that sense, the council deems necessary the role of NADBANK in finding ways to finance energy projects that could benefit communities along both sides of the border. Another recommendation, which appears to be consistent with Trump's stance, is to streamline the environmental review process of different agencies to support the development of cross-border energy infrastructure (DOC 2018a). It is unknown if the council's advice has influenced the administration of Trump in this respect, but the fact is that numerous federal agencies—including the U.S. Department of Commerce (DOC), the U.S. Department of Energy (DOE), the Federal Energy Regulatory Commission (FERC), and the U.S. Department of Transportation (DOT)—have signed an MOU to comply with a presidential executive order dealing with this matter (White House 2017, 2018). The HLED may have lost momentum, although that does not appear to be the case for some of the objectives it set at first.

Institutions and Regulations

The restructuring of Mexico's framework in the realm of energy indicates that institutional governance has recently gone through greater changes than the energy sector in the United States—which is already exceptional in the world for its decentralized regulatory apparatus. In this regard, Mexico's experience is much more limited—and it is likely that President Andrés Manuel López Obrador will reverse some of the more decentralizing aspects of energy regulation in Mexico. Even so, Mexico has strengthened and even created new energy regulatory organizations. On top of opening all activities of the value chain to private participation, the other significant amendment of Mexico's reform is connected to the array of institutions, existing and new, that nowadays regulate the industry and its participants and encourage energy activities.

The 2013–14 reform transformed the institutional scaffolding of the energy sector, and that included engraving the regulatory character of federal entities such as the Comisión Nacional de Hidrocarburos (CNH) and the Comisión Reguladora de Energía (CRE, Energy Regulatory Commission) in the Constitution; the reform also mandated the creation of the Agencia de Seguridad, Energía y Ambiente (ASEA, Agency for Safety, Energy and Environment, also known as the National Agency for Industrial Safety and Environmental Protection), which is a regulatory entity with federal jurisdiction, and the Centro Nacional de Control del Gas Natural (CENAGAS, National Center for Natural Gas Control) to operate the country's largest natural gas pipeline system.[17]

As noted, the most influential institutions in border states are embedded in the structure of the federal government and have a rather limited operational presence locally. The point is that entities at the state level, in contrast, are left with little clout over energy activities, at least from a regulatory standpoint. Hence, such a division of authority is viewed as a top-down structure that has contributed to crafting a context where governance issues are perceived as more complex and diverse in many respects. For example, federal institutions are short in resources to assist firms with (un)expected complications at the local level, as in the case of natural gas pipelines whose construction has been delayed due to opposition by local communities; while at the same time local institutions like state energy commissions, some of which were established recently, have no influence on the subject of regulations to help firms enter the energy sector and/or materialize investments.[18] In circumstances like these where the interest of stakeholders such as firms and local communities is affected, greater cooperation and coordination between state and federal institutions is perceived as an important part of the answer. In that regard, it is evident that in practice a lot more needs to be done.

Additionally, it must be stressed that the federal institutional scaffolding that emerged from the 2013–14 reforms is not alone in shaping border energy governance. Several initiatives in all Mexican border states have arisen in recent years with the goal to seize the opportunities and manage the risks associated with the energy reform in Mexico and the cross-border trade of commodities. The setting up of state energy commissions, like in the case of Tamaulipas, and the creation of industry associations such as the Clúster Energía Coahuila (Coahuila Energy Cluster), are a testament that the number of stakeholders being part of the dialogue around energy issues, at least on the Mexican side, has increased substantially, even though this has not necessarily translated into effective coordination and cooperation to tackle common challenges (*Periódico Oficial del Estado de Tamaulipas* 2017).[19]

Mexico's federal institutions overseeing the energy sector exercise a great deal of influence over border governance; and given the economic potential of reforms, the response at the local level is to strengthen and create institutions such as industry associations and state agencies to help promote investment and manage risks, among other matters. In that respect, SENER estimates that firms will have committed investments of around US$200 billion in projects by the end of 2018, and that includes natural gas pipelines, power transmission lines, solar and photovoltaic farms, gas-fired power plants, and the exploration and production of hydrocarbons in border states (SENER 2018). That amount of resources reveals that Mexico is likely to face challenges in terms of balancing out the interests of the different stakeholders involved.

Concerning the United States, institutions at the federal and state level such as the FERC and the Railroad Commission of Texas (RRC) are known to represent diverse regulatory attributes that make their role complementary in practice.[20] Therefore, what appears to have an impact on governance of the border is the so-called shale revolution, which, by stimulating a wave of investments that in turn translates into higher volumes of energy goods being sent over the southern border, is stirring a shift in the long-established configuration of trade with Mexico, as explained previously.

Natural gas is certainly the most helpful example as to how Mexico and the United States are forging a more interdependent relationship. Whereas Mexico relies considerably on imports via pipelines from the United States, shale gas producers count on Mexico's demand to withstand the effects of abundant supply over domestic prices (EIA 2018a). From that perspective, the function of governance in addressing the delay in the construction of pipelines on the Mexican side is instrumental since it helps address issues of energy security, in Mexico's case, and enables access to the most important export market for the U.S. natural gas industry (Guerra Luz and DiSavino 2018).

The same logic applies to other border energy issues, such as risk management concerning infrastructure and social opposition to energy activities. If the purpose is to better overcome these border challenges, strengthening governance structures is a goal worth pursuing. And that is not only associated with cross-border cooperation; the relationships established among local actors are also of significance.

Final Remarks

As an emerging driver of a need for border governance, the energy sector at large is perhaps even more strategic in economic terms than other subjects, such as migration and security, or other areas that have received much more attention. It has been shown in this text that the U.S.-Mexico energy trade has lately undergone a deep transformation—primarily because trade in energy has grown exponentially and is likely to continue. This is even more so because Mexico's exports of crude oil are now dwarfed by imports of natural gas and petroleum products from the United States, meaning that under prevailing conditions of supply and consumption, Mexico finds itself in a vulnerable position in terms of energy security. U.S. energy now fuels Mexico's productive capacity, especially in manufacturing, gasoline for transportation, light oil for more efficient refining, and so on. In that regard, the steady cross-border supply of natural gas from the United States to Mexico is far more critical than the movement of crude oil from Mexico to its northern neighbor via vessels. Thanks to its increasing output and thriving private sector, the United States is better equipped to find alternative sources to substitute Mexico's crude oil in case of supply interruptions. Mexico, on the contrary, resembles a captive buyer of U.S. natural gas and petroleum products, given that geographical proximity, the expansion of border pipeline connectivity, and the plummet in production exacerbates its dependency on imports. That is why the border and its energy infrastructure are strategic for Mexico's energy security.

Under that logic, an analysis of the importance of the kind of good governance that border stakeholders and residents require must not overlook the explosion of the fuel pipeline in the state of Hidalgo in January 2019 that killed 132 individuals who were taking gasoline in ersatz containers in order to sell it and profit from what was essentially an illegal tap. In reviewing the evolution of events that led to the tragedy, the fragile rule of law and the lack of cooperation and coordination among the different institutions revealed weak governance structures in the locality. In the border and elsewhere, what happened in Hidalgo illustrates that all sorts of conflicts involving local communities and energy firms could be better addressed through enhancing governance mechanisms.

Notes

1. For example, Mexico is currently the most important export market for Texas, New Mexico, California, and Arizona, and these four states together represent 55 percent of all U.S. exports to their southern neighbor (Wilson 2017). Cross-border trade accounted for US$460 billion in 2017, according to an analysis of U.S. Census Bureau data (USTradeNumbers 2017).

2. This was noted by energy pundits and media outlets during the negotiations. See Caruso 2018; Green 2018.

3. Petroleum products refer to gasoline, distillate fuel oil, and natural gas liquids (ethane, propane, normal butane, isobutane, natural gasolines).

4. The price per barrel in January–February 2020 averaged US$50.77 (EIA n.d. ["F.O.B. Costs"]).

5. Mexico's dry gas production in August 2019, the latest figure reported, was 2.67 Bcf/d (CNH n.d. ["Mexico's Natural Gas Balance"]). U.S. exports of natural gas to Mexico averaged 5.08 Bcf/d in January–February 2020. Figures refer to U.S. pipeline exports (EIA n.d. ["U.S. Natural Gas Exports"]).

6. Mexico's imports of liquefied natural gas amounted to US$382 million in 2019, down from US$1.696 billion in 2018, of which US$1.314 billion corresponded to the United States. In 2012 the value stood at US$477.7 million, of which US$57.8 million was imported from the United States (UN Comtrade Database n.d. ["Mexico's Imports of Natural Gas"]).

7. As of August 2019, Mexico's Secretaría de Energía (SENER, Secretariat of Energy) reports that refineries operated at 37.7 percent of installed capacity (SENER n.d.).

8. Export volumes for 2012 are as follows: gasoline (0.201 MMb/d), distillate fuel oil (0.133 MMb/d), and natural gas liquids (0.050 MMb/d) (EIA n.d. ["U.S. Exports of Petroleum Products"]).

9. The Center for Transportation Analysis is part of the Department of Energy's National Transportation Research Center.

10. Volumes are for petroleum crude (16); gasoline, aviation turbine fuel, and ethanol (kerosene and fuel alcohol) (17); fuel oils (diesel, Bunker C, and biodiesel) (18); and other coal and petroleum products not elsewhere classified (natural gas and petroleum coke) (19). The numbers in parentheses refer to codes according to DOT 2011.

11. From 2012 to 2016, there has been a shift in trade routes between Mexico and the United States. The volume of U.S. exports across the border in 2016 is 33.4 percent lower than 2012, while the volume of petroleum products shipped to Mexico via vessels has increased by 56.4 percent. In Mexico's case, sagging production of crude oil and petroleum products means that the volume of cross-border exports in 2016 has declined by 83.3 percent in comparison to 2012, while exports via vessels (mostly crude oil) have fallen by 36.6 percent (DOT 2011).

12. This forecast refers to commodities included in codes 16, 17, 18, and 19 described in note 10.

13. This analysis includes pipelines, trucks, and rail and refers to codes 16, 17, 18, and 19 of the Standard Classification of Transported Goods (SCTG) (DOT 2011).

14. However, in August 2015 the United States and Mexico opened a new rail link that is dubbed to be the first in more than a century (FRA 2017).

15. It is understood that the level of detail with which FAF4 presents the information depends on its sources, which at the same time have their own restrictions in terms of confidentiality and financial information (CTA n.d.).

16. The online platform was launched at the North American Energy Ministerial Meeting on November 14, 2017, in Houston, Texas. See https://www.nacei.org/#!/overview.

17. The regulatory authority of the CNH and the CRE is now inscribed in Article 28 of the Constitution, which states that "the Executive Power will count on the coordinated regulatory entities in the energy field, named National Hydrocarbons Commission and Regulatory Energy Commission, in the terms provided by the law" (SEGOB 2013). ASEA is responsible for environmental protection and regulating and supervising industrial and operational safety in energy industry activities (SEGOB 2014).

18. Nine pipelines under construction in Mexico are facing an average delay of more than four hundred days (Wyeno and Hilfiker 2018).

19. The Clúster Energía Coahuila is an initiative defined as a multi-stakeholder association that is made up of firms, education institutions, research centers, civil associations, and municipal, state, and federal agencies (Clúster Energía Coahuila n.d.).

20. For an overview of regulatory attributes, see FERC n.d.; RRC n.d.

References

Banco Central de México (Banxico). 2019. "Balanza de Productos Petroleros." Accessed May 6, 2020. https://bit.ly/2WD78pi.

Bureau of Transportation Statistics (BTS). n.d. "Transborder Freight Data." Accessed May 6, 2020. https://www.bts.gov/transborder.

CartoCrítica. 2017. "Ductos, ¿por dónde circulan los hidrocarburos en México?" July. http://www.cartocritica.org.mx/2017/ductos/.

Caruso, Guy F. 2018. "Commitment to NAFTA Vital for Energy Markets." *Houston Chronicle*, February 12.

Center for Transportation Analysis (CTA). n.d. "Freight Analysis Framework Data Tabulation Tool (FAF4)." Accessed May 6, 2020. https://faf.ornl.gov/faf4/Extraction4.aspx.

Clúster Energía Coahuila. n.d. "¿Qué es el Clúster?" Accessed November 18, 2019. https://clusterenergia.org/quienes-somos-2/.

Comisión Nacional de Hidrocarburos (CNH). n.d. "Mexico's Natural Gas Balance." Accessed May 6, 2020. https://hidrocarburos.gob.mx/media/3043/balance-gas-natural.pdf.

Comisión Nacional de Hidrocarburos (CNH). n.d. "Tablero de producción de petróleo y gas." Accessed May 6, 2020. https://produccion.hidrocarburos.gob.mx/.

Federal Energy Regulatory Commission (FERC). n.d. "Overview of FERC." Accessed November 18, 2019. https://www.ferc.gov/about/ferc-does/overview.asp.

Federal Railroad Administration (FRA). 2017. "Federal Railroad Administration Report to House and Senate Appropriations Committees: International Border Passenger and Freight Rail Study." June. https://railroads.dot.gov/sites/fra.dot.gov/files/fra_net/17163/FRA%20-%20International%20Border%20Passenger%20and%20Freight%20Rail%20Study%20-2017.pdf.

Green, Mark. 2018. "NAFTA Modernized in the Right Way Would Boost U.S. Economic, Security Interests." *Energy API*, February 21. https://www.api.org/news-policy-and-issues/blog/2018/02/21/nafta-modernized-would-boost-economic-security-interests.

Guerra Luz, Andres, and Scott DiSavino. 2018. "Rising U.S. Natural Gas Exports Capped by Pipe Delays." Reuters, August 10. https://reut.rs/2KUzzra.

Morales, Isidro. 2016. "Continental Energy Integration in North America: The Emergence of Nonconventional Fuels and the Restructuring of Integrative Trends." In *The Rule of Law and Mexico's Energy Reform*, edited by Tony Payan, Stephen P. Zamora, and José Ramón Cossio Díaz, 269–306. Mexico City: Tirant Lo Blanch.

North American Cooperation on Energy Information (NACEI). 2014. "Memorandum of Understanding Among the Department of Energy of the United States of America and the Department of Natural Resources of Canada and the Ministry of Energy of the United Mexican States Concerning Cooperation on Energy Information." December 15. https://www.nacei.org/content/documents/DOE-NR_Canada-United_States_Mexican_MOU_Energy%20Information_12-15-2014.pdf.

Office of the United States Trade Representative. n.d. United States-Mexico-Canada Agreement. Accessed January 20, 2019. https://ustr.gov/trade-agreements/free-trade-agreements/united-states-mexico-canada-agreement.

Parfomak, Paul W., Richard J. Campbell, Robert Pirog, Michael Ratner, Phillip Brown, John Frittelli, and Marc Humphries. 2017. "Cross-Border Energy Trade in North America: Present and Potential." Congressional Research Service, January 30. https://fas.org/sgp/crs/misc/R44747.pdf.

Periódico Oficial del Estado de Tamaulipas. 2017. "Decreto gubernamental mediante el cual se crea la Comisión de Energía de Tamaulipas, como un Organismo Público Descentralizado del Gobierno del Estado de Tamaulipas." February 17. http://po.tamaulipas.gob.mx/wp -content/uploads/2017/02/cxlii-Ext.2-170217F.pdf.

Petróleos Mexicanos (Pemex). n.d. "Estadísticas Petroleras." Accessed April 25, 2020. https:// bit.ly/3dndZdd.

Railroad Commission of Texas (RRC). n.d. "Railroad Commission Authority and Jurisdiction." Accessed January 20, 2019. http://www.rrc.state.tx.us/about-us/resource-center/faqs /railroad-commission-authority-and-jurisdiction-faq/.

Secretaría de Energía (SENER). 2015. "Mapa 'Infraestructura nacional de petrolíferos.'" https:// www.gob.mx/sener/articulos/mapa-infraestructura-nacional-de-petroliferos-31065.

Secretaría de Energía (SENER). 2018. "Con los proyectos de este año las inversiones totales comprometidas con la Reforma Energética rebasaran los 200 mil millones de dólares: PJC." Press release no. 8, February 8.

Secretaría de Energía (SENER). 2019. "Estatus de gasoductos." October. https://www.gob.mx /cms/uploads/attachment/file/497827/Estatus_de_gasoductos_octubre_2019.pdf.

Secretaría de Energía (SENER). n.d. "Producción." Accessed May 6, 2020. http://estadisticashi drocarburos.energia.gob.mx/Producci%C3%B3n.aspx.

Secretaría de Gobernación (SEGOB). 2013. "Decreto por el que se reforman y adicionan diversas disposiciones de la Constitución Política de los Estados Unidos Mexicanos, en materia de energía." *Diario Oficial de la Federación*, December 20. http://dof.gob.mx/nota_detalle .php?codigo=5327463&fecha=20/12/2013.

Secretaría de Gobernación (SEGOB). 2014. "Ley de la Agencia Nacional de Seguridad Industrial y Protección al Medio Ambiente del Sector Hidrocarburos." *Diario Oficial de la Federación*, August 11. http://www.diputados.gob.mx/LeyesBiblio/pdf/LANSI_110814.pdf.

Sistema de Información Energética (SIE). n.d. "Balance de Gas Natural Seco." Accessed May 6, 2020. https://bit.ly/2xFcmII.

UN Comtrade Database. n.d. "Mexico's Imports of Natural Gas." United Nations International Trade Statistics Database. Accessed May 6, 2020. https://comtrade.un.org/data/.

UN Comtrade Database. n.d. "U.S. Imports of Crude Oil from Mexico." United Nations International Trade Statistics Database. Accessed May 6, 2020. https://comtrade.un.org/data/.

U.S. Department of Commerce (DOC). 2018a. "Department of Commerce Hosts Fourth Meeting of U.S.-Mexico Energy Business Council." June 15. https://www.trade.gov /press/press-releases/2018/department-of-commerce-hosts-fourth-meeting-of-us-mexico -energy-business-council-061518.asp.

U.S. Department of Commerce (DOC). 2018b. "U.S., Mexico Energy Leaders Meet to Discuss Cross-Border Cooperation, Industry Needs." November 7. https://www.trade.gov/press /press-releases/2018/us-mexico-energy-leaders-meet-to-discuss-cross-border-cooperation -110718.asp.

U.S. Department of State (DOS). 2016. "Application of Borrego Crossing Pipeline, LLC for a Presidential Permit Authorizing the Construction, Operation, and Maintenance of Pipeline Facilities at the International Boundary Between the United States and Mexico." August 12. https://2009-2017.state.gov/e/enr/applicant/applicants/borregopipeline/261151.htm.

U.S. Department of State (DOS). 2019. "Sixth Meeting of the U.S.-Mexico Energy Business Council." https://mx.usembassy.gov/sixth-meeting-of-the-u-s-mexico-energy-business-council/.

U.S. Department of Transportation (DOT). 2011. "2012 Commodity Flow Survey: Standard Classification of Transported Goods (SCTG)." https://bhs.econ.census.gov/bhs/cfs /Commodity%20Code%20Manual%20(CFS-1200).pdf.

U.S. Energy Information Administration (EIA). 2017a. "In New Trend, U.S. Natural Gas Exports Exceeded Imports in Three of the First Five Months of 2017." August 8. https://www .eia.gov/todayinenergy/detail.php?id=32392.

U.S. Energy Information Administration (EIA). 2017b. "United States, Canada, and Mexico Launch North American Energy Information Website." December 1. https://www.eia.gov /todayinenergy/detail.php?id=33952.

U.S. Energy Information Administration (EIA). 2018a. "U.S. Net Natural Gas Exports in First Half of 2018 Were More Than Double the 2017 Average." October 1. https://www.eia.gov /todayinenergy/detail.php?id=37172.

U.S. Energy Information Administration (EIA). 2018b. "The Value of U.S. Energy Exports to Mexico Exceeded Import Value for Third Year in a Row." *Today in Energy*, March 14. https://www.eia.gov/todayinenergy/detail.php?id=35332.

U.S. Energy Information Administration (EIA). 2019. "U.S. Energy Trade with Mexico Involves Importing Crude Oil, Exporting Petroleum Products." *Today in Energy*, April 22. https:// www.eia.gov/todayinenergy/detail.php?id=39172.

U.S. Energy Information Administration (EIA). n.d. "F.O.B. Costs of Imported Crude Oil by Area." Accessed May 6, 2020. https://www.eia.gov/dnav/pet/pet_pri_imc1_k_m.htm.

U.S. Energy Information Administration (EIA). n.d. "U.S. Dry Natural Gas Production." Accessed May 6, 2020. https://www.eia.gov/dnav/ng/ng_prod_sum_a_EPG0_FPD_mmcf _a.htm.

U.S. Energy Information Administration (EIA). n.d. "U.S. Exports of Petroleum Products to Mexico." Accessed May 6, 2020. https://www.eia.gov/dnav/pet/pet_move_expc_a_EPP0 _EEX_mbblpd_a.htm.

U.S. Energy Information Administration (EIA). n.d. "U.S. Imports by Country of Origin." Accessed May 6, 2020. https://www.eia.gov/dnav/pet/hist/LeafHandler.ashx?n=pet&s =mcrimusmx1&f=m.

U.S. Energy Information Administration (EIA). n.d. "U.S. Imports from Mexico of Crude Oil." Accessed May 6, 2020. https://www.eia.gov/dnav/pet/hist/LeafHandler.ashx?n=PET&s =MCRIMUSMX2&f=A.

U.S. Energy Information Administration (EIA). n.d. "U.S. Natural Gas Exports by Country." Accessed May 6, 2020. https://www.eia.gov/dnav/ng/ng_move_expc_s1_a.htm.

USTradeNumbers. n.d. "Mexico." Accessed January 20, 2019. https://www.ustradenumbers.com/country/mexico/.

White House. 2016. "Joint Statement: 2016 U.S.-Mexico High Level Economic Dialogue." Office of the Vice President, February 25. https://obamawhitehouse.archives.gov/the-press-office/2016/02/25/joint-statement-2016-us-mexico-high-level-economic-dialogue.

White House. 2017. "Presidential Executive Order on Establishing Discipline and Accountability in the Environmental Review and Permitting Process for Infrastructure." August 15. https://www.whitehouse.gov/presidential-actions/presidential-executive-order-establishing-discipline-accountability-environmental-review-permitting-process-infrastructure/.

White House. 2018. "Memorandum of Understanding Implementing One Federal Decision Under Executive Order 13807." April 10. https://www.whitehouse.gov/wp-content/uploads/2018/04/MOU-One-Federal-Decision-m-18-13-Part-2-1.pdf.

Wilson, Christopher. 2017. "A NAFTA Update for the Border Region." Wilson Center, August 18. https://www.wilsoncenter.org/article/nafta-update-for-the-border-region.

Wyeno, Ross, and John Hilfiker. 2018. "Impulsora Pipe Begins Gas Injections as Nueva Era Project Looks Toward Start Later This Month." S&P Global, June 6. https://www.spglobal.com/platts/en/market-insights/latest-news/natural-gas/060618-impulsora-pipe-begins-gas-injections-as-nueva-era-project-looks-toward-start-later-this-month.

Conclusion

Uneven Institutional Development and Governance at the U.S.-Mexico Border

Tony Payan

The project that gave rise to the book you now have in your hands attempted a wide-ranging exploration of key areas that need more understanding—specifically the institutional development at the U.S.-Mexico border and the quality of governance that existing binational or bilateral institutions produce in spaces where these two sovereign nations with a complicated history meet. Although the central concern of all participants in this project was the U.S.-Mexico border, the region may hold important lessons for many other regions of the world, given that all borderlands appear to have enormous difficulties creating effective institutions and achieving good governance. To examine the state of institutional development and governance at the U.S.-Mexico border overall—and to extract the lessons for other border regions—the leaders of this project called upon prominent experts to conduct thorough studies of as many binational issues as possible in an effort to gain just that broad view of the state of institutional development and the quality of governance they yield in the border region straddling the United States and Mexico. These foremost experts on various border issues produced valuable contributions that, when taken together, render just such comprehensive understanding of institutions and governance in this complicated corner of the world. By the end of the project, a much clearer picture of the state of institutions and governance at the border did indeed emerge. And the picture is mixed.

In general, students of border issues tend to underestimate the complicated nature of governance—and the institutional requirements for the production of good governance—in places of exclusive territorial demarcations and sovereignties. At the end of this book, that certainly appears to be the case at the U.S.-Mexico border. We also tend to ignore the serious problem of leadership and political will in this area—and the role of creativity. In fact, we often deal with issues as if they were structural and inevitable. Thus, one of the important lessons of this exercise has been that, by definition, divided territories and sovereignty are foundational institutions that demand above-the-ground hard work to carefully negotiate arrangements that bridge territories and pool sovereignty so as to respond jointly to common and often urgent issues while preserving the prerogatives and priorities of *national* governance. This is no mean feat, and it is a tension that is not easily resolved. And when the task is exacerbated by a lack of agency, it often results in uneven institutional development and inconsistent and even poor governance—much as we have discovered in most areas explored in this volume. In a space as full of activity and dynamism as the U.S.-Mexico border, where things are further complicated by differences in language, social norms, history, economic development, political traditions, geostrategic positions, uneven interdependence, and so on, the absence of a binational vision for border management can only result in wanting institutions and meager governance, making everyone worse off. Now, to be sure, this is not unique either. Europe is full of borders in much the same condition—characterized by dramatic differences and historical conflicts—and yet it has found the political will to take these differences and build on and around them. And this is what we conclude has been lacking at our border. Chapter by chapter, issue by issue, the reader quickly realizes that the U.S.-Mexico border, now approaching two centuries, constitutes a place where all institution-building efforts have had to navigate not only hard concepts—such as territory, sovereignty, and an ever-hardening borderline—but also the intricacies of issues at hand as well as the structural differences and historical disagreements between the two countries. Under nearly all circumstances, but certainly under the structural and historical conditions of the U.S.-Mexico border, institution building and governance are not only a science; they are also an art. Thus, for any observer of the border, the space sometimes appears chaotic and lawless, but it does contain patterns of interaction, which can be captured theoretically and understood in their most subjective dimensions. It is possible to understand border institutions and governance over time if one traces a model of governance over border activity, as Sergio Peña explores in his chapter. Moreover, all actors have to deal with bristly issues, sailing between contradictory interests, overlapping jurisdictions, and ideological preferences—in addition to the historical cargo prevailing in the subregion or the issue at hand. And sometimes they have to do so in the midst of crises—security threats, irregular migration flows, spikes in organized criminal activity, and so forth. In the end, the border is governed by reaction, not proaction. Consequently, border institutions and governance resemble a patchwork of complicated bits and pieces of demands and responses that must somehow fit together incongruously, and the border works not because of them but in spite of them.

At the end of this study, one of the most important lessons is that borderlanders, and perhaps border scholars and leaders, should want to advocate for a redefinition of the border as a *binational commons*—that is, the idea that the border is best reconceived as a shared space that requires solid institutions to govern the region and can provide solutions to problems as a whole instead of providing solutions to individual problems separately. Our assessment is that the way we have approached the border— prioritizing the nation-state and its existential interests—has produced a border that is considerably more inefficient than it should be and detracts from both security and prosperity not only for borderlanders but for both nations. We are aware that there is important resistance to bridged border gaps and pooling sovereignty, but reconceiving the border as a binational commons might in fact set us on a different path, one where we view problems as wholes rather than two halves and conceive of solutions as integral rather than ensembles of bits and pieces that end up creating structural inefficiencies without resolving any issues and sometimes making them worse. Even when institutions have been built, as Irasema Coronado and Stephen Mumme show, these are often put at risk by stubbornly focusing on national solutions rather than cooperative frameworks. For that, however, governments would have to find relatively consistent definitions of the border region, where they would pool sovereignties to address issues jointly—something that is not at all easy to do. Interestingly, for a quarter of a century, Washington, D.C., and Mexico City set a new route, propped up by the North American Free Trade Agreement—one that conceived both countries (together with Canada) as allies in a single North American platform. But that appears to have run out of steam under both Donald Trump (United States) and Andrés Manuel López Obrador (Mexico). The two countries had eyed each other with more suspicion than trust for many years and appeared to have bridged that—a prerequisite for the creation of holistic answers to common problems—but now, they seem to be reverting to the status quo ante. The border wall that Trump wants to build is perhaps the greatest symbol of that reversal.

Here, a question emerges: What prevents these two countries, with all the historical knowledge and all the accumulated experience on border institution building and governance, especially in the last quarter century, from reconceiving the borderlands and the issues they face for better overall border management? The chapters included in this volume show that there are several problems with the border—and not problems related to the attitudes of borderlanders, bureaucrats, cross-border entrepreneurs, and so on but problems that are much more related to agency and politics and need to be part of a broader conversation about the border region—something not likely soon but necessary in the future. The next sections explore some of these obstacles to efficient and efficacious border institution building and governance.

Talking Past Each Other

One of the greatest issues facing border institution building is that the United States and Mexico appear to be talking past each other. First, their policy priorities are not the same or there is no comprehensive list of joint priorities. Whereas Mexico's priority is economic development, the United States' main focus is security. Only under great pressure has Mexico been persuaded and sometimes forced to acknowledge security as a major issue. Even so, the levels of mutual trust vary wildly over time, with the United States making it clear that Mexican law enforcement and security authorities are hardly trustworthy. Similarly, the United States has hardly ever given a second thought to Mexico's economic development. Even when immigration from Mexico was at its height, the United States never really acknowledged the economic forces behind the exodus. Thus collaboration on fundamental issues, such as border security and economic development, remains patchy at best. Worse than that, as Tony Payan and Pamela Cruz's chapter shows, there seems to be no clear agreement on a definition of the border—territorially or jurisdictionally. The border varies, depending on the issue at hand or the activities of the regional player. Even when an issue has been acknowledged as a joint issue, other priorities step in to limit what can be done. Such is the case with binational cooperation on water and the environment, where institutions that were built over a century have now been placed at risk, cracking under other players' demands (see Coronado and Mumme's chapter). This does not bode well for a binational dialogue that will necessarily demand a renegotiation of the water and environmental agreements to respond to a changed climate as the twenty-first century advances. The same is true of cross-border infrastructure, binational border public health, energy development, human mobility needs, and so forth. Even the institutions that exist often operate isolated from one another, with no overarching coordinating mechanism, and those that could potentially serve as such are not empowered to do so, including the Conference of Border Governors, the Legislative Border Conference, or the Border Mayors Association.

To be sure, it is hardly possible to create a single overarching framework or coordinating mechanism or even to achieve a single definition of the border—different issues demand different territorial or substantive characterizations of *the border*—but it is possible to expand the channels of communication and dialogue and craft, over time, better problem meanings, reinforce understanding and trust, and eventually generate joint solutions to problems that the dearth of such channels makes appear intractable. In the complex century ahead, it is not sufficient to vaguely and ambiguously coordinate for border governance, every now and then, and on this issue or that issue—where the objective is simply to get out of each other's way—but it is necessary to collaborate on problem scoping and solution generation. That of course may require that the federal governments reconsider their relationship with local governments and seek to empower them to contribute meaningfully to border management—something that so far they have not been willing to do. In fact, there is a monopoly on border management in the hands of federal authorities. Even powerful governors hardly ever have a significant say on border governance. Yet, without local government input, it will be much more difficult to pair problem definition with resource provision to create a more prosperous and secure border region. In the end, where the forums for establishing dialogue are few and far between—and largely uncoordinated and isolated by issue—the two countries will continue to talk past each other and the distrust that today exists will compound, exacerbating the problems of the border and reinforcing its image as a threat rather than an opportunity.

Failure of Leadership

Talking past each other and failing to create channels for true communication on border management are not the only serious concerns when it comes to the basis of cross-border institution building and governance at the U.S.-Mexico border. To the observer of the border, it is clear that there is also a clear failure of leadership. The border has in fact many critics but few champions. And where there are champions, these are divided and often working at cross-purposes. For a border that is crossed by hundreds of millions of individuals each year—pedestrians, vehicles, trucks, trains, planes—and the kind of economic activity that it encompasses, the lack of political entrepreneurship around its management and governance is astounding. There is in fact a serious deficiency in institutional innovation, something that, in the face of increasingly complex challenges, has led to poor governance. There is indeed very little novel, useful, and legitimate change at the border, with law enforcement being increasingly dominant. A clear instance of this is the state of cross-border infrastructure, as the chapter by Kimberly Collins explores. The growth of cross-border activity has far surpassed the growth of the infrastructure that supports it. This has made the wait times at the ports of entry increasingly unbearable by border users—it is becoming more normal to wait two, three, and even four or five hours to cross a bridge that is at most a quarter of a mile long. To the industry, the border has become a transaction cost rather than a clear advantage to doing business. Moreover, the bodies charged with coordinating infrastructure building and expansion are clearly dated in their ability to expedite the permitting process, the financing, the construction, and the management of cross-border infrastructure. This is reflected in the hundreds of millions of dollars lost on human hours wasted waiting—and we are talking about legal and legitimate trade and travel—and the fuel and wear and tear of vehicles across the board.

When we have seen political entrepreneurship, it has been limited in power and scope and generally reactionary—that is, in response to crises that can no longer wait for a response. Such is the case of security. Even then, this cooperation on security is fragile in its institutionalization levels and built on a need-to-use basis, as it has not come accompanied by true collaboration on problem definition, resolution crafting, and joint implementation. The relationship on security issues, though it has an enormous impact on the border, continues to be largely managed from the national capitals and following national priorities. The human security of borderlands always takes a backseat to those broader goals. Another instance of this kind of approach is the recent crisis of immigration at the border—Central American and other asylum seekers who have arrived at the border. The approach did not consist in joint management, although there was communication and coordination. The approach was essentially a threat from the United States on Mexico to contain these migrants or face trade tariffs. Mexico had no choice but to comply and further risk the safety and security of these migrants by leaving them stranded along the border, cutting them off at its southern border, or deporting them in large numbers. That is hardly joint management. That was a unilateral decision by one party imposed on the other, who complied out of weakness, not out of a common interest.

This is not to say that the border has no political champions. There are plenty. And they have tried to mount a defense of border interests and to advocate for the border region. However, they do not have the statutory power to influence border institutional development and do not have the resources and skills to overcome federal power, especially law enforcement power, over border governance. Entities like the Border Governors Conference, the Border Mayors Association, and the Border Legislative Conference, although composed of legitimately elected leaders, appear almost powerless and can, at most, agree to push certain agendas vis-à-vis specific authorities that do have the power—when they manage to organize meetings, show up, and agree on anything! Their ability to influence public policy at the border is in fact quite low.

Interestingly, whereas the ability of the border champions to "move the needle" on border interests is relatively low, the grip that national leaders and their rhetoric can have over the border region is quite powerful. Indeed, the border is a space extremely vulnerable to political opportunism and populist impulses at the national level. For decades now, politicians of all stripes in Washington, D.C., have found the border a convenient issue to enhance their political trajectory, focusing much of their responses to a variety of issues—including trade, terrorism, security, drug policy, and so on—on the border, even when they are only tangentially related to the border itself. The region has proven quite a good stage for politicians to make their point on a variety of issues that may not even originate or end at the border. All of them—from Bill Clinton to George W. Bush to Barack Obama to Donald Trump—have pursued increasingly militaristic policies toward the border, presumably in an effort to control issues that they are under pressure to resolve. They have in the process placed a heavy burden on borderlanders. And although President Trump has been particularly vociferous about the border as a major threat to the United States, the reality is that the border has already been the focal point for much presidential rhetoric well before Trump. If economic sanctions are *the lazy statesman's foreign policy*, it can be said that the border is the *lazy statesman's problem dump*. In the end, the weakness of local actors and the vulnerability of the border to national rhetoric have served to make the border an increasingly difficult place to live and to do business. As Víctor Daniel Jurado Flores and Cecilia Sarabia Ríos show, civil society is even weaker and more poorly organized than the entrepreneurial cross-border community—although it is evident that even the business community is relatively weak compared to law enforcement agencies. Civil society simply stands no chance at resistance against national priorities, however misguided they may be in regard to the border's true nature and character. In the end, the border is seen as a source of problems and not as an opportunity. The border is, at the end of the day, less deserving of consultation and democracy than other parts of the country.

Governing Complexity

This chapter does not argue that the border is a simple, Euclidean space. It is not. Governing the border is, in a way, solving for exponential complexity. Chapter by chapter, the reader surely observed how different and complex each of the issues are—from security (Guadalupe Correa-Cabrera and Evan D. McCormick; Octavio Rodríguez Ferreira) to transportation infrastructure (Collins) to public health (Eva M. Moya, Silvia M. Chavez-Baray, and Miriam S. Monroy) to water and the environment (Coronado and Mumme) to migration and human mobility (Payan, Cruz, and Carla Pederzini Villarreal) to energy (Adrián Duhalt), and on and on. The sheer number of issues and the complexity of these issues are but one layer of a composite space. In addition to the issues themselves, which crisscross in many different directions, there are also active competing visions of the border. While some actors prefer a more open and fluid border (e.g., business interests and human rights activists), others prefer a border that is much more closed and tightly controlled (security bureaucracies and many politicians). The border is managed somewhere in between, with increasing controls that sometimes attempt to balance prosperity and security but generally favor a closed border over a more efficiently run border. This tension is juxtaposed over each and every issue explored in this volume. One could think of a flat plane where many different issues interact or of a series of spheres that sometimes overlap and sometimes clash, unable to resolve the issues where they touch because the synapses are missing. The borderlands are, therefore, spaces that are continuously contested and negotiated—each actor seeking to carve out spaces of privilege for itself. This individual action, however, prevents broader coalitions from either pushing in the direction of a more open border or entirely prevailing with a vision of a more tightly controlled border. Collective action, in general, is fairly weak at the border. Thus, the border history is a continual process of construction and contestation—with some actors trying to "fix" the border and others continually resisting these efforts.

The result is a border that is institutionalized at many different speeds. While the management of some areas is fairly well, although never fully well, institutionalized (e.g., boundary and water issues), others are handled nearly unilaterally (e.g., human mobility), and others are barely functioning cooperative arrangements (e.g., security). Yet others are emerging organically with few regulations and trying to figure out their place at the border (e.g., energy, whose governance is largely driven by market forces). In the end, the institutions that *govern* the border are uneven in their evolution and character and do not constitute a system of good *comprehensive* governance. This, unfortunately, leaves many spaces open—gray spaces—where darker forces flourish, including human smugglers and illegal drug traffickers. If there is a pattern, however, it is one where government, economic, and social actors all move at different speeds in many different corners of the border, with poor coordination, sometimes cooperating, and seldom truly collaborating on border governance.

Mutual understanding and the will to find this understanding are also impediments to collaboration and add yet another layer to the complexity of the border. As Manuel A. Gutiérrez and Kathleen Staudt argue, the borderlands' news coverage is irregular and inconsistent. Print media and local radio and television stations appear to operate in ways that would signal, to the uneducated observer, that they do not really know each other, they hardly ever talk to each other, and so forth—specifically *across* the border. This in turn translates into a generally poor understanding of one community among the members of the other—or at least a very deficient understanding of how politics, the economy, and society work on one side or the other. This, in our estimation, should add to the inability of local communities to bind together for collective action.

In addition to the issues at hand, the many speeds at which they move, the myriad of actors, and the dearth of mutual knowledge—at least systematized knowledge—of each other, the foci also vary wildly. Some actors focus on the flows, legal and illegal, and they center their attention on the activities around these flows. Others focus on the quality of life in the border space—for example, human rights groups and local governments to some extent. And yet others focus on sovereignty maintenance, often at the expense of inhabitability of the borderlands—for example, law enforcement. And while some want more efficiently managed cross-border flows, others are more focused on containing such flows. While some want to focus on a more inclusive and human space, others are focused on punishing and deterring action in the border space. And the rules for each of these foci and interests vary wildly. Thus, this adds yet another layer of complexity to an already difficult, multilayered space that is challenging to understand. And in the middle of all this, the numbers around cross-border activity are staggering and continue to grow, demanding better governance. For example, nearly 300 million individual crossings complicate the ability of authorities to sort each crossing and determine the level of threat coming from each. This is not to say that systems have not been put in place to do so—the designated commuter lane and SENTRI programs are one way to sort out the trusted traveler and cargo from that which requires additional inspection. But the system is clearly overwhelmed and sometimes the price to participate in these programs is prohibitive. Consequently, the wait times at the ports of entry are increasing rapidly, with no one in the governance system putting any additional thought to efficiency in border management. Part of the failure of leadership, of course, consists in the inability of politicians and bureaucrats to really think outside the box. They seem to lack imagination and they are quite conservative in the way they view the border—generally as a chaotic, lawless place that needs to be controlled. The possibility of a free circulation border is nearly impossible to conceive, for example. Upon its mere mention, border enforcement agencies jump into panic mode. A free border threatens the perceptions of border agents of what the borderlands are and it would endanger the entire institutional scaffolding they have built around the border as a threat. It would certainly threaten their own livelihood if the border were ever an open space where people could obtain permits to work, study, invest, and so on, on one side or the other without the need for inspection at the port of entry. A European-style border region would simply be unthinkable. Yet a better-managed, freer border would likely resolve many of the tensions that today make the border a good target for political grandstanding and opportunism. And it might unleash some of the enormous economic potential of a region that could benefit from a different set of rules for integration.

Democratic Deficit

Governing through institution building is the more durable way to ensure that everyone and every interest is represented in all decision-making processes and outcomes.

But it is also important to consider that institution building without citizen participation will always be lacking in legitimacy and will always be perceived as authoritarian governance. Democratic governance—that is, inclusive of those governed—is a better way to respond to issues anywhere. But at the borderlands, it is clear that citizens' views on the issues matter considerably less. Borderlanders are hardly ever consulted and hardly ever asked about their own vision of the border and the way it should be governed. Governance at the border is nearly always authoritarian. Political organization across the border is discouraged and institution building follows a pattern of exclusion of the perceptions, aspirations, and needs of the residents of the region. The institutional architecture at the border is, almost by definition, exclusive of what its residents might think—and it is so by design. They, especially national politicians and law enforcement agencies, do not want borderlanders to express themselves and to participate. Thus, when an observer of the border asks, Who counts? the answer is generally the federal government and national political actors and the bureaucracies that enforce the border on their behalf, but hardly ever do the local communities and border residents count. Much of the opinion of borderlanders and the cross-border civil society they have built is invisible. Faced with this lack of participation, it is truly remarkable that local societies are as resilient as they are and continue to find spaces to interact with each other, even up against the odds of actors that view the border as a threat.

Unfortunately, it is also true that border society as a whole is divided. The interests of the business elite reign supreme. They have found ways to interact with the hegemonic actors of the border and have found channels of interaction that helped them carve spaces of privilege for themselves and their economic drivers. That is, business interests do not align with the interests of the rest of civil society because they tend to view them as more radical and unable to put together a coherent message that they can then bring to the few channels of negotiation that exist between the political and bureaucratic actors that govern the border and the rest of border society. That necessarily dictates that business interests prefer to put space between them and the rest of civil society and negotiate the border for themselves rather than for the entire community.

Under the national lens through which the border is conceived and understood, local features are devalued and unappreciated. Local actors are not seen as potential contributors to the solution of border issues but as players constantly willing to subvert the system of surveillance and control that now prevails along the border. They are seen not as a force that needs to be unleashed but as a menace that needs to be tethered. Interestingly, this way of viewing citizens and citizenship at the border is contradictory to the original view of the founding of the United States, where citizens were viewed as central to the political system and the key players in all institutions. At the border, citizens are viewed more as perils to the system that some actors have built for themselves—namely, the security bureaucracies that have acquired enormous discretionary power over the region. At the border, civil society is the enemy, not the reserve of ideas, talent, and skills that needs to be included and accessed for stronger, more legitimate institution building. Bureaucracies prefer their silence and compliance over their participation. Their protest is certainly never welcome.

Mind the Gap!

The border has a structural advantage that has been turned against it. There is a gray area, a zone that exists but is not easily seen. As one crosses the international line at the ports of entry, it is easy to look down and see small and large markers that tell you that you are stepping from one country into another. There is no gap. The line is clear. Yet floating above the international boundary line is an area where the two political systems meet only very uneasily, where the institutions do not necessarily interlock well, and where governance is ill-matched. This can be compared to a vacuum, a place where neither country has control. Over that line, a keen observer of the border can see the consequences of policy—good or bad policy. While border management is stuck in traditional public administration, for example, border problems have moved ahead of the ability of the nation-state to manage them through the tools of traditional public administration. Security issues flow back and forth, escaping the reach of border agencies as they cross the borderline; global warming affects residents on both sides; epidemics travel undetected by the naked eye of border agents; and so forth. But as issues float above the borderline and go back and forth across the line on the ground, the mechanisms to deal with them are blind. There is little trust. The channels of communication and interaction have been built largely in response to specific issues within the *national scale*, with hardly any understanding of the complexity of issues that straddle the line and occupy the gray zone created by the inability of institutions to fit together and fill in the gap irradiating from the borderline. This type of governance has led to poor quality of life along the border. In fact, it has been said that if the border counties on the U.S. side were a state, they would rank at the bottom, right along with Mississippi, on most economic and social indicators. The gap created by ill-fitting institutions has led to poor quality of life because issue governance is simply not there, is unevenly crafted, or is at risk of being lost where it exists.

On only very few issues does border governance value technical and diplomatic expertise. It prefers to reinforce the line, criminalize behavior, squash dreams and aspirations of a better border, and prevent people from using the border as what it is: a resource. In the end, the entire border is poorly managed. This has been the path the border was put on from the very beginning. Although able technicians and diplomats were called upon in the nineteenth century to draw the lines on the ground, there has hardly ever been another effort to call on able technicians and diplomats to contribute to border governance on a comprehensive basis. Where they participate, such as in the International Boundary and Water Commission, their mandate is limited, their resources curtailed, and their ability to bring additional issues to the table restricted. And a border that is badly managed is likely to continue to be badly managed, precisely because too many vested interests emerge in bad governance. Those who benefit from a border governed in a certain way—for example, national politicians and law enforcement bureaucracies—will naturally resist change, especially systemic change to border governance; in other words, they will naturally resist institution building. They in fact appear to profit from defective institutions and poor governance. And along this path of poor governance development, where history has an enormous weight, the border crumbles under its inefficiency, underinvestment, and increasing inhabitability. It is no surprise that the border region is underperforming other national regions in both the United States and Mexico today. Where the border should be an enormous resource, it has become a transaction cost, a limitation, a place to be contained, and a problem to be managed and more recently used for political profit. Institutions look inward, away from the border, rather than forward, at each other, to close the gray zones, the gaps, which produce suspicion, distrust, and even dread.

Precisely because innovation has not come to institution building at the U.S.-Mexico border, the only response has been to continue to define and redefine the border as a major threat or a source of threats to the United States and to reinforce the same mechanisms of control, introducing more boots on the ground, greater budgets, and more high-tech gadgets, all of which have proven insufficient to control the border. The latest, the border wall proposed by President Trump, is not likely to stop drug smuggling through tunnels, by drone, or in containers at ports of entry, and it is not likely to stop migrants who will come to the ports of entry and make claims of asylum or who will be willing to pay high dollars to be smuggled by sea or underground. When faced with those challenges, the bureaucracies that govern the border, however, are likely to ask for more of the same—personnel, money, and technology. This has created a spiral of poor governance, and profiteering from it, so that the border is now managed in a path-dependent mode that is unlikely to change unless political leadership steps in to reconceive the border.

In all, places where there are gaps in institutional development do not perform as well. Good governance is a factor of institutional development. Without the right institutions to respond to the increasing array of challenges, the border will continue to be poorly governed and more of a burden to its residents. It will also continue to be a place of political marginalization, poor social capital, and economic underperformance.

Reconceiving the Border

One of the major lessons learned over the course of this project is that institutional development at the U.S.-Mexico border is fairly uneven, depending on the issue at hand, the actors, the times, and so on, and that poor (and authoritarian) governance is generally associated with a dearth of institutions. To change this, however, it is not enough to push against the actors that, taking advantage of the lack of institutions, seize governance for their own vested interests. It is necessary to change the very way we see the border. In a century that is as complex as the twenty-first century, the border can no longer be seen as two different and mutually exclusive spaces—each with its own dynamics by the fiat of those who would control it. It must be reconceived as a whole; it must be reconceived as a commons. If we do not first think of the border region as a whole, it will be impossible to rethink issues collectively so that the correct institutions to respond to them can be built and *good* democratic governance achieved. Unique spaces require unique institutions, and borders are not like any other region in a given country. Borders are special spaces, precisely because they are spaces where common problems need to be dealt with by common institutions. The chapters by James Gerber and Jorge Eduardo Mendoza Cota and Payan and Cruz show clearly that such an idea has not even crossed the minds of policy makers. There is no common definition of the border, territorially or otherwise, and the data gathered is often incompatible. Thus, it is necessary to reconceive the border as a whole to be able to focus on the problems through joint definitions of issues and solutions.

To accomplish this, however, both central governments have to acknowledge that the border requires a deeper degree of coordination than it has today—one where the data gathered is comparable, where the problems are defined together, and where the institutions are truly binational and not just bilateral. There has to be an acknowledgment as well that the region needs to be politicized at the local level, by introducing a degree of local participation that is well structured and carefully considered and depoliticized at the national level, where political and rhetorical opportunism often prevail. The borderlands must be seen as a commons that requires shared responsibility and therefore more solid institutions to produce better governance. Only then will the border become a true resource not only for borderlanders but also for both nations as a whole.

Conceptualizing a New Framework for Cross-Border Action

Understanding the border as a binational commons rather than as two units that just happen to abut each other can also help figure out a new way of governing. It will no longer be a matter of coordination (different objectives and different means and working to simply stay out of each other's way) or even cooperation (different goals but the same means, with a clear need to work together to accomplish such goals), but collaboration (defining goals together and defining means together). The highest stage of these cannot be achieved if the space and the issues are not seen as a matter of managing a binational commons, instead of managing two segments of the same land as a whole and sometimes up against each other. This is not to say that sovereignty should be transcended; it can simply be pooled so that institutions where workers from both countries work issues shoulder to shoulder in the same office space and on the same budgets might result in a better border for the future. Reconceiving the border as such allows for capacity building for managing issues, such as health and energy; infrastructure; and action, such as security cooperation, at a much higher level. This observation stems from the fact that this is no longer an issue of policy coordination but the very idea that policy delivery must be done jointly if the border is to work to the advantage of borderlanders and both countries. Europe has learned to do just that, and there is hardly any reason why the United States and Mexico cannot move in that direction. Of course, many inertias and vested interests will have to be tamed or broken down, but it is entirely possible to do so and in the long run it may be even more productive.

The Future of the Border

To be able to understand the future of the border, we first need to understand the past of the border. Although there is much rhetoric about the border in the national political environment, the reality is that few Americans truly understand what the border is like. Over its history, especially its recent history, the border has become a place of order, law-abiding citizens, and rule compliance. The peak of undocumented migration, for example, occurred in 2007 and has been dropping since. The agencies that surveil and control the border have achieved an unprecedented degree of operational control. The number of border crossings that are both legal and legitimate far surpasses any illegal activity going on at the border. And most of the issues that show up at the border generally originate away from the border and come to the border because it is the obligated passage for their final resolution—illegal drug consumption, for example, has a pull on illegal drug production, which must cross the border;

undocumented migration has pushed forces at their points of origin, which relate to the border because it is the obligated passage for many of the individuals expelled by violence or economic crisis, and so forth. And all the economic activity that crosses the border makes both countries richer than they would otherwise be. Yet the border is an easy place to focalize all these anxieties, most of which stem from a failure of leadership and our inability to create the institutions that can create a much more livable space. Border cities moved into the rank of safe cities in America—with many of them being at the very top, including El Paso and Laredo, Texas. In other words, the border is by far an asset but is never viewed as such.

What the future of the border requires is an overall assessment of its value to both countries. Institutions should be built with the idea that the border is an asset, and both countries should increase binational investment in connectivity, including infrastructure. Borderlanders should be educated with the idea that they belong in a complex region and are citizens who can contribute to the overall well-being of the entire region. Countries should move to a free trade zone with even market regulations and can help everyone partake of a dynamic cross-border economy. Permanent bodies that can jointly tend to persistent problems such as security and migration should be created—considering that technology can help build trust and interaction among government actors to mitigate illegal activities that flourish in the gray areas created by the borderline. Institution building at the border, however, must be created with a clear use of the latest technology to facilitate the flows of capital, services, ideas, information, goods, and people with enormous efficiency. With such changes, border residents would be allowed greater access to each other's communities under frameworks that can allow them to work legally, shop, visit, and study across the border.

Unless we understand that the forces of globalization will not stop, governments will continue to engage in resistance to public policy, attempting to control the borderline in ways that will be ever-more expensive, not just in terms of the resources that such control implies but also in the cost to borderlanders, who could save time and individual, family, and business resources by being permitted a more fluid border. The border will continue to get more complex, as it grows in population and as external forces—such as climate change—put pressure on the region, and governments will have to harness the forces of globalization *for* the benefit of the border rather than exhaust themselves trying to resist them. As the border stands today, the costs of vigilance and control are beginning to outweigh the benefits obtained from dealing with problems that could be solved differently. The current state of fragmented political action will continue to be insufficient to govern the border, and hegemonic players will likely continue a reactive, crisis-driven mode of operation and will be unable to emerge above water to create good governance institutions. If the border is not institutionalized to be governed democratically and dynamically, it will become an enormous burden to all borderlands and a growing perceived threat to both nations. It will become a wasted opportunity for a more prosperous and secure North America.

Final Lessons

What we learned over the course of the academic exercise that gave rise to this book is that there is hardly any region of the country that is more poorly managed than the border region. That has to do with the facts that continue to fit the border into a *national* straitjacket, when it is really a shared, unique place—a binational commons. This approach to the border has led to uneven institutional development, which has in turn led to poor governance and a growing democratic deficit. And this has in turn led to a continued criminalization of border users and a repression of the social and economic forces generated by cross-border differentials, which should be an asset rather than a threat. Interestingly, the dearth of institutions at the border has also fed additional fears about the border and created opportunities for political opportunism, as we have seen during the Trump administration, which has painted a picture of the border that is uniquely negative with the intention of keeping his electoral base fired up. Uneven institutional development has also created opportunities for specific players to define the border for their own organizational benefits—border security agencies now define the border as an enormous security threat, which allows them to capture ever-more resources to maintain their dominion over the border region and to reduce resistance to their approach to border management. This in turn creates an increasingly unlivable space, as borderlanders have few or no recourses of resistance.

The border today faces a bleak future. Only strong political will and effective leadership can help turn its fate around. It begins by making people who do not live at the border understand that the region is unique and deserves a special formal recognition of its uniqueness and institutions that are uniquely crafted to resolve issues that are shared. Without an effort to change the views of the border in regions far away from the border, political support for those who would make the border an excuse to push their own agendas will continue and borderlanders will continue to pay a very high price.

CONTRIBUTORS

Silvia M. Chavez-Baray has a PhD in clinical psychology. She is an adjunct faculty and a postdoctoral fellow in the Department of Social Work at the University of Texas at El Paso. She is a mental health advisor of the Mexico Section of the U.S.-Mexico Border Health Commission and the founder of the psychoeducational group Breaking the Cycle of Violence for victims and survivors of intimate partner violence. Chavez-Baray received certification from the State of Texas as a Community Health Worker trainer. She served as the coordinator for the Ventanilla de Salud of the Mexican Consulate in El Paso and the advisor for the Instituto de los Mexicanos en el Exterior on gender studies. Her research focuses on gender, migration, TB, violence, health inequalities, and the use of Photovoice method.

Kimberly Collins is the executive director of the Barbara and William Leonard Transportation Center (LTC) at California State University, San Bernardino. She is also a professor of public administration at CSUSB and the faculty liaison for CLADEA (Latin American Commission for Administration Schools). Collins's current research focuses on social equity, sustainability, networks, and democracy in communities, particularly borderlands. She was appointed to the Good Neighbor Environmental Board in 2018 and is the North American regional editor for the *Journal of Borderlands Studies*. Collins received her PhD in 2006 from El Colegio de la Frontera Norte in Tijuana, Baja California, and an MA in political science with a focus on international relations from San Diego State University.

Irasema Coronado, PhD, is a professor and the director of the School of Transborder Studies at Arizona State University. Her research focuses on the politics of the

U.S.-Mexico border region, including environmental policy, activism, human rights, and the role of women in politics. She served as executive director of the Commission for Environmental Cooperation of North American from 2013 to 2015. She is the co-author of *Fronteras No Más: Toward Social Justice at the U.S.-Mexico Border* (2002). She served on the U.S. Environmental Protection Agency's National Advisory Council for Environmental Policy and Technology from 2016 to 2019.

Guadalupe Correa-Cabrera is an associate professor in the Schar School of Policy and Government at George Mason University. She is a Global Fellow at the Woodrow Wilson International Center for Scholars and a nonresident scholar at the Center for the United States and Mexico at Rice University's Baker Institute for Public Policy. Correa-Cabrera is also a co-editor of the *International Studies Perspectives (ISP)* journal.

Pamela L. Cruz is the research analyst for the Center for the United States and Mexico at Rice University's Baker Institute for Public Policy. She works with the director and affiliated scholars to carry out research on Mexico's policy issues and U.S.-Mexico relations. She also served as a Peace Corps Volunteer in Mali, West Africa, where she worked as a water sanitation extension agent. Cruz holds a master's degree in political science from the University of Texas at El Paso.

Adrián Duhalt is a postdoctoral fellow in Mexico energy studies for the Center for Energy Studies and the Center for the United States and Mexico at Rice University's Baker Institute for Public Policy. In 2012 he received his PhD in economic geography from the University of Sussex and received the Best PhD Thesis Award from the Economic Geography Specialty Group of the Association of American Geographers. His professional/academic interests have long intertwined with that of the energy sector in Mexico and North America.

James Gerber is a professor emeritus of economics at San Diego State University. He is the author of *International Economics* (2018), a best-selling textbook now in its 7th edition, and numerous works on U.S.-Mexico economic relations, including *Fifty Years of Change on the U.S.-Mexico Border: Growth, Development, and Quality of Life* (with Joan B. Anderson, 2008), which won the Association of Borderlands Studies Book Award.

Manuel A. Gutiérrez received his MA in political science from the University of Texas at El Paso in 2014. Since then, he has had the opportunity to work as a research specialist and campaign consultant in Mexico. He is currently pursuing a PhD in political science at Arizona State University with a focus on independent candidates in the postreform Mexican legislative process. His research interest is in comparative politics, especially the Mexican political system, institutions, and social issues.

Víctor Daniel Jurado Flores, PhD, is a professor and researcher of social sciences and spatial analysis at El Colegio de Tamaulipas. He has a PhD in social sciences with a specialty in regional studies from El Colegio de la Frontera Norte in Tijuana. His research focuses on social geography and network analysis.

Evan D. McCormick is an associate research scholar with the Obama Presidency Oral History project at Columbia University. He received his PhD in history from the University of Virginia (2015) and an MA in international relations from Yale University (2007). He has held postdoctoral fellowships from the Center for Presidential History at Southern Methodist University and the Clements Center for National Security at the University of Texas at Austin.

Jorge Eduardo Mendoza Cota obtained his PhD in economics from the University of Utah. He is a full-time researcher in the Economic Studies Department at El Colegio de la Frontera Norte in Tijuana, Mexico. He is also a professor of international trade in the Department of Economics at San Diego State University. He has published articles on the economic impacts of the U.S.-Mexico economic integration on the Mexican economy and other economic issues related to the northern border region of Mexico.

Miriam S. Monroy has an MPH from the University of Texas at El Paso, where she was a graduate assistant in the Department of Social Work. She is a native of Peru, with extensive experience on community organization and environmental justice. She is presently practicing public health in Arizona.

Eva M. Moya is an associate professor in the Department of Social Work at the University of Texas at El Paso. She received an MSSW from the University of Texas at Austin and a PhD in interdisciplinary health sciences from the University of Texas at El Paso. Her experience includes working as a senior project officer for Project Concern International and training health and human service professionals in the use of Photovoice and person-centered approaches. She is the executive director of the U.S. Section of the U.S.-Mexico Border Health Commission, the director of the Border Vision Fronteriza Initiative with the University of Arizona, and the director of the Tuberculosis Photovoice project in El Paso, Texas. Her teaching courses include Policy Welfare, Macro Practice, and Social and Health Inequalities. Her research interests include Photovoice, sexual and reproductive health, homelessness, HPV, stigma, tuberculosis, and intimate partner violence. She is an alumna of the Kellogg Leadership Fellowship Program.

Stephen Mumme is a professor of political science at Colorado State University and an affiliated faculty member in the School of Global Environmental Sustainability. He is the author or co-author of more than 140 journal articles, chapters, books, and monographs, including *Statecraft, Domestic Politics, and Foreign Policy Making: The El Chamizal Dispute* (1988). He is also a nonresident scholar at the Center for the United States and Mexico at Rice University's Baker Institute for Public Policy.

Tony Payan, PhD, is the Françoise and Edward Djerejian Fellow for Mexico Studies and the director of the Center for the United States and Mexico at Rice University's Baker Institute for Public Policy. He is also a professor at the Universidad Autónoma de Ciudad Juárez. Between 2001 and 2015, Payan was a professor of political science at the University of Texas at El Paso. Payan's research focuses primarily on border studies, particularly the U.S.-Mexico border. His work includes studies of border governance, border flows and immigration, and border security and organized crime. Payan earned an MBA from the University of Dallas Graduate School of Management in 1994 and a PhD in international relations from Georgetown University in 2001.

Carla Pederzini Villarreal, PhD, has been a professor at the Universidad Iberoamericana in Mexico City since 2002. She served as president of the National Demographic Society from 2013 to 2015 and in 2011 was a visiting scholar at ISIM (Georgetown University). Pederzini Villarreal co-edited *Migration and Remittances from Mexico: Trends, Impacts, and New Challenges* (2012) and has published several articles and reports on migration from Mexico to the United States, Central American migration, and Mexican schooling and youth. She received her PhD in population studies from El Colegio de México in Mexico City.

Sergio Peña holds a PhD in urban and regional planning from Florida State University. He is a professor in the Department of Urban and Environmental Studies at El Colegio de la Frontera Norte in Ciudad Juárez. His research is focused on studying cross-border planning, governance processes, and collaboration mechanisms between the United States and Mexico. He is the co-editor of the *Journal of Borderlands Studies*.

Octavio Rodríguez Ferreira is a native of Aguascalientes, Mexico. He is a researcher and the executive director of Justice in Mexico, a research and policy program at the

University of San Diego's (USD) Department of Political Science and International Relations. He is also a lecturer in the College of Arts and Sciences and an adjunct at the School of Law, both at USD. He received a master's in legal science and a PhD from the School of Law at the Universidad Panamericana (UP), Mexico, and has graduate diplomas in human rights from the Universidad de Castilla-La Mancha in Spain and in procedural law from UP. Rodríguez Ferreira has written and co-authored several studies on security, organized crime, violence, policing, judicial reform, and human rights.

Cecilia Sarabia Ríos, PhD, is a professor and researcher in the Department of Public Administration Studies at El Colegio de la Frontera Norte in Ciudad Juárez, Chihuahua. She holds a PhD in government and public administration from the Ortega y Gasset University Research Institute. Her research focuses on democracy, electoral processes, and local governments.

Kathleen Staudt, PhD, is a professor emerita of political science and former Endowed Professor of Western Hemispheric Trade Policy Studies at the University of Texas at El Paso. Her research interests, published in more than one hundred journal articles and chapters in books, include borders, women/gender in international development, immigration, education, activism, and violence. She has authored and edited twenty-one books, the latest of which is *Hope for Justice and Power: Broad-Based Community Organizing in the Texas Industrial Areas Foundation* (2020).

INDEX